▶◀ Speech Communication

Ronald L. Applbaum
CALIFORNIA STATE UNIVERSITY, LONG BEACH

Owen O. Jenson
CALIFORNIA STATE UNIVERSITY, LONG BEACH

Richard Carroll
LONG BEACH CITY COLLEGE

Speech
Communication

A BASIC ANTHOLOGY

Macmillan Publishing Co., Inc.
NEW YORK

Collier Macmillan Publishers
LONDON

MACMILLAN PUBLISHING CO., INC.
866 Third Avenue, New York, New York 10022

COLLIER-MACMILLAN CANADA, LTD.

Library of Congress Cataloging in Publication Data

Applbaum, Ronald L.   comp.
  Speech communication.

  Includes bibliographical references.
  1. Communication—Addresses, essays, lectures.
I. Jenson, Owen Oscar, 1931–   joint comp.
II. Carroll, Richard, 1945–   joint comp. III. Ti-
tle.
P90.A82   001.5   74.2641
ISBN 0-02-303700-8

Printing: 1 2 3 4 5 6 7 8   Year: 5 6 7 8 9 0

◄ Preface

As our title suggests, this book is an anthology of readings concerned with the process of communication with an emphasis on oral communication. The articles present ideas and information that should aid you in (1) understanding human communication and (2) developing your own communication skills in a variety of communicative situations. The text was developed with a belief that an understanding of the communication process provides one of the most important learning experiences. Understanding and learning to apply the ideas presented in this text have a direct relationship to one's personal, social, economic, and technological success.

This text should be viewed as an introduction to the primary concepts and areas covered in the field of speech communication. It is intended for college students who are beginning their study of the communication process and human communication activities.

In selecting the articles and essays for this text, we used a number of guidelines. First, because communication is studied by scholars in a number of disciplines, our selections were drawn from writings in speech communication, social psychology, psychology, linguistics, and business. Second, we attempted to provide a balance between articles that are regarded as classics in the area of communication and those that represent new and different approaches. For example, Jack Gibb's "Defensive Communication" has had considerable influence in our field and has been reprinted in a number of collections. Irving Janis's "Groupthink," a more recent contribution, poses some significant questions about the role of communication in our society. Third, we sought out eight scholars engaged in teaching speech communication and asked them to contribute original essays that would provide information and answer questions not previously addressed. We believe that these articles assist in providing focus and integrating ideas presented in the various sections of the text. Fourth, we attempted to include articles that would require little or no prior understanding of communication theories or procedures.

The text is divided into five parts. Part I explains the problems of attempting to define what we mean by the term *communication*. Part II examines the intrapersonal process of speech communication. The concepts of language, perception, and meaning are the main concerns of this section. Part III provides insight into interpersonal communication, exploring the process underlying communication between two individuals. Part IV deals with group communication. Group member awareness, nonverbal communication, conformity, conflict, culture, and leadership are examined. Part V examines the role of communication in law, organizations, mass media, political campaigning, advertising, and the future.

At the beginning of each reprinted article or original essay is a set of questions to guide you in reading the selection. They can also be used as a basis for in-class discussion.

We are deeply indebted to Dr. Lawrence B. Rosenfeld, Dr. Robert F. Forston, Dr. Richard E. Porter, Dr. Karl W. E. Anatol, Dr. Gary M. Richetto, Dr. Robert K. Avery, Dr. William B. Lashbrook, and Dr. Michael D. Scott for having spent the time and effort preparing significant original essays. We are also grateful to those who granted us permission to reprint articles and textual materials. Finally we would like to thank Lloyd Chilton of Macmillan for his encouragement and assistance.

R. L. A.
O. O. J.
R. C.

◄ Contents

1 Communication: Defining Our Terms

We usually take for granted our own ability to speak and write and to understand the speaking and writing of others. We give little thought to the nature and function of human communication. It is not surprising, therefore, that we sometimes fail to realize the impact of communication on society and its role in producing that society.

Let us imagine ourselves sitting at home with a group of friends preparing for an examination. We read through our class notes attaching meaning to the words spoken by the teacher and arrange these meanings into a logical pattern. We also incorporate the meanings attached to the words written in the textbook assignment. We may ask one of our friends the meaning he has attached to the teacher's lecture. Our friend, in turn, will take our question, reconstruct a version of that question, and respond in light of his interpretation. If we can detach ourselves from this situation for a moment, we will realize that without our ability to communicate we could not study for an examination, interact with other human beings, or, in more general terms, learn about our environment.

Without the ability to communicate—to share experiences, to exchange ideas, and to transmit knowledge from one generation to another—mankind could not survive and develop. It is speech communication that sets us apart from animals, assisting us in developing reasoning structures and influencing the ways in which our societies have developed.

Mere words on a page can never fully explain the importance of studying human communication. It is only when we finally recognize how much we depend on communicating with others and the insights into our society provided by communication that we can actually appreciate the impact of communication. Once we have reached that point, it becomes obvious why we *must* study communication.

Since one goal of this text is to provide an overview of some of the most important aspects of human communication, our first task is to see how we may define the term *communication*.

The Concept of Communication, by Frank E. X. Dance, examines the many different definitions of communication drawn from different disciplines and diverse publications. From these definitions Dance was able to distinguish fifteen conceptual components. Perhaps, most significant was the finding that no one definition covers the entire range of behaviors studied by all of those who purport to be students of communication. This difference in viewing what is *communication* can lead to contradictory statements, dissension, and theoretical divisiveness.

Franklin H. Knower's *What Do We Mean—Communication?*, rather than defining the term *communication*, examines nine ways in which communication is studied in our colleges and universities. These nine categories or ways of approaching the study of communication are based principally upon the way that communication is studied and practiced in academia.

After reading this section, we should realize that the word *communication* can be used in many different ways. We cannot, in all honesty, say that one definition is totally correct or incorrect. Rather, the way we define and interpret the term *communication* will be largely determined by our needs and our personal view of communication.

▶◀ The "Concept" of Communication

FRANK E. X. DANCE

Abstract

This essay examines multitudinous definitions of 'communication' in the light of the meaning of 'concept' as reflected in the literature of the philosophy of science. The examination produced 15 main themes from the definitions. Among the 15 conceptual components there are three upon which the definitions rather critically divide. These three points of conceptual split are examined for their impact on theory construction in communication. Some suggestions are made for conceptual clarification.

In the process of theory construction a concept determines the behavioral field observed which, in turn, affects the principles derived which, in turn, affect the hypotheses generated which, in turn, affect the laws and the system of laws stated which, all together, compose the theory constructed[1]. The concept is basic to any study of communication or the communicative process. The concept determines the field which the theorist, experimenter, or historian will choose to study[2]. The concept of communication with which one starts will substantively affect any additions to an already extant theory of communication or any efforts directed toward the development of a new theory. Concepts serve as a real, if unstated, rule for making observations and organizing experience[3]. Although psychologists and psycholinguists have considered and studied concept-*formation* it is the scholars in the philosophy of science who have concentrated on the study of the "concept." Abraham Kaplan observes that "What makes a concept significant is that the classification it institutes is one into which things fall, as it were, of themselves"[4].

"The 'Concept' of Communication," by Frank E. X. Dance, from the *Journal of Communication*, Vol. 20 (June, 1970), No. 2, pp. 201–210.

The concept is basic to theory and theory construction since it is the point of research origination and, as is the case with all points of origination or departure, radically affects the determination and reaching of the desired destination or goal.

The main purpose of this essay is to examine the multitudinous definitions of communication in the light of the meaning of "concept" as reflected in the literature of the philosophy of science. One possible result of such an examination is the derivation of the essential components of the concept of communication as reflected in the definitions. A second, though admittedly less plausible, result would be the synthesis of the components into a single definition of the concept of communication.

A concept is the result of a generalizing mental operation. The initial apprehension and perception of individual acts, or realities, lead to the grouping. The grouping is the concept, and the name, or "term," serves as the label for a specific concept. A concept is a generic mental image abstracted from percepts and generally relies on an originally inductive process rooted in objective reality. Everyday concepts, such as "dog" or "food," seem manifest to all. Other concepts depend on cognitive structuring for their existence. Herein is the difference between ordinary, common concepts and extraordinary or scientific concepts. "Some features of the world *stand out*, almost begging for names. Concepts of clouds, thunder, table, dog, wealth, hunger, color, shape, and the like, name differentiated slices of reality that impinge willy-nilly on all of us. The terms of common sense name these obtrusive daily experiences. Other features of the world have to be *cut out*, as it were. They are discerned only by a more subtle and devious examination of nature, man, and society than is made in everyday life. These more covert aspects of experience are named by the concepts of science. Terms like *mass* and *momentum*, *IQ* and *primary group, anomie* and *repression* name attributes that do not stand out as do *love* and *hunger, green, round*, and *huge*"(5). Kaplan, by implication, raises two questions which can be fruitfully asked of our concepts of communication. First, are the concepts objective? and second, do the concepts mark out paths which help us move freely in both logical and experiential space? "The word 'object', it has been said, can be understood as referring to that which objects. That is objective which insists on its own rights regardless of *our* wishes, and only experience can transmit its claim to us." Subjectivity is held in check with the question, "Do *you* see what I see?"(6) One way of assessing the usefulness of any given concept of communication is to see if our experience "objects" to it—to decide whether or not, based upon our experience, we recall instances which contradict the essence of the concept. Such contradictions do exist in certain published concepts of communication and shall be alluded to later in this essay. "The function of scientific concepts is to mark the categories which will tell us more about our subject matter than any other categorical sets"(7). Do our definitions of communication so serve us? The examination reported in this essay does not so indicate.

The definitions of communication examined were drawn from diverse fields and diverse publications. In order to be included, each definition had to have been published, thus assuring its being subjected to some prior scrutiny and expert evaluation(8). The definitions were subjected to a content analysis for their main themes. The substantive terms of each definition were listed and then collated into a master list which provided evidence of repetition and redundancy of themes. Out of approximately 4,560 words or tokens comprising approximately 2,612 types, thirty different terms were classified from which were derived 15 of what were considered to be distinct conceptual components. Below are presented the 15 conceptual components, each accompanied by a definition representative of those definitions including the component. Included are both intensional and extensional components. No componential valuation is intended by the order of presentation. Almost every definition contained more than one conceptual component and the sample definitions are not intended to represent only the component for which they serve as examples.

1. *Symbols/Verbal/Speech:* "Communication is the verbal interchange of thought or idea." John B. Hoben. "English Communication at Colgate Re-Examined." *Journal of Communication* 4:76–86, 1954, p. 77.

2. *Understanding:* "Communication is the process by which we understand others and in turn endeavor to be understood by them. It is dynamic, constantly changing and shifting in response to the total situation." Martin P. Andersen. "What Is Communication." *Journal of Communication* 9:5, 1959.

3. *Interaction/Relationship/ Social Process:* "Interaction, even on the biological level, is a kind of communication; otherwise common acts could not occur." George Herbert Mead. "Mind, Self, and Society." In *Sociology.* 3rd Ed. (Edited by Leonard Broom and Philip Selznik). New York: Harper & Row, 1963, p. 107.

4. *Reduction of Uncertainty:* "Communication arises out of the need to reduce uncertainty, to act effectively, to defend or strengthen the ego." Dean C.

5. *Process:*

Barnlund. "Toward a Meaning-Centered Philosophy of Communication." *Journal of Communication* 12:197–211, 1964, p. 200.

"Communication: the transmission of information, ideas, emotions, skills, etc., by the use of symbols—words, pictures, figures, graphs, etc. It is the *act* or process of transmission that is usually called communication." In Bernard Berelson and Gary A. Steiner. *Human Behavior.* New York: Harcourt, Brace and World, 1964, p. 254.

6. *Transfer/Transmission/ Interchange:*

". . . the connecting thread appears to be the idea of something's being transferred from one thing, or person, to another. We use the word "communication" sometimes to refer to what is so transferred, sometimes to the means by which it is transferred, sometimes to the whole process. In many cases, what is transferred in this way continues to be shared; if I convey information to another person, it does not leave my own possession through coming into his. Accordingly, the word "communication" acquires also the sense of participation. It is in this sense, for example, that religious worshipers are said to communicate." A. J. Ayer. "What Is Communication?" In *Studies in Communication.* Communication Research Centre, University College, London : Martin Secker and Warburg, 1955, 11–28, p. 12.

7. *Linking/Binding:*

"Communication is the process that links discontinuous parts of the living world to one another." Jurgen Ruesch. "Technology and Social Communication." In *Communication Theory and Research* (Edited by Lee Thayer). Springfield, Ill.: Charles C Thomas, 1957, 452–81, p. 462.

8. *Commonality:*

"It (communication) is a process that makes common to two or several what was the monopoly of one or some." Alex Gode. "What Is Communication." *Journal of Communication* 9:5, 1959.

9. *Channel/Carrier/ Means/Route:*

"(pl.) . . . the means of sending military messages, orders, *etc.* as by telephone, telegraph, radio, couriers." *The American College Dictionary.* New York: Random House, 1964, p. 244.

10. *Replicating Memories:*

"Communication is the process of conducting the attention of another person for the purpose of replicating memories." F. A. Cartier and K. A. Harwood. "On Definition of Communication." *Journal of Communication* 3:71–75, 1953, p. 73.

11. *Discriminative Response/ Behavior Modifying/ Response/Change:*

"Communication is the discriminatory response of an organism to a stimulus." S. S. Stevens. "A Definition of Communication." *Journal of the Acoustical Society of America* 22:689–90, 1950, p. 689.

"So, communication between two animals is said to occur when one animal produces a chemical or physical change in the environment (signal) that influences the behavior of another . . ." Hubert Frings. "Animal Communication." In *Communication: Concepts and Perspectives* (Edited by Lee Thayer). Wash., D.C.: Spartan Books, 1967, 297–329, p. 297.

12. *Stimuli:*

"Every communication act is viewed as a transmission of information, consisting of a discriminative stimuli, from a source to a recipient." Theodore M. Newcomb. "An Approach to the Study of Communicative Acts." In *Communication and Culture* (Edited by Alfred G. Smith). New York: Holt, Rinehart and Winston, 1966, 66–79, p. 66.

13. *Intentional:*

"In the main, communication has as its central interest those behavioral situations in which a source transmits a message to a receiver(s) *with conscious intent to affect the latter's behaviors.*" Gerald A. Miller, "On Defining Communication: Another

	Stab." In *Journal of Communication* 16:88–98, 1966, p. 92.
14. *Time/Situation:*	"The communication process is one of transition from one structured situation-as-a-whole to another, in preferred design." Bess Sondel, "Toward a Field Theory of Communication." In *Journal of Communication* 6: 147–53, 1956, p. 148.
15. *Power:*	". . . communication is the mechanism by which power is exerted." S. Schacter. "Deviation, Rejection, and Communication." In *Journal of Abnormal and Social Psychology* 46:190–207, 1951, p. 191.

Among these 15 conceptual components there are three upon which the definitions rather critically divide. These three points of critical conceptual differentiation provide points upon which the definitions split. Given that definitions are descriptions of concepts, definitional split reflects conceptual split and conceptual split alters the behavioral field to which the concepts direct us, thus substantially affecting the theories drawn from these conceptual beginnings.

The three points of conceptual cleavage are (1) the level of observation; (2) the presence or absence of intent on the part of the sender; and (3) the normative judgment (goodness-badness/successful-unsuccessful) of the act.

(1) If we choose to examine all animate matter we accept a task far broader than if we narrow our observational field to include only human beings. The definitions of communication reflect fields at almost every conceivable level ranging from *all* behavior to *meaningful, purposive behavior* of *human beings* in *conscious interaction.* In addition, some definitions center on themes (such as "process") which cut vertically through all levels. Obviously, the theories needed and the theories predicated will differ greatly depending upon the level of observation. The definitions reflect interest in different levels of systems and yet distinct system levels will include wide variations in behavioral fields and probably in the number and interpretation of observations and resultant theory construction.

(2) The conceptual component of "intentionality" markedly reduces the behavioral field and substantially alters a theory's range and power. The concept of "intentionality" is one of those instances in which experience and reality seem to object to the conceptual component. If one chooses to include only acts which are characterized by sender intent as communication then how does one classify acts wherein there is manifest deception, or accident, but which result in the acquisition of information, or the altering of behavior

on the part of one organism as a result of the behavior (including verbal messages) of another organism?

(3) Even more selective is the conceptual component of normative judgment. If we choose only to include *successful* interaction (defined as that kind of interaction in which the intent of the sender is achieved as a result of the communicative event) as representative of communication then our behavioral field and the resultant observations and final theory is cripplingly restricted.

Clearly not one of the 95 definitions reviewed adequately covers the entire range of behaviors studied by these who are identified, or who identify themselves, as communication scholars or theoreticians. In addition, the concept of communication as reflected in the 95 definitions is too loose, indeed includes contradictory components as expressed in the points of cleavage mentioned above, to allow the synthesization of a single, internally consistent definition that would contain all 15 conceptual components. "A concept means what its definition says it means. If it does not say this clearly so that we know when we do or when we do not have an instance of it, then the concept may be criticized legitimately as being inadequately defined" (9). It is difficult to determine whether communication is over-defined or under-defined but certainly its definitions lead the experimentalist, the historian, and the theoretician alike in different and sometimes contradictory directions.

The looseness of the concept of communication is reflected in the looseness of the field or fields identified with the study of communication. In many ways such diversity is enriching, but such diversity can also lead to dissension, academic sniping, and theoretical divisiveness. A variety of approaches and methodologies is often beneficial when dealing with a concept as complex as communication and we should beware of seeking or, worse, of finding a single, rigid, exclusive definition. On the other hand, it is essential to remain sensitive to the importance of concepts and of their effect upon our scholarly research and professional behavior.

We are trying to make the concept of "communication" do too much work for us. The concept, in its present state, is overburdened and thus exhibits strain within itself and within the field which uses it. What may help is the creation of a family of concepts(10). Certainly concepts relate to experience, but they also, within a theory, relate to other concepts. A family of concepts should also facilitate the treatment of communication in a systems fashion. We can spread the work through a family of communication concepts. The members of the family may include "attitudes," "opinions," and "beliefs" on one level and then on another level members such as "communication," "Animal Communication," "Human Speech Communication," and even "Effective Communication." The identification of the familial members is a task still to be completed.

Given such a family of communication concepts perhaps those who identify as communication theoreticians or communication scholars could better systematize their scholarly and teaching pursuits, move towards reducing their professional dissonance, work toward eliminating conceptual inconsistencies and contradictions and, in the end, come closer toward producing a satisfactory, systematic theory of communication.

NOTES

1. Although the vocabulary of meta-theory is subject to many interpretations, one schema for theory construction suggests the following system:
1. *Assumptions* underlie all behavior and theory building; 2. *concepts* and their corresponding definitions structure 3. *observed behaviors* from which 4. *principles* (general observations not stated in testable form) are drawn, from which a 5. *hypothesis,* or theorem (a general observation stated in testable form), is extracted, based upon which a 6. *law(s)* (a statement expressing tested relationships between facts) is formulated, a number of which laws constitute a 7. *system* (a concatenation of laws), leading to a 8. *theory* (an interrelated system of laws capable of explanation and prediction).

2. Ernest Bormann states it this way: "The setting up of classes in such a way that knowledge can be ordered, related, and explained is dependent upon concept formation." Ernest G. Bormann. *Theory and Research in the Communicative Arts.* New York: Holt, Rinehart and Winston, 1965, p. 84.

3. Margaret J. Fisher. A *Methatheoretical Analysis of the Literature on Theory-Construction in Speech-Communication.* Master's Thesis. Milwaukee: University of Wisconsin, 1969, p. 26.

4. Abraham Kaplan. *The Conduct of Inquiry.* San Francisco: Chandler Publishing Co., 1964, p. 50.

5. May Brodbeck. "General Introduction." In *Readings in the Philosophy of the Social Sciences* (Edited by May Brodbeck). Toronto: Collier-Macmillan Canada, Ltd., 1968, I–II, p. 3–4.

6. Kaplan, op. cit., p. 35.

7. Ibid., p. 52.

8. A limited number of copies of the definitions and their sources is available, at cost, upon request from the author.

9. Brodbeck, op. cit., p. 5.

10. "The meaning of a term is a family affair among its various senses." Kaplan, op. cit., p. 48.

STUDY GUIDE
QUESTIONS

1. What are the nine different usages of the word *communication?*
2. Which categories best describe the approach to communication used in your class?
3. How do the areas, goals, and categorical subsystems overlap?
4. How would you relate the concepts of communication in the previous article to the categories of communication?

▶◀ What Do You Mean – Communication?

FRANKLIN H. KNOWER

Some consider the modern study of communication to be a discipline. Others prefer to call it a field of study. For many it designates one of the many variables within a discipline. A variant of the later usage is one in which the word refers to a part or subsystem within the larger system of interrelated variables. Again the word is identified as synonymous with the label of a larger system of variables as in the statement that "communication is culture," or "communication is behavior." The word is also used metaphorically in the attempt to simplify the designation of some similar object, process, or event. The state of the art suggests that we make an effort to reduce its level of ambiguity. This is not a task for authoritarian pronouncements. Two suggestions may be helpful. One is the review of the great variety of current usages of the word. The second is a clear statement of our own intentions in this matter.

In our colleges and universities at this time communication is studied in at least nine different major ways, with many subvariants. Of course, most scholars with some justifications will defend their own practice as best. It is not our intention to stake a claim for any of these approaches as justifying a monopoly. Indeed, there is some overlapping of most of the nine areas, goals, and categorical systems and subsystems. A chart which follows illustrates the nature of these approaches to study and practice in our field.

Communication is studied as process. There is an inherent linearity over time which is an important variable in the communication event. There are two other useful ways of conceiving of the word process as used in communication. The first involves the variables or subsystems in the integrated whole. The second is the social interaction process involving at least

Franklin H. Knower, "What Do You Mean—Communication?" *Central States Speech Journal*, **XXI** (Spring, 1970), 18–23. By permission.

two persons in mutual and circular symbolic stimulus response behavior. To identify process with the concept of universal cause may at once be both an obvious oversimplification and a barrier to the development of knowledge.

There are many subsystem processes in communication. Any communication reflects to some extent the cultures and sub-cultures of which it is a part. The content and quality of the message processing system may be considered the heart of any communication. The ways in which the participants perceive the situation shape their method of operation. What people know and how they use their knowledge in perceiving and reasoning influence the way the message is developed.

Some communications "code" the message. Far more frequently, it is best understood as represented and interpreted. In most cases both linguistic and non-verbal symbols are used. The communicator and the communicatee as total and unique persons with resources, purposes, and responsibilities will make personal adjustments they consider fitting. They may be concerned with artistic and ethical processes. The total operation of the communication phenomenon takes a form or pattern deemed appropriate for the particular message system and situation. Each and all of these processes as used in communication is a learned and learning process. Total communication behavior is itself an integration process of behavior variables into a perceptual unity.

Categories in the Study of Communication

1. AS PROCESS	2. AS TYPE OF BEHAVIOR	3. AS FIELD OF DISCIPLINE	4. AS LEVEL OF INTERACTION
Cultural	A Language	The Arts	Interpersonal
Message	Literature Written and Spoken	Humanities	Small Group
Knowing	Speaking	Behavioral Sciences	Organizational and Institutional
Reasoning	Listening	Physical Sciences	Public
Linguistic	Writing	Biological Sciences	Mass
Non-Verbal Symbolic	Observing	Technologies	
Personal	Reading Silent Oral	Human Applications	

1. AS PROCESS	2. AS TYPE OF BEHAVIOR	3. AS FIELD OF DISCIPLINE	4. AS LEVEL OF INTERACTION

Ethical	Art
	  Performing
	  Graphic
	  Music		

Artistic	Broadcasting		
Form and Pattern	Journalism		
Channel	Film-Making and Viewing		
Social Learning	Management		

5. AS LEVEL OF ACHIEVEMENT	6. AS CONTENT	7. AS EFFECT	8. AS RESEARCH METHODOLOGY	9. AS A COMMUNICOLOGY
Remediation to Excellence	Agriculture	Information	Historiography	
Elementary School	Medicine	Attitudes	Criticism	

Secondary
  School
	Business	Problem
		  Solving
			Description	

College	Religion	Action	Experimentation	

Graduate
  School
	Political
	  Science
		Numbers	Creativity	

There are other ways of categorizing the processes as variables in communication. Many of these processes are also sub-units of other disciplines or fields of study. This does not mean that as these processes function in communication, any discipline has a monopoly on the information about them.

Communication is studied as a type of activity or behavior. All communication behavior is to a greater or lesser degree an interaction process. The various languages such as English, German or French are types of communication behavior. Any piece of literature including recorded speeches is a segment of communication forms. Some arts, both performing and graphic, are looked upon as merely expression, and some of them are considered communication. The history of the study of modern speaking seems to be moving in the direction of greater concern for communication whereas the history of art seems to show it to be less concerned with communicating today than formerly.

Broadcasting is a form of communication behavior, as is journalism, and film-making or viewing. Management may be looked upon as largely communication activity. This approach to communication as behavior along with the process approach discussed first has tended to dominate recent ways of categorizing communication in courses of instruction.

A third way of categorizing communication study is to relate it to a field of disciplines. In many colleges and universities courses of study in communication can be found in most of the major categories of the disciplines. Some forms of communication are much studied as an art. These and others have long been associated with the arts and humanities. There have been growing numbers of scholars in speech and in other behavioral sciences who have found some of the problems of communication particularly amenable to study by behavioral science methodologies. Other communication problems are of special interest to the physical and biological scientist. Some aspects of communication are of a technological nature, and others fall largely within the realm of human development and organization.

Communication scholars must have some academic home base, yet they must have the freedom to develop the knowledge of this most central of all man's concerns as their academic responsibilities direct them. For anyone, much less communication scholars themselves, to think narrowly about the needs for freedom in the study of communication is unrealistic. Some units for the study of communication are still organized as disciplines. A growing number recognize the value in a multidisciplinary pattern of organization.

A fourth way to study communication is on the basis of levels of social interaction. It will be noticed by some that we do not begin here with a level recently referred to as "intrapersonal communication." We consider the crux of this problem to be a matter of taxonomy rather than typology. There can be no doubt that communication involves such variables as referred to under the heading of the process approach in the earlier chart. We perceive the *message, knowing, reasoning,* and *personality* as important at all levels of social interactive communication. To classify these matters in one level of interaction appears to exclude them from other levels. As communication variables they can be conceived as applying to all levels. Thus intrapersonal variables in communication are not excluded, but considered in a way in which their rich contributions to such behavior receives maximum identification and realization.

The simplest level of social interaction commonly conceived to be "communicative," that is to have some commonness, is interpersonal communication. It is the prototype that every level must have as its minimal unit, one person communicating with another. It is conceivable at each of the other levels that the higher forms may include each of the lower levels. This level is characterized by such patterns as conference, interview, teaching, the letter, the memo, etc. It has the power to produce all the agonies and ecstasies of life for the individual of which the higher forms of communication are capable. In a society where there is no value superior to the maintenance of the individual life, there can be no more important category for study.

Small group communication is illustrated by the activities of discussion groups, committees, boards, and commissions. Organizational communication is essentially institutionalized and largely determined by the needs and interests of the organization. To the extent that an individual is committed to an organization, his communication may be the life and the essence of the organization. Whereas some organizational communication may be public, much of it is shielded from public exposure.

Public communication today may be limited only by the number who by design or chance happen to receive it. Whereas organizational communication may be designed only for its members, public communication is not so limited. Although mass communication is essentially public, not all public communication is mass communication. Both public and mass communication tend to be institutionalized. Interpersonal, small group, and organizational communication can be thought of as at least partially private.

Educational programs for the study of communication are organized for the development of levels of achievement. The needs of students for the understanding of communication are not limited to those who are deficient or misguided. The speech correctionist is essentially a teacher, but the speech pathologist is primarily concerned with the curing of an illness or overcoming an impediment. Although he works with the subnormal, many of the people he works with are superior in intellectual aptitudes. Most educators in other areas of communication set goals of excellence in the mastery of principles at the level of the student in our school systems from the elementary through the graduate school.

There are a number of branches of communication study in which scholarship is focused on the content to be communicated. Colleges of agriculture, medicine, and dentistry have communication programs set up to help professionals communicate their subject matter more effectively to practitioners in the field. The development of concepts of the dissemination of innovation had its origin largely in agriculture. Colleges of commerce have developmental programs in business communication. Political Science has developed techniques of content analysis as a road to better understanding of the communicative acts of governments.

A seventh way in which communication studies are organized centers around the concept of communication purposes and effects. Some take the position that all communication persuades. It would appear that to the extent that we accept this way of thinking that we do not need both words.

The phrase persuasive communication is then redundant. A series of arguments can be advanced for recognizing more precise objectives and effects. The traditional categories include interest, information, attitudes, and actions. One objection to this system makes the claim that the categories aren't strictly logical; they overlap. They do. But, if we demand this standard, few categories in education or human behavior could be maintained. Are they based on a false mind-body dichotomy? This dichotomy is not defended today. But psychology makes extensive use of the concepts of cognitive, affective and motor response. Of course these categories overlap but they are useful. If we reject this system we shall need to reject the differentiation of information testing, attitude testing, and motor testing. We shall have to give up the time honored distinction between knowledge and belief, between fact and opinion, between theory and involvement, between education and indoctrination, between research and development, and indeed between instrumental and consummatory response. Many people find these distinctions useful. As constructs of convenience, they provide general goals for achievement as well as categories of response. They may well provide guides to differences in message construction from which the purposes of a communicator can be inferred. One may challenge the argument that such an analysis is based on a false "mind-body dichotomy," and "an appeal to the body" as illustrations of the fallacies of the straw man, and a *reductio ad absurdum*. Because information is a unique commodity exchanged among men and a new concept of wealth and power, the number of persons receiving a message may well be recognized as an additional dimension of the goals and dimensions of communication in general, just as it now is in education and broadcasting.

A comment on the limitations of pragmatism as the sole standard of communication is in order. We must note that some students of communication defend concepts of internal standards of quality as adequate standard for communication. We must recognize that slight or delayed evidence of effect on a major subject may be far more significant than an apparent achievement of an incidental and trivial message. A sometimes fickle or politically minded audience cannot be considered a good guide to the recognition of the social significance of a message.

Communication studies may be organized according to general categories of research methods. The first of these may be designated as historiography. Many modern students of communication not only ignore its legitimate multiplicity of approaches but seem totally lacking in its history and perspective. Speech may be said to be the oldest discipline subject to organized academic study. We, more than any other group of modern scholars, ought to know the mistakes that can be made. We have an excellent record of the study of historical approaches to this subject. This should give us perspective which indeed points to the recognition of the value of breadth of procedure as well as substantive interests in our scholarship.

While historiography is critical, not all criticism need be historical. Indeed all our research, yes, even the scientific and the creative, must also be critical. Carefully reasoned discourse is the very foundation and the goal of all research. Research is but that body of scholarly method aimed at explanation, problem solving, and prediction. These are thinking processes for which research seeks the reliable knowledge with which reason operates.

Descriptive research in communication is carried out to refine our analysis of facts and processes in the total process-events of our concern. It may be qualitative or quantitative in nature. As we become more exact in the way we conceive our world, we can make sharper and sharper discriminations about it. This is a significant part of what education is all about. Descriptive research has the advantage of the use of case and field study techniques which are useful in the analysis of certain dimensions of communication not available when other methods are employed.

Experimental method, through the manipulation of variables, has as its major objective the speeding up of the understanding of the world in which we live by a better understanding of what is related to what. Without experimentation such variables might become exposed to man's evaluation as a matter of chance at some distant time. Experimentation allows us to telescope time that we may learn today that which otherwise we might not know until too late, at least for some. There are other functions of experimentation. It may be an economical means of study. It may enable us to be more exact in our thinking about variables than some other study procedures.

Finally there are methods of exploration of the world of communication which are creative in nature. While all research in some way should be creative, communication with its responsiveness to imagination as well as fact, to myth as well as reality, has the potential of an instrument for the formulation of new mixes of meanings in which creative ideas may emerge. Here, as in space research, a little step for man can be a giant step for mankind.

Our final reminder of the ways in which communication may be studied looks at the field of communication in yet another way. This is a radically different concept. The simple word communication won't do for it. It is the way of a dream, a goal. We have been discussing communication analytically as a world of processes, variables, and approaches. Yet, when people communicate, they engage in unified experienceable wholes, suggested by the common language sentence, "I hear what you say, but you're not communicating with me." Someplace in education there ought to be a place where consideration is given to the synthesis of variables into this whole. To have an interest in the contour of one of the pieces of a jigsaw puzzle may be important but it's not enough to tell us what the big picture is all about. Only a realistic understanding of the whole as it operates in the lives of men is acceptable as the ultimate goal. Specialists in the separate parts, we need. Most men can't and don't need to know all that the experts in the specializations of communication need to know. What all men need to know is the generally significant information about the whole. This is the goal of a communicology.

We have referred to the fact that categorizing systems used in the taxonomy of communication are not formally logical. Neither are the logician's categories of inference. Those used consist of the types of categories that reflect the field of speech and communication as it is understood. To be parsimonious we need to keep major categories few in number and simple in type. In indexing publications and dissertation titles, we have cut across various approaches suggested here. One deals with sub-processes and the simpler examples of communication as process, four deal with types of behavior and activity, and two deal essentially with levels of academic study and factors in learning.

One final distinction may be useful. Some scholars in communication are primarily concerned with the study of one or more types of subsystem behaviors with which ends are achieved. Others are also interested in the relationships of the referents and the ends of communication to the means by which they are achieved. The word *communication* is now widely used to refer, sometimes indiscriminately, to either set of referents. Perhaps we need discriminating terms to refer to the study and to the integrated and ultimate achievements of the processes. But we need most of all to understand the state of ambiguity of our terminology.

II Intrapersonal Communication

Quite often when we think of communication we think of one person talking to another person or a group of people talking to each other. What we usually forget is that in each of these situations there are *individual* people involved, that there is a single person talking to other single persons. It is the individual person who is the center of focus in intrapersonal communication. Intrapersonal communication deals with what goes on inside the individual. It is concerned with how the person perceives things, how information is processed inside the individual, how meaning is attached to the information that has been processed, how this meaning and information is added into the already existing patterns and processes that have been established by the individual inside his own head, and how the person behaves and/or communicates as a result of the information perceived and processed. In short, intrapersonal communication is the communicative functions that take place inside the individual, the process an individual goes through to make sense out of the world he lives in.

In making sense out of the world, an individual is free to pick and choose what he is going to pay attention to. He has a number of stimuli in his external world that are available to him at any given moment and he may choose to perceive any single stimulus or any number of these stimuli. He is, at the same time, free to ignore any stimulus or number of stimuli. Whatever he does choose to perceive is then transformed into the internal processes of the individual. At this point the person is also free to pick and choose any internal stimulus or number of stimuli he finds that apply to what he has taken from the external environment. He may choose to include internal physiological functions, such as hunger or other physical states, or he may choose to include psychological functions such as feelings and motivations. These internal stimuli are coupled with the external stimuli, and are both transmitted to the brain where meaning is attached and interpretation is made.

19

In the process of intrapersonal communication, then, the individual is free to choose whatever stimuli he believes are necessary in order to make sense out of the world at any given moment. The person may choose to perceive any external stimuli that he thinks are important out of the immediate environment and combine them with any internal stimuli that seem to apply at the moment and to fit them together inside himself in order to develop a meaningful pattern. Behavior, communication, and continued existence is then based on the meaningful pattern that is developed by the individual.

Much intrapersonal communication takes place at the symbolic level. The way an individual places meaning on these symbols and the way the symbols are combined and arranged help determine the sense a person makes out of the world. This is why language and the words a person chooses to use are so important in his intrapersonal communication. The language units that each person uses to describe his world to himself help determine what the person perceives about that world both externally and internally, and thus helps to shape the sense he makes out of that world.

In turn, the way the person behaves in the world, the way he interacts with other objects and people, is determined by the patterns and arrangements that are constructed inside himself. Thus, intrapersonal communication becomes the basis of all other forms of communication. Communication between two people (interpersonal communication) is determined and guided by each individual's intrapersonal communication patterns. Each individual selects, combines, and attaches meaning to stimuli in his own way and interacts on the basis of how he is reacting to and interpreting data inside himself. It could be said that interpersonal communication is simply two or more intrapersonal communication systems interacting. It is for this reason that understanding of intrapersonal communication is so important. Unless one understands how a person communicates within himself it would be difficult, if not impossible, to fully understand how one person communicates with another.

In an effort to understand how intrapersonal communication might work, let us look at an example of it in action. Think back to the last time you found yourself in a new or different situation. Let us say it was at a party that you and some of your friends attended. Suppose that you arrived a little late and most of the people were already there. As you entered the room you were able to look at the people assembled; note who they were; how they were dressed; the patterns of interaction that had already formed before you arrived; the location of furniture, food, and beverages; and a host of other impressions that your senses picked up for you. These external stimuli that you choose to perceive are coupled with what is going on inside you at the moment. Perhaps you are a little apprehensive about being there, or a little embarrassed about arriving late, or maybe you are a little hungry.

What you have seen and heard from outside yourself is coupled with what is inside yourself, and on the basis of these two sets of stimuli you decide on your course of action, your pattern of behavior. You may want to go to the food table or join a particular group of people. You may want to talk about inconsequential matters or apologize for your lateness. Or you may want to do any or all of these in a particular order. Whatever behavior you exhibit, whatever you do or say will be based on your intrapersonal communication system and the sense you make out of your world at that moment.

The articles and essays presented in the following portion of this reader are brought together in an attempt to make the process of intrapersonal communication more understandable and meaningful.

William V. Haney, in *Perception and Communication*, explains what he thinks perception is. He explains how differing environments, stimuli, sensory receptors, internal states, and evoked sets influence our perceptions. Haney discusses how each individual's frame of reference and self-image affects that person's perceptions and why we all defend our own personal perceptions.

In *Perception, Communication, and Educational Research: A Transactional View*, Hans Toch and Malcolm S. MacLean, Jr., present a transactional view of perception. They present a discussion of various views of perception and discuss the similarities and differences in peoples' perceptions. They also explain the working assumptions of a transactional approach to perceptions and the implications of this approach.

Owen O. Jenson, in *Language and Perception: Two Interrelated Characteristics of Human Behavior*, discusses the part that language plays in our perception of the world. He presents information on how language works, how we attach meaning to words, and the relationship between what we say about people and things and our perception of those people and things.

Don Fabun, in *The Trouble With Is, Is Is*, talks about the difficulties we have with the word *is*. In this article we are reminded that we are describing something inside our heads rather than something outside ourselves when we use this word.

In *How We Know What We Know*, S. I. Hayakawa discusses the process of abstracting, the act of perceiving objects based on the level of specificity of the language we use in describing the things we perceive.

Taken together, these articles present an attempt to help the reader understand the process of intrapersonal communication.

STUDY GUIDE	1. What is meant by the term *perception*?
QUESTIONS	2. How do differing environments, stimuli, sensory receptors, internal states, and evoked sets change our perceptions?
	3. Why do we become defensive in terms of our perceptions?
	4. What is the relationship of our frame of reference to our perceptions?
	5. How does our self-image effect our perceptions?

◄ Perception and Communication

WILLIAM V. HANEY

"This is nothing. When I was your age the snow was so deep it came up to my chin!"

Reprinted from Redbook *with the permission of cartoonist, Gerry Marcus.*

Dad is right, of course—*as he sees it.* And in this seemingly innocuous self-deception lies one of the most interesting and perhaps terrifying aspects of human experience: *We never really come into direct contact with reality.* Everything we experience is a manufacture of our nervous system.

Reprinted with permission from Haney, *Communication and Organizational Behavior* (Rev. Ed.; Homewood, Ill.: Richard D. Irwin, Inc.) pp. 51–78.

For practical purposes we should acknowledge that there is a considerable range of similarity between reality and one's perception of it. When an engineer is measuring, testing, and the like, usually with the aid of precise gauges and instruments, his perceptions may be an extremely close approximation of reality. This is basically why bridges, tunnels, and skyscrapers not only get built but generally stay built.

But when the engineer, or anyone else, is relating to and communicating with other human beings,—when he is operating in a world of feelings, attitudes, values, aspirations, ideals, and emotions—he is playing in a very different league and the match between reality and perceptions may be far from exact.

Just what is going on and just what is this concept "perception" we have been alluding so casually? "Perception" is a term we perhaps shouldn't be using at all. There seems to be very little agreement as to what it entails. It evidently is a complex, dynamic, interrelated composite of processes which are incompletely and variously understood. Allport, for example, describes some 13 *different* schools of thought on the nature of perception, listing, among others, core-context theory, gestalt theory, topological field theory, cell-assembly, and sensory-tonic field theory(1). In the face of such irresolution I will be so bold as to define perception in unsophisticated language as the process of *making sense out of experience—of imputing meaning to experience*(2).

Obviously what kind of "sense" one makes of a situation will have great bearing on how he responds to that situation so let us examine the phenomenon more closely.

A Model of Perception

March and Simon suggest a model (see Figure 2-1) which seems well supported by research. First of all, they regard man as a complex, information-processing system—"a choosing, decision-making, problem-solving organism that can do only one or a few things at a time, and that can attend to only a small part of the information in its memory and presented by the environment"(3).

They argue that one's behavior, through a short interval of time, is determined by the interaction between his *internal state*(4) (which is largely a product of one's previous *learning*) at the beginning of the interval and his *environment*.

When the interval is very short only a small part of one's internal state and a small part of his environment will be active, i.e., will significantly influence his behavior during the interval. In information theory terms, the eye can handle about 5 million bits per second, but the resolving power of the

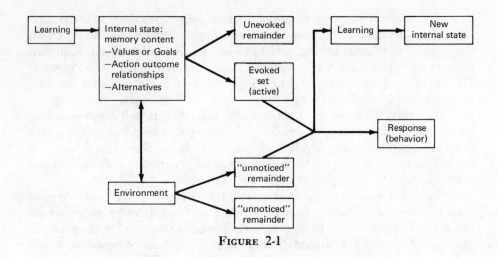

FIGURE 2-1

brain is approximately 500 bits per second. *Selection* is inevitable. How then, are these active parts determined? As stated above, they are selected through the interaction of one's internal state and his environment at the beginning of the time interval. The active part of the internal state is called the *set*(5) which is evoked by the environment leaving the *unevoked remainder* which plays no significant role in affecting the behavior at that time. Similarly, the active part of the environment is selected by the internal state and is called the *stimuli*; the residue is the "unnoticed" remainder. Munn gives a relevant illustration:

> I once had a colony of white rats in the attic of the psychology building. One afternoon I found several rats outside of their cages. Some were dead and partly eaten. It occurred to me that, however the rats had escaped, they must have been eaten by wild rats. I went downstairs to get some water and was climbing the stairs again when I saw before me, and directly in front of the cages, a large wild gray rat. It was standing tense and trembling, apparently having heard me ascend the stairs. Very slowly I raised a glass jar that was in my right hand, and aimed it at the rat. Much to my surprise, the animal failed to move. Upon approaching the object, I discovered it to be a piece of crumpled-up-grayish paper. Without the set induced by my suspicion that gray rats were in the attic, I should undoubtedly have seen the paper for what it was, assuming that I noticed it at all(6).

Let us examine Munn's behavior, asserting a chain of *sets* and *stimuli*. To start at an arbitrary point, he was *set* to notice the white rats among other reasons because they were presumably why he went to the attic in the first place. Thus, the partly eaten white rats readily became *stimuli* which in turn triggered still another *set*—the expectation of wild gray rats. Any part of his environment which bore a reasonable resemblance to a wild gray rat thus became a candidate for becoming his new *stimuli*. The crumpled paper qualified. It was not only selected as a *stimulus* (supposedly it had been part of the "unnoticed remainder" of the environment on his first trip to the attic) but was interpreted as a wild gray rat.

The result of the interplay of environment and internal state is one's *response* (behavior) and his *internal state* at the beginning of the next time interval. This new internal state can be considered as modified by the *learning* derived from the experience of the previous interval.

Just what is active or passive in one's internal state and environment is a function of time, among other factors. For a very short period, there will be very few active elements in set and stimuli. For a longer period, a larger portion of the memory content will likely be evoked and a large number of environmental events will influence behavior at some time during the interval. Thus, phrases such as "definition of the situation" and "frame of reference" are more appropriate than "set" in discussing longer time periods.

If one's response is a function of interrelated variables it follows that a variation in any or all of them would normally affect the response. Therefore we shall examine some of these variables in greater detail.

Differing Environments

Hold up a die between us. If you see three dots I will see four. As obvious as it should be, the phenomenon of differing environments, which would preclude our receiving the same stimuli, seems to contribute to a great deal of unnecessary and destructive conflict.

I have had the rewarding experience of serving for several years as a consultant to the Federal Mediation and Conciliation Service. Any number of the commissioners, men who are constantly concerned with union-management controversies, have asserted to me that a significant portion of the lack of communication, understanding, and harmony between the two parties stems from the simple fact that neither side is given full and direct access to the private environment—including the pressures, complexities, and restrictions—of the other. Thus, from the very outset of the negotiation the parties are exposed to substantially different environments and therefore are, in many respects, responding to different stimuli.

Differing Stimuli

Presume a mutual environment and there is still no guarantee that your responses and mine will be influenced by the same stimuli. Our respective evoked sets will have a considerable bearing on which parts of the environment will significantly impinge upon us as stimuli. Munn's story of the rat is a case in point.

Differing Sensory Receptors

Another reason why parts of the environment either never become stimuli or are experienced differently is that our sensory "equipment" varies. It has long been recognized that individuals differ markedly in sensory thresholds and acuity. While there has been gratifying progress in the prevention, correction, and amelioration of sensory limitations there is still much to be learned.

An interesting demonstration of differing sensory equipment is to give a bit of paper to each person in a group and request each to determine the taste of the paper. The group does not know it but the paper is impregnated with phenylthiocarbamide (PTC). If the group is representative, a significant portion will experience a distinctly bitter sensation. But some will taste it as sweet, others as sour, and still others as salty. And about half will find it utterly tasteless!

PTC, a chemical used by geneticists to trace heredity traits, reveals dramatically that we simply do not all inherit identical sensory apparatus. Add to this variations of the nervous system due to disease and injury and it is clear that our senses are inclined to be neither infallible nor uniform. I have a personal example to contribute in this regard. I have had a few mild disputes with my wife who "alleged" a shrill whistle in the television set. Since I did not hear it I denied that it existed. Somewhat later I had an autiometric examination and discovered that, like many others who were around artillery during the war, I had lost the capacity to hear tones of extremely high pitch.

Differing Internal States

One's *internal state* is the product of his *learning processes* and it is obvious that the "lessons" acquired by one person can differ markedly from those of another. Imagine a number of individuals observing a man drinking liquor. If the observers are candid and sufficiently representative we can expect a gamut of reactions. Some will regard the man as sinful; others as extravagant. Others will associate his drinking with friendliness and congeniality. Some will view it as a character flaw—a way of avoiding unpleasantness, running from problems. Still others may perceive it as a relaxant. And people in the distilling industry—and the Alcohol and Tobacco Tax Division of the Internal Revenue Service—may relate it to a job!

For a more dramatic example of the role of learning compare cultures. One's culture is an extraordinarily effective teacher. First, it teaches us unrelentingly—every waking moment. Second, it is a most subtle, even insidious teacher—which detracts not at all from its effectiveness. Immersed in it constantly, we are seldom conscious of what it has been teaching us until we contrast its lessons with those taught by other cultures. The perceptive traveler, for example, as he visits foreign countries, learns a good deal about *himself* and the special lessons his culture has taught him.

For example, anthropologists tell us that we learn from our respective cultures how to perceive a misbehaving child. This is revealed by how we speak to the child. English-speaking people generally consider misbehavior as "bad" or "naughty," a suggestion of immorality, and admonish the child with "Johnny, be *good!*" Italian- and Greek-speaking people say the equivalent. The French, however, tend to say "Jean, sois sage!"—be *wise*. Their culture teaches that the child who misbehaves is being stupid, foolish, imprudent, injudicious. The Scandinavians have another concept expressed by the Swedish, "Jan, var snell!" and the Norwegian, "Jan, ble snil!"—be *friendly*, be *kind*. Germans have learned still differently. With them it is "Hans, sei artig!" *get back in step*. *Sei artig* is literally "be of your own kind"—in other words, "conform to your role as a child"(7).

Clearly, individuals from these various cultures could observe the same child misbehaving but regard him very differently because they had been *trained* to do so. Grant that different people learn different "lessons" from life and it is readily apparent that individualized learning plays a subtle but critical role in one's communication with others.

Differing Evoked Sets

One's set, according to the model, is dependent upon three other variables: that which is available in the internal state, the stimuli which trigger the set, and, though less directly, the processes of learning. March and Simon clarify the role of learning in this regard:

When one of these elements (values or goals, action-outcome relationships and alternatives) is evoked by a stimulus, it may also bring into the evoked set a number of other elements with which it has become associated through the learning processes. Thus, if a particular goal has been achieved on previous occasions by execution of a particular course of action, then evocation of that goal will be likely to evoke that course of action again. Habitual responses are extreme instances of this in which the connecting links between stimulus and response may be suppressed from consciousness. In the same way, the evocation of a course of action will lead by association to evocation of consequences that have been associated with the action(8).

This helps to account for the apparent self-perpetuating nature of sets which others have observed.

Our concept of causal texture implies that definitions and relations, once they have been adopted, influence interpretations of subsequent events. Early definitions of the conditions under which a task will be accomplished are apt to take precedence over later definitions(9).

The tendency to distort messages in the direction of identity with previous inputs is probably the most pervasive of the systematic biases(10).

Sebald confirmed a hypothesis "that largely only those meanings are being perceived and recalled which reinforce prior images"(11). He also suggested "that selective distortion takes place in order to screen out dissonant features—features which are apt to disturb pre-conceived images"(12).

The concept of differing sets helps to explain the abyss which so frequently separates superiors and subordinates. A man looking downward in an organization may often have a very different set from the man below him looking up. For example, Likert reports that 85 percent of a sampling of foremen estimated that their men "felt very free to discuss important things about the job with my superior." However, only 51 percent of their men shared this view(13). Seventy-three percent of the foremen felt they "always or almost always get subordinates' ideas" on the solution of job problems. Only 16 percent of their subordinates agreed with this appraisal(14). Ninety-five percent of the foremen said they understood their men's problems well but only 34 percent of the men felt that they did(15).

The gulf between superiors' and subordinates' sets is documented further by Maier(16) who reports a study of 35 pairs from four large firms. A pair consisted of a manager, third echelon from the top, and one of his immediate subordinates. Each partner in each pair was questioned regarding the subordinate's job. On only one aspect was there substantial agreement—the content of the subordinate's duties. However, there was little agreement on the order of importance of these duties. There was only fair agreement on the job's requirements and almost complete disagreement on their priority ranking. Finally, there was virtually no agreement on the problems and obstacles of the subordinate. These findings were discussed with all participants. Several months later a questionnaire was sent to each participant asking if the superior and his respective subordinate had gotten together to discuss their differences. Only 22 pairs replied. Six of them agreed that they had gotten together; nine agreed that they had not; and seven pairs could not agree on whether they had or had not gotten together!

In Summation

The perception model suggests why it is impossible for one to be in simple, direct contact with reality, why he lives in a personalized world and why, in the words of St. Paul, "We see through a glass darkly." Indeed, there are a number of interrelated variables (differing environments, stimuli, sensory receptors, internal states, and evoked sets) which intervene between perception and reality. Thus, individuals are led to respond differently to events and, in general, complicate the process of communication enormously— particularly *if the role of such factors is ignored or misunderstood.*

the prime obstacle of every form of communications . . . is simply the fact of *difference.* On this point most serious students of communication are in agreement, the great gap is the gap in background, experience, and motivations between ourselves and those with whom we would communicate.

It is a gap that will remain. . . . But if we cannot close the gap, we must at least acknowledge it. For this *acknowledgment of difference* is the vital preface to all the efforts that follow. . . .(17).

DEFENSIVENESS

The "acknowledgment of difference"—a simple phrase but how difficult to practice! Perhaps the most appropriate adjective to describe much of the behavior of people communicating and relating to one another in organizational settings would be *defensive.* A fundamental reason for defensive behavior appears to be the inability of so many people to *acknowledge differences* —differences between their perceptions and reality and differences between their perceptions and those of others. Their prevailing, albeit largely unconscious, presumption is that "the world is as I see it." He who harbors this notion will find life continuously threatening for there are many others who share his notion—but not *his* "*world!*" Such people find it perpetually necessary to protect their "worlds" and to deny or attack the other fellow's.

Admittedly, the premise that one deals only indirectly and often unreliably with reality can be disturbing. To those who crave a certain, definite, and dependable world (and that includes all of us in varying degrees) the admission that we respond only to *what it appears to be* rather than *what it is* necessarily lessens our *predictability* about the "real world." Even those who *intellectually accept* the perception model and the roles that stimuli, set, learning, and so on, play in determining responses may have difficulty converting the concept into performance. A good test of the extent to which one has truly internalized such awareness occurs when he becomes emotionally involved with others.

For instance, suppose you and I work in the same organization and we observe Joe, one of our colleagues, taking home company supplies—such as paper pads, paper clips, and pencils—not in large quantities but it is obvious to us that he will not use them exclusively for official purposes. He will let the the children have them, use them for his private affairs, and so on.

Now, let us say that you are the product of a rigorous religious upbringing. It is likely that you will be *set* to regard Joe as dishonest. But suppose that I have had none of your training and that the only part of my background that is particularly relevant was the three years I spent in the Army in World War II. There I learned a code that was unwritten but very pervasive. It was in effect, "You may rob the Army blind!—but you must not steal a nickel from another serviceman." I would be quite inclined to regard Joe as honest and could readily consider his acquisitions as normal prerequisites.

Let us examine the *communication* issue. (Permit me to disregard the moral issue without denying that there is one.) Consider the tremendous difficulty you and I would have in discussing Joe if in our increasingly vehement statements—"Joe's dishonest!" "No, he's not!"—we failed to realize that neither of us was talking about *Joe*. We were talking about *you* and *me* and our *respective* "inside-the-skin" experiences. Our respective worlds were different from the outset and there was no reason to expect them to be identical—and no *rational* reason to have to protect them. Why, then, did we protect them so ardently?

Let us begin with an assertion: Most reasonably mature people can tolerate fairly well differences in value judgments, opinions, attitudes, points of view—*so long as they can recognize them as such*. If I can realize that your "reality" is not the same as mine then your statement about *your* "reality" is no threat to *mine*.

But no one can tolerate differences on matters of objectivity—matters which submit to corroborable measurement and are capable of general agreement. To illustrate, suppose you and I have a mutual superior and he comes to us and says: "This may sound silly but I'm serious. I want you two to estimate the length of that 2 × 4 over there (about 20 feet away) on the ground. You have to estimate because you can't use any kind of measuring device and you can't get any closer to it than you are now. Now, I want a good estimate and only one between you—so get to it!"

(Now suppose the piece of lumber is actually 7 feet long but neither of us knows this.) So we start sizing up the situation and you say, "Looks about 6½ or 7 feet." And I say, "No, no—you're way short—that's a lot closer to 14 feet!" Unless you had admirable constraint you would probably blurt out, "You're crazy!"

Now, why were you moved to feel I was crazy?

Was it not partly because my statement was at least a slight threat to your sense of reality and, therefore, your sanity? In other words if (I said *if*) I were indeed right—i.e., if the board actually were 14 feet and everything were twice as big as you perceive it—would you not begin to have serious misgivings about *your* "contact with reality"? "You're crazy!", then, is your understandable if impulsive way of defending yourself against an attack on your sanity.

Actually, we would be unlikely to have such a disparity (unless one or both of us *were* losing touch with reality) because our perceptual lessons, when we initially learned to perceive the inch, the foot, and the yard, were likely to have been very similar regardless of where or when we learned them. And even if we were to disagree on matters such as distance, speed, and weight we could resolve our differences by using standardized measuring devices.

But when we encounter Cezanne and Dali, Tolstoi and Faulkner, Mozart and Cole Porter, we are unlikely to have had identical learning experiences and where is the "standardized measuring device"? Will someone resolve a controversy with "Why, that Van Gogh is 87 percent beautiful!"? Even professional critics are unable to provide universally acceptable and applicable criteria.

The point is that not only can we not tolerate differences in matters of objectivity (but what differences there may be are generally minor or re-solvable by objective measurement) but we cannot accept differences on matters of subjectivity (value judgments, opinions, and so on) if we uncon-sciously *treat them* as matters of objectivity. There are many important aspects of our lives such as art, music, architecture, religion, politics, morals, fashions, foods, economic and political theory, which (1) are not taught to us in standardized lessons and (2) are not, by and large, measurable by standardized scales or gauges. It is in such areas that we find it easiest to threaten one another. And when one is threatened he tends, if he does not run, to fight back—the threatener is now threatened and bootless conflict generally follows.

Defensiveness appears to be so pervasive and potentially so destructive to organizational communication and interpersonal relationships that we shall examine it in more detail in terms of the communicator's *frame of reference*.

Frame of Reference

Frame of reference is the term March and Simon used for longer intervals of time in lieu of "set." It has been defined as:

A system of standards or values, usually merely implicit, underlying and to some extent controlling an action, or the expression of any attitude, belief, or idea(18).

Carl Rogers offers several propositions(19) which serve as a rationale for the validity and utility of the frame of reference construct.

1. *Every individual exists in a continually changing world of experience of which he is the center.*

Rogers holds that each of us is at the core of his own world and every-thing else is happening, developing, occurring about him—(not unlike Ptolemy's homocentric notion of the earth as the center of the universe). It is painfully obvious that man is the most egocentric organism on earth, and surely no one can be more self-centered than the human infant. The baby will outgrow much of this, of course, but hardly all of it. But it would seem that one who is approaching emotional maturity has already recognized that egocentrism is a substantial part of being human. Once one accepts this frailty he is in an excellent state to begin to compensate for it and to grow beyond it. The truly arrogant person, however, is the man or woman who has never made and perhaps cannot make this admission. For so long as one can shield himself from a recognition of his fallibility, he need not expend energy in growing and he need not submit to the unknowns and possible pain of *change*.

2. *The individual reacts to his world as he experiences and perceives it and thus this perceptual world is, for the individual, "reality."*

Rogers put quotes around *reality* to indicate that it is not the "real" reality. Consider these definitions of perception: "The point of reality contact, the door to reality appraisal"(20); the "structuring of stimuli"(21) and the "organization of stimuli"(22), and "the way in which the person structures his world and himself"(23). But regardless of how invalid and incomplete it may be, one's personalized reality is the only one he has and therefore the only one to which he responds.

3. *The individual has one basic tendency and striving which is to actualize, maintain, and enhance himself.*

Rogers writes of the *actualizing tendency* as "the inherent tendency of the organism to develop all its capacities in ways to serve to maintain or enhance the organism. It involves not only the tendency to meet . . . 'deficiency needs' for air, food, water, and the like, but also more generalized activities. . . . It is development toward autonomy and away from heteronomy, or control by external forces"(24). He subscribes to Angyal's statement: "Life is an autonomous event which takes place between the organism and the environment. Life processes do not merely tend to preserve life but transcend the momentary status quo of the organism, expanding itself continually and imposing its autonomous determination upon an ever increasing realm of events(25).

More specifically, Rogers refers to *self*-actualization. We will discuss his concept of the self-image later in this chapter and for the moment will merely suggest that much of the individual's perceiving is in the service of preserving or enhancing his self-image.

According to Frenkel-Brunswick:

It would appear that we do **not** always see ourselves as we are but instead perceive the environment in terms of our own need. Self-perception and perception of the environment actually merge in the service of these needs. Thus, the perceptual distortions of ourselves and the environment fulfill an important function in our psychological household(26).

The role of *needs* and *motivation* in influencing perception and therefore behavior is clearly important enough to require the separate chapter which follows this one.

4. *Therefore, the best vantage point for understanding another's behavior is from that person's internal frame of reference.*

This conclusion follows logically from Rogers' preceding propositions but this does not necessarily make it easy to utilize the frame of reference concept. The individual's internal frame of reference *is* his subjective world. "Only he knows it fully. It can never be known to another except through empathic inference and then can never be perfectly known."(27).

Probably the greatest single deterrent to one's accurately visualizing another's frame of reference is his *own*. An analogy will suggest why this is so.

Analogy of the Box

Visualize each of us as the sole and constant tenant of a box with a top, a bottom, and four sides. There is just one window in this box—one's frame of reference, loosely speaking—through which he views the outside world.

A Restricted Window   This suggests immediately that one's view is restricted—he cannot see what is happening in back of him, above, to the sides, and so forth. One obviously cannot be ubiquitous and therefore his view is inevitably limited. But there is another restriction that he can overcome to an extent—the *size* of the window. We all have our "narrownesses"—our areas of naïveté. I, for example, was born and reared in a suburb. Suppose you are a country boy and we go out to a farm. We would share the same environment but I would expect that your stimuli and evoked sets would greatly outnumber mine. You would have the preparation, the memory content, to make so much more significance out of the experience than I.

But I have the capacity to learn. Given the time and provided I have the motivation I can acquire some of your sophistication. In short I can *expand* my window.

Stained-Glass Window   Not only is one's window frame restricted (but expandable largely at his will) but it also does not contain a pane of clear glass. It is rather like a stained-glass church window with various, peculiarly shaped, tinted, and refracting lenses. In one's frame of reference these lenses are his experiences, biases, values, needs, emotions, aspirations, and the like. They may all be distorting media to an extent but are we powerless to overcome these distortions? Hardly, but let us establish one point first.

Does anyone grow up with a clear window? Can anyone be without bias for example? Quite unlikely, for everyone had to be born at a particular time and in a particular place. Thus he was exposed to particular people and situations all of whom and which taught him *special* lessons regarding values, customs, mores, codes, and so on.

But again man has viability and the capacity to adjust and compensate— he can *clarify* his window. A pencil in a glass of water appears to bend abruptly but if one *understands* something about the nature of refraction he can compensate for the distortion, aim at where the pencil appears not to be, and hit it. So it is more profoundly with a man himself—if he can *understand himself* he can *compensate* for his distorted frame of reference and, in effect, clarify his window.

The Self-Image

But there is at least one extremely formidable obstacle in the way of a man's truly understanding himself. We return to Carl Rogers for this. A key concept of the Rogerian therapeutic approach is the premise that as a person grows up he develops a *self-image* or *self-concept*—a picture of himself. Hayakawa asserted: "The mode of human behavior is not self-preservation but self-concept. The self-concept is who you think you are and the self is who you are. Values determine people's self-concept and self-concept determines social experience"(28). Rogers uses *self, concept of self*, and *self-structure* as terms to refer to

the organized, consistent conceptual gestalt composed of perceptions of the characteristics of the "I" or "me" and the perception of the relationships of the "I" or "me" to others and to various aspects of life, together with the values attached to these perceptions. It is a fluid and changing gestalt, a process, . . . The term self or self-concept is more likely to be used when we are talking of the person's view of himself, self-structure when we are looking at this gestalt from an external frame of reference(29).

On Coping with Guilt.   The self-image helps to explain how one copes with guilt.

One of man's most compelling needs is the need to justify himself. Moreover, most of us tolerate guilt very poorly. Guilt is painful—acutely so. Therefore, as pain-avoidance organisms most of us have devised highly facile and sophisticated means for eliminating or diminishing the pain of guilt. Test this assertion, if you can tread a painful route, by tracing back to an event in which you did something that you *knew* was *wrong*; that you *could not justify* by rationalizing that the end warranted the means; and that *was not beyond your control.*

Most of us have great difficulty remembering such events objectively and yet almost all of us have been guilty of them. The pain of guilt is so noisome that we have developed great skill in justifying our behavior before, during, or after the act.

At the core of this behavior appears to be the overriding motive to "actualize, maintain, and enhance" one's self-image. It is clear that the individual can distort experience to satisfy this powerful need. For example, suppose Mike treats Tom unjustly—at least as Tom perceives it. Tom will likely become angry and want revenge. If Tom were to analyze himself he might find that what he wants most of all is for Mike to experience remorse, true contrition—the pain of guilt—at least commensurate with the pain he inflicted upon Tom. However, Mike as a pain-avoider, has already begun to justify his behavior and is unlikely, therefore, to tender a sincere apology. Failing to receive evidence of Mike's acceptance of his own guilt, Tom may be moved to retaliate in kind or to attempt to wrench an apology from Mike. In either event, Tom's behavior, as Mike perceives it, is sufficiently obnoxious to complete his self-justification. "You see how Tom is acting? That _____ deserved to be treated that way in the first place!"

No matter how unreasonable, irrational, or immoral another's behavior may appear to us it is generally a good assumption that it is quite reasonable, rational and moral *in his world*. Epictetus wrote: "The appearances of things to the mind is the standard of action of every man."

One's self-image is perhaps most profoundly important to the individual in the sense that it serves as *his contact with himself*. In fact, when he talks or thinks about *himself* he is usually not referring to his limbs, torso, and head but rather to an abstraction he usually labels as "my *self*." Thus, it is by his self-image that he *knows* himself.

Images of Others   But we also need to know and understand others and thus we form images of them as well—particularly those with whom we are most interdependent—parents, spouse, children, superiors, subordinates. Such image formation, whether one is conscious of it or not, requires considerable energy output and the marshaling of much psychological intelligence about the individual of whom one is forming an image. The prime motive for the effort is that we need to build a good base for understanding and predicting the behavior of the other person. And only by predicting the other's behavior reasonably accurately can we confidently control our own behavior and deal effectively with the other person(30). This helps to explain why one becomes confused and upset when another's behavior suddenly contradicts his image of that other person. He has lost or risks the loss of his base for predicting and thus for controlling himself in dealing with the other.

And this holds even when the other's behavior is *more favorable* than anticipated. Suppose you have a superior—a father, a teacher, a boss—who is a veritable tyrant. And suppose one day he greets you with a broad smile, a friendly clap on the back, and an encouraging comment. Is your initial response—"Wonderful, the old buzzard has finally turned over a new leaf!"? Or is it—"What's he up to now!"? As a friend in business put it, "You can work for an s.o.b.—provided he's a *consistent* s.o.b. It's the one who turns it on and off unpredictably that gives you the ulcers!"

Self-Image Challenged   Now if we are troubled by another person's jeopardizing our predictability about him then how much more traumatic is it for one to have his *own self*-image challenged. He stands the risk of losing the ability to predict, control, and *know himself*. It is difficult to imagine a greater internal upheaval than suddenly not to *know oneself—to lose contact with oneself*. It may not be inaccurate to say that our mental institutions are filled with people who have lost contact with themselves more or less permanently.

It is no wonder, then, that the loss of a self-image is generally warded off at almost any cost. And yet few of us have gone through life unscathed. Anyone who has experienced a deeply traumatic experience at one time or another—whether related to a parent, a spouse, a child, school, religion, vocation, narcotics, alcoholism, job security, illness, injury, lawsuit—will probably find on retrospection that his self-image was being severely threatened.

A Personal Case. My own experience is a case in point. As a high school freshman I hit upon chemical research for a career. I suppose this was encouraged by an older boy I admired who also aspired to chemistry. He had built a laboratory in his basement so, of course, I had to have one too. I remember collecting hundreds of jars and bottles and scores of other treasures that might somehow be useful in my lab. I can also recall spending hour after hour thoroughly enjoying mixing potions of every description—and some beyond description. (I recall without quite so much relish the time I brewed some chlorine and nearly gassed myself unconscious!)

I *devoured* the chemistry course in my junior year. I must admit feeling rather smug during this period for I had a ready answer to the recurrent question, What are you going to be? Most of my friends had either a hazy answer or none at all. My self-image in this regard was forming and solidifying.

I was graduated from high school during World War II and immediately entered the service. Somehow the Army gave little shrift to young men who were long on aspiration but short on experience and consequently I had three years of singularly nonchemical experience—but this did not dissuade me. Finally, the war ended and I was discharged. I immediately enrolled in a chemical technology program at a university reputed for this field.

Suddenly, reality began to catch up with my self-image. I had not realized that a chemist was also expected to be a pretty fair mathematician. I had done well enough in high school math courses but the last three years were nonmathematical as well as nonchemical. At any rate I foolishly disregarded the math refresher course (my self-image said I didn't need a "crutch") and charged headlong into college algebra where I was in competition with fellows fresh from high school math. While I was rusty, it would be unfair to say that I didn't get the math; I did get it but about a week after the exams, which is poor timing! Net result—the first D I had ever received in my life. What was the consequence—did I trade in my self-image for a new model? Hardly; rather than yield, I fought tenaciously and found a ready explanation for my plight: Aside from the Army's causing me to "forget my math" the instructor "had it in for me." Among other evidences he had a Scottish name and I was convinced he was anti-Irish!

I was practicing what some writers call "perceptual defense," a form of perceptual distortion which "demonstrates that when confronted with a fact inconsistent with a stereotype already held by a person, the perceiver is able to distort the data in such a way as to eliminate the inconsistency. Thus, by perceiving inaccurately, he defends himself from having to change his stereotypes"(31). Haire and Grunes suggest that we "blinder" ourselves to avoid seeing that which might trouble us(32). As communication authority David K. Berlo paraphrased the Bible—"Seek and ye shall find—whether it is there or not!"

The next quarter? A C in math. This instructor had an Irish name but he didn't like me either! In the middle of the third quarter and another math D, my self-image had withstood all the onslaught from harsh reality that it could. And for two to three weeks (at the time it seemed like six months) I was in a state of unrelieved depression. I became very nervous and had difficulty eating, sleeping, and studying (which only intensified my problem). Figuratively, a large section of my self-image had been shot away and *I had nothing to replace it.* The most appalling aspect of the experience was that I realized that *I didn't know myself.* To give the story a happy ending I took a battery of aptitude tests, changed to another major, and very gradually began to construct another self-image.

Resistance to Image Change Anyone who has undergone such a trauma will understand why the individual generally resists image change—particularly sudden change. And herein lies one of the greatest obstacles to the full development of an effective communicator and, for that matter, an effective person. The central premise of an excellent book(33) by psychiatrist Karen Horney is that the neurotic process is a special form of human development which is the antithesis of healthy growth. Optimally, man's energies are directed toward realizing his own potentialities. But, under inner stress, he becomes estranged from his *real self* and spends himself creating and protecting a false, idealized self, based on pride, but threatened by doubts, self-contempt, and self-hate. Throughout the book the goal of liberation for the forces that lead to true self-realization is emphasized.

Take the case of a high school friend. After graduation he, too, went into the service but was more fortunate (in a sense), for the Army put him through three years of an engineering curriculum. Then the war was over and he was discharged. But he decided he did not care for engineering and could not bring himself to take a final year of course work to earn an engineering degree. And yet he could not bear the thought of starting all over again in another field. The net result was that, for all practical purposes, he did nothing. He took a clerical job in a nearby insurance firm and has been there for 20 years. Through the years, his perhaps largely unconscious philosophy of life has evidently been: "I can't stand another failure [he probably regarded not completing the engineering degree as a failure] and one sure way not to lose a race is not to enter it." In sum, here is a man who apparently has protected his self-image at the cost of a stunted life.

The handicap of inaccurate self-knowledge and the unwillingness to reconstruct a more realistic self-image seem to be very widespread. In 15 years of organizational research and consulting I have known scores, if not hundreds of men, particularly in the middle echelons of their organizations, who seemed to have all the requisites for continued success: intelligence, education, experience, drive, ability, ambition. But they had one vital failing—*they did not know themselves.* The image they held of themselves was pitifully out of phase with that which they were projecting to others. They seemed chronically annoyed and/or bewildered by the reactions of others to them. What was happening? As unrealistic as their self-images were it was nevertheless too threatening to entertain contrary cues from other people. Fending off the reactions of others variously as "those malicious/crazy/misinformed/ornery/perverse/stupid people!" they had been successful in perpetuating and even reinforcing their respective self-myths. Thus, they ineffectualized themselves; squandered their nervous energies in a kind of internal conflict, protecting their fallacious self-images(34). The masterful Robert Burns captured the poignancy of self-deception almost two centuries ago.

> Oh wad some power the giftie gie us
> To see oursels as ithers see us!
> It wad frae monie a blunder free us,
>   An' foolish notion.

ON COPING WITH DEFENSIVENESS

We have discussed defensive behavior as a critical obstacle to effective interpersonal communication. What, in the final analysis, are people defending *against?* In a word, *perceived threat*—the threat of change or harm to their self-images, to their personalized worlds. This would suggest that whatever reduced perceived threat would reduce the need to defend against it—to enable one to reduce his defenses accordingly. What threat-reducing techniques or aproaches, then, are available to us?

After an eight-year study of recordings of interpersonal discussions, Jack Gibb delineated two communication climates—one threatening ("defensive"); the other nonthreatening ("supportive"). (See Table 2-1.) Gibb defined his paired categories of perceived behavior as follows(35):

Evaluation. To pass judgment on another; to blame or praise; to make moral assessments of another; to question his standards, values and motives and the affect loadings of his communications.

Tᴀʙʟᴇ 2-1

CATEGORIES OF BEHAVIOR CHARACTERISTIC OF SUPPORTIVE AND
DEFENSIVE CLIMATES IN SMALL GROUPS *

Defensive Climates	Supportive Climates
1. Evaluation	1. Description
2. Control	2. Problem orientation
3. Strategy	3. Spontaneity
4. Neutrality	4. Empathy
5. Superiority	5. Equality
6. Certainty	6. Provisionalism

* Jack R. Gibb, "Defensive Communication," *Journal of Communication*, Vol. 11, No. 3, Sept., 1961, p. 143.

Description. Nonjudgmental; to ask questions which are perceived as genuine requests for information; to present "feelings, events, perceptions, or processes which do not ask or imply that the receiver change behavior or attitude."

Control. To try to do something to another; to attempt to change an attitude or the behavior of another—to try to restrict his field of activity; "implicit in all attempts to alter another person is the assumption of the change agent that the person to be altered is inadequate."

Problem Orientation. The antithesis of persuasion; to communicate "a desire to collaborate in defining a mutual problem and in seeking its solution" (thus tending to create the same problem orientation in the other); to imply that he has no preconceived solution, attitude, or method to impose upon the other; to allow "the receiver to set his own goals, make his own decisions, and evaluate his own progress—or to share with the sender in doing so."

Strategy. To manipulate others; to use tricks to "involve" another, to make him think he was making his own decisions, and to make him feel that the speaker had genuine interest in him; to engage in a stratagem involving ambiguous and multiple motivation.

Spontaneity. To express guilelessness; natural simplicity; free of deception; having a "clean id"; having unhidden, uncomplicated motives; straightforwardness and honesty.

Neutrality. To express lack of concern for the welfare of another; "the clinical, detached, person-is-an-object-of-study attitude."

Empathy. To express respect for the worth of the listener; to identify with his problems, share his feelings, and accept his emotional values at face value.

Superiority. To communicate the attitude that one is "superior in position, power, wealth, intellectual ability, physical characteristics, or other ways" to another; to tend to arouse feelings of inadequacy in the other; to impress the other that the speaker "is not willing to enter into a shared problem-solving relationship, that he probably does not desire feedback, that he does not require help and/or that he will be likely to try to reduce the power, the status, or the worth of the receiver."

Equality. To be willing to enter into participative planning with mutual trust and respect; to attach little importance to differences in talent, ability, worth, appearance, status, and power.

Certainty. To appear dogmatic; "to seem to know the answers, to require no additional data"; and to regard self as teacher rather than as co-worker; to manifest inferiority by *needing to be right*, wanting to win an argument rather than solve a problem, seeing one's ideas as truths to be defended.

Provisionalism. To be willing to experiment with one's own behavior, attitudes, and ideas; to investigate issues rather than taking sides on them, to problem solve rather than debate, to communicate that the other person may have some control over the shared quest or the investigation of ideas. "If a person is genuinely searching for information and data, he does not resent help or company along the way."

It would appear that if one were to offer another the most supportive climate possible his behavior should be descriptive, problem oriented, spontaneous, and so on, and should avoid attempting to evaluate, control, employ stratagems, and so forth. But the situation is a bit more complex.

First of all, the above are *perceived* behaviors. Therefore, the *perceptions* of the *perceiver* rather than the *intentions* of the perceived will be the final arbiter as to how defensive or supportive the perceiver regards the climate. Moreover, as a person becomes more defensive he becomes less able to assess accurately the motives, values, and emotions of the other person. Conversely, as he grows less defensive, the more accurate his perceptions become(36).

The more "supportive" or defense reductive the climate, the less the receiver reads into the communication distorted loadings which arise from projections of his own anxieties, motives, and concerns. As defenses are reduced, the receivers become better able to concentrate upon the structure, the content, and the cognitive meanings of the message(37).

Another qualification on Gibb's classifications is that while the defensive categories *generally* arouse defensiveness and the supportive categories *ordinarily* generate defense reduction, the degree to which these responses occur depends upon the *individual's level of defensiveness* as well as the *general climate of the group at the time*(38).

Still another qualification is that the behavior categories are *interactive*. For example, when a speaker's behavior appears *evaluative* it ordinarily increases defensiveness. But if the listener feels the speaker regards him as an *equal* and was being direct and *spontaneous*, the evaluativeness of the message might be neutralized or not even perceived. Again, attempts to *control* will stimulate defensiveness depending upon the degree of *openness* of the effort. The suspicion of hidden motives heightens resistance. Still another example, the use of *stratagems* becomes especially threatening when one attempt seems to be trying to make strategy *appear spontaneous*.

Openness

A central theme running throughout Gibb's findings is the importance of *openness*—the willingness to be receptive to experience. Rogers considered openness as the polar opposite of defensiveness.

In the hypothetical person who is completely open to his experience, his concept of self would be a symbolization in awareness which would be completely congruent with his experience. There would, therefore, be no possibility of threat(39).

One who is open to experience evaluates threat more accurately and tolerates change more graciously. This is why the frame of reference concept can be so helpful in reducing defenses and in keeping them low. Because the frame of reference obviates the mine-is-the-only-valid-world presumption it makes defense of one's personalized world unnecessary. Nondefensive, one is not compelled to attack or counterattack—thus he is more able to contribute to a supportive climate in his relations with others.

In a supportive climate people are more able to explore their own and each other's decision premises(40) and thus get down to the real grounds of controversy (or to discover that there was no real basis for conflict). Even if there are genuine differences, under conditions of openness people themselves more capable of dealing with them maturely.

Rogers offers this practical suggestion:

The next time you get into an argument with your wife, or your friend, or with a small group of friends, just stop the discussion for a moment and for an experiment, institute this rule. "Each person can speak up for himself only *after* he has first restated the ideas and feelings of the previous speaker accurately, and to that speaker's satisfaction." You see what this would mean? It would simply mean that before presenting your own point of view, it would be necessary for you to really achieve the other speaker's frame of reference—to understand his thoughts and feelings so well that you could summarize them for him. Sounds simple, doesn't it? But if you try it you will discover it one of the most difficult things you have tried to do. However, once you have been able to see the other's point of view, your own comments will have to be drastically revised. You will also find the emotion going out of the discussion, the differences being reduced, and those differences which remain being of a rational and understandable sort(41).

SUMMARY

We have depicted human behavior as the product of the internal state of the individual and the environment in which he finds himself. His behavior, then, is only indirectly a response to reality. One who cannot tolerate this basic uncertainty of life and who assumes *his world is the only real world* may find that "world" in almost constant jeopardy. Closed and defensive he may respond to the "threats" with irrational attack and/or flight.

We have conceded that many organizations are populated to an extent with more or less defensive (and thus often aggressive) people. Therefore, the challenge to anyone who aspires to be an effective leader or member of an organization (or more broadly, wishes to live an emotionally mature and deeply satisfying life) might be phrased as follows:

1. Can he come to accept that *his* and everyone else's "reality" is subjective, incomplete, distorted, and unique? Can he, therefore, muster the courage to become open and nondefensive—to permit even contrary cues to reach him and to begin to revise, update, and make more valid his self-image?
2. Having clarified his own frame of reference can he learn to assess accurately the frames of reference of others? Can the manager, for example, realize the simple but profound truth that his subordinates' worlds have him in it as a boss—his world does not?

NOTES

1. F. H. Allport, *Theories of Perceptions and the Concept of Structure* (New York: John Wiley & Sons, Inc., 1955).

2. Perception has been defined as "the more complex process [as distinguished from sensation] by which people select, organize, and interpret sensory stimulation into a meaningful and coherent picture of the world." B. Berelson and C. A. Steiner, *Human Behavior: An Inventory of Scientific Findings* (New York: Harcourt Brace Jovanovich, Inc., 1964), p. 88.

3. J. G. March and H. A. Simon, *Organizations* (New York: John Wiley & Sons, Inc., 1958), p. 11.

4. His internal state is mostly contained in his memory which "includes [but is not limited to] all sorts of partial and modified records of past experiences and programs for responding to environmental stimuli." Thus, the memory consists, in part, of:

a) Values or goals: criteria that are applied to determine which courses of action are preferred among those considered.

b) Relations between actions and their outcome; beliefs, perceptions, and expectations as to the consequences that will follow from one course of action or another. . . .

c) Alternatives: possible courses of action.

Ibid., pp. 10–11.

5. *Set* is generally regarded as the readiness of the organism to respond in a particular way.

6. Normal L. Munn, *Psychology: The Fundamentals of Human Adjustment* (Boston: Houghton Mifflin Co., 1947), p. 327. Reprinted by permission.

7. L. Sinclair (ed.), "A Word in Your Ear," *Ways of Mankind* (Boston: Beacon Press, 1954), pp. 28–29. For a fascinating account of cultural differences interfering with interpersonal communication see E. T. Hall, *The Silent Language* (Garden City, N.Y.: Doubleday & Co., Inc., 1959).

8. March and Simon, op. cit., p. 11.

9. H. B. Pepinsky, K. E. Weick, and J. W. Riner, *Primer for Productivity* (Columbus, Ohio: The Ohio State University Research Foundation, March, 1964), p. 54.

10. D. T. Campbell, "Systematic Error on the Part of Human Links in Communication Systems," *Information and Control*, Vol. 1 (1958), p. 346.

11. H. Sebald, "Limitations of Communication: Mechanisms of Image Maintenance in Form of Selective Perception, Selective Memory and Selective Distortion," *Journal of Communication*, Vol. XII, No. 3 (September, 1962), p. 149.

12. Ibid.

13. Rensis Likert, *New Patterns in Management* (New York: McGraw-Hill Book Co., 1961), p. 47.

14. Ibid., p. 53.

15. Ibid., p. 52.

16. N. R. F. Maier, "Breakdown in Boss-Subordinate Communication," *Communication in Organizations* (Ann Arbor, Mich.: The Foundation for Research on Human Behavior, 1959).

17. "Is Anybody Listening," *Fortune*, September 1950, p. 83. The italics are mine.

18. H. B. English and A. C. English, *A Comprehensive Dictionary of Psychological and Psychoanalytical Terms* (New York: Longmans, Green & Co., 1958).

19. Paraphrased from C. R. Rogers, *Client-Centered Therapy* (Boston, Mass.: Houghton Mifflin Co., 1951), pp. 483, 484, 487, 494.

20. G. S. Klein, "The Personal World through Perception," *Perception: An Approach to Personality*, ed. R. R. Blake and G. V. Ramsey (New York: The Ronald Press Co., 1951), pp. 328–29.

21. C. M. Solley and G. Murphy, *Development of the Perceptual World* (New York: Basic Books, Inc., Publishers, 1960), p. 26.

22. F. A. Beach, "Body Chemistry and Perception," Blake and Ramsey, op. cit., p. 56.

23. U. Bronfenbrenner, "Toward an Integrated Theory of Personality," Ibid., p. 207.

24. C. R. Rogers, "A Theory of Therapy, Personality, and Interpersonal Relationships, as Developed in the Client-Centered Framework," *Psychology: The Study of a Science*, Vol. 3, *Formulations of the Person and the Social Context*, ed. Sigmund Koch (New York: McGraw-Hill Book Co., 1959), p. 196.

25. A. Angyal, *Foundations for a Science of Personality* (New York: Commonwealth Fund, 1941).

26. Else Fenkel-Brunswick, "Personality Theory and Perception" chap. 13 in Blake and Ramsey, op. cit., p. 379.

27. C. R. Rogers, "A Theory of Therapy . . . ," op. cit., p. 210.

28. S. I. Hayakawa, participating in the 1965 Student Symposium, "Spectrum of Perspectives," Northwestern University.

29. C. R. Rogers, "A Theory of Therapy . . . ," op. cit., p. 200.

30. The process we call *forming impressions of personality* is sometimes called *persons perception*. Bruner [J. S. Bruner, "Social Psychology and Perception," *Readings in Social Psychology*, ed. E. Maccoby, T. M. Newcomb, and E. L. Hartley (3rd ed.; New York: Henry Holt, Inc., 1958), pp. 85–94] has argued that the "process of perception tends, in general, to accomplish two things: (1) a recording of the diversity of data we encounter into a simpler form that brings it within the scope of our limited memory; (2) a going beyond the information given to predict future events and thereby minimize surprise." Roger Brown, *Social Psychology* (New York: The Free Press, 1965), p. 611.

Social psychologists, in particular, have been concerned with how we perceive or infer the traits and intentions of others. For a sampling of experimental and theoretical works in "social perception" or "person perception" see: I. E. Bender and A. H. Hastorf, "On Measuring Generalized Emphatic Ability (Social Sensitivity)," *Journal of Abnormal and Social Psychology*, Vol. 48 (1958), pp. 503–506; V. B. Cline and J. M. Richards, Jr., "Accuracy of Interpersonal Perception—A General Trait?", *Journal of Abnormal and Social Psychology*, Vol. 60 (1960), pp. 1–7; F. Heider, *The Psychology of Interpersonal Relations* (New York: John Wiley & Sons, Inc., 1958); W. C. Schutz, *FIRO: A Three-Dimensional Theory of Interpersonal Behavior* (New York: Holt, Rinehart and Winston, Inc., 1960); R. Taft, "The Ability to Judge People," *Psychological* Bulletin, Vol. 52 (1955), pp. 1–23; R. Tagiuri and L. Petrullo (eds.), *Person Perception and Interpersonal Behavior* (Stanford, Calif.: Stanford University Press, 1958).

31. S. S. Zalkind and T. W. Costello, "Perception: Some Recent Research and Implications for Administration," *Administrative Science Quarterly* (September, 1962), p. 227.

32. M. Haire and W. F. Grunes, "Perceptual Defenses: Processes Protecting an Original Perception of Another Personality," *Human Relations*, Vol. 3 (1958), pp. 403–12.

33. Karen Horney, *Neurosis and Human Growth: The Struggle toward Self-Realization* (New York: W. W. Norton & Co., Inc., 1950).

34. This is why Brouwer was moved to write: "Manager development means change in the manager's self-image." Paul J. Brouwer, "The Power to See Ourselves," *Harvard Business Review*, Vol. 42, No. 6 (November–December, 1964), p. 156.

35. Jack R. Gibb, op. cit., pp. 142–148.

36. J. R. Gibb, "Defense Level and Influence Potential in Small Groups," L. Petrullo and B. M. Bass (eds.), *Leadership and Interpersonal Behavior* (New York: Holt, Rinehart and Winston, 1961), pp. 66–81.

37. J. R. Gibb, "Defensive Communication," op. cit., p. 142.

38. J. R. Gibb, "Sociopsychological Processes of Group Instruction," N. B. Henry (ed.), *The Dynamics of Instructional Groups* (Fifty-ninth Yearbook of the National Society for the Study of Education) (1960), Part II, 115–35.

39. C. R. Rogers, "A Theory . . . ," op. cit., p. 206.

40. H. A. Simon, *Administrative Behavior* (2d ed.; New York: Macmillan Publishing Co., Inc., 1957).

41. C. R. Rogers, "Communication: Its Blocking and Its Facilitation," a paper delivered at Northwestern University Centennial Conference on Communications, Evanston, Illinois, Oct. 11–13, 1951. Northwestern University *Information*, Vol. XX, No. 25.

1. What is perception according to the transactional view?
2. Why are there similarities in perception among people?
3. What causes differences in perception between people?
4. What are the working assumptions of the transactional view of perception?
5. What are the implications of the transactional viewpoint?

▶ Perception, Communication and Educational Research: A Transactional View

HANS TOCH AND MALCOLM S. MACLEAN, JR.

The transactional approach to perception has relatively limited aspirations. It does not pretend to offer a systematic set of principles concerning the mechanics of the perceptual process. Instead, it supplies a point of regard or emphasis or perspective—or, if you please, a *bias*. This transactional bias has been described as (among other things) neo-Gestalt, neo-behaviorist, radical empiricist and common sense. None of these labels can be totally rejected, but reservations may be entered to all of them.

Common Sense and Perception

Of most interest is common sense: Perception viewed through the eyes of common sense is clearly a passive affair. The eye is the equivalent of a motion picture camera, and hearing functions in the fashion of a tape recorder. The chemical senses act in the manner of variegated litmus paper; the mechanical senses register physical weights and measures. In other words, perception unassumingly transcribes on the slate of our awareness whatever the world presents to us. It dispassionately and uncritically records the gamut of bewildering impressions which reach us—mostly from without, but sometimes from within. This information, having been duly recorded, is then sorted, edited, and evaluated subsequently and—very importantly—elsewhere.

In due fairness, one must add that common sense, when pressed, may

Hans Toch and Malcolm S. MacLean, Jr., "Perception, Communication and Educational Research: A Transactional View," *Audio-Visual Communication Review*, 10 (1962), 55–77. Reprinted by permission.

admit that there is probably more to the story. The senses, for example don't appear to receive impressions at random: the eyes must be directed at some portion of the world, and the glass of wine must be sipped before anything of consequence is perceived in either case. Moreover, there is obviously some measure of control over the quality of the product: the languid gaze, the shameless stare, and the vacant look don't transmit comparable data. Sophisticated common sense also discovers that there is some question as to whether we always perceive equally well. Assuming, for example, that the cochlea responds with the same precision when a person sits in a concert hall or in his living room immersed in his newspaper, everyone knows that auditory awareness clearly differs in these situations.

These and other observations of perception in action may suggest to common sense that the process is not altogether passive nor invariant. Perception seems to provide, within limits, the type of information the perceiver needs. Perception, in other words, is invoked, suppressed, and modified in the context of what the rest of the person is about. In order to be instrumental in this fashion, perception must be flexible and active. The vocabulary is full of words which imply recognition of this truism. The eye, for example, does not merely mirror or transmit; it scans, peeks, watches, stares, scrutinizes, and inspects. Such terms reflect a recognition of directionality, selection, or variability in perception.

Transactional Departure from Common Sense

At this point, however, common sense assumes that it is the "user" of the perceptual process who is active, while perception itself is simply being manipulated. In other words, the perceptual apparatus is seen to subject to the same type of manipulation as the motion picture camera which may be switched on and off, variously aimed, and possibly even changed to different speeds at the whim of its owner and the flick of a switch. These manipulations, of course, would be viewed as extrinsic to the process of receiving and recording information. The transactional view does not accept this argument. It regards perception as continuously and inextricably enmeshed in the enterprise of living. Do we ever encounter perception as a "pure" process? Or, for that matter, can we conceive of a person behaving without perceiving? Is not behavior both an outcome of past perceptions and a starting point for future perceptions? And is not the "user" of perception himself a perceptual result? This conclusion would clearly follow from the fact that every human being is a product—a constantly changing product—of the situations through which he moves. Each encounter with life leaves its chink in the armor or its depression in the hide; the person who arises in the morning is never the same one who returns to his pillow that evening. His successor may be broadened, chastised, wiser, or warier; his jaw may be more set or his brow more furrowed

—more likely, he may see things a little differently or feel somewhat different. Whatever the change, it represents a deposit of perceptions and will, in turn, affect future perceptions.

Perception, then—in transactional parlance—is so wedded to the rest of the human enterprise that it has no meaning outside this context. If common sense finds this conception hard to deal with, the next step may prove even harder to take. Because unlike common sense, which assumes that a person perceives the world, the transactional view denies the independent existence of both the perceiver and his world. The term "transaction" was first used by Dewey and Bentley to distinguish this new view of epistemology from the common sense "interaction" conception. Dewey and Bentley summarize their transactional approach to perception by saying, "Observation of this general (transactional) type sees man-in-action not as something radically set over against an environing world, nor yet as merely action 'in' a world, but as action *of* and *by* the world in which the man belongs as an integral constituent (7:228)." Ittelson and Cantril illustrate the meaning of this statement by considering the case of a baseball batter:

It is immediately apparent that the baseball batter does not exist independent of the pitcher. We cannot have a batter without a pitcher. It is true that someone can throw a ball up in the air and hit it with a bat, but his relationship to the batter in the baseball game is very slight. Similarly, there is no pitcher without a batter. The pitcher in the bull-pen is by no means the same as the pitcher in the game. But providing a pitcher for a batter is still not enough for us to be able to define and study our batter. The batter we are interested in does not exist outside of a baseball game, so that in order to study him completely we need not only pitcher, but catcher, fielders, teammates, officials, fans, and the rules of the game. Our batter, as we see him in this complex transaction, simply does not exist anywhere else independent of the transaction. The batter is what he is because of the baseball game in which he participates and, in turn, the baseball game itself is what it is because of the batter. Each one owes its existence to the fact of active participation with and through the other. If we change either one, we change the other (15:3–4).

Another baseball analogy bearing on the meaning of the perceptual transaction is cited by Cantril, who quotes the following story about three umpires swapping views as to their professional function:

The first umpire said, 'Some's balls and some's strikes and I calls 'em as they is.' The second umpire said, 'Some's balls and some's strikes and I calls 'em as I sees 'em.' While the third umpire said, 'Some's balls and some's strikes but they ain't nothin' till I calls 'em (4:126).'

This story nicely illustrates the basic characteristic of the transactional view of perception, which may be summarized as follows: Each percept, from the simplest to the most complex, is the product of a creative act. The raw material for this creation is lost to us since in the very act of creating, we modify it. We can never encounter a stimulus before some meaning has been assigned to it by some perceiver. Moreover, the perceiver himself becomes available to us only when he has entered into his task and has been modified in the process.

Both of these statements hold true because meanings are given to things in terms of all prior experience the person has accumulated. Therefore, each perception is the beneficiary of all previous perceptions, in turn, each new perception leaves its mark on the common pool. A percept is thus a link between the past which gives it its meaning and the future which it helps to interpret.

Neo-behaviorist View

Perception, in other words, is a form of learning. This view makes it possible to speak of the transactional position as a neo-behaviorist approach. And transactionalism clearly approximates behaviorism not only in its emphasis on learning, but also in its conception of how learning takes place. According to behavioristic learning theory, learning is stimulated and strengthened by rewards (reinforcing situations) and inhibited by punishments or disappointments. The transactional conception is analogous. Each experience or perception helps to provide us with unconscious expectations or assumptions about reality. We expect the world to behave in accord with these assumptions. Like the data supplied in a racing form about the performance of horses under particular conditions, the accumulation of our past experiences provides the basis for bets as to success or failure of our intended enterprises. These bets are repeated or discontinued depending on whether they pay off or fail to pay off.

Just as a horse which has a long record of "wins" becomes a favorite and is assigned a high probability of success, certain interpretations come to be endowed with considerable confidence because of their repeated accuracy in the past. I have no hesitation in sitting down on what appears to me to be a chair, and I point my pencil at the paper in front of me with little doubt about the physical outcome. In other situations, however, past experience has not been as fully rewarding, and interpretations became long shots. The trustworthiness of friends, the reliability of colleagues, and the receptivity of students are not necessarily as punctually encountered as the seats of chairs. And even relatively simple perceptual dimensions such as size or distance may be incorrectly deduced—as has been the sad experience of many motorists. As a rule, however, perception results in confirmation, in the sense that our assumptions lead to successful conduct, thereby reinforcing our images of reality and our confidence in them.

Gestaltist View

The scheme we have just outlined differs from the thinking of students of learning only in its emphasis on personal experience, which behaviorism has traditionally refused to discuss. In turn, Gestalt psychologists, who share the transactionalist bias favoring perceptual experiences as the basis of human conduct, reject the premise that such experiences are essentially learned. According to Gestalt thinking, the essential qualities of experience are, rather, built into the process of perception. The following statement by Wolfgang Köhler illustrates the Gestaltist rejection of the assumption that perceived meanings are acquired through past experience:

When I see a green object, I can immediately tell the name of the color. I also know that green is used as a signal on streets and as a symbol of hope. But from this I do not conclude that the color green as such can be derived from such knowledge. Rather, I know that, as an independently existent sensory fact, it has acquired secondary meanings, and I am quite willing to recognize the advantages which these acquired meanings have in practical life. In exactly the same fashion, Gestalt Psychology holds, sensory units have acquired names, have become richly symbolic, and are now known to have certain practical uses, while nevertheless they have existed as units before any of these further facts were added. Gestalt Psychology claims that it is precisely the original segregation of circumscribed wholes which makes it possible for the sensory world to appear so utterly imbued with meaning to the adult; for, in its gradual entrance into the sensory field, meaning follows the lines drawn by natural organization; it usually enters into segregated wholes (20:139).

Beside the difference, apparent in this quote, between the Gestalt emphasis on innate perceptual qualities as against the transactional stress on learning, there is another divergence in emphasis between these two views of perception. This difference rests in the fact that perception, in transactional parlance, is *functional,* in the sense that it exists to enable the perceiver to carry out his purposes, whereas Gestalt thinking sometimes assumes that man strives for veridicality or accuracy for its own sake.

There is, however, an even greater difference between the transactional premise that perception derives its meaning from the human enterprise and the contention of some people that needs and fears can shape perceptual products. Unlike these New Look theorists, the advocates of the transactional view do *not* assume that we tend to see steaks when hungry, or that we have difficulty in hearing threatening language. In fact, the transactional assumption would be that it is never in the long-run interest of people to see what they want to see or to fail to perceive what doesn't meet their fancy, just as the deer is not aided by failing to notice the jumping lion. The greatest survival value lies in accurate perception. The purpose of perception is to help us cope with the world by assigning meanings to it which can stand the test of subsequent experiences.

PERCEPTION AND COMMUNICATION

The above exposition of what—essentially—the transactional view is and is not, makes possible a few statements about perception which might have special bearing on non-verbal communication. Sample experiments illustrating some of these statements may help clarify them.

Shared Experiences Result in Perceptual Communalities

There are many types of experience which people have in common, almost by virtue of their human condition. These range from the elements of geometry to their intimate exposures to other human beings which create the beginning of social awareness. Common human experiences create similarities in perception and make possible easy communication. Universally shared meanings, in fact, are the *simplest* means of communication because they require little translation from one person's frame of reference into another. When A offers B a chair, when B smiles at C, or when C makes love to D, communication problems are minimized.

Probably the most famous of the "Ames Demonstrations" (so-called because they were originated by Adelbert Ames, Jr.) is the "Rotating Trapezoidal Window" Demonstration. This device helps to show the perceptual role of assumptions which have their origin in relatively universal human experiences. The demonstration consists of a trapezoidally-shaped window which can be slowly rotated, and which is invariably perceived as a rectangle (in perspective) oscillating from side to side. If a rod is placed in the window, it will appear to fold around it or to cut through it while the window is in motion. A box attached to one corner of the apparatus seems to take to flight. Why do those illusions occur? Ames himself offers this explanation:

In his past experience the observer, in carrying out his purposes, has on innumerable occasions had to take into account and act with respect to rectangular forms, e.g., going through doors, locating windows, etc. On almost all such occasions, except in the rare case when his line of sight was normal to the door or window, the image of the rectangular configuration formed on his retina was trapezoidal. He learned to interpret the particularly characterized retinal images, that exist when he looks at doors, windows, etc., as rectangular forms. Moreover, he learned to interpret the particular degree of trapezoidal distortion of his retinal images in terms of the positioning of the rectangular form to his particular viewing point (2:14).

These assumptions about rectangularity are in most situations not apparent because they lead to accurate perceptions, so that the perceiver can argue, "I see X (rectangular) because it *is* X (rectangular)." The "trapezoidal window" reveals assumptions because it is deliberately designed to be misleading.

Differences in Experience Cause Perceptual Divergence

The "trapezoidal window" depends for its effect on universal human experiences with rectangular objects in perspective. But are experiences such as these really equally shared by every human being? In the case of rectangularity, for instance, some people may be more intensively exposed to rectangular objects than others. Zulu members of the Bantu culture in South Africa stand out as having relatively little experience with man-made rectangles.

Huts are invariably round (rondavels) or else beehive shaped, whereas in other Bantu tribes they are sometimes square or rectangular. Round huts arranged in a circular form with round stockades to fence in animals, constitute a typical African homestead (kraal). Fields follow the irregular contours of the rolling land, and never seem to be laid out in the neat rectangular plots so characteristic of western culture. The typical Zulu hut has no windows, and no word for such on aperture exists. In the more primitive beehive grass huts, doors are merely round entrance holes; in the round mud huts, doors are amorphous, seldom if ever really rectangular. Cooking pots are round or gourd-shaped . . . (1:106).

When tested with the "trapezoidal window", in a study by Allport and Pettigrew, non-westernized Zulus tended to perceive the illusion less frequently —under sub-optimal conditions—than did westernized persons who have more intensive experience with rectangularity (1). One can infer from this fact that differences in experience, even in cumulative experience that is common to people, can create subtle differences in the way the world is perceived.

Perceptual Differences Can Be Readily Produced

Social psychologists are frequently concerned with attitudes, values, and habits that are prevalent among groups of people and are transmitted from generation to generation. Less obviously, ways of perceiving also come to be acquired and transmitted collectively. Two experiments, both involving a relatively new research technique, may serve to illustrate this fact:

In 1955, a psychologist named Engel published a set of observations involving subjects who had been exposed to two different pictures—one to the left eye and the other to the right (9). One effect he discussed is that of perceptual dominance by more familiar pictures when they are paired with less familiar pictures. "A 'right side up' face, for instance, tends to perceptually prevail over the same face 'upside down.' "

This observation has given rise to a number of experiments, one of which included matched Mexican and American observers. These persons were exposed to several sets of pictures, in each of which a typically American scene (such as a baseball game) was paired with a typically Mexican view (like a bullfight). The investigator, Bagby, concludes:

Ss report scenes of their own culture as predominant in binocular rivalry over scenes from another culture. The national cultural differences appear critical in affecting perceptual predominance in the majority of the stereogram slide pairs . . . Differences in ways of perceiving come about as a consequence of differences in past experiences and purposes. These in turn emerge from influences in the home, in the school, and in the various groups with which an individual identifies. Thus, under conditions of perceptual conflict as found in the binocular rivalry situation those impingements possessing the more immediate first-person meaning would be expected to predominate in visual awareness (3:334).

This statement, of course, need not be confined to past experiences associated with different cultures. Subgroups in the same culture also frequently become differentially indoctrinated, and such differences in indoctrination should leave their mark on perception.

To test for this possibility, terminal candidates in a Midwestern police training program were presented with a set of slides, each of which featured a violent scene for one eye, and a similar but non-violent picture for the other. Beginning students in the training program and comparable liberal arts students served as control groups. The persons trained in police work saw a number of "violent" pictures in this situation. The investigators comment:

Assuming that extremely violent scenes are comparatively unfamiliar, we would thus expect violence to be relatively infrequently perceived in true binocular rivalry. We would predict the type of result we obtained from our Control Groups. We could assume that law enforcement training *supplements* this experiential deficit in the area of violence and crime. Unusual experiences, after all, become 'familiar' in the course of *any* specialization. The funeral director or the medical intern, for instance, may learn to accept corpses as part and parcel of everyday experience. The dedicated nudist may acquire a special conception of familiar attire. The air pilot may come to find nothing unusual about glancing down out of a window at a bank of clouds. In the same fashion, law enforcement training can produce a revision of unconscious expectations of violence and crime. This does not mean that the law enforcer necessarily comes to exaggerate the prevalence of violence. It means that the law enforcer may come to accept crime *as a familiar personal experience*, one which he himself is not surprised to encounter. The acceptance of crime as a familiar experience in turn increases *the ability or readiness to perceive violence where clues to it are potentially available* (29:392).

Subtle perceptual differences of this sort, although universally present, only manifest themselves for our inspection under special conditions such as binocular rivalry. At other times, we may deal with people under the assumption that their perceptions coincide with ours, although in fact differences in past experience have produced fundamental divergences in outlook.

The same point holds true over time, since research shows that subtle *changes* in perception continuously take place without our being aware of them. To illustrate: Two photographs, each of a different face, were mounted in a stereoscopic device. When the observer first looked into the stereoscope, he was presented with just one of the faces with normal illumination. Then the illumination was cut. Next, he was given the first face normally lit, with the second face under very low illumination. The procedure was repeated with a slight increase in light on the second face, and so on until the subject was observing both faces each with the same normal light. At each step he was asked whether any change had taken place in what he saw. Most said they saw no change! But the second phase of the experiment was even more startling. In the same way, by small steps, the light on the first photograph was reduced to zero. At this point, the observer was looking at the second face, quite different from the first. He continued to claim that no change had taken place, that he was still looking at the same face. Engel reports that observers were much perplexed when they were again presented with the original face (8).

Any Given Event Is Differently Perceived by Different People

The more complex a perceptual situation becomes, the greater the tendency for variations in perception to occur. Whereas a chair, for instance, provides a minimum of opportunity for differences in perception—at least, for members of our Western culture—any standard *social* situation constitutes a veritable perceptual cafeteria. This is the case not only because complexity multiplies the opportunity for the perceiver to assign meanings—for instance, one can choose to attend to one of many aspects of a complex situation in preference to others—but also because complexity usually evokes a wide gamut of personal experiences and needs which enter into the assignment of meaning.

Hastorf and Cantril illustrate this process in their study of the infamous football game between Dartmouth and Princeton which took place on November 23, 1951. The events which occurred in this game are conservatively catalogued as follows:

A few minutes after the opening kick-off, it became apparent that the game was going to be a rough one. The referees were kept busy blowing their whistles and penalizing both sides. In the second quarter, Princeton's star left the game with a broken nose. In the third quarter, a Dartmouth player was taken off the field with a broken leg. Tempers flared both during and after the game. The official statistics of the game, which Princeton won, showed that Dartmouth was penalized

70 yards, Princeton 25, not counting more than a few plays in which both sides were penalized (13:129).

The sequel of these events was a prolonged and intense exchange of recriminations between players, students, coaches, administrative officials, student publications, alumni and partisans of the two universities each of whom claimed to have sustained the brunt of the injuries.

Hastorf and Cantril submitted a questionnaire concerning the games to both Princeton and Dartmouth students and alumni, the results of which confirmed the divergent position of the two sides relating to the game. A film of the game also was shown to some 100 students; it yielded widely discrepant reports of the number of infractions committed by each side and the seriousness of these infractions. The Princeton students, for instance, "saw" the Dartmouth team make more than twice the number of infractions "seen" by Dartmouth students in watching the same film. They also "saw" two "'flagrant" to each "mild" infraction for the Dartmouth team, and one "'flagrant" to three "mild" offenses for their own team, a ratio considerably dissimilar to that of ratings by Dartmouth students. Hastorf and Cantril conclude:

the 'same' sensory impingements emanating from the football field, transmitted through the visual mechanism to the brain, obviously gave rise to different experiences in different people. The significances assumed by different happenings for different people depend in large part on the purposes people bring to the occasion and the assumptions they have of the purposes and probable behavior of other people involved (13:132). . . .

It is inaccurate and misleading to say that different people have different 'attitudes' concerning the same 'thing.' For the 'thing' simply is *not* the same for different people whether the 'thing' is a football game, a presidential candidate. Communism, or spinach. We do not simply 'react to' a happening or to some impingement from the environment in a determined way (except in behavior that has become reflexive or habitual). We behave according to what we bring to the occasion, and what each of us brings to the occasion is more or less unique (13:133).

All Aspects of a Percept Are Related to Each Other

A fundamental discovery of Gestalt psychology was that the basic unit of perception is the organized configuration which the perceiver perceives. Perceptual objects, in other words, function as indivisible units. This statement extends beyond the geometric or formal properties of stimuli. Thus, the perceived motion of the Ames "trapezoidal window" results from its perception as a rectangle in perspective: Object-identification and movement-direction are dependent on each other.

Hastorf has shown that the perceived size of a white square can range widely, depending on whether it is identified as an envelope or a calling card (12). This perceived size, in turn, can determine the apparent distance of the figure from the observer.

Less obviously, positive or negative feelings can also determine perceived size and distance. Thus, G. H. Smith set out to determine whether "faces regarded as friendly or pleasant" would be seen as "larger than those regarded as unfriendly or unpleasant in order to appear opposite the same target post (27:47)." His findings confirmed these expectations. He concludes:

Ss responded to the meaning which faces elicited in this situation; and . . . this meaning emerged out of the assumptions, attitudes, expectations, purposes, and special sensitizations which Ss had acquired through experience. . . . The fact that 'pleasant' or 'liked' faces were made larger (closer) than others indicates that attributed meaning, rather than size of retinal image alone, determined the responses . . . perception of a human face literally changed before the eyes of the Ss as a function of alterations in beliefs, assumptions, etc. (27:60–61).

Another set of experiments showing a relationship between affective significance and the perceptions of physical properties was provided by the "honi phenomenon" (30). This effect was first observed in an Ames Demonstration known as the "monocular distorted room," which is a geometrically distorted structure that looks square when viewed with one eye. Since the room appears to be normal (although it is in fact distorted), any face viewed through a window of the room becomes expanded or contracted. The "honi phonomenon" was born one day when this customary illusion did not materialize. The face which refused to change belonged to a New York attorney, and the viewer was his devoted wife. Subsequent investigation showed that it is not uncommon for newlyweds to perceive their marital partners as relatively unchanged when optical distortions have in fact taken place. Similar phenomenon can occur involving other kinds of affects (as with amputees and authority figures). The lesson to be drawn from such instances is that the apparent physical properties of a percept cannot be divorced from its other connotations.

PERCEPTION AND EDUCATIONAL RESEARCH

Working Assumptions

What difference might the viewpoint expounded above make in the ways we think about and treat audiovisual communication and learning resources development? How would it affect our research into problems in these areas? Before trying to answer these questions, we might follow the tradition of restating our teaching points. We will present these views so as to have at hand some statements we can readily refer to.

Here we go:

- There is no behavior without perception.
- Behavior is both an outcome of past perceptions and a starting point for future perceptions.
- Every human being is a constantly changing product of the situations through which he moves.
- The perceiver and his world do not exist independently.
- Each percept is the product of a creative act.
- We never find a stimulus with unassigned meaning.
- Meanings are given to things by the perceiver in terms of all prior experience he has accumulated.
- A percept is a link between the past which gives it its meaning and the future which it helps to interpret.
- Each experience or perception helps to provide us with expectations or assumptions about "reality." We expect the world to behave in accord with these assumptions.
- We make bets on the outcomes of our behavior and continue or modify these bets according to our assessment of the pay off.
- How assured we are in our bets depends on the amount and consistency of past relevant experience.
- We are often surer in our assumptions about simple physical things than we are about complex social relationships.
- Perceptual experiences are personal and individual, and they are learned.
- Perception is functional. It exists to enable the perceiver to carry out his purposes. It helps him to cope with the world by assigning meanings to it which can stand the test of subsequent experiences.
- Though no two persons can have exactly the same meanings for things-observed, common experiences tend to produce shared meanings which make communication possible.
- Most failures in communication are due to mistaken assumptions about correspondence of meanings.
- Systematic differences in experiences arising from cultural and sub-cultural differences create reliable differences in perception.
- Those things that have been tied in most closely and most often with past personal experience predominate perceptually over the unusual or the unfamiliar.
- The more complex a situation-observed, the more we are likely to differ in our situation perceptions. We will likely attend to somewhat different aspects and draw on much wider ranges of personal experience.
- The thing-observed can never be exactly the *same* thing for two different people or for the "same" person at two different times (since he cannot be the same person).
- Apparent physical properties of a percept (size of retinal image, for example) cannot be divorced from its other connotations.

There are other pertinent transactional views. Let's look at them briefly:

- Impingements on the senses are not uniquely determined. Many different distorted rooms, for example, can look to an observer like the same "normal" room.

• There is no revealed reality.

• The object is not necessarily less an abstraction than the word which refers to it.

• Since two people cannot be in the same place at the same time, they must see at least slightly different environments.

• Experience is cumulative and compounding in its effects on our perceptions.

• Though we work with subjective, functional probabilities, in acting we must deal with them as absolutes. In order to make decisions from one moment to the next, we act as though our assumed world is the real world.

• We tend to hold on to assumptions which were reliable in the past even when we are experiencing situations in which they no longer appear reliable (18).

• We remember past events as directly as we perceive present events. A poor memory is similar to unreliable perception (26).

• There can be no such thing as pure objectivity in terms of the meanings most people seem to assign to this concept.

• The only world we know is determined by our assumptions.

• Science is an activity designed by man to increase the reliability and verifiability of his assumptive world.

• Behaviors are present events converging pasts into futures (5:26).

• We can change the behavior of others only to the extent that we can help to produce situations and experiences which lead them to modify relevant assumptions.

• If common assumptions are not available, the only possibility of coming to perceptual agreement lies in making them available through common experience (17:288).

Some people get pretty angry when presented such statements.

"Nonsense!" they say. "Just a bagful of mystical philosophy. There are real things. We can see them and touch them and we can measure them. The aim of science is to reveal to us what they really are and how they really behave. Don't tell *us* that ours is a world of assumptions."

At least part of the resistance to transactional thinking stems from the implications it holds for many of our professional vested interests.

Implications

What are some of the implications of transactional viewpoints?

They seem to say about any field: One of the most vital continuing activities we can perform is to examine our assumptions about what we are doing, our values, our beliefs, what we "know" about the world. This examination may be especially required where things don't seem to be working as well as we would like. But there is a danger here. Especially in education and communication we may be blithely assuming that things are working well while events are leading us toward crisis. A change in viewpoint, a tentative revision of assumptions might allow us to see the makings of crises we had been blind to before. Many of us go along talking chiefly with people who believe and think pretty much as we do. We have roughly similar philosophies of education, audiovisual communication, civil liberties, male-female relationships or what-have-you. We all "know" what is true and right and good, we know what works and how and why . . . we think. Then, whamo! We get mixed up with people from other cultures or other specialties. (Finn's letter to President Griswold of Yale University (10) makes explicit some of the assumptions underlying pro and con audiovisual education arguments.)

You are a researcher, a teacher, an audiovisual specialist, a you-name-it. Suppose, one of these fine days, even though you feel quite well, the best medical specialists tell you that you have at most six weeks still to live. What would you do?

Perhaps you have already had some experience which led you to re-examine seriously your values, your purposes in life. Most people apparently put off or avoid entirely such considerations of their own value systems. They get caught up in the busyness of their work and play and continue along, sometimes with even rather severe discontent. Questioning the adequacy of one's own values seems to be one of the hardest of human tasks.

Toch and Cantril conducted a simple demonstration experiment in which experimental subjects were given a contrived letter (28). This letter from "Steve" merely asked the subject to put himself in the shoes of a man with only six weeks to live and to write notes on what he would do. Control subjects were given a crossword puzzle to solve. Most of the experimental subjects found even this minor excursion into personal values a tough but rewarding experience. Those subjects who worked individually on the problem found it more fun than did those who did so in groups.

Transactional viewpoints suggest that both our research and our educational efforts might much more than they do presently take into account our own purposes and assumptions and those of our students. They suggest, too, that our modern, rapidly developing world requires more contemplation of our own and others' values and greater readiness to modify our assumptions creatively.

Kelley has indicated some implications of transactional views for education (16). Much of our school work, he says, seems to be based on the assumption that we adults know things as they really are. Thus, we can show the child the correct or true version of life. We act as though there are bodies of knowledge somehow distinct from observers. We seem to assume that if you tell the child he will know.

Though we give frequent lip service to the fact that all humans are different, our educational efforts often assume that they are highly similar in the ways that they learn and the kinds of things they grasp as meaningful and salient.

Some of the new developments in self-instruction may be very helpful here—especially those that take into account some of those assumptions which seem to be relatively common in the culture where they are used. In addition, they must allow some flexibility in starting from somewhat different assumptions.

The Educational Transaction   Knowledge is what we know after we have learned and not some object outside of us. Kelley suggests the following procedures and ways of looking at education:

1. Let us find out what our learner is like. What are his values, purposes, beliefs, assumptions, *etc.?*

2. As teachers, let us consider ourselves as persons who facilitate growth. What experiences can we lead our learners through to help them test and modify their assumptions about the world?

3. Let us give our learners plenty of opportunity and freedom for honest creative expression. Let us not assume that the "reality" we know is necessary better and more workable than the "reality" they know.

4. If we seriously put into question our assumptions concerning the efficacy of the lecture, we may wind up severely modifying this approach or getting rid of lectures altogether.

5. Let us remember that a learner can put meaning into reading matter— or for that matter films or slides or self-instruction programs—only when he has something in experience and purpose to put into them.

6. Let's get rid of the artificial separation of process and subject matter, as how and the what of learning experience.

7. One is always learning. We teachers can simply help to determine the rate, direction, and quality by the variety and richness of experiences we lead our students into.

The Audiovisual Transaction

In the first issue of *AV Communication Review*, Norberg suggested some implications of transactional research for audiovisual education (24). If we can say, Norberg writes, that we learn from a "look" at something only when this "look" stands in a series of experiences linked together in a course of purposeful action, then our production, utilization, and research should reflect this.

We might, for example, more often present things in slides or films from various points of view, perhaps starting with those points of view most likely to relate to viewers' previous personal experience.

Since words and memories, as well as present physical objects or pictures or sounds, all play a part in our perceptual experience, and since this experience always involves an abstracting process, we may be kidding ourselves when we consider the "thing" or the picture to be more concrete than the word or the memory. Norberg writes:

We cannot say what an individual will learn from any discrete visual presentation, as such, and aside from a context of other experiences, in time. Learning results from a *series* of purposeful acts carried out with continuity of purpose and direction. All action is not overt or 'physical,' but to maintain and carry forward a line of purposeful action, in time, requires adequate conditions of sensory contact with the environment. We learn *from* visual presentations in so far as they make it possible, or easier, for us to carry out our purposes. As we learn *from* perceptions, and *to* new ways of perceiving things, our 'assumptive form' world changes and this involves the most complex organizations of our behavior including social attitudes and conceptions.

We cannot learn without acting. We cannot act without perceiving (24:28).

A current research-educational project developed by Elizabeth Drews and her colleagues presents some interesting applications of transactionalism. Dr. Drews for a number of years has been working with and studying gifted children. She noticed that many such children seemed seriously limited by their values and assumptions in their own creative expression and in accepting creativity by others. For example, some children believe that most adults who are highly creative in their work are also emotionally sick. They tend to reject other children around them who express odd or unusual ideas.

Under a Title VII grant, Drews and her team produced a series of films showing highly creative adults at work, at play, talking with their families, *etc.* They also prepared a catalog of biographies, essays, novels, and magazine articles. These are all being used in experimental "careers" courses at the ninth-grade level along with such things as class discussions, the writing of essays and diaries, and the preparation of scrapbooks.

The major purpose of this course is to modify some of those assumptions about the future adult world which might seriously restrict students in their educational and career choices. Some children seem to think that there is only one occupational niche into which they will be able to fit. Some girls practically exclude certain professions (that of judge, for example) from their thinking about careers because they are "men's work." (Half of the films present personalized biographies of professional women, including a woman judge.) In the same way, Negro children may have a potentially self-fulfilling prophecy about the kinds of careers open to them (14). A child may feel, even in the ninth grade, that he ought to make a career choice now and stick to it. The whole project has been set up to discover what kinds of assumptions the children are making and to move them purposefully through a set of related experiences designed to help modify assumptions which are likely to be debilitating.

The experimental courses will be compared with "typical" traditional careers courses taught by the same teachers. The careers courses common to many high schools simply present lectures and outside readings about different jobs and have the students write a research report on one occupation of their choice. The experimental course is expected to:

- reduce unfavorable stereotypes of artists and scientists
- increase awareness of the existence of successfully creative adults
- increase acceptance of creative qualities and potential in self and in others
- increase the number and variety of careers perceived by students as open and rewarding to them
- strengthen the value of intellectual creativity as a purpose in life
- develop a more open and flexible process view of career choice
- perceive work on the job and other aspects of life more as an integrated whole
- engage voluntarily in more independent, creative projects
- talk more with peers about goals and careers and creative values.

Our assumptions about how the Drews course may modify students' assumptions about adult life remain to be tested. We feel, however, that the focus on evaluation of assumptions and on their modification is likely to prove a great deal more enlightening and useful than that regains in factual information.

Multiple Transactions

Gerbner describes well how points of view, contexts, and assumptions become complex in mass media communication (11). We frequently observe somebody else's observation of somebody else's observation *etc.*, and then we tell somebody about it from our own point of view. Writes Gerbner:

The analysis of communications is, therefore, compounded observation: In looking at a picture, for example, we do not merely observe a 'thing'; we observe an observation.

What's in a picture? A 'thing' viewed from a 'built-in' point of view, in a certain context, and probably on the basis of some implicit assumptions about the nature of the object or event portrayed. For example, the angle of the camera and the position of the lights used to take a photograph (and used to convey, implicitly, a point of view) are just as much objective elements of the picture as is the 'thing' portrayed. If we are unaware of the fact that we are observing the picture *through the eye of a camera* (or of an artist), we have lost some of our own power of observation; we fall in, unwittingly, with a 'given' point of view (11:271-2).

In a study of group photographs of the kind commonly seen in newspapers, Oshiki found (25) that camera viewpoint, lighting, and the arrangement of persons mattered much less in people's "like-dislike" ratings of the pictures than did smiles resulting from the photographer's simple instruction:

"Smile, please!" Koch-Weser got similar results in a study of "ideal self-identification" with persons portrayed in advertising photographs (19). In Q sorts, most subjects ranked pictures of people smiling, especially "happy" family groups, considerably higher than those of "serious" people. Some recent work by Randall Harrison using cartoon faces indicates that when a smiling mouth is accompanied by eyebrows in a modified V, quite a different result obtains. People usually assume that a "normal" smile means that the person portrayed is happy and friendly, while they interpret the smile with the V eyebrows as meaning that the person is fiendish or happy with evil intentions. The latter expression is typical of the Charles Addams cartoons.

Transactional views and experimentation seem to support the widely held assumption that visuals which present things simply and relevantly (to the purposes and experiences of both teacher and learner) and with functional viewpoints and contexts, will best facilitate meaningful perception and learning. In diverse studies and teaching programs, it has been found that the learning of materials defined by instructors as irrelevant to their purposes can take place at the expense of materials defined as relevant (6 and 21).

Some other assumptions commonly held by audiovisual specialists may not be so well supported. For example, most such specialists argue that teachers, if they are to have their students obtain full value from a film, say, must introduce it before the showing and encourage discussion of it afterward. There is some evidence that students do indeed learn more "facts" from a film when this is done. But there is also some evidence which should lead to at least a more sophisticated view of what we may be doing when we introduce a film. Several transactional demonstration-experiments using the distorted rooms have indicated that verbal explanations of the distortion have tended to *inhibit* rather than facilitate re-interpretation of the forms perceived (18). It may well be that the subjects who were given the verbal explanation would be better able to repeat this back in a verbal test of "facts." But the finding is that they could less readily shift to a functionally more adequate perception of the distorted rooms. Too much attention to the map may keep one from learning the territory (1).

The Learning Resources Transaction

Another area which we believe may be suffering from traditional assumptions rigidly held is that of learning resources development. Most educators who discuss this subject seem to be picturing learning resources merely as a kind of bolstered audiovisual center-library-computer-combination in the context of the school-as-is, but with more than the usual number of students around. We suggest that if our educational administrators can break away no further than this from traditional assumptions, we face extravagant waste of time and money. Here, intensive creative effort and bold, dramatic experimentation might really pay off (22). We need to examine our instrumental and ultimate values. We need to examine the assumptions underlying present and proposed techniques. Why do students have to come to a university, for example, rather than the university coming to them?

The Research Transaction

Transactional views imply a great deal of research, but research well integrated with action, research with purpose. They raise doubts about some of our traditional ways of viewing science. Take "validity," for example. Many textbooks define this term as "the degree to which our instruments measure what we say they measure." The transactionalist is not alone in considering this a ridiculous, non-functional kind of statement since it assumes an objective reality "out there" isolated from the observer and his measures. Rather, we think in terms of the predictive reliability of our assumptions. Meaning is not in events or words nor is it in people, somehow isolated from events. Beauty, say, is not in the sunset but it may very well be in the sunset-observed. "Science is an activity designed by man to increase the reliability and verifiability of his assumptive world (5:9)." Man, the scientist, or just plain man is in a continuing process something like the following:

1. He senses inadequacies in certain of his assumptions. They don't seem to hold as well as they did in the past. This is problem awareness.
2. He tries to locate those aspects of phenomena *except for* which the functional activities in question would not exist.
3. He chooses those aspects he feels are most crucial.
4. He works out some methods for changing those aspects and experimenting with the changes.
5. He modifies his assumptions on the basis of empirical evidence.

Notice that values are implied at each step. The notion that science is value-free—that is, purely objective—is a strange one, indeed.

Since the assumptive worlds of ourselves and the people we study are so complex, good research requires a great deal of speculation about research problems. We must explore different ways of viewing them and speculate about different potential outcomes for various alternative actions. Many experiments suffer from insensitivity to many of the crucial circumstances operating in the situations they investigate. In purifying and controlling, the experimenter may squeeze so much of the life blood out of the situation that the results provide us little help in dealing with our real-life worlds (23).

These are reasons why the present writers prefer, in research on complex problems, some of the more open-ended, comprehensive methods such as focused interviewing, inventories of relevant past experience, theme analysis, group interviews, Q methodology, field studies, and the like. Not that we would discard the controlled experiment. Not at all. Confirmation or disconfirmation of assumptions requires such research. But we wish to jump into the strictures of controlled experimentation only when we feel reasonably sure that we can take into account those aspects of the phenomena under study which are likely to be functionally crucial.

SUMMARY

We have not presented a transactional theory, since, so far as we know, there is no one such theory to present. Instead, we have outlined some transactional viewpoints which we consider potentially useful in audiovisual communication, learning resources development, and research in these areas. We have suggested some implications and advantages of transactional assumptions.

NOTES

1. A similar finding was obtained by the Norwegian psychologist R. Rommetveit in experiments involving concept formation by children. "Verbalized" concepts, according to Rommetveit, can inhibit the perception of relevant dimensions of problems. (R. Rommetveit's report delivered at 1961 Meetings of Michigan Psychology Association, Detroit.)

REFERENCES

1. Allport, G. W., and Pettigrew, T. F. "Cultural Influence on the Perception of Movement: the Trapezoidal Illusion among Zulus." *Journal of Abnormal and Social Psychology* 55:104–13; 1957.
2. Ames, A., Jr. "Visual Perception and the Rotating Trapezoidal Window." *Psychological Monographs* 65:1–31; 1951.
3. Bagby, J. W. "A Cross-cultural Study of Perceptual Predominance in Binocular Rivalry." *Journal of Abnormal and Social Psychology* 54:331–34; 1957.
4. Cantril, H. "Perception and Interpersonal Relations." *American Journal of Psychiatry* 114:119–26; 1957.
5. Cantril H., Ames, A., Hastorf, A. H., and Ittelson, W. H. "Psychology and Scientific Research." *Explorations in Transactional Psychology*, edited by F. P. Kilpatrick. New York: New York University, 1961. p. 6–35.
6. Deutschmann, P. J., Barrow, L. C., Jr., and McMillan, A. "The Efficiency of Different Modes of Communication." *AV Communication Review* 10:3; 176–78; May–June 1962.
7. Dewey, J., and Bentley, A. F. *Knowing and the Known*. Boston: Beacon Press, 1943.
8. Engel, E. "Binocular Methods in Psychological Research." *Explorations in Transactional Psychology*, edited by F. P. Kilpatrick. New York University Press, 1961. p. 290–305.
9. Engel, E. "The Role of Content in Binocular Resolution." *American Journal of Psychology* 69:87–91; 1956.
10. Finn, J. D. "Some Notes for an Essay on Griswold and Reading." *AV Communication Review* 7:111–21; 1959.

11. Gerbner, G. "Education and the Challenge of Mass Culture." AV *Communication Review* 7:264–78; 1959.

12. Hastorf, A. H. "The Influence of Suggestion on the Relationship Between Stimulus Size and Perceived Distance." *Journal of Psychology* 29:195–217; 1950.

13. Hastorf, A. H., and Cantril, H. "They Saw A Game: A Case Study." *Journal of Abnormal and Social Psychology* 49:129–34; 1954.

14. Hayakawa, S. I. "How to Be Sane Though Negro." *Contact I.* Sausalito, California: Angel Island Publications, 1958. p. 5–20.

15. Ittelson, W. H., and Cantril, H. *Perception: A Transactional Approach.* New York: Doubleday and Company, 1954.

16. Kelley, E. C. "Education is Communication." *Etc.* 12:248–56; 1955.

17. Kilpatrick, F. P. "Assumptions and Perception: Three Experiments." *Explorations in Transactional Psychology*, edited by F. P. Kilpatrick. New York: New York University Press, 1961. p. 257–89.

18. Kilpatrick, F. P. "Perception Theory and General Semantics." *Etc.* 12:257–64; 1955.

19. Koch-Weser, Elke. "A Q-Study in Role Identification Using a Sample of Advertising Photographs." Master's Thesis. Michigan State University, 1961.

20. Köhler, W. *Gestalt Psychology.* New York: Liveright Publishing Corporation, 1947.

21. Kumata, H. "Teaching Advertising by Television—Study II." Mimeo. East Lansing Communications Research Center, Michigan State University, 1958.

22. Kumata, H., and MacLean, M. S., Jr. "Education and the Problems of the New Media in the United States of America." *The Year Book of Education.* Tarrytown-on-Hudson, New York: World Book Company, 1960.

23. MacLean, M. S., Jr. "Critical Analysis of 12 Recent Title VII Research Reports." *Research Abstracts and Analytical Review*, Installment 4. p. A-102–14. (AV *Communication Review*, Vol. 10, No. 3; May–June 1962.)

24. Norberg, K. "Perception Research and Audio-Visual Education." AV *Communication Review* 1:18–29, 1953.

25. Oshiki, K. "Effects of Smiles, Subject Arrangement, and Lighting on Reader Satisfaction from Pictures of Groups of People." Master's Thesis. University of Wisconsin, 1956.

26. Pratt, D. A. "The Import of the Word 'Transaction' in Dewey's Philosophy." *Etc.* 12:299–308; 1955.

27. Smith, G. H. "Size-distance Judgments of Human Faces." *Journal of Genetic Psychology* 49:45–64; 1953.

28. Toch, H., and Cantril, H. "The Learning of Values: An Experimental Inquiry." *Explorations in Transactional Psychology*, edited by F. P. Kilpatrick. New York: New York University Press, 1961. p. 321–31.

29. Toch H., and Schulte, R. "Readiness to Perceive Violence as a Result of Police Training." *British Journal of Psychology* 52:389–93; 1961.

30. Wittreich, W. J., Grace, M., and Radcliffe, K. B., Jr. "Three Experiments in Selective Perceptual Distortion." *Explorations in Transactional Psychology*, edited by F. P. Kilpatrick. New York: New York University Press, 1961. p. 188–202.

1. What is the nature of language?
2. How is meaning attached to our words?
3. According to Warr and Knapper, what are three components of perception?
4. How do the words we use about things change our perception of those things?

▶◀ Language and Perception: Two Interrelated Characteristics of Human Behavior

OWEN O. JENSON

In our world, communication between people has become very important. This communication includes individuals talking to other individuals. It is important that we understand how each individual communicates with himself before we can fully understand how the individual communicates with others. This individualized, or intrapersonal, communication deals with how each person endeavors to make sense out of the world for himself. In order to accomplish this the individual talks to himself about his perception of the world around him. An individual's language and his perception are two important, interrelated characteristics of his intrapersonal communication. In order to understand intrapersonal communication it is important to look at language and perception and the interrelationships between them.

THE NATURE OF LANGUAGE

Our world has become very symbolically oriented. People have allowed many things to stand for or represent other things, such as a big car or a fancy address representing wealth in certain societies. In this way cars and addresses become symbols of prosperity. In the same manner, Phi Beta Kappa keys become symbols of intelligences and particular kinds of clothing may become symbols of group membership. Language is the biggest and most important

"Language and Perception: Two Interrelated Characteristics of Human Behavior," by Owen O. Jenson. Reprinted with permission of the author. This original essay appears here in print for the first time.

symbol system we have. In language, words represent or stand for things. Since it is difficult for us to communicate directly by pointing or showing people what we mean, we use words/language as our vehicle of communication. These words become symbols representing our thoughts or things that are in our reality. But language cannot truly or fully represent the complexities of our reality. Language by its very nature is limited, and even the most extensive vocabulary contains only a limited number of words, whereas the world moves and shifts and changes in a multidimensional process.

Not only is language limited in scope but often people tend to confuse the word with the thing it represents. In the mind, quite often, the linguistic symbol and the part of reality it represents become blended together as a whole thing, and soon the word becomes the thing. We then begin to manipulate language as if we are manipulating things, react to language as if words were the realities they represent, and live in a world of words rather than in a world of things. In time, we all seem to begin to react to words and to live with them sometimes to the exclusion of the "real" world that surrounds us. In order to keep proper perspective and to make sense out of the world, we need to be able to distinguish between words and the things they stand for. And, since words are the basis of our communication, we need to understand how they work. We need to be aware of how words are learned, how meaning is developed for words, and how language and perception are related.

How Language and Meaning Are Learned

When we were born we did not have a language. We had to learn language just as we have had to learn many other things in our lives. We learned our language through a process of imitation and reinforcement. As we grew and developed we heard our family using words to communicate. When we were capable of making noise, we attempted to duplicate these words. When our attempts seemed to be similar to the words used by our family, they rewarded us with excitement, hugs, and kisses. This positive reinforcement led us to attempt to imitate the word again and to, again, receive the reinforcement when we were successful. As we grew older we learned not only the language of our family but the language usage of our peers and our instructors. We were taught the words and what they represented. We learned our language through our experiences with that language.

We learned meanings for words in the same way. Very early in life we noted how words were used and what meanings seemed to go along with the words. We watched, listened, and experienced and slowly meanings were formed for us. At first we copied our parent's meanings and later on we picked up meanings from our peers and teachers. If we weren't certain what others meant by certain things, we asked and incorporated the answers into our developing meaning system. As we grew older we soon started developing meanings for ourselves until finally we had our own unique meaning system. Out of our experiences we developed our meaning system, just as we developed our grasp of the language. This process of learning meaning has been over-simplified to make it easily understandable. But learning language is much more complicated than it appears and deserves further explanation.

Meaning for any given word or symbol is learned through experience with that word or symbol. Meaning for a word becomes a product of all our past experiences with that word. As we are exposed to a word either by hearing it said or by reading it, we couple with the word whatever part of the environment we deem important at the time. The part of the environment that we consider important may be the person saying the word, the situation in which it is being said, the circumstances surrounding the saying of the word, the other words being used, and so forth. Whatever we perceive outside ourselves as being important and relevant to that word becomes a part of the word and its meaning at the time.

Just as we incorporate this perception of what is outside ourselves into the meaning of the word, we also incorporate what is inside ourselves at the time as part of the meaning. Our recollection of past experiences with the word, or other similar or related words, how we feel about the word and the person saying the word, how we feel about the situation or circumstances surrounding the saying of the word, our physical and mental state at the moment, and anything else inside ourselves that may be related to the word or situation is coupled with our perceptions and added to our meanings for the word. Then everything that we perceive outside ourselves at the moment is added together with all of our experiences with the word in order to develop our meaning for the word at that time.

Viewed this way, meaning becomes a situational phenomenon. Each situation in which we encounter that particular word is different, and our meanings for words change from situation to situation. Each time we encounter the word our internal states are different and our meanings are changed by this. Every time we have an experience with the word this experience is added to our previous experiences and thus meaning becomes a changeable thing.

Perhaps a personal experience may help clarify this concept of meaning. I was born and raised in a city. Consequently, my meaning for the word *horse* was developed through books about horses, discussions in school about horses, and my father's accounts of the use of horses on the farm where he spent his childhood. I had never seen a horse or had an experience with one myself, but from others I learned that horses were big, beautiful, gentle, cooperative animals used to help man on the farm. The summer I was nine I was invited to spend my vacation on a farm owned by the uncle of my best friend. At last I would have a personal experience with that wonderful animal, the horse.

During my first day on the farm I was introduced to the horse. He had just finished a full day of work and wasn't particularly interested in me, but my perceptions of him and my internal joy at seeing a horse coupled with all my past "storybook" experiences with horses made him seem magnificent to me. All of my expectations were met and my meanings were reinforced. Later my friend and I decided to ride the horse, a decision the horse did not appreciate. To show his lack of appreciation, the horse tried to bite us. My perception of this unexpected behavior of the horse coupled with my internal state of fear of those big teeth began to dramatically change my meaning for the word *horse*. Two days later my friend and I decided to ride the horse again. This time the horse seemed to feel that biting was not enough to discourage us, so he stepped on my foot with his foot and broke my instep. Again, my perception of the menacing, dangerous horse, coupled with the fear and pain that was inside me, drastically changed my meaning for *horse*. To this day, whenever horses are discussed, and even though I have had pleasant experiences with horses since, my meaning system reflects that experience when I was nine.

It is obvious that if the situational view of meaning in language is accepted, our perception of the world is an important part of language. But at the same time our language helps shape our perception.

SOME CHARACTERISTICS OF PERCEPTION

In the two preceding articles in this portion of the reader, Haney and Toch and MacLean examine many of the aspects of perception. Warr and Knapper present three other components, the attributive, the expectancy, and the affective, which are well worth considering (1). All three components are directly related to language.

The attributive portion of perception includes those characteristics that we choose to place upon the object or person being perceived. These attributed characteristics may or may not be present in the thing perceived—they are attributed by the perceiver based on his or her past experiences.

We also have certain expectations about those things we perceive. These expectancies are also based on our past experiences. We do not expect rocks to walk or people to be frozen because we have not had such experiences in the past.

We also have feelings about the objects or people we perceive. These feelings about our perceptions come out of our past experiences with whatever we are perceiving, the characteristics we attribute to those things perceived, and our expectancies about what is perceived.

All three of these components of perception are influenced by the language we use in describing our perceptions to ourselves. We categorize our perceptions through language, and this categorizing influences our perception.

Let us take an example and see how language might influence our perceptions. Suppose we are driving through the desert on a dark night and our headlights reveal an object in the road ahead. Seeing the general outline of the object we might categorize or label it as a large rock in the road. If we thus label it, we might attribute certain characteristics to it such as sharp outlines, jagged portions, solidness, and hardness. After attributing these characteristics to the object, we might expect the object to remain where it is and to do damage to the automobile if hit. We might also have feelings about this object such as that it is something to avoid or something to be apprehensive about. All of these attributes, expectancies, and emotions have grown out of our labeling of the object we have perceived, and our reactions to that object are based on the label or language category *rock*.

On the other hand, suppose we chose to label the object in the road ahead as a tumbleweed. We would then attribute other characteristics to the object such as branches, mobility, and lightness in weight. We would expect the object to be easily moved and would not expect it to do damage to the car if hit. We might also feel excitement at seeing a large tumbleweed, anticipation toward seeing it moved by the passage of the car, and so on. Again, our perception of the object is shaped by the word we have used to categorize the object.

We might even decide to label the object in the road as an injured person. Again the characteristics attributed to, our expectancies about, and our feelings toward the object would be changed according to the label we use for the object.

Not many of us may drive through the desert at night and see an object in the road, but we all come into contact with objects and persons every day. Our perceptions of these things are influenced by the word categories we use to label them. If an object is labeled a *horse*, certain characteristics are attributed to it, certain expectancies are developed about that object, and certain feelings are generated toward that object. If the horse is further labeled as "gentle," the attributes, expectancies, and feelings are pointed in one direction, whereas if that same horse is labeled *hostile*, the attributes, expectancies, and feelings go in another direction. In short, our perception of objects and people is influenced by the words we use in describing the thing or the person being perceived.

The Interrelationships Between Language and Perception

As can be seen by what has been said, language and perception are two interrelated and interdependent variables in behavior. The example of the horse is a case in point. The meaning developed for the symbol *horse* is based on past experiences with the word *horse* and the *horse* coupled with the perception of horses in particular situations. At the same time the perception of horses is colored by the same past experiences coupled with the meanings attached to the symbol. The interdependency causes meaning to be colored by perception and perception to be colored by meaning. The interrelatedness of these two characteristics helps influence the sense we make out of the world and affects our behavior in the world. Any label or linguistic unit we attach to any object or person we perceive in the world colors our perception of that object or person and dictates the characteristics we perceive. At the same time the characteristics we perceive help dictate the meanings we attach to those labels.

It seems to be natural for us to want to have a name for everything. In fact, we often feel that we cannot really understand something unless we have a label for it. Have you ever heard music that you like on the radio and been upset when the announcer did not identify that music? This tendency to want to name or label everything may be an outgrowth of our training in school where grades are awarded based on our ability to learn the names of things. Or it may be due to the fact that we like to systematize our experiences in order to make better sense out of the world for ourselves. For whatever the reason, we like to label and categorize our world. In their book *Person Perception*, Hastorf, Schneider, and Polefka discuss it this way:

One of the most salient features of the person's participation in structuring his experiential world can be described as a categorizing process. He extracts stimuli from the world and forces them into a set of categories. We have here a powerful example of the effects of linguistic coding on the structuring of experience. . . . The categories we use are derived from our past history and are dependent on our language and our cultural background (2).

This categorizing process is a prime example of the interrelationship of perception and language. When we are exposed to a new experience, object, or person that we have not known before we are open to as many perceptual inputs as possible in an attempt to categorize it. All possible stimuli are perceived in an attempt to fit the experience, object, or person into our linguistic system. These perceptions are checked against past perceptions until some sort of agreement or correspondence is discerned between what we now are perceiving and something in our past, and then a label is attached. Once a label is attached, those perceptions that do not reinforce the label are dropped as irrelevant. Future perceptions are then based on the category into which the new experience, object, or person has been placed. Perhaps an example may help clarify this process. Think back to a birthday on which you might have received a number of wrapped presents. Perhaps you received a present early and were curious about its contents. You may have checked the size and weight of the package. Perhaps you shook the package to see if it rattled or gurgled. You paid attention to all of these perceptions in order to categorize the present. Suppose that you learned that the gift was a shirt or a blouse. Suddenly the weight and noise the gift made were immaterial. Your perceptions of the object were then directed to other stimuli because of the category into which the gift was placed. Your perceptions were now directed to the color, the style, the fit, and the ability of the gift to match your other clothes.

As we are exposed to new experiences, we perceive in terms of trying to categorize that experience. Once categorized, the experience is perceived in terms of the category and details are dropped out of our perceptions in order that we concentrate our perceptions on details that reinforce our categorization. We fit our perceptions into categories in order to make sense out of the world, and our categories help determine our perceptions.

Another example of the interrelationship between perception and language is in the area of stereotyping. This is a case of prejudgmental categorizing. We develop our stereotypes out of our background, either cultural, familial, or experiential. We may have cultural stereotypes developed out of the culture in which we are raised, based on feelings toward other cultures. Our stereotypes might be developed out of family feelings for certain groups. Or our personal experiences with one individual from a certain group might structure our stereotype of all members of that group. Whatever the cause of our stereotypes, we tend to perceive members of particular groups based on our stereotypes of that group. We may feel that certain groups are characterized by stinginess, or by being in the clothing business, or by a natural sense of rhythm or a host of other characteristics. Once we developed stereotypes we have a tendency to want to perceive in terms of those stereotypes. If we meet a person that we can place in a stereotype category (for whatever reason), we tend to perceive that person in terms of our stereotypes. We attribute characteristics, we expect certain qualities, and we feel toward the person in terms of the stereotype. The individual involved may not have these characteristics, or may have some of them, or may have many more characteristics, but we tend to perceive in terms of the characteristics we have come to associate with that stereotype. We reinforce our linguistic categories through selective perception.

Each person makes sense out of the world for himself. In developing the sense, each individual must fit his perceptions into some meaningful pattern. Language patterns help the individual arrange his perceptions. Language and perception become two interrelated characteristics of human behavior in this systematic development.

NOTES

1. P. B. Warr and C. Knapper, *The Perception of People and Events* (New York: John Wiley & Sons, Inc., 1968), pp. 7–16.

2. A. H. Hastorf, D. J. Schneider, and J. Polefka, *Person Perception* (Reading, Mass.: Addison-Wesley Publishing Co., Inc., 1970), p. 6.

STUDY GUIDE
QUESTIONS

1. In what way does the word *is* imply that we are discussing something "out there" rather than our personal experience?
2. Why does using *is* indicate that we are choosing the best way to describe something?
3. What do we mean when we say *is* may often be used as an equal sign?

◄ The Trouble With Is, Is Is

DON FABUN

If we were to track down and corner in its lair what we believe to be one of the chief causes of problems in everyday communications, we would describe it as the misuse of the word . . . "is."

Behind the unqualified use of the word "is" lurk a number of assumptions, each of which can lead to trouble. (We use the word "unqualified" because there certainly appear to be places in our common speech where trying to avoid using the word "is" is—see?—not worth the effort it takes).

So what's so bad about "is"?

For one thing, what we consider "bad" are the many ways in which it can be misused in every day speech:

"It *is* good . . ."
"He *is* lazy . . ."
"That *is* a rock . . ."

all have one thing in common. The "is" implies that we are describing something "out there" that has a certain quality—"goodness," "laziness," or "rocklike"—which exists independently of our personal experience of it. And the next implication is that you must agree because "obviously" that *is* what it *is*.

But what we really are describing is an internal experience . . . which may have validity only for us.

One way out of this dilemma may be to say:

"I *think* it is good . . ."

"I *believe* he is lazy . . ."

"It *looks to me* like a rock . . ."

or, if we don't actually say it out loud, we can at least think this way to ourselves, as a reminder that what we describe is not "out there" but an experience inside ourselves.

Another thing we imply when we use the word "is" seems to be that we have examined the subject (whatever it may be) thoroughly, and have determined how best it can be described. But, in reality, we can only have examined

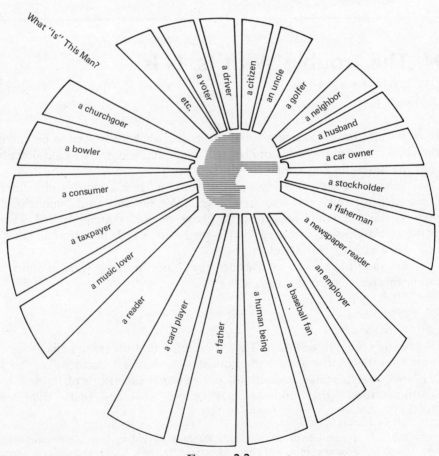

FIGURE 2-2

a limited number of possibilities (an expert may be defined as a person "who knows how much he does not know"). Of these possibilities, we have chosen one (or several) for a personal reason that may have validity only for us.

In our everyday speech, in memos, and letters and conferences and conversation, we hear or read pronouncements like, "He is an organization man," or, "He is unimaginative," rendered with the air of finality that would be more proper coming from the Princeton Institute of Advanced Learning.

If you take a look at [Figure 2-2] which partially lists some of the things that might be said about an individual (just as many things could be said about the company you work for, or an organization you belong to, or your neighborhood) you will see that they represent a wide spectrum of different experiences that different people have had at different times with this one individual. To choose *one* and to speak of it as if it characterized the real, living person, is to imply "all." When you imply "all" you seem to have closed the subject; you have, in effect, said, "He's_____, and that's all there is to it."

Now, no one believes you should try to say all about a subject every time you say something about it; that would be nonsensical, even if it were possible. But you *can* describe your reaction to a person or situation in such a way as to make it clear that you are making an inference . . . based on your own limited personal experience.

You can say, "I've only seen him a few times but he seemed to be a nice guy," (instead of, "He is a good guy,") or you could say, "I've seen him several times at club meetings and he strikes me as a loudmouth," (instead of, "He is a loudmouth.")

When we make clear the limitations of our experience and that we are talking about that experience rather than the person, event or thing, we leave open the way to further discussion (rather than disagreement and argument.) No one can seriously question that that was what *you* felt; but everyone can— and most people do—argue with the categorical statement, "That *is* ———."

There is still another way in which we sometimes use "is" that can lead to trouble. We may use it in the sense of "identities"—as in the phrase "2+2 = 4." We substitute "is" for the "=" sign and say "2+2 *is* 4." They are not the same thing at all. "2+2 *is* 2+2." But it does not appear to be "4." "4" is something else altogether. The arithmetical expression simply says that we can use the symbol "4" instead of "2+2" in certain types of agreed upon operations. It is permissive but it is not descriptive.

When we use "is" as if it was an "=" sign in common speech, as in "truth *is* beauty" or "knowledge *is* power" we begin to wander rather far afield from the world we actually experience.

This all may sound so obvious as to be almost childlike. Yet the "fact" remains that many of us, every day, use "is" as if it were some kind of a weapon. In doing so, we replace the richness and diversity of human experience with a dull and lifeless monochrome. We kill the animal and dry its skin and nail it to the temple wall, and in the end reduce the world we describe to a two-dimensional diagram—sans color, sans depth, sans motion—sans everything.

Stamp Out Is!

STUDY GUIDE   1. What is meant by the process of abstracting?
QUESTIONS   2. What are the various levels in the process of abstracting?
                              3. Why is it necessary that we abstract?
                              4. What is an operational definition?
                              5. What is "dead-level abstracting"?

◄ How We Know What We Know

S. I. HAYAKAWA

Bessie, the Cow

The universe is in a perpetual state of flux. The stars are growing, cooling, exploding. The earth itself is not unchanging; mountains are being worn away, rivers are altering their channels, valleys are deepening. All life is also a process of change, through birth, growth, decay, and death. Even what we used to call "inert matter"—chairs and tables and stones—is not inert, as we now know, for, at the submicroscopic level, it is a whirl of electrons. If a table looks today very much as it did yesterday or as it did a hundred years ago, it is not because it has not changed, but because the changes have been too minute for our coarse perceptions. To modern science there is no "solid matter." If matter looks "solid" to us, it does so only because its motion is too rapid or too minute to be felt. It is "solid" only in the sense that a rapidly rotating color chart is "white" or a rapidly spinning top is "standing still." Our senses are extremely limited, so that we constantly have to use instruments, such as microscopes, telescopes, speedometers, stethoscopes, and seismographs, to de-

---

tect and record occurrences which our senses are not able to record directly. The way in which we happen to see and feel things is the result of the peculiarities of our nervous systems. There are "sights" we cannot see, and, as even children know today with their high-frequency dog whistles, "sounds" that we cannot hear. It is absurd, therefore, to imagine that we ever perceive anything "as it really is."

Inadequate as our senses are, with the help of instruments they tell us a great deal. The discovery of microörganisms with the use of the microscope has given us a measure of control over bacteria; we cannot see, hear, or feel electromagnetic waves, but we can create and transform them to useful purpose. Most of our conquest of the external world, in engineering, in chemistry, and in medicine, is due to our use of mechanical contrivances of one kind or another to increase the capacity of our nervous systems. In modern life, our unaided senses are not half enough to get us about in the world. We cannot even obey speed laws or compute our gas and electric bills without mechanical aids to perception.

To return, then, to the relations between words and what they stand for, let us say that there is before us "Bessie," a cow. Bessie is a living organism, constantly changing, constantly ingesting food and air, transforming it, getting rid of it again. Her blood is circulating, her nerves are sending messages. Viewed microscopically, she is a mass of variegated corpuscles, cells, and bacterial organisms; viewed from the point of view of modern physics, she is a perpetual dance of electrons. What she is in her entirety, we can never know; even if we could at any precise moment say what she was, at the next moment she would have changed enough so that our description would no longer be accurate. It is impossible to say completely what Bessie or anything else really *is*. Bessie is not a static "object," but a dynamic process.

The Bessie that we experience, however, is something else again. We experience only a small fraction of the total Bessie: the lights and shadows of her exterior, her motions, her general configuration, the noises she makes, and the sensations she presents to our sense of touch. *And because of our previous experience, we observe resemblances in her to certain other animals to which, in the past, we have applied the word "cow."*

The Process of Abstracting

The "object" of our experience, then, is not the "thing in itself," but *an interaction between our nervous systems (with all their imperfections) and something outside them.* Bessie is unique—there is nothing else in the universe exactly like her in all respects. But we automatically *abstract* or select from the process-Bessie those features of hers in which she resembles other animals of like shape, functions, and habits, and we *classify* her as "cow."

Abstraction Ladder

Start reading from the bottom *up*

8. "wealth"

8. The word "wealth" is at an extremely high level of abstraction, omitting *almost* all reference to the characteristics of Bessie.

7. "asset"

7. When Bessie is referred to as an "asset," still more of her characteristics are left out.

6. "farm assets"

6. When Bessie is included among "farm assets," reference is made only to what she has in common with all other salable items on the farm.

5. "livestock"

5. When Bessie is referred to as "livestock," only those characteristics she has in common with pigs, chickens, goats, etc., are referred to.

4. "cow"

4. The word "cow" stands for the characteristics we have abstracted as common to cow_1, cow_2, cow_3 . . . cow_n. Characteristics peculiar to specific cows are left out.

3. "Bessie"

3. The word "Bessie" (cow_1) is the *name* we give to the object of perception of level 2. The name *is not* the object; it merely *stands for* the object and omits reference to many of the characteristics of the object.

2.

2. The cow we perceive is not the word, but the object of experience, that which our nervous system abstracts (selects) from the totality that constitutes the process-cow. Many of the characteristics of the process-cow are left out.

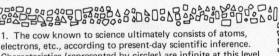

1. The cow known to science ultimately consists of atoms, electrons, etc., according to present-day scientific inference. Characteristics (represented by circles) are infinite at this level and everchanging. This is the *process level*.

Figure 2-3

When we say, then, that "Bessie is a cow," we are only noting the process-Bessie's resemblances to other "cows" and *ignoring differences*. What is more, we are leaping a huge chasm: from the dynamic process-Bessie, a whirl of electro-chemico-neural eventfulness, to a relatively static "idea," "concept," or *word*, "cow." In this connection, the reader is referred to the diagram entitled "The Abstraction Ladder" [Figure 2-3].

As the diagram illustrates, the "object" we see is an abstraction of the lowest level; but it is still an abstraction, since it leaves out characteristics of the process that is the real Bessie. The *word* "Bessie" (cow_1) is the lowest *verbal* level of abstraction, leaving out further characteristics—the differences between Bessie yesterday and Bessie today, between Bessie today and Bessie tomorrow—and selecting only the similarities. The word "cow" selects only the similarities between Bessie (cow_1), Daisy (cow_2), Rosie (cow_3), and so on, and therefore leaves out still more about Bessie. The word "livestock" selects or abstracts only the features that Bessie has in common with pigs, chickens, goats, and sheep. The term "farm asset" abstracts only the features Bessie has in common with barns, fences, livestock, furniture, generating plants, and tractors, and is therefore on a very high level of abstraction.

Our concern here with the process of abstracting may seem strange since the study of language is all too often restricted to matters of pronunciation, spelling, vocabulary, grammar, and sentence structure. The methods by which composition and oratory are taught in old-fashioned school systems seem to be largely responsible for this widespread notion that the way to study words is to concentrate one's attention exclusively on words.

But as we know from everyday experience, learning language is not simply a matter of learning words; it is a matter of correctly relating our words to the things and happenings for which they stand. We learn the language of baseball by playing or watching the game *and studying what goes on*. It is not enough for a child to learn to *say* "cookie" or "dog"; he must be able to use these words in their proper relationship to nonverbal cookies and nonverbal dogs before we can grant that he is learning the language. As Wendell Johnson has said, "The study of language begins properly with a study of what language is about."

Once we begin to concern ourselves with what language is about, we are at once thrown into a consideration of how the human nervous system works. When we call Beau (the Boston terrier), Pedro (the chihuahua), Snuffles (the English bulldog), and Shane (the Irish wolfhound)—creatures that differ greatly in size, shape, appearance, and behavior—by the same name, "dog," our nervous system has obviously gone to work *abstracting* what is common to them all, ignoring for the time being the differences among them.

Why We Must Abstract

This process of abstracting, of leaving characteristics out, is an indispensable convenience. To illustrate by still another example, suppose that we live in an isolated village of four families, each owning a house. A's house is referred to as *maga*; B's house is *biyo*; C's is *kata*, and D's is *pelel*. This is quite satisfactory for ordinary purposes of communication in the village, unless a discussion arises about building a new house—a spare one, let us say. We cannot refer to the projected house by any one of the four words we have for the existing houses, since each of these has too specific a meaning. We must find a *general* term, at a higher level of abstraction, that means "something that has certain characteristics in common with *maga, biyo, kata,* and *pelel,* and yet is not A's, B's, C's, or D's." Since this is much too complicated to say each time, an *abbreviation* must be invented. So we choose the noise, *house.* Out of such needs do our words come—they are a form of shorthand. The invention of a new abstraction is a great step forward, since it *makes discussion possible*—as, in this case, not only the discussion of a fifth house, but of all future houses we may build or see in our travels or dream about.

A producer of educational films once remarked to the writer that it is impossible to make a shot of "work." You can shoot Joe hoeing potatoes, Frank greasing a car, Bill spraying paint on a barn, but never just "work." "Work," too, is a shorthand term, standing, at a higher level of abstraction, for a characteristic that a multitude of activities, from dishwashing to navigation to running an advertising agency to governing a nation, have in common. The special meaning that "work" has in physics is also clearly derived from abstracting the common characteristics of many different kinds of work. ("A transference of energy from one body to another, resulting in the motion or displacement of the body acted upon, in the direction of the acting force and against resistance." Funk and Wagnalls' *Standard College Dictionary.*)

The indispensability of this process of abstracting can again be illustrated by what we do when we "calculate." The word "calculate" originates from the Latin word *calculus*, meaning "pebble," and derives its present meaning from such ancient practices as putting a pebble into a box for each sheep as it left the fold, so that one could tell, by checking the sheep returning at night against the pebbles, whether any had been lost. Primitive as this example of calculation is, it will serve to show why mathematics works. Each pebble is, in this example, an abstraction representing the "oneness" of each sheep—its numerical value. And because we are abstracting from extensional events on clearly understood and uniform principles, the numerical facts about the pebbles are also, barring unforeseen circumstances, numerical facts about the sheep. Our x's and y's and other mathematical symbols are abstractions made from numerical abstraction, and are therefore abstractions of still higher level. And they are useful in predicting occurrences and in getting work done because, since they are abstractions properly and uniformly made from starting points in the extensional world, the relations revealed by the symbols will be, again barring unforeseen circumstances, relations existing in the extensional world.

On Definitions

Definitions, contrary to popular opinion, tell us nothing about things. They only describe people's linguistic habits; that is, they tell us what noises people make under what conditions. Definitions should be understood as *statements about language*.

House. This word, at the next higher level of abstraction, can be substituted for the more cumbersome expression, "Something that has characteristics in common with Bill's bungalow, Jordan's cottage, Mrs. Smith's guest home, Dr. Jones's mansion. . . ."

Red. A feature that rubies, roses, ripe tomatoes, robins' breasts, uncooked beef, and lipsticks have in common is abstracted, and this word expresses that abstraction.

Kangaroo. Where the biologist would say "herbivorous mammal, a marsupial of the family Macropodidae," ordinary people say "kangaroo."

Now it will be observed that while the definitions of "house" and "red" given here point *down* the abstraction ladder (see the charts) to *lower* levels of abstraction, the definition of "kangaroo" remains at the same level. That is to say, in the case of "house," we could if necessary go and *look* at Bill's bungalow, Jordan's cottage, Mrs. Smith's guest home, and Dr. Jones's mansion, and figure out for ourselves what features they seem to have in common; in this way, we might begin to understand under what conditions to use the word "house." But all we know about "kangaroo" from the above is that where some people say one thing, other people say another. That is, when we stay at the *same* level of abstraction in giving a definition, we do not give any information, unless, of course, the listener or reader is already sufficiently familiar with the defining words to work himself down the abstraction ladder. Dictionaries, in order to save space, have to assume in many cases such familiarity with the language on the part of the reader. But where the assumption is unwarranted, definitions at the same level of abstraction are worse than useless. Looking up "indifference" in some cheap pocket dictionaries, we find it defined as "apathy"; we look up "apathy" and find it defined as "indifference."

Even more useless, however, are the definitions that go *up* the abstraction ladder to higher levels of abstraction—the kind most of us tend to make automatically. Try the following experiment on an unsuspecting friend:

"What is meant by the word *red*?"

"It's a color."
"What's a *color?*"
"Why, it's a quality things have."
"What's a *quality?*"
"Say, what are you trying to do, anyway?"

You have pushed him into the clouds. He is lost.

If, on the other hand, we habitually go *down* the abstraction ladder to *lower* levels of abstraction when we are asked the meaning of a word, we are less likely to get lost in verbal mazes; we will tend to "have our feet on the ground" and know what we are talking about. This habit displays itself in an answer such as this:

"What is meant by the word *red?*"
"Well, the next time you see some cars stopped at an intersection, look at the traffic light facing them. Also, you might go to the fire department and see how their trucks are painted."

"Let's Define Our Terms"

An extremely widespread instance of an unrealistic (and ultimately superstitious) attitude toward definitions is found in the common academic prescription, "Let's define our terms so that we shall all know what we are talking about." The fact that a golfer, for example, cannot define golfing terms is no indication that he cannot understand and use them. Conversely, the fact that a man can define a large number of words is no guarantee that he knows what objects or operations they stand for in concrete situations. Having defined a word, people often believe that some kind of understanding has been established, ignoring the fact that the words in the definition often conceal even more serious confusions and ambiguities than the word defined. If we happen to discover this fact and try to remedy matters by defining the defining words, and then, finding ourselves still confused, we go on to define the words in the definitions of the defining words, and so on, we quickly find ourselves in a hopeless snarl. The only way to avoid this snarl is to keep definitions to a minimum and to point to extensional levels wherever necessary; in writing and speaking, this means giving specific examples of what we are talking about.

Operational Definitions

Another way to keep extensional levels in mind, when definitions are called for, is to use what physicist P. W. Bridgman called "operational definitions." As he says,

To find the length of an object, we have to perform certain physical operations. The concept of length is therefore fixed when the operations by which length is measured are fixed. . . . In general, we mean by any concept nothing more than a set of operations; *the concept is synonymous with the corresponding set of operations* (2).

The operational definition, then, as Anatol Rapoport explains, is one that tells you *"what to do* and *what to observe* in order to bring the thing defined or its effects within the range of one's experience." He gives the following simple example of how to define "weight"; go to a railroad station or drugstore, look for a scale, stand on it, put in a penny, read the number at which the pointer comes to rest. *That* is your weight. But supposing different scales give different readings? Then your weight can be said to be within the range of, say, 140 to 145 pounds. With more accurate scales you might get closer readings, such as 142 pounds plus-or-minus one. But there is no "property" called weight that exists apart from the operations measuring it. As Rapoport says, "If the only way we can be aware of the amount of weight is by means of the scale, then the very definition of weight, has to be in terms of the scale" (3).

Such, then, is the scientific, or "operational," point of view towards definition—one that attempts rigidly to exclude non-extensional, non-sense statements. We can extend this idea from science to the problems of everyday life and thought. Just as there is no such thing as "length" apart from the operations by which length is measured, just as there is no "weight" apart from the operations by which weight is determined, there is likewise no "democracy" apart from the sum-total of democratic *practices,* such as universal franchise, freedom of speech, equality before the law, and so on. Similarly, there is no such thing as "brotherhood" apart from brotherly behavior, nor "charity" apart from charitable actions.

The operational point of view does much to keep our words meaningful. When people say things like, "Let's have no more of *progressive* methods in our schools," "Let's get back to *sound business principles* in running our county government," "Let's try to do the *Christian* thing," "Let's put father back as head of the family," we are entitled to ask, "what do you mean—*extensionally speaking?*" To ask this question often—of ourselves as well as of others—is to do our bit towards reducing the vast amount of non-sense that is written, spoken, and shouted in this incredibly garrulous world.

The best examples in everyday life of operational definitions are to be found in cookbooks, which describe the *operations* by means of which the entity defined may be extensionally experienced. Thus: *"Steak Diane.* Slice tenderloin beef very thin and give it a few whacks with a meat mallet to flatten it even more; sprinkle with salt and pepper to taste. Have your pan very hot. . . ." (*The Sunset Cook Book.*) Writers and speakers would do well to study cookbooks occasionally to increase the clarity and verifiability of their utterances.

Chasing Oneself in Verbal Circles

In other words, the kind of "thinking" we must be extremely wary of is that which *never* leaves the higher verbal levels of abstractions, the kind that never points *down* the abstraction ladder to lower levels of abstraction and from there to the extensional world:

"What do you mean by *democracy?*"
"Democracy means the preservation of human rights."
"What do you mean by *rights?*"
"By rights I mean those privileges God grants to all of us—I mean man's inherent privileges."
"Such as?"
"Liberty, for example."
"What do you mean by *liberty?*"
"Religious and political freedom."
"And what does that mean?"
"Religious and poltical freedom is what we enjoy under a democracy."

Of course it is possible to talk meaningfully about democracy, as Jefferson and Lincoln have done, as Frederick Jackson Turner does in *The Frontier in American History* (1950), as Karl R. Popper does in *The Open Society and Its Enemies* (1950), as T. V. Smith and Eduard Lindeman do in *The Democratic Way of Life* (1939)—to name only the first examples that come to mind. The trouble with speakers who never leave the higher levels of abstraction is not only that their audiences fail to notice when they are saying something and when they are not; but also that they themselves lose their ability to discriminate. Never coming down to earth, they frequently chase themselves around in verbal circles, unaware that they are making meaningless noises.

This is by no means to say that we must never make extensionally meaningless noises. When we use directive language, when we talk about the future, when we utter ritual language or engage in social conversation, we often make utterances that have no extensional verifiability. It must not be overlooked that our highest ratiocinative and imaginative powers are derived from the fact that symbols *are* independent of things symbolized, so that we are free not only to go quickly from low to extremely high levels of abstraction (from "canned peas" to "groceries" to "commodities" to "national wealth") and to manipulate symbols even when the things they stand for cannot be so manipulated ("If all the freight cars in the country were hooked up to each other in one long line . . ."), but we are also free to manufacture symbols at will even if they stand only for abstractions made from other abstractions and not for anything in the extensional world. Mathematicians, for example, often play with symbols that have no extensional content, just to find out what can be done with them; this is called "pure mathematics." And pure mathematics is far from being a useless pastime, because mathematical systems that are elaborated with no extensional applications in mind often prove to be applicable later in useful and unforeseen ways. But when mathematicians deal with extensionally meaningless symbols, they usually know what they are doing. We likewise must know what we are doing.

Nevertheless, all of us (including mathematicians), when we speak the language of everyday life, often make meaningless noises without knowing that we are doing so. We have already seen what confusions this can lead to. The fundamental purpose of the abstraction ladder . . . is to make us aware of the process of abstracting.

The Distrust of Abstractions

We may, using our abstraction ladder, allocate statements as well as words to differing levels of abstraction. "Mrs. Levin makes good potato pancakes" may be regarded as a statement at a fairly low level of abstraction, although, to be sure, it leaves out many elements, such as (1) the meaning of "goodness" in potato pancakes, and (2) the infrequent occasions when her pancakes fail to turn out well. "Mrs. Levin is a good cook," is a statement at a higher level of abstraction, covering Mrs. Levin's skill not only with potato pancakes, but also with roasts, pickles, noddles, strudels, and so on, nevertheless omitting *specific* mention of what she can accomplish. "Chicago women are good cooks," is a statement at a still higher level of abstraction; it can be made (if at all) only from observation of the cooking of a statistically significant number of Chicago women. "The culinary art has reached a high state in America," would be a still more highly abstract statement and, if made at all, would have to be based not only on observation of the Mrs. Levins of Chicago, New York, San Francisco, Denver, Albuquerque, and Chattanooga, but also on observation of the quality of meals served in hotels and restaurants, the quality of training in high school and college departments of home economics, the quality of writings on culinary art in American books and magazines, and many other relevant factors.

Unfortunately, though understandably, there is a tendency in our times to speak with contempt of "mere abstractions." The ability to climb to higher and higher levels of abstraction is a distinctively human trait, without which none of our philosophical or scientific insights would be possible. In order to have a science of chemistry, one *has* to be able to think of "H_2O," leaving out of consideration for the time being the wetness of water, the hardness of ice, the pearliness of dew, and the other extensional characteristics of H_2O at the objective level. In order to have a study called "ethics," one has to be able to think of what elements in ethical behavior have in common under different conditions and in different civilizations; one has to abstract that which is common to the behavior of the ethical carpenter, the ethical politician, the ethical businessman, and the ethical soldier—and that which is common to the laws of conduct of the Buddhist, the Orthodox Jew, the Confucian, and the Christian. Thinking that is most abstract can also be that which is most generally useful. The famous injunction of Jesus, "And as ye would that men should do to you, do ye also to them likewise," is, from this point of view, a brilliant generalization of more particular directives—a generalization at so high a level of abstraction that it appears to be applicable to all men in all cultures.

But high-level abstractions acquire a bad reputation because they are so often used, consciously or unconsciously, to confuse and befuddle people. A grab among competing powers for oil resources may be spoken of as "protecting the integrity of small nations." (Remember Japan's "Greater East Asia Co-prosperity Sphere"?) An unwillingness to pay social security taxes may be spoken of as "maintaining the system of free enterprise." Depriving the Negro of his vote in violation of the Constitution of the United States may be spoken of as "preserving states' rights." The consequence of this free, and often irresponsible, use of high-level abstractions in public controversy and special pleading is that a significant portion of the population has grown cynical about *all* abstractions.

But, as the abstraction ladder has shown, *all we know are abstractions*. What you know about the chair you are sitting in is an abstraction from the totality of that chair. When you eat white bread, you cannot tell by the taste whether or not it has been "enriched by vitamin B" as it says on the wrapper; you simply have to trust that the process (from which the words "vitamin B" are abstracted) is actually there. What you know about your wife—even if she has been your wife for thirty years—is again an abstraction. Distrusting all abstractions simply does not make sense.

The test of abstractions then is not whether they are "high-" or "low-level" abstractions, but *whether they are referrable to lower levels*. If one makes a statement about "culinary arts in America," one should be able to refer the statement down the abstraction ladder to particulars of American restaurants, American domestic science, American techniques of food preservation, down to Mrs. Levin in her kitchen. If one makes a statement about "civil rights in Wisconsin," one should know something about national, state, and local statutes; one should also know something about the behavior of policemen, magistrates, judges, academic authorities, hotel managers, and the general public in Wisconsin, all of whose acts and whose decisions affect that minimum of decent treatment in the courts, in politics, and in society that we call "civil rights." A preacher, a professor, a journalist, or politician whose high-level abstractions can systematically and surely be referred to lower-level abstractions is not only talking, he is saying something. As *Time* would say, no windbag, he.

"Dead-Level Abstracting"

Professor Wendell Johnson of the University of Iowa, in his *People in Quandaries* (1946), discusses a linguistic phenomenon which he calls "dead-level abstracting." Some people, it appears, remain more or less permanently stuck at certain levels of the abstraction ladder, some on the lower levels, some on the very high levels. There are those, for example, who go in for "persistent low-level abstracting":

Probably all of us know certain people who seem able to talk on and on without ever drawing any very general conclusions. For example, there is the back-fence chatter that is made up of he said and then I said and then she said and I said and then he said, far into the afternoon, ending with, "Well, that's *just* what I told him!" Letters describing vacation trips frequently illustrate this sort of language, detailing places seen, times of arrival and departure, the foods eaten and the prices paid, whether the beds were hard or soft, etc.

A similar inability to get to higher levels of abstraction characterizes certain types of mental patients who suffer, as Johnson says "a general blocking of the abstracting process." They go on indefinitely, reciting insignificant facts, never able to pull them together to frame a generalization that would give a meaning to the facts.

Other speakers remain stuck at higher levels of abstraction, with little or no contact with lower levels. Such language remains permanently in the clouds. As Johnson says:

It is characterized especially by vagueness, ambiguity, even utter meaninglessness. Simply by saving various circulars, brochures, free copies of "new thought" magazines, etc. . . . it is possible to accumulate in a short time quite a sizable file of illustrative material. Much more, of course, is to be found on library shelves, on newsstands, and in radio programs. Everyday conversation, classroom lectures, political speeches, commencement addresses, and various kinds of group forums and round-table discussions provide a further abundant source of *words cut loose from their moorings.* [Italics supplied.]

(The writer once heard of a course in esthetics given at a large Middle Western university in which an entire semester was devoted to Art and Beauty and the principles underlying them, and during which the professor, even when asked by students, persistently declined to name specific paintings, symphonies, sculptures, or objects of beauty to which his principles might apply. "We are interested," he would say, "in principles, not in particulars.")

There are psychiatric implications to dead-level abstracting on higher levels, too, because when maps proliferate wildly without any reference to a territory, the result can only be delusion. But whether at higher or lower levels, dead-level abstracting is, as Johnson says, always dull:

The low-level speaker frustrates you because he leaves you with no directions as to what to do with the basketful of information he has given you. The high-level speaker frustrates you because he simply doesn't tell you what he is talking about. . . . Being thus frustrated, and being further blocked because the rules of courtesy (or of attendance at class lectures) require that one remain quietly seated until the speaker has finished, there is little for one to do but daydream, doodle, or simply fall asleep.

It is obvious, then, that interesting speech and interesting writing, as well as clear thinking and psychological well-being, require the constant interplay of higher- and lower-level abstractions, and the constant interplay of the verbal levels with the nonverbal ("object") levels. In science, this interplay goes on constantly, hypotheses being checked against observations, predictions against extensional results. (Scientific *writing*, however, as exemplified in technical journals, offers some appalling examples of *almost* dead-level abstracting —which is the reason so much of it is hard to read. Nevertheless, the interplay between verbal and nonverbal experimental levels does continue, or else we would not have science.) The work of good novelists and poets also represents this constant interplay between higher and lower levels of abstraction. A "significant" novelist or poet is one whose message has a high level of *general* usefulness in providing insight into life; but he gives his generalizations an impact and a persuasiveness through his ability to observe and describe actual social situations and states of mind. A memorable literary character, such as Sinclair Lewis' George F. Babbitt, has *descriptive* validity (at a low level of abstraction) as the picture of an individual, as well as a *general* validity as a picture of a "typical" American businessman of his time. The great political leader is also one in whom there is interplay between higher and lower levels of abstraction. The ward heeler knows politics only at lower levels of abstraction: what promises or what acts will cause what people to vote as desired; his loyalties are not to principles (high-level abstractions) but to persons (e.g., political bosses) and immediate advantages (low-level abstractions). The so-called impractical political theorist knows the high-level abstractions ("democracy," "civil rights," "social justice") but is not well enough acquainted with facts at lower levels of abstraction to get himself elected county register of deeds. But the political leaders to whom states and nations remain permanently grateful are those who were able, somehow or other, to achieve simultaneously higher-level aims ("freedom," "national unity," "justice") *and* lower-level aims ("better prices for potato farmers," "higher wages for textile workers," "judicial reform," "soil conservation").

The interesting writer, the informative speaker, the accurate thinker, and the sane individual, operate on all levels of the abstraction ladder, moving quickly and gracefully and in orderly fashion from higher to lower, from lower to higher—with minds as lithe and deft and beautiful as monkeys in a tree.

NOTES

1. The "Abstraction Ladder" is based on "The Structural Differential," a diagram originated by Alfred Korzybski to explain the process of abstracting. For a fuller explanation both of the diagram and of the process it illustrates, see his *Science and Sanity: An Introduction to Non-Aristotelian Systems and General Semantics* (1933), especially Chapter 25.

2. *The Logic of Modern Physics* (1927), p. 5.

3. *Operational Philosophy* (1953), p. 25.

III Interpersonal Communication

Interpersonal communication, that is, communication taking place between people, is what most of us usually consider when we use the term *communication*. By now, however, we are aware that communication is far more complex than most of us probably realized. Interpersonal communication is just one type of communication, and, like the rest, it too has many varied aspects.

Wendell Johnson's *The Fateful Process of Mr. A Talking to Mr. B* provides us with a diagram of interpersonal communication. Johnson breaks the process down into stages and discusses the limitations and problems within each stage. His diagram serves as a bridge between intrapersonal and interpersonal communication since he discusses both processes and demonstrates how they interrelate. Through the study of the diagram and the stages discussed by Johnson, we come to realize some of the complexity of the interpersonal communication process.

Communication, Communicative Process, Meaning: Toward a Unified Theory by Robert S. Goyer discusses these three terms and demonstrates how these three concepts are interrelated. Unlike some other definitions, Goyer's are interpersonally oriented and show an emphasis upon the interaction between individuals and their purposeful sharing of meaning.

Charles Kelly's article, *Empathic Listening*, stresses the importance of one aspect of interpersonal communication. Kelly feels that perhaps listening has received too little attention and he suggests that we should not only listen more but listen emphatically rather than deliberately. He offers us suggestions on how we can improve our listening habits and thereby enhance our communication with others.

Jack Gibb, in *Defensive Communication*, discusses a particular type of communication behavior. Gibb feels that defensive behavior, that is, behavior aimed primarily at defending our own egos, can be aroused by improper communication. Such defensive behavior has a detrimental effect upon communication and should be avoided. Gibb suggests how we can create supportive rather than defensive communication climates and thus improve our interpersonal communication.

Rather than discuss one basic aspect or one particular type of interpersonal communication, *Interpersonal Communication: Some Working Principles*, by Samovar and Rintye, discusses what the authors believe to be the twelve basic principles of interpersonal communication. These principles consider various aspects of the communication process and once again demonstrate how interpersonal and intrapersonal communication interrelate. The authors suggest how perception, fidelity, and communication context are affected by these principles. Additionally they consider the ways that man's symbol system affects communication.

Persuasion is the topic of Campbell and Hepler's article, *Persuasion and Interpersonal Relations*. Here the authors offer the view that all communication is directed at changing behavior. They discuss how the amount of shared experience can affect interpersonal communication. Furthermore, they relate the ways in which our perception of ourselves, as well as one another, can affect us when we communicate.

Finally, Richard Carroll's article, *Transactional Analysis: A Different Perspective of Communication*, considers the applications of Transactional Analysis to the field of communication theory. Carroll discusses how an understanding and application of the basics of Transactional Analysis can give us added insight into certain communication characteristics and help us improve our communication habits.

STUDY GUIDE
QUESTIONS

1. What are the functions of the various stages in Johnson's diagram?
2. What problems can occur in the various stages of Johnson's diagram?
3. What roles do limited sensory capacity and filtering play in perception?
4. Why does Johnson call communication an art?

▶◀ The Fateful Process of Mr. A Talking to Mr. B

WENDELL JOHNSON

It is a source of never-ending astonishment to me that there are so few men who possess in high degree the peculiar pattern of abilities required for administrative success. There are hundreds who can "meet people well" for every one who can gain the confidence, goodwill, and deep esteem of his fellows. There are thousands who can speak fluently and pleasantly for every one who can make statements of clear significance. There are tens of thousands who are cunning and clever for every one who is wise and creative.

Why is this so? The two stock answers which I have heard so often in so many different contexts are: (1) administrators are born, and (2) administrators are made.

The trouble with the first explanation—entirely apart from the fact that it contradicts the second—is that those who insist that only God can make a chairman of the board usually think themselves into unimaginative acceptance of men as they find them. Hence any attempt at improving men for leadership is automatically ruled out.

Meanwhile, those who contend that administrators can be tailor-made are far from omniscient in their varied approaches to the practical job of transforming bright young men into the inspired leaders without which our national economy could not long survive. Nevertheless, it is in the self-acknowledged but earnest fumblings of those who would seek out and train our future executives and administrators that we may find our finest hopes and possibilities.

"The Fateful Process of Mr. A Talking to Mr. B," by Wendell Johnson, from *Harvard Business Review*, Vol. 31, No. 1, pp. 49–56.

This article does not propose to wrap up the problem of what will make men better administrators. Such an attempt would be presumptuous and foolhardy on anyone's part; there are too many side issues, too many far-reaching ramifications. Rather, this is simply an exploration into one of the relatively uncharted areas of the subject, made with the thought that the observations presented may help others to find their way a little better. At the same time, the objective of our exploration can perhaps be described as an oasis of insight in what otherwise is a rather frightening expanse of doubt and confusion.

The ability to respond to and with symbols would seem to be the single most important attribute of great administrators. Adroitness in reading and listening, in speaking and writing, in figuring, in drawing designs and diagrams, in smoothing the skin to conceal and wrinkling it to express inner feelings, and in making the pictures inside the head by means of which thinking, imagining, pondering, and evaluating are carried on—these are the fundamental skills without which no man may adequately exercise administrative responsibilities.

Many of the more significant aspects of these administrative prerequisites may be brought into focus by means of a consideration of what is probably the most fateful of all human functions, and certainly the one function indispensable to our economic life: communication. So let us go on, now, to look at the process of communication and to try to understand the difficulties and disorders that beset us in our efforts to communicate with one another.

The Process Diagramed

Several years ago I spent five weeks as a member of a group of university professors who had the job of setting up a project concerned with the study of speech. In the course of this academic exploring party we spent a major part of our time talking—or at least making noises—about "communication." By the second or third day it had become plain, and each day thereafter it became plainer, that we had no common and clear notion of just what the word "communication" meant.

After several days of deepening bewilderment, I recalled an old saying: "If you can't diagram it, you don't understand it." The next day I made a modest attempt to bring order out of the chaos—for myself, at least—by drawing on the blackboard a simple diagram representing what seemed to me to be the main steps in the curious process of Mr. A talking to Mr. B. Then I tried to discuss communication by describing what goes on at each step—and what might go wrong. Since sketching that first diagram on the blackboard eight or nine years ago, I have refined and elaborated it, and I have tried from time to time, as I shall again here, to discuss the process of communication in terms of it (see Figure 3-1) (1).

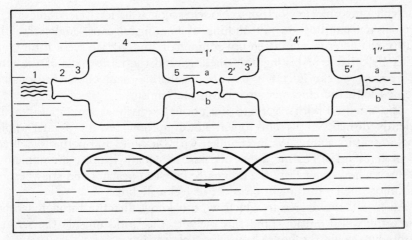

FIGURE 3-1. The process of communication. Key: Stage 1, event, or source of stimulation, external to the sensory end organs of the speaker; Stage 2, sensory stimulation; Stage 3, pre-verbal neurophysiological state; Stage 4, transformation of pre-verbal into symbolic forms; Stage 5, verbal formulations in "final draft" for overt expression; Stage 1', transformation of verbal formulations into (a) air waves and (b) light waves, which serve as sources of stimulation for the listener (who may be either the speaker himself or another person); Stages 2' through 1" correspond, in the listener, to Stages 2 through 1'. The arrowed loops represent the functional interrelationships of the stages in the process as a whole.

INSIDE MR. A

What appears to take place when Mr. A talks to Mr. B is that first of all, at Stage 1, some event occurs which is external to Mr. A's eyes, ears, taste buds, or other sensory organs. This event arouses the sensory stimulation that occurs at Stage 2. The dotted lines are intended to represent the fact that the process of communication takes place in a "field of reality," a context of energy manifestations external to the communication process and in major part external to both the speaker and the listener.

The importance of this fact is evident in relation to Stage 2 (or Stage 2'). The small size of the "opening" to Stage 2 in relation to the magnitude of the "channel" of Stage 1 represents the fact that our sensory receptors are capable of responding only to relatively small segments of the total ranges of energy radiations.

Sensory Limitations

The wave lengths to which the eye responds are but a small part of the total spectrum of such wave lengths. We register as sound only a narrow band of the full range of air vibrations. Noiseless dog whistles, "electronic eyes," and radar mechanisms—to say nothing of homing pigeons—underscore the primitive character of man's sensory equipment. Indeed, we seem little more than barely capable of tasting and smelling, and the narrowness of the temperature range we can tolerate is downright sobering to anyone dispassionately concerned with the efficiency of survival mechanisms.

The situation with regard to the normal individual may appear to be sufficiently dismal; let us not forget, however, how few of us are wholly normal in sensory acuity. We are familiar with the blind and partially sighted, the deaf and hard of hearing; we notice less the equally if not more numerous individuals who cannot taste the difference between peaches and strawberries, who cannot smell a distraught civet cat or feel a fly bite.

All in all, the degree to which we can know directly, through sensory avenues, the world outside (and this includes the world outside the sensory receptors but inside the body) is impressively restricted.

Any speaker is correspondingly limited in his physical ability to know what he is talking about. Relatively sophisticated listeners are likely to judge a speaker's dependability as a communicating agent by the degree to which he discloses his awareness of this limitation. The executive who demonstrates a realistic awareness of his own ignorance will in the long run acquire among his peers and subordinates a far better reputation for good judgment than the one who reveals his limitations by refusing to acknowledge them.

Pre-Verbal State

Once a sensory receptor has been stimulated, nerve currents travel quickly into the spinal cord and normally up through the base of the brain to the higher reaches of the cortex, out again along return tracts to the muscles and glands. The contractions and secretions they cause bring about new sensory stimulations which are "fed back" into the cord and brain and effect still further changes. The resulting reverberations of stimulation and response define what we may call a pre-verbal state of affairs within the organism. This state is represented at Stage 3 of the diagram.

Two statements about this pre-verbal state are fundamental: (1) we need to realize that our direct knowledge of this state is slight; (2) at the same time we are justified in assuming that it does occur.

No one has ever trudged through the spinal cord and brain with gun and camera, at least not while the owner of those organs was alive. Nevertheless, we are reasonably sure of certain facts about the nervous system. Observations have been reported by neurosurgeons, electroencephalographers, nerve physiologists, and anatomists. Thousands of laboratory animals have been sacrificed on the altars of scientific inquiry. We know that there are nerve currents, that they travel at known rates of speed, exhibit certain electrical properties, and are functionally related to specified kinds of loci of stimulation and to specified kinds and loci of response.

Thus, though our factual information is meager as yet, certainly it is sufficient to demonstrate that the nervous system is not merely a hypothetical construct. We can say with practical assurance that stimulation of our sensory end organs is normally followed by the transmission of nerve currents into the central nervous system, with a consequent reverberation effect, as described above, and the resulting state of affairs within the organism.

Two specific observations about this state of affairs are crucial: (1) it is truly pre-verbal, or silent; (2) it is this noiseless bodily state that gets transformed into words (or other symbols). Therefore—and these next few words should be read at a snail's pace and pondered long and fretfully—besides talking always to ourselves (although others may be listening more or less too), and whatever else we may also be striving to symbolize, *we inevitably talk about ourselves.*

The Individual's Filter

What the speaker—whether he be a junior executive or the general manager—directly symbolizes, *what he turns into words,* are physiological or electrochemical goings-on inside his own body. His organism, in this sense, operates constantly as a kind of filter through which facts (in the sense of things that arouse sensory impulses) must pass before they can become known to him and before they can be *communicated* by him to others in some symbolic form, such as standard English speech.

It follows, to present a single, seemingly trivial, but quite representative example, that when the junior executive says to the general manager, "It's certainly a fine day," he is exhibiting an elaborate variety of confusion; indeed, he appears literally not to know what he is talking about. In the meantime, he is talking about himself—or at least about the weather only as "filtered" by himself. He is symbolizing an inner state, first of all. In this he is the brother of all of us who speak.

I do not mean to imply that we talk solely about our inner states. We often talk about the world outside; but when we do, we filter it through our inner states. To the degree that our individual filters are standardized and alike, we will agree in the statements we make about the world outside—allowing, of course, for differences in time, place, observational set, equipment, sensory acuity, perceptive skill, and manner of making verbal reports.

The existence of the filter at Stage 3 of the process of communication is the basic fact. We may differ in our manner of appreciating and interpreting the significance of the filter, and in so doing make ourselves interesting to each other. But when the administrator—when anyone at all—simply never learns that the filter is there, or forgets or disregards it, he becomes, as a speaker, a threat to his own sanity and a potential or actual menace in a public sense.

Self-Projection

Because the filter is there in each of us, self-protection is a basic bodily process that operates not only in all our speaking but in other kinds of communicative behavior. To claim to speak literally, then, a person must always say "as I see it," or "as I interpret the facts," or "as I filter the world" if you please, or simply "to me."

An administrator whose language becomes too "is"-y tends to persuade himself that what he says the facts are is the same thing as the facts, and under the numbing spell of this illusion he may become quite incapable of evaluating his own judgments. If he is aware of projection, he must make clear, first of all to himself that he is not speaking about reality in some utterly impersonal or disembodied and "revealed" sense, but only about reality as the prism of his own nervous system projects it upon the gray screen of his own language—and he must realize that this projection, however trustworthy or untrustworthy, must still be received, filtered, and reprojected by each of his listeners.

Sufficient contemplation of this curious engineering scheme renders one sensitive to the hazards involved in its use. As with any other possibility of miracle, one is well advised not to expect too much of it.

Patterns and Symbols

Stage 4, the first stage of symbolization, is represented in our diagram as a great enlargement in the tunnel through which "the world" passes from Stage 1 to Stage 1'. The words ultimately selected for utterance (at Stage 5) are a very small part of the lush abundance of possible verbalizations from which they are abstracted. Moreover, the bulge is intended to suggest that the state of affairs at Stage 3 becomes in a peculiarly human way much more significant by virtue of its symbolization at Stage 4.

At Stage 4 the individual's symbolic system and the pattern of evaluation reflected in its use come into play. The evaluative processes represented at this stage have been the object of much and varied study and speculation:

Freud Here, it would appear, was the location of Freud's chief preoccupations, as he attempted to explain them in terms of the so-called unconscious depths of the person, the struggle between the Id and the Super-Ego from which the Ego evolves, the ceaseless brewing of dreamstuff, wish and counterwish, the fabulous symbolism of the drama that we call the human personality (2). Indeed, at this stage there is more than meets the eye—incredibly more so far as we may dimly but compellingly surmise.

Korzybski Here, too, were the major preoccupations of the founder of general semantics, Alfred Korzybski: the symbol; the creation of symbols and of systems of symbols; the appalling distortions of experience wrought by the culturally imposed semantic crippling of the young through the witless and artful indoctrination of each new generation by the fateful words of the elders —the words which are the carriers of prejudice, unreasoning aspiration, delusional absolutes, and the resulting attitudes of self-abandonment. But also here we find the unencompassable promise of all that *human* can suggest, and this Korzybski called upon all men to see, to cherish, and to cultivate with fierce tenderness (3).

Pavlov The father of the modern science of behavior, Pavlov, also busied himself with ingenious explanations of occurrences at what we have called Stage 4 (4). In human beings, at least, the learning processes, as well as the drives and goals that power and direct them, appear to function at this stage of incipient symbolization.

It seems useful to conjecture that perhaps the general *patterns* of symbolic conditioning are formed at Stage 4 in contrasts to the conditioning of specific symbolic responses (i.e., particular statements) produced at Stage 5. We may put it this way: at Stage 4 the syllogism, for example, as a *pattern* or *form* of possible symbolic response, is laid down, while at Stage 5 there occur the specific verbal responses patterned in this syllogistic mold.

Again, at Stage 4 we find the general form, "X affects Y"; at Stage 5 we see its specific progeny in such statements as "John loves Mary," "germs cause disease," "clothes make the man," and so on. In this relationship between general forms or patterns at Stage 4 and the corresponding specific utterances at Stage 5 we find the substantial sense of the proposition that our language does our thinking for us.

In fact, one of the grave disorders that we may usefully locate at Stage 4 consists in a lack of awareness of the influence on one's overt speech of the general symbolic forms operating at Stage 4. The more the individual knows about these forms, the more different forms he knows—or originates—and the more adroit he is in the selective and systematic use of them in patterning specific statements at Stage 5, the more control he exercises over "the language that does his thinking for him." The degree of such control exercised over the verbal responses at Stage 5 represents one of the important dimensions along which speakers range themselves, all the way from the naïvete of the irresponsible robot—or compulsive schizophrenic patient—to the culture-shaping symbolic sophistication of the creative genius.

(Generally speaking, most of the disorders of abstracting described and emphasized by the general semanticists are to be most usefully thought of as operating chiefly at Stage 4. These disorders include those involving identification or lack of effective discrimination for purposes of sound evaluation [5].)

The Final Draft

The fact has been mentioned, and should be emphasized, that the "final draft" formulated at Stage 5, the words that come to be spoken, represents as a rule a highly condensed abstract of all that might have been spoken. What enters into this final draft is determined, in a positive sense, by the speaker's available knowledge of fact and relationship, his vocabulary, and his flexibility in using it, his purposes, and (to use the term in a broad sense) his habits. What enters into it is determined negatively by the repressions, inhibitions, taboos, semantic blockages, and ignorances, as well as the limiting symbolic forms, operating at Stage 4.

Mr. A to Mr. B

As the communication process moves from Stage 5 to Stage 1', it undergoes another of the incredible transformations which give it a unique and altogether remarkable character: the words, phrases, and sentences at Stage 5 are changed into air waves (and light waves) at Stage 1'. At close quarters, Mr. A may at times pat the listener's shoulder, tug at his coat lapels, or in some other way try to inject his meaning into Mr. B by hand, as it were, but this transmission of meaning through mechanical pressure may be disregarded for present purposes.

Inefficiency of Air Waves

In general, it seems a valid observation that we place an unwarranted trust in spoken words partly because we disregard, or do not appreciate, the inefficiency of air waves as carriers of information and evaluation. The reasons for this inefficiency lie both in the speaker and in the listener, of course, as well as in the air waves themselves. What the listener ends up with is necessarily a highly abstracted version of what the speaker intends to convey.

The speaker who sufficiently understands this—the wise administrator —expects to be misunderstood and, as a matter of fact, predicts quite well the particular misunderstandings with which he will need to contend. Consequently, he is able not only to forestall confusion to some extent but also to give himself a chance to meet misunderstanding with the poise essential to an intelligent handling of the relationships arising out of it. A minimal requirement for the handling of such relationships is that either the speaker or the listener (or, better, both) recognize that the fault lies not so much in either one of them as in the process of communication itself—including particularly the fragile and tenuous air waves, whose cargo of meaning, whether too light to be retained or too heavy to be borne, is so often lost in transit.

Such an executive takes sufficiently into account the fact that words, whether spoken or written, are not foolproof. He will do all he can, within reason, to find out how his statements, his letters and press releases, his instructions to subordinates, and so on are received and interpreted. He will not take for granted that anyone else thinks he means what he himself thinks he means. And when he discovers the misunderstandings and confusions he has learned to expect, he reacts with disarming and constructive forbearance to the resentments and disturbed human relationships that he recognizes as being due, not to men, but to the far from perfect communications by means of which men try to work and live together.

Inside Mr. B

The air waves (and light waves) that arrive at Stage 2'—that is, at the ears and eyes of the listener—serve to trigger the complex abstracting process which we have just examined, except that now it moves from 2' through 5' instead of 2 through 5. That is, the various stages sketched in the speaker are now repeated in the listener. To understand speech, or the communication process in general, is to be aware of the various functions and the disorders operating at each stage in the process—and to be conscious of the complex pattern of relationships among the various stages, as represented schematically by the double-arrowed loops in the diagram.

Effect of Feedback

Always important, these relationships become particularly significant when the speaker and listener are one and the same individual. And this, of course, is always the case, even when there are other listeners. The speaker is always affected by "feedback": he hears himself. What is significant is precisely the degree to which he is affected by feedback. It may, in fact, be ventured as a basic principle that the speaker's responsiveness to feedback— or, particularly important, the *administrator's* responsiveness to feedback—is crucial in determining the soundness of his spoken evaluation. It is crucial also, in determining his effectiveness in maintaining good working relationships with his associates.

Application to Problems

This view of the process of Mr. A speaking to Mr. B may be applied to any one of a great many specific problems and purposes. The diagram can be used especially well as a means of directing attention to the disorders of communication, such as those encountered daily in the world of trade and industry.

Preventing Troubles

In this connection, let me call attention to the fact that Professor Irving Lee of the School of Speech at Northwestern University has written a book on *How to Talk with People* (6), which is of particular interest to anyone concerned with such disorders. Its subtitle describes it as "a program for preventing troubles that come when people talk together." The sorts of troubles with which Professor Lee is concerned in this book are among those of greatest interest and importance to personnel managers and business administrators and executives generally, and there would seem to be no better way to make my diagram take on a very practical kind of meaning than to sketch briefly what Professor Lee did and what he found in his studies of men in the world of business trying to communicate with one another.

Over a period of nearly ten years Professor Lee listened to the deliberations of more than 200 boards of directors, committees, organization staffs, and other similar groups. He made notes of the troubles he observed, and in some cases he was able to get the groups to try out his suggestions for reducing such troubles as they were having; and as they tried out his suggestions, he observed what happened and took more notes.

Among the many problems he describes in *How to Talk with People* there are three of special interest, which can be summarized thus:

(1) First of all, misunderstanding results when one man assumes that another uses words just as he does. Professor Quine of Harvard once referred to this as "the uncritical assumption of mutual understanding." It is, beyond question, one of our most serious obstacles to effective thinking and communication. Professor Lee suggests a remedy, deceptively simple but profoundly revolutionary: better habits of listening. We must learn, he says, not only how to define our own terms but also how to ask others what they are talking about. He is advising us to pay as much attention to the righthand side of our diagram as to the lefthand side of it.

(2) Another problem is represented by the person who takes it for granted that anyone who does not feel the way he does about something is a fool. "What is important here," says Lee, "is not that men disagree, but that they become disagreeable about it." The fact is, of course, that the very disagreeable disagreer is more or less sick, from a psychological and semantic point of view. Such a person is indulging in "unconscious projection." As we observed in considering the amazing transformation of the physiological goings-on at Stage 3 into words or other symbols at Stage 4, the only way we can talk about the world outside is to filter it through our private inner states. The disagreeable disagreer is one who has never learned that he possesses such

a filter, or has forgotten it, or is so desperate, demoralized, drunk, or distracted as not to care about it.

A trained consciousness of the projection process would seem to be essential in any very effective approach to this problem. The kind of training called for may be indicated by the suggestion to any administrator who is inclined to try it out that he qualify any important statements he makes, with which others may disagree, by such phrases as "to my way of thinking," "to one with my particular background," "as I see it," and the like.

(3) One more source of trouble is found in the executive who thinks a meeting should be "as workmanlike as a belt line." He has such a business-only attitude that he simply leaves out of account the fact that "people like to get things off their chests almost as much as they like to solve problems." Professor Lee's sensible recommendation is this: "If people in a group want to interrupt serious discussion with some diversion or personal expression—let them. Then bring them back to the agenda. Committees work best when the talk swings between the personal and the purposeful."

Constructive Factors

Professor Lee saw something, however, in addition to the "troubles that come when people talk together." He has this heartening and important observation to report:

"In sixteen groups we saw illustrations of men and women talking together, spontaneously, cooperatively, constructively. There was team-play and team-work. We tried to isolate some of the factors we found there: (1) The leader did not try to tell the others what to do or how to think; he was thinking along with them. (2) No one presumed to know it all; one might be eager and vigorous in his manner of talking, but he was amenable and attentive when others spoke. (3) The people thought of the accomplishments of the group rather than of their individual exploits."

This can happen—and where it does not happen, something is amiss. The diagram presented in Figure 3-1, along with the description of the process of communication fashioned in terms of it, is designed to help us figure out what might be at fault when such harmony is not to be found. And it is intended to provide essential leads to better and more fruitful communication in business and industry, and under all other circumstances as well.

CONCLUSION

Mr. A talking to Mr. B is a deceptively simple affair, and we take it for granted to a fantastic and tragic degree. It would surely be true that our lives would be longer and richer if only we were to spend a greater share of them in the tranquil hush of thoughtful listening. We are a noisy lot; and of what gets said among us, far more goes unheard and unheeded than seems possible. We have yet to learn on a grand scale how to use the wonders of speaking and listening in our own best interests and for the good of all our fellows. It is the finest art still to be mastered by men.

NOTES

1. The diagram, with a discussion of it, was first published in my book *People in Quandaries* (New York, Harper & Brothers, 1946), Chapter 18, "The Urgency of Paradise." I developed it further in *The Communication of Ideas*, edited by Lyman Bryson (New York, Harper & Brothers, 1948), Chapter 5, "Speech and Personality." It was also reproduced in *Mass Communications*, edited by Wilbur Schramm (Urbana, University of Illinois Press, 1949), pp. 261–274. The most recent statement is to be found in my article, "The Spoken Word and the Great Unsaid," *Quarterly Journal of Speech*, December, 1951, pp. 419–429. The form of the diagram reproduced here, together with a substantial portion of the text, are used by permission of the *Quarterly Journal of Speech*.

2. Sigmund Freud, *A General Introduction to Psychoanalysis*, translated by Joan Riviere (New York, Liveright Publishing Corporation, 1955).

3. Alfred Korzybski, *Science and Sanity: An Introduction to Non-Aristotelian Systems and General Semantics* (Lancaster, Pennsylvania, Science Press, 3rd ed. 1948).

4. I. P. Pavlov, *Conditioned Reflexes: An Investigation of the Physiological Activity of the Cerebral Cortex*, translated and edited by G.V. Anrep (London, Oxford University Press, 1927).

5. See Alfred Korzybski, *op. cit.*, and Wendell Johnson, *People in Quandaries*, particularly Chapters 5 through 10.

6. New York, Harper and Row, Publishers, 1952.

◄ Communication, Communicative Process, Meaning: Toward Unified Theory

ROBERT S. GOYER

Abstract

This paper attempts to dispel some of the prevailing ambiguity regarding related concepts of communication by suggesting: (1) a perspective for approaching the study of communicative process, and (2) a behavioral focus for the examination and classification of the process elements.

The term "communication" is defined as the sharing of experience, observable as the extent to which the responses of a generator and perceiver are systematically correlated to a referent stimulus. "Communicative process" is described in relatively discreet terms as a unique class of intentful stimulus-response behavior, represented by the model $G^s \rightarrow p^a$. "Meaning" is defined as a discriminative response to a stimulus, and provides the criterion for determining whether or not communication occurs in a given situation.

The implication of the proposed system of inquiry is that any observably definable communicative event, regardless of its context or complexity, is potentially subject to systematic, verifiable analysis for purposes of critical investigation, empirical explanation, and useful prediction of behavior.

I

The object of the discussion which follows is to suggest a structural pattern for approaching the study of communicative behavior.

Assertions are found in the literature that an integrated theory of communicative process is necessarily either futile or unfeasible [5]. However,

"Communication, Communicative Process, Meaning: Toward a Unified Theory," by Robert S. Goyer, from *The Journal of Communication*, Vol. 20 (March 1970), pp. 4–16.

given a viable operational base for defining the three initial terms in the title of this paper, I am persuaded that some of the ambiguity and confusion surrounding the use of these terms can be eliminated, and their points of conceptual similarity and commonality emphasized. I do not propose to examine differentially the various theories and definitions found throughout the published literature as partially represented in the list of references included in this discussion. Instead, I shall offer a theoretical position for describing any observably definable communicative event, regardless of its content or environment, and explicate the derivation and implications of that position for related concepts.

The use of the phrase "toward a unified theory" reflects my present conviction that a series of statements of the relations prevailing in a comprehensive body of observable communicative events is within our reach, if not entirely within our present grasp. The emphasis placed on "observable" events should not be interpreted as denying the usefulness or value of private, unique, intuitive experiences as a source of questions and answers. However, until such experiences are systematically sharable and thus verifiable in a public sense, their usefulness as a basis for general application and prediction is extremely limited.

II

The efforts of living organisms to influence and to accommodate to their environments depend substantially upon their abilities to share experiences (communicate) with other living organisms. Man's ability to "share experience" observably is not unique among living organisms, but his ability to share experiences indirectly and vicariously by means of surrogates (signs/symbols) is perhaps the most uniquely characteristic of his "human" qualities.

It must be a truism to note that communicative process is a (if not *the*) basic ingredient in virtually all interaction among and between living organisms. Denotative definitions of the term "communication" and its various derivative forms are numerous, ranging from the very general to the very specific [2, 6]. Connotative definitions are surely legion. Some writers conceive of communicative process as involving only humans, while others are inclined to a much broader view. Many writers use the term "communication" as synonymous with "influence," as in the sense that any response to any stimulus involves communicative process. These advocates suggest that communication occurs in its most primitive form whenever an organism responds, discriminatively or otherwise, to any stimulus event; no distinction is made between the influential behavior of either animate or inanimate objects as parties to the process. Neither is it inherent in this position to distinguish between intentful and nonintentful behaviors.

The most serious and frequent charge levied against such a broad definition is that it excludes nothing from itself, and thus fails pragmatically to define anything. Such all-inclusiveness invites ambiguity unnecessarily by tending to rob the term of its usefulness as a unique and viable label for what shall be described later as a unique combination of events. As a base line for the systematic examination and public discussion of the process of communication, such a definition is therefore unsatisfactory.

To use the term "communication" (whether in noun, verb, or adjectival form) as a synonym for "message" (e.g., "the communication was received") and/or as a synonym for the transmitting act (e.g., "the message was communicated") and/or as a synonym for the entire process (e.g., "the communicative environment was disrupted"), etc., is avoidable and contributes to the ambiguity which unfortunately and unnecessarily is often found in the literature in this field. Similarly, the dual use of the word "communication" as both noun and adjective is ambiguous and potentially confusing; restricting "communication" to usage as a noun, and employing "communicative" or "communicational" as the adjectival form should help increase precision in usage.

In the discussion that follows, "to communicate" shall mean "to make common" (to share) experience, regardless of the nature of the experiential event, or the method of its transmission or projection. "Communication" is therefore that particular event which culminates in some degree of shared experience. The experience for the involved parties may be either "direct" in terms of the time and space dimensions of the event, or it may be "vicarious" (indirect), involving the processing of surrogate elements (ranging from arbitrarily different to highly related) which are substitutes for the original direct experience, and which occur at a point in time and/or space removed to some degree from the original event. In this context, the direct communicative event can be experienced by any living organism interacting with another living organism at the most elementary biochemical level. The vicarious sharing of experiences, however, by definition occurs only through the sharing of sign/symbol surrogates. Published observations suggest that only a very few species of animals are capable of this sophisticated kind of symbol manipulation behavior, and *homo sapiens* is far superior to all others in this respect.

Experiences are said to be shared when commonality of "meaning" occurs between the organisms involved. Behavioral evidence of such occurrence is defined operationally in terms of the correlation of responses made to the stimulus event by the organisms involved [3].

Like other living organisms, man exhibits the ability to *directly* share experiences with others of his species. In addition he often shares experiences with other living things. Implied in this statement is that living organisms constitute relatively "open" behavior systems capable of some degree of self-organizing ability (i.e., the ability to generate behavior change), while non-living objects are incapable of any sort of generative behavior, including "sharing." Thus, it would be inaccurate to say that a man "communicates with" a rock or with any other non-living substance, although such an object and substance may very well be a common *referent* for man's communicative behavior with some other living organism. Similarly, such non-living objects may be manipulated by man as processing and/or transmitting agents (e.g., computers) in the total process, but such objects are manifestly "closed" systems in the sense that their capabilities are controlled and programmed at their genesis by a living organism. Whether or not man can communicate with living plants, or even whether plants communicate with plants, is highly speculative and not pertinent to our purposes here. However, perhaps man's most unique attribute is his manifest ability to generate, store, and subsequently employ a high order of sign/symbol behavior * by way of implementing *vicarious* experience with other men, and some other animals. By means of man's symbol-generating activity, he typically represents his world and interacts with it by means of a consciously employed, conventional set of symbols combined according to specified rules. This generation of symbol systems is *by definition* inevitably purposeful and intentful from the generator's standpoint, rather than accidental and random. These symbol systems are typically referred to as *language codes*, and may be either verbal (the "English" language, etc.) or nonverbal (music, dance, etc.). A language code thus consists of any systematic combination of sensory, symbolic stimuli. The direct physical sharing of an event thus may require *no* language employment, although neither does it prevent its generation; on the other hand, the vicarious sharing of experience depends on a language of some sort. "Language" thus constitutes the currency which makes possible the vicarious sharing of experiences.

Although the communicative behavior of man in a given situation may involve a number of language codes (both verbal and nonverbal), it is perhaps obvious that his ability to employ sophisticated *verbal* language codes is of central importance in his daily existence. Our present state of knowledge suggests that those organisms beneath man on the evolutionary ladder of biological development are quite capable of engaging in communicative behavior of a "direct experience" (biochemical) nature, but they are severely limited in their ability to share experiences vicariously.

---

* Although various writers have attempted to distinguish between a "sign" and a "symbol," the position taken here is that operationally they are both observable as *substitute*, or *surrogate*, representations of some other object or event. To say that "signs" are involuntarily and automatically exhibited, while "symbols" are learned artifacts which are "signs of signs," may be accurate, but irrelevant to this discussion.

III

If "communication" shall be the label used to name that event in which experience is shared between living organisms, what shall the phrase "communicative process" imply? What is proposed below is a theory of communicative process which is applicable to any living organism at any point on the direct-vicarious continuum, the mechanics of which are demonstrable not only in living biological systems, but also in some artificial systems created by man and used by him as subsets of the more inclusive process.

The sequence of events which must occur to produce a communicative event may be viewed as involving a minimum of five sequential ingredients: (1) a generator of a (2) stimulus which is (3) projected to a (4) perceiver which (5) responds discriminatively (assigns meaning). Thus the basic unit in communicative process can be represented by the model $G^s \rightarrow P^R$, where: G represents the generator, S represents a stimulus, P represents a perceiver, R represents a differential response, and $\rightarrow$ represents projection in time.

Although it is very possible that additional ingredients may be present in a given communicative situation which influence the process in some way by affecting its quality, efficiency, etc. (e.g., feedback, channel noise, filters), such ingredients are not inherently necessary for the process to occur, even though they may be highly desirable or even probable in a given situation.

According to the elemental model proposed here, the ability to participate in this basic communicative event is not restricted to man alone. Also, the response of a living organism to *any* kind of stimulus does *not* necessarily result in a communicative event in that: (1) the stimulus may not have been initially generated by a living organism, and (2) the response may not have been discriminative. These qualifications are intended to distinguish the communicative event from the general class of stimulus-response behavior in which a given stimulus, regardless of its origin, may evoke a response which is unshared. Similarly, the responses that the perceiver makes must be discriminative (as contrasted with random, or indiscriminate) with respect to the generator's stimuli, as evidence that "meaning" has resulted. *Random* responses on the part of the perceiver therefore would be described as "meaningless" responses (and vice versa) from the perceiver's standpoint, although such responses on the part of the perceiver might be *interpreted* otherwise by the generator or other observer.

In dealing with the communicative behavior of human beings, we have traditionally been most concerned with a particular kind of stimulus initiated by the generator: his verbal symbols. It is this behavior which makes possible vicarious experience, and permits man to deal with objects and events which are not physically present, nor are in fact "material" in any referential sense.

In terms of the vicarious sharing of experience, *communication* thus occurs with reference to G and P whenever the response of P to a sign/symbol stimulus projected by G, is consistent or correlated with the response intended by G; that is, when the referent responses of G and P to the sign/symbol stimulus are systematically related. The greater the correlation between the response intended by G and the response provided by P, the more "effective" is the communicative event. To put it algebraically, when P meaning/G meaning = 1, communication is whole and complete. Clearly fractional effectiveness is also possible. In fact, *perfect* sharing of meaning in terms of vicarious experience probably occurs only by chance, since the backgrounds and experiences of individuals are so infinitely varied.

In terms of the operational model discussed above, *meaning* is thus defined as the discriminative response of each participant in the communicative process to the sign/symbol stimulus. Some degree of communication thus occurs when the "meanings" (discriminative responses) of G and P are shared (overlap). Thus, communicative process can occur without much *communication* occurring, although the reverse could not hold. Notice that any stimulus, whether or not it is generated by a living organism, is capable of evoking a "meaningful" response in a perceiver, depending upon the conditioning history (direct and vicarious experiences) of the perceiver. But the unique requirement that the stimulus be generated by a living organism narrows the range of our concern with communicative behavior to those generators and perceivers with similar response potentialities. Notice that we are concerned with the response potentialities of the *participants* not of the *referent*, although on occasion the referent also may be a participant.

Although the elemental G-P model described above may accurately reflect the most basic unit of communicative process, it is potentially misleading in terms of its lack of emphasis on the dynamic characteristics of the process. The multivariate nature of communicative process as represented should be perceived as occurring along a time continuum which results in behavioral change in the parties involved.

Models of this process with respect to human communicative behavior have developed historically from many sources [7]. Descriptions and explanations of more current contributions are found in a variety of publications [1, 2, 3, 4, 6, 9].

Using the time dimension as an axis, a model of communicative process emphasizing its dynamic nature might be represented by analogy to the structure of the deoxyribonucleic acid molecule (DNA). This "coil of life" molecule is pictured as a double helix [8]. In [Figure 3-2], the points of communicative interaction occur as indicated, with the qualification that the roles of G and P may be reversed at any given point (i.e., G becomes P¹ and P becomes G¹).

In an *intra*personal (intradependent) sense, it can be speculated that the processing of information (both the immediately sensory and that which the individual's conditioning history provides) occurs along a time dimension

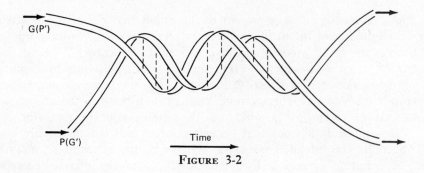

G(P')

P(G')

Time

FIGURE 3-2

which permits him to generate, organize and further process data, and subsequently respond in a manner suggested by the model. In an *inter*personal (interdependent) sense, the model provides a somewhat more obvious fit.

If we can assume that one strand of this double helix represents a G and the other strand a P, and that the hyphenated lines connecting them represent specific points of interaction between the organisms, it becomes more apparent how the G and P potentially respond to one another in communicative processes, albeit not always in as orderly a fashion as the model suggests. If one visualizes this event as occurring in an environment replete with a variety of simultaneously competing stimuli from the standpoint of both G and P (some of which are shared and some of which are not), a more representative picture emerges. Nevertheless, if it is accurate to assume that each perceiver tends to respond primarily to a single stimulus at a given time, and that the primary stimulus in his environment at a given time is the stimulus behavior provided by a generator, then the helical model above provides a limited representation of the communicative event. Furthermore, the model's suggestion that the event is inherently a dyadic one is no accident. It is quite incidental to the process unit that the generator and perceiver may exist in an environment devoid of other organisms, or in a crowded environment. As far as interpersonal communicative process is concerned, the point here is that it is in essence personal and dyadic in nature, regardless of the total environment in which the process operates. This is *not* to suggest that the presence or absence of other organisms, or the nature of the projection technique, or the quality of the symbol system employed (if any), etc., doesn't potentially affect the event. It *is* to suggest, however, that the necessary and sufficient conditions for the occurrence of a communicative event are represented by the G-P model.

The question concerning whether or not "intent" is a necessary ingredient for communicative process to occur has long been a subject of debate. The position implicit in the G-P model is that intent on the part of the generator is indeed necessary, whether the communicative event is direct or vicarious. Perceiver intent is present to the extent that the perceiver attends to the stimulus, but intent in the sense of preconceived *perceiver* purpose is not necessary for the communicative process to function. Without some degree of *generator* intent, however, the generator's behaviors by definition would be random and unstructured, and although the perceiver may respond discriminatively to such stimuli, no communication between the organisms is possible if no "sharing" is possible from the standpoint of the generator.

It is probably obvious that generator intent will not necessarily be so identified by the intended perceiver; conversely, the generator's "message" may be fortuitously perceived by organisms other than the intended perceiver. The latter situation, however, does not mean that the generator's stimulus behavior was unintentional; it simply means that a given (one or more) perceiver was unintended. (See Section IV below.)

An artificial and highly abstracted representation of communicative process is mechanically represented by the modern computer system. It is artificial in that the computer is incapable of initially generating intentful and adaptive behavior of its own volition; someone pushes that first button which starts the total programmed process, no matter how sophisticated and complex the mechanics ultimately become. Similarly, the "final" response of the computer is produced ultimately for "someone," directly or indirectly. The computer provides an excellent abstraction of the mechanics of the G-P model, however, in that all elements are present in form, if not in kind (e.g., neither g nor p are living organisms; environmental stimuli other than the one(s) programmed at a given instant are excluded from both g and p, so that virtually no competing stimuli are present). As a result, the computer functions in effect as part of the larger projection process of the G-P model, and is employed by the G as a means to an end in the larger process:

$$G^s \; (g^s \rightarrow p^r : g^s \rightarrow p^r : g^s \rightarrow p^r : etc.) \; P^R.$$
$$\xrightarrow{\hspace{6cm}}$$

As is often the case, the projection technique here affects (and perhaps refines) the message (e.g., the sign/symbol stimulus) while it is being mediated. Thus the computer represents a mechanical abstraction, albeit restricted and perhaps refined, of the parent model.

IV

The immediately preceding discussion has been concerned with "communicative process," defined as the sequential combination of ingredients which is designed to culminate in some degree of communication between organisms. In Section II above, "communication" was defined as "shared experiences (behaviors, responses)," or "commonality of meaning." The question now is, how can we come to grips with the concept "meaning"; more specifically, how can we put it into operation?

In terms of the model $G^s \rightarrow P^R$, "meaning" is defined as the discriminative response by an organism to a stimulus [3]. Although many stimuli evoke discriminative responses (and are therefore verifiably "meaningful"), they are not necessarily part of any communicative process. However, if the stimulus is intentfully generated, projected, and discriminatively responded to, then the possibility exists that communication has occurred. Thus, "meaning" can certainly occur in the absence of communicative process *per se*, but communication cannot occur in the absence of "meaning."

What is the relationship between meaning and generator intent, or lack of it? This question was raised in Section III above.

In human terms, the meaning (discriminative behavioral responses) of persons perceiving a message *not* intended for their ears does not imply that meaning has not been evoked or can not be assigned to these events by these accidental perceivers. All of us respond discriminatively to a variety of events and objects in our environments, whether verbal or nonverbal, real or imagined, that are not particularly "intended" for us. In this sense the P can respond to the G's message in much the same way as P would respond to any non-intentfully generated stimulus in his environment. Communication may or may not have occurred in that there may be no correlation between G_{ri} (*response intended* by the generator) and P_{rm} (*response made* by the perceiver). The basic criterion against which communicative *effectiveness* is evaluated pragmatically must be the intent of the G; on the other hand, whether or not meaning *in any sense* has resulted, must depend inevitably upon the nature of the response made by the P. Although the G never may be in a position to know the nature of P's response, and therefore never be in a position to judge the effectiveness of his own efforts, this in no sense means that communication may not have occurred. Similarly, when the G is in a position to evaluate P's response to G's sign/symbol stimulus, G must conclude on the basis of P's observable behavior whether or not the response made (rm) is consistent with response intended (ri).

Thus, the P's observable response is defined from the standpoint of G (or some other observer) as the "meaning" which P assigns to the sign/symbol stimulus. This is not to say that P's observable physical response is the "true" meaning, or that the G interprets P's response behavior accurately; but it is to say that P's response behavior provides the only independently verifiable indication which G can use as a criterion. Although the P may be engaging in unobservable mental/physical activities which are more valid indicators of the "real" meaning which P assigns, until some way is found to observe that which is now unobservable, the behavioral manifestations of P's mental/physical activities provide the public evidence that meaning has resulted. To the extent that the background experiences (conditioning histories) of both

G and P are similar, so that the shared symbol evokes similar responses from both parties, the probabilities of effectiveness of the communicative event are improved. Conversely, the more dissimilar or ambiguous the real or vicarious experiences associated by each party with the particular symbol, the lower the probability that effective or "successful" communication will result.

V

This discussion reflects an effort to provide (1) a perspective for approaching the study of communicative process, and (2) a behavioral focus for the examination and classification of its elements. While recognizing that communicative process probably does not occur in isolation from a larger environment, it has been my intent to identify those ingredients which are the *sine qua non* of the process, regardless of the event's content, environment, media, or circumstances.

Briefly, I have suggested that "communication" be defined as the sharing of experience, observable as the extent to which the responses of a generator and perceiver (both of which are necessarily living organisms) are systematically correlated to a referent stimulus. "Communicative process" can be described in relatively discreet terms as a special class of intentful stimulus-response behavior, represented by the model $G^S \rightarrow P^R$. "Meaning" is defined as a discriminative response to a stimulus, and provides the criterion for determining whether or not communication occurs in a given situation. Thus, to share meaning is to share experience, which is to communicate.

Notes

1. Barnlund, D. C. *Interpersonal Communication: Survey and Studies.* Boston: Houghton Mifflin, 1968.

2. Dance, Frank E. X. *Human Communication Theory: Original Essays.* New York: Holt, Rinehart and Winston, 1967.

3. Fink, John B. and Goyer, R. S. "Behavioristics and Communication Process." In *Communication—Spectrum '7: Proceedings of the 15th Annual Conference of NSCC.* Lawrence, Kansas: Allen Press, 1968, p. 92–98.

4. Goyer, Robert S. "Communication Process: An Operational Approach." In *Perspectives on Communication* (Edited by C. Larson and F. Dance). Milwaukee, Wisconsin: University of Wisconsin, Speech Communication Center; 1968, pp. 20–23.

5. Krippendorf, Klaus. "Values, Modes and Domains of Inquiry into Communication." *Journal of Communication* 19:105–33, 1969.

6. Smith, A. G. *Communication and Culture.* New York: Holt, Rinehart and Winston, 1966.

7. Smith, R. L. *General Models of Communication.* Communication Research Center Special Report No. 15: Purdue University, 1962.

8. Steiner, R. F. *The Chemical Foundations of Molecular Biology*. Princeton, N.J.: D. Van Nostrand, 1965.

9. Thayer, Lee. *Communication and Communication Systems*, Homewood, Illinois: Richard D. Irwin, 1968.

<table>
<tr><td>STUDY GUIDE
QUESTIONS</td><td>1. What emphasis has been placed on listening in the past?
2. What characterizes deliberative and empathic listening?
3. Why does the author suggest that empathic listening is preferable to deliberative?
4. What suggestions can we utilize to improve our listening?</td></tr>
</table>

▶ Empathic Listening

CHARLES M. KELLY

In a research project exploring listening behavior, industrial supervisors gave the following reasons for communication problems in large management-level meetings and conferences: "things discussed here are often side issues that don't interest everyone," "I think about my job upstairs," "they get off the subject," and "a lot of people like to hear themselves talk." A content analysis was made of these and other responses dealing with the perceived deficiencies of meetings and discussions. Results indicated that most of the dissatisfaction centered around the general feeling that many different issues were discussed at a typical meeting, and that usually some of these issues were not directly related to all of the participants (1).

Complaints such as the above are not unusual, and frequently are justified. Every text of discussion and conference methodology deals with the problems of keeping the discussion on relevant and significant issues, and of motivating the participants. However, most of the emphasis in the past has dealt with the obligations of the discussants (both leaders and participants) as *speakers*, rather than as *listeners*. This unbalanced emphasis, especially as it actually affects persons in real discussions, could be an important *cause* of

"Empathic Listening," by Charles M. Kelly, from *Small Group Communication*, L. A. Samovar and R. S. Cathcart, eds. (Dubuque, Iowa: William C. Brown, 1970), pp. 251–259. Reprinted with permission of author.

the problems that speaking is supposed to cure: e.g., the reason a discussion leader may have difficulty clarifying the comments of another, may be that he did not listen carefully to begin with; when one is overly concerned about what *he* is *going* to say, he really can't devote his full attention to what *is* being said by others. If a person in a group preoccupies himself by privately bemoaning the irrelevancies that inevitably occur in discussion, he may be less able to get the group back on the track; he misses opportunities for constructive action because he lacks an *accurate* analysis of the flow of ideas, even the irrelevant ones.

Of course, listening is a multi-faceted activity and it can be considered from different viewpoints, but at least two ways of categorizing listening seem especially fruitful for theoretical analysis: *deliberative listening* and *empathic listening*. Most recent writers have treated listening as a unitary skill, i.e., as a rather definite and "deliberative" ability to hear information, to analyze it, to recall it at a later time, and to draw conclusions from it. Commercially-published listening tests and most listening training programs are based on this, the deliberative listening, viewpoint. On the other hand, empathic listening occurs when the person participates in the spirit or feeling of his environment as a communication *receiver*. This does not suggest that the listener is uncritical or always in agreement with what is communicated, but rather, that his primary interest is to become fully and accurately aware of what is going on. (See Figure 3-3.)

It should be observed that the terms "deliberative listening" and "empathic listening" are not mutually exclusive or exhaustive. Their main purpose is to differentiate between two basic ways of viewing the same listening activity. The desired result of both deliberative and empathic listening is identical: accurate understanding of oral communication. However, this understanding is achieved by different routes. The deliberative listener *first* has the desire to critically analyze what a speaker has said, and secondarily tries to understand the speaker (this can be the result of personal inclination or of training which emphasizes procedure at the expense of listening). The empathic listener has the desire to understand the speaker first, and, as a result, tries to take the appropriate action.

The former kind of listening is characteristic of the discussant who is predisposed to be disagreeable, or to summarize, or to clarify—even when there is little that is significant to disagree with, when there is no need to summarize, or when further clarification is a waste of the group's time. The latter kind of listening is characteristic of the person who is able to adapt quickly to the real needs of a situation because he has a presence of mind and a greater confidence in the accuracy of his awareness—he does not handicap himself by deciding in advance that he does not have to listen to a particular person who is poorly dressed, or that he must be sure to explore all faulty reasoning if he is to demonstrate his competence.

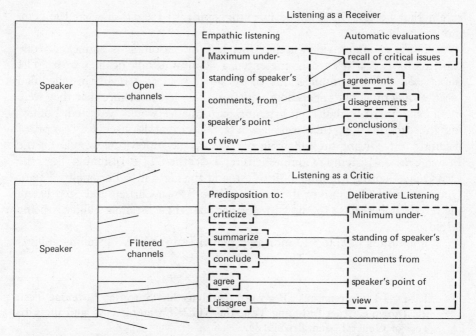

FIGURE 3-3. The differences between empathic listening and deliberative listening are primarily motivational. Both listeners seek the same objective: accurate understanding of the communication from another. The model suggests that the motivation to receive information is superior to the motivation to use critical skills. The empathic listener lets his understanding of the speaker determine his modes of evaluation, which are automatic; the deliberative listener's understanding of the speaker is filtered through his predetermined modes of selective listening, and actually spends less time as a communication receiver. The empathic listener is more apt to be a consistent listener, and is less prone to his own or other distractions. This theory is correct, only if the assumption is true that persons can and do think critically without deliberate effort—*while listening*. (Of course, if persons do not make the effort to listen *per se*, little or no understanding will occur.)

This is not to say that various skills in critical thinking are less important than empathic listening. Without critical analysis, listening in a problem-solving discussion would be useless. The point is, however, that a person uses quite naturally whatever critical skills he has already acquired, as long as he is interested and actively listening; to the extent that he is not listening, critical skills will be of little value. Actually, a case can be made that "deliberative listening" is a self-contradiction and a misnomer—and that "empathic listening" is a redundancy. To the extent that one is deliberating (mentally criticizing, summarizing, concluding, preparing reports, etc.) he is *not listening*, but formulating his own ideas. And listening, by its very nature, *has* to be empathic; a person understands what he has heard, only to the extent that he can share in the meaning, spirit, or feeling of what the communicator has said.

There is some evidence that this line of reasoning is correct. In one experiment (2), a researcher presented a 30-minute talk dealing with "The Supervisor and Communication" to 28 supervisors at a regularly scheduled business meeting. The supervisors were in no way led to believe that they were in an experiment or that their listening performance would be tested. Following the presentation, they were given a 30-item multiple-choice "surprise" listening test. During the following two weeks, the supervisors were given the Brown-Carlsen Listening Comprehension Test, the STEP Listening Test, the Otis Quick-Scoring Mental Ability Test, and the Cattell 16 Personality Factor Questionnaire. (Because of the nature of the Brown-Carlsen and Step listening tests, subjects have to know in advance that their listening ability is being tested.)

The results (Table 3-1) indicated that the supervisors' "listening ability"

TABLE 3-1. Correlations (Pearson r) Among the "Surprise" Listening Test, the Brown-Carlsen Listening Test, the STEP Listening Test, and the Otis Test of General Mental Ability [a]

	BROWN-CARLSEN	STEP	OTIS
Surprise Listening test	.79	.78	.70[bc]
Brown-Carlsen		.82	.85[b]
STEP			.85[c]

[a] All correlations are significant at the .01 level.
[b] The difference between the two correlations so designated is significant at the .05 level, t = 2.205.
[c] The difference between the two correlations so designated is significant at the .05 level, t = 2.162.

(as measured by the Brown-Carlsen and the STEP) was indistinguishable from general mental ability (as measured by the Otis) when they knew in advance that their listening was being tested. In fact, the listening tests correlated *lower* with each other, than each did with the test of mental ability. In other words, when the supervisors had the extra motivation of a test, or were constantly listening, they made full use of their general mental ability, and the listening tests became orally presented tests of general mental ability, rather than of "listening." On the other hand, when the supervisors did not know their listening was being tested, their listening performance was significantly less related to general mental ability.

Further insight can be gained by analyzing the results in terms of personality variables (Table 3-2). Again, the Brown Carlsen and STEP listening

TABLE 3-2. Statistical Significance of Differences (Chi Square with Yates' Correction) Between "High" and "Low" Criterion Groups (as Determined by Scores on Each of Four Tests) on the Cattell 16 PF Scales

CATTELL SCALE LOW SCORE VS. HIGH SCORES	SURPRISE LISTENING TEST [bcd]	BROWN- CARLSEN [b]	STEP [c]	OTIS [d]
Aloof vs. Outgoing	.14	.00**	.14	.00
Dull vs. Bright (intelligence factor)	.57	5.16	2.29	2.29
Emotional vs. Mature	3.57***	1.28	3.57***	1.28
Submissive vs. Dominant	.14	.00	.00	.15
Glum vs. Enthusiastic	.14	.00	.00	.00
Casual vs. Conscientious	.00	.00	.00	.00
Timid vs. Adventurous	9.19*	.57	2.29	.57
Tough vs. Sensitive	.00	.00	.00	.57[a]
Trustful vs. Suspecting	.57[a]	.00	.00	.00
Conventional vs. Eccentric	.00	.00	.00	.00
Simple vs. Sophisticated	3.65***	1.31	1.31	1.31
Confident vs. Insecure	.00	.57[a]	.00	.00
Conservative vs. Experimenting	.00	.59[a]	.00	.00
Dependent vs. Self-sufficient	.00	.00	.00	.00
Lax vs. Controlled	2.29	.00	.00	.00
Stable vs. Tense	7.00*[a]	.14[a]	1.31[a]	2.29[a]

* X^2 of 6.64 = 1% level.
** X^2 of 3.84 = 5% level.
*** X^2 of 2.71 = 10% level.
[a] High scorers on the test scored low on the Cattell personality scale.

Using the sign test for statistical significance, the following differences were observed between tests, on the basis of personality scales (intelligence scale, "Dull vs. Bright," was not included):

[b] difference between tests so designated was significant at p = .03
[c] p = .008
[d] p = .055

tests are indistinguishable from the Otis, when compared on the basis of personality variables; the same personality factors appear about equally important (as expressed in chi square values) in the test of general mental ability as in the tests of listening ability. However, the "surprise" listening test showed significantly more substantial personality differences between good and poor listeners than did the other three tests.

The most significant differences between good and poor listeners, when they had no unusual motivation to listen because of test awareness, were that good listeners were more adventurous (receptive to new ideas), (emotionally) stable, mature, and sophisticated. Although the other six differences in Table 3-2 (under "surprise listening test") were not statistically significant, it is interesting to note that all were in the same direction, with the good listeners being more emotionally mature: outgoing, bright, dominant, enthusiastic, trustful and controlled (will control). The opposite ends of the personality scales, describing the poor listeners in the surprise listening test, were: aloof, dull, emotional, submissive, glum, timid, suspecting, simple, lax, and tense.

This and other studies (3) strongly indicate that when persons know that their listening comprehension is being tested, differences between individuals are primarily matters of general mental ability; when they do not know their listening performance is being tested, differences are due to personality differences (including motivation to listen), as well as general mental ability. Of these two kinds of research situations, the latter is more representative of realistic listening events.

It is likely that most communication problems arise either because of participant inattention (poor motivation), or because of a lack of general mental ability—not because of anything that can be called "listening ability." Do teachers in a faculty meeting miss the details of registration because of a lack of listening ability, or because of a lack of motivation? Does an engineer fail to understand an explanation of a new process because he lacks listening ability, or because he simply has not yet been able to visualize unfamiliar relationships? In the rare cases when a discussion is vitally important to everyone and motivation is high (as in a listening test), there is little chance of an important point (or its significance) being missed, unless the listener simply lacked the mental ability to understand or appreciate it to begin with. But in most of the everyday discussions that deal with the nagging problems of industrial production, proposed new school construction, traffic safety, curriculum changes, etc., motivation to participate (and, hence, listen) is moderate at best and is not evenly distributed among the discussants—and with some persons, inattention seems to be habitual.

In terms of *listening* theory, it is far more important to stress empathic, rather than deliberative, listening in discussion. This observation in no way depreciates the need for education and practical experience in critical analysis, debate, general semantics—or in any of the various mental skills brought into play *while* listening. But it is a mistake to consider these skills *as* listening, since this viewpoint suggests that the listener's analysis is part of the receiving process.

The degree to which one is able to listen, and to perform other mental acts at the same time is an open question; research into the exact nature of listening, as it relates to other general mental abilities, is unclear at best. However, because of the obvious difficulties that occur in discussion when listener motivation is poor or nonexistent, and in view of the probability that problems in discussion are due to factors other than listening *ability* when participant motivation is high, the following suggestions seem warranted:

Remember the characteristics of the poor listener. It is easy to sit back in your chair and complain to yourself that the discussion is boring or unimportant. However, the description of the kind of person who habitually does this is not very flattering, and should serve as an incentive to better listening; research suggests that the poor listener is less intelligent, and less emotionally mature than the good listener. Obviously, there are times when a person may be just as well off *not* listening, but the poor listener tends to make this a crutch for the easy way out of difficult listening events.

Make a firm initial commitment to listen. Listening is hard work and it takes energy. If you have had difficulty listening in the past, and now decide merely to *try* to listen and to participate in the spirit of the discussion as long as you can, you will soon fall into old habits. Above all, don't make an initial decision *not* to listen; if discussions in the past have proved deficient, according to your standards, accurate listening will better enable you to correct them in the future.

Get physically and mentally ready to listen. Sit up, and get rid of distractions; put away paper you were reading, books, pencils, papers, etc., unless you plan to use them. Try to dismiss personal worries, fears, or pleasant reverie until a later time. Will these kinds of thoughts be more productive of personal gain than your participation in this discussion?

Concentrate on the other person as a communicator. View the others in a discussion as sources of ideas and information, not as personalities. If you are reacting to another as being dishonest, unethical, stupid, tedious—or as a college professor, or Republican, or student rioter, or disgruntled parent—it will be difficult for you to accurately perceive what he is trying to say. There is little to fear in such an open approach. Shoddy thinking or speaking needs no label to be recognized, and fewer good ideas will be discarded because they were never really listened to. Of course, it goes without saying that persons communicate with gestures as well as with their voices, and the listener is concerned with perceiving the total communication environment as accurately as possible.

Give the other person a full hearing. Avoid interrupting another person unless you are sure you understand him fully, and that it is necessary. If you feel that you aren't sure you understand him, a well phrased question is usually more appropriate than an attempt by you to clarify his position. Impatience with others can lead to false understanding or agreement, and eventually leads to greater difficulties.

Use analytical skills as supplements to, not instead of, listening. To the degree that successful participation in discussion requires your understanding of others, rather than your speaking contributions, it is important not to be distracted by our own note taking, mental review of main points, critical analysis, or preparation for argumentative "comeback." An especially dubious recommendation frequently found in articles on listening is that, since listeners can listen faster than speakers can talk, the extra time should be used to review main points, "read between the lines," etc. Whether this conscious effort is exerted between words, sentences, or major ideas is never made clear. However, interviews with subjects following "surprise" listening tests have indicated that one of the major causes of listener distraction was a speaker's previous point: "I suddenly realized that I didn't know what he was talking about, because I was still thinking about what he had said before."

Omitted from this list are the many sound suggestions that have been made by other writers about: analyzing the speaker's intent, figuring out what he is going to say or what he has not said, note taking, mental reorganization of a speaker's comments, etc. These, and others, are perfectly valid tools to be used in an oral communication setting, but their success is due to factors other than listening. For example, a discussion leader may wisely decide to mentally review the progress of a discussion while "listening" to a certain person unnecessarily repeating himself—but the wisdom of his action is due to his prior analysis, not to "listening ability." While listening to a specific individual, he may briefly jot down the person's main ideas for future reference; if he has developed an efficient note-taking skill, he may not miss anything significant—but he is effective because he is able to take notes with very little or no conscious effort, not because note taking is a *listening* activity. Other less talented persons may never be able to take notes without distracting them from what is truly listening.

Conclusion

Many factors make up a discussion, and listening is only one of them; however, it is an extremely important factor, and it has been diluted in the past by a shift of its meaning from one of reception to one of critical analysis.

Empathic listening cannot of itself make a good speaker out of a poor one, a clear thinker out of a dull thinker, or a good discussion out of a bad discussion. But to the extent that problems result from a lack of participant reception and understanding of the discussion interaction, empathic listening appears to be the best answer.

Notes

1. Charles M. Kelly, "Actual Listening Behavior of Industrial Supervisors as Related to Listening Ability, General Mental Ability, Selected Personality

Factors and Supervisory Effectiveness," Unpublished Ph.D. Dissertation, Purdue University, 1962, 129.

    2. This study is reported in detail: Charles M. Kelly, "Mental Ability and Personality Factors in Listening," *Quarterly Journal of Speech*, XLIX, (April, 1963), 152–156.

    3. For a detailed analysis of this issue, see: Charles M. Kelly, "Listening: Complex of Activities—and a Unitary Skill?" *Speech Monographs*, XXXIV, (November, 1967), 455–466.

STUDY GUIDE   1. What is defensive behavior?
QUESTIONS   2. How does defensiveness affect communication?
                      3. How can a supportive climate affect communication?
                      4. What characterizes both defensive and supportive climates?

▶◀ Defensive Communication

JACK R. GIBB

One way to understand communication is to view it as a people process rather than as a language process. If one is to make fundamental improvement in communication, he must make changes in interpersonal relationships. One possible type of alteration—and the one with which this paper is concerned—is that of reducing the degree of defensiveness.

Definition and Significance

    Defensive behavior is defined as that behavior which occurs when an individual perceives threat or anticipates threat in the group. The person who behaves defensively, even though he also gives some attention to the common task, devotes an appreciable portion of his energy to defending himself. Besides talking about the topic, he thinks about how he appears to others, how he may be seen more favorably, how he may win, dominate, impress, or escape punishment and/or how he may avoid or mitigate a perceived or an anticipated attack.

"Defensive Communication," by Jack R. Gibb, from *The Journal of Communication*, Vol. 11, No. 3 (September, 1961), pp. 141–148.

Such inner feelings and outward acts tend to create similarly defensive postures in others; and, if unchecked, the ensuing circular response becomes increasingly destructive. Defensive behavior, in short, engenders defensive listening, and this in turn produces postural, facial, and verbal cues which raise the defense level of the original communicator.

Defense arousal prevents the listener from concentrating upon the message. Not only do defensive communicators send off multiple value, motive, and affect cues, but also defensive recipients distort what they receive. As a person becomes more and more defensive, he becomes less and less able to perceive accurately the motives, the values, and the emotions of the sender. The writer's analyses of tape recorded discussions revealed that increases in defensive behavior were correlated positively with losses in efficiency in communication (1). Specifically, distortions became greater when defensive states existed in the groups.

The converse, moreover, also is true. The more "supportive" or defensive reductive the climate the less the receiver reads into the communication distorted loadings which arise from projections of his own anxieties, motives, and concerns. As defenses are reduced, the receivers become better able to concentrate upon the structure, the content, and the cognitive meanings of the message.

Categories of Defensive and Supportive Communication

In working over an eight-year period with recordings of discussions occurring in varied settings, the writer developed the six pairs of defensive and supportive categories presented in Table 3-3. Behavior which a listener perceives as possessing any of the characteristics listed in the left-hand column arouses defensiveness, whereas that which he interprets as having any of the qualities designated as supportive reduces defensive feelings.

TABLE 3-3. Categories of Behavior Characteristic of Supportive and Defensive Climates in Small Groups

DEFENSIVE CLIMATES	SUPPORTIVE CLIMATES
1. Evaluation	1. Description
2. Control	2. Problem orientation
3. Strategy	3. Spontaneity
4. Neutrality	4. Empathy
5. Superiority	5. Equality
6. Certainty	6. Provisionalism

The degree to which these reactions occur depends upon the personal level of defensiveness and upon the general climate in the group at the time (2).

Evaluation and Description

Speech or other behavior which appears evaluative increases defensiveness. If by expression, manner of speech, tone of voice, or verbal content the sender seems to be evaluating or judging the listener, then the receiver goes on guard. Of course, other factors may inhibit the reaction. If the listener thought that the speaker regarded him as an equal and was being open and spontaneous, for example, the evaluativeness in a message would be neutralized and perhaps not even perceived. This same principle applies equally to the other five categories of potentially defense-producing climates. The six sets are interactive.

Because our attitudes toward other persons are frequently, and often necessarily, evaluative, expressions which the defensive person will regard as nonjudgmental are hard to frame. Even the simplest question usually conveys the answer that the sender wishes or implies the response that would fit into his value system. A mother, for example, immediately following an earth tremor that shook the house, sought for her small son with the question: "Bobby, where are you?" The timid and plaintive "Mommy, I didn't do it" indicated how Bobby's chronic mild defensiveness predisposed him to react with a projection of his own guilt and in the context of his chronic assumption that questions are full of accusation.

Anyone who has attempted to train professionals to use information-seeking speech with neutral affect appreciates how difficult it is to teach a person to say even the simple "who did that?" without being seen as accusing. Speech is so frequently judgmental that there is a reality base for the defensive interpretations which are so common.

When insecure, group members are particularly likely to place blame, to see others as fitting into categories of good or bad, to make moral judgments of their colleagues, and to question the value, motive, and affect loadings of the speech which they hear. Since value loadings imply a judgment of others, a belief that the standards of the speaker differ from his own causes the listener to become defensive.

Descriptive speech, in contrast to that which is evaluative, tends to arouse a minimum of uneasiness. Speech acts which the listener perceives as genuine requests for information or as material with neutral loadings is descriptive. Specifically, presentations of feelings, events, perceptions, or processes which do not ask or imply that the receiver change behavior or attitude are minimally defense producing. The difficulty in avoiding overtone is illustrated by the problems of news reporters in writing stories about unions, communists, Negroes, and religious activities without tipping off the "party" line of the newspaper. One can often tell from the opening words in a news article which side the newspaper's editorial policy favors.

Control and Problem Orientation

Speech which is used to control the listener evokes resistance. In most of our social intercourse someone is trying to do something to someone else —to change an attitude, to influence behavior, or to restrict the field of activity. The degree to which attempts to control produce defensiveness depends upon the openness of the effort, for a suspicion that hidden motives exist heightens resistance. For this reason attempts of nondirective therapists and progressive educators to refrain from imposing a set of values, a point of view, or a problem solution upon the receivers meet with many barriers. Since the norm is control, noncontrollers must earn the perceptions that their efforts have no hidden motives. A bombardment of persuasive "messages" in the fields of politics, education, special causes, advertising, religion, medicine, industrial relations and guidance has bred cynical and paranoidal responses in listeners.

Implicit in all attempts to alter another person is the assumption by the change agent that the person to be altered is inadequate. That the speaker secretly views the listener as ignorant, unable to make his own decisions, uninformed, immature, unwise, or possessed of wrong or inadequate attitudes is a subconscious perception which gives the latter a valid base for defensive reactions.

Methods of control are many and varied. Legalistic insistence on detail, restrictive regulations and policies, conformity norms, and all laws are among the methods. Gestures, facial expressions, other forms of nonverbal communication, and even such simple acts as holding a door open in a particular manner are means of imposing one's will upon another and hence are potential sources of resistance.

Problem orientation, on the other hand, is the antithesis of persuasion. When the sender communicates a desire to collaborate in defining a mutual problem and in seeking its solution, he tends to create the same problem orientation in the listener; and, of greater importance, he implies that he has no predetermined solution, attitude, or method to impose. Such behavior is permissive in that it allows the receiver to set his own goals, make his own decisions, and evaluate his own progress—or to share with the sender in doing so. The exact methods of attaining permissiveness are not known, but they must involve a constellation of cues and they certainly go beyond mere verbal assurances that the communicator has no hidden desires to exercise control.

Strategy and Spontaneity

When the sender is perceived as engaged in a strategem involving ambiguous and multiple motivations, the receiver becomes defensive. No one wishes to be a guinea pig, a role player, or an impressed actor, and no one likes to be the victim of some hidden motivation. That which is concealed, also, may appear larger than it really is with the degree of defensiveness of the listener determining the perceived size of the suppressed element. The intense reaction of the reading audience to the material in the *Hidden Persuaders* indicates the prevalence of defensive reactions to multiple motivations behind strategy. Group members who are seen as "taking a role," as feigning emotion, as toying with their colleagues, as withholding information, or as having special sources of data are especially resented. One participant once complained that another was "using a listening technique" on him!

A large part of the adverse reaction to much of the so-called human relations training is a feeling against what are perceived as gimmicks and tricks to fool or to "involve" people, to make a person think he is making his own decision, or to make the listener feel that the sender is genuinely interested in him as a person. Particularly violent reactions occur when it appears that someone is trying to make a stratagem appear spontaneous. One person has reported a boss who incurred resentment by habitually using the gimmick of "spontaneously" looking at his watch and saying, "My gosh, look at the time—I must run to an appointment." The belief was that the boss would create less irritation by honestly asking to be excused.

Similarly, the deliberate assumption of guilelessness and natural simplicity is especially resented. Monitoring the tapes of feedback and evaluation sessions in training groups indicates the surprising extent to which members perceive the strategies of their colleagues. This perceptual clarity may be quite shocking to the strategist, who usually feels that he has cleverly hidden the motivational aura around the "gimmick."

This aversion to deceit may account for one's resistance to politicians who are suspected of behind-the-scenes planning to get his vote, to psychologists whose listening apparently is motivated by more than the manifest or content-level interest in his behavior, or to the sophisticated, smooth, or clever person whose "oneupmanship" is marked with guile. In training groups the role-flexible person frequently is resented because his changes in behavior are perceived as strategic maneuvers.

In contrast, behavior which appears to be spontaneous and free of deception is defense reductive. If the communicator is seen as having a clean id, as having uncomplicated motivations, as being straightforward and honest, and as behaving spontaneously in response to the situation, he is likely to arouse minimal defense.

Neutrality and Empathy

When neutrality in speech appears to the listener to indicate a lack of concern for his welfare, he becomes defensive. Group members usually desire to be perceived as valued persons, as individuals of special worth, and as objects of concern and affection. The clinical, detached, person-as-an-object-of-study attitude on the part of many psychologist-trainers is resented by group members, Speech with low affect that communicates little warmth or caring is in such contrast with the affect-laden speech in social situations that it sometimes communicates rejection.

Communication that conveys empathy for the feelings and respect for the worth of the listener, however, is particularly supportive and defense reductive. Reassurance results when a message indicates that the speaker identifies himself with the listener's problems, shares his feelings, and accepts his emotional reactions at face value. Abortive efforts to deny the legitimacy of the receiver's emotions by assuring the receiver that he need not feel bad, that he should not feel rejected, or that he is overly anxious, though often intended as support giving, may impress the listener as lack of acceptance. The combination of understanding and empathizing with the other person's emotions with no accompanying effort to change him apparently is supportive at a high level.

The importance of gestural behavioral cues in communicating empathy should be mentioned. Apparently spontaneous facial and bodily evidences of concern are often interpreted as especially valid evidence of deep-level acceptance.

Superiority and Equality

When a person communicates to another that he feels superior in position, power, wealth, intellectual ability, physical characteristics, or other ways he arouses defensiveness. Here as with the other sources of disturbance whatever arouses feelings of inadequacy causes the listener to center upon the affect loading of the statement rather than upon the cognitive elements. The receiver then reacts by not hearing the message, by forgetting it, by competing with the sender, or by becoming jealous of him.

The person who is perceived as feeling superior communicates that he is not willing to enter into a shared problem-solving relationship, that he probably does not desire feedback, that he does not require help, and/or that he will be likely to try to reduce the power, the status, or the worth of the receiver.

Many ways exist for creating the atmosphere that the sender feels himself equal to the listener. Defenses are reduced when one perceives the sender as being willing to enter into participative planning with the mutual trust and respect. Differences in talent, ability, worth, appearance, status, and power often exist, but the low defense communicator seems to attach little importance to these distinctions.

Certainty and Provisionalism

The effects of dogmatism in producing defensiveness are well known. Those who seem to know the answers, to require no additional data, and to regard themselves as teachers rather than as co-workers tend to put others on guard. Moreover, in the writer's experiment, listeners often perceived manifest expressions of certainty as connoting inward feelings of inferiority. They saw the dogmatic individual as needing to be right, as wanting to win an argument rather than solve a problem, and as seeing his ideas as truths to be defended. This kind of behavior often was associated with acts which others regarded as attempts to exercise control. People who were right seemed to have low tolerance for members who were "wrong"—i.e., who did not agree with the sender.

One reduces the defensiveness of the listener when he communicates that he is willing to experiment with his own behavior, attitudes, and ideas. The person who appears to be taking provisional attitudes, to be investigating issues rather than taking sides on them, to be problem solving rather than debating, and to be willing to experiment and explore tends to communicate that the listener may have some control over the shared quest or the investigation of the ideas. If a person is genuinely searching for information and data, he does not resent help or company along the way.

Conclusion

The implications of the above material for the parent, the teacher, the manager, the administrator, or the therapist are fairly obvious. Arousing defensiveness interferes with communication and thus makes it difficult—and sometimes impossible—for anyone to convey ideas clearly and to move effectively toward the solution of therapeutic, educational, or managerial problems.

NOTES

1. J. R. Gibb, "Defense Level and Influence Potential in Small Groups," in L. Petrullo and B. M. Bass (eds.), *Leadership and Interpersonal Behavior* (New York: Holt, Rinehart and Winston, Inc., 1961), pp. 66–81.

2. J. R. Gibb, "Sociopsychological Processes of Group Instruction," in N. B. Henry (ed.), *The Dynamics of Instructional Groups* (Fifty-ninth Yearbook of the National Society for the Study of Education, Part II, 1960), pp. 115–135.

STUDY GUIDE
QUESTIONS

1. What are the twelve principles basic to interpersonal communication?
2. How do certain of these principles affect communication perception and fidelity?
3. How is the communication context affected by some of these principles?
4. In what way do certain characteristics of man's symbol system affect communication?

▶◀ Interpersonal Communication: Some Working Principles

LARRY A. SAMOVAR AND EDWARD D. RINTYE

In the age of communication hardware as sophisticated as the Telstar and global television network, perhaps it is not surprising that much intellectual energy has also been directed toward solving the mysteries of human interpersonal communication (1). Whether or not the effort to understand the human factors in communication is equal to the intensity devoted to mastering electronic extensions of man is debatable. There is no doubt, however, that interpersonal communication is the subject of great interest to those in industry, government, and the academic world.

Yet, as one examines the literature on human communication, he may be frustrated by the realization that communication theory is not a well-defined and unified body of thought. Indeed, it is an amorphous collection

Interpersonal Communication: Some Working Principles, by Larry A. Samovar and Edward D. Rintye, from *Small Group Communication*, L. A. Samovar and R. S. Cathcart, eds. (Dubuque, Iowa: William C. Brown, Publishers, 1970), pp. 278–288. Reprinted with permission of authors.

of writings from disciplines as diverse as mathematics, semantics, physiology, social psychology, anthropology, rhetoric, existential philosophy, and political science (2). Because of the interdisciplinary nature of the resource materials, it is impossible at this stage to designate any single book, department, or discipline as representative of communication theory. To study human communication, one must seek out his principles, theories, and procedures where he may; and it seems probable that many more years will elapse before any integrative theoretical framework will evolve. It is this thought which prompts the authors to offer the following summary.

The study presented is an attempt to bring together in summary form several "working principles" of human interpersonal communication. Drawn from many disciplines, these principles are by no means exhaustive of all pertinent insights in communication theory. But they do represent to the authors a basic core or foundation of assumptions which requires recognition in any sound theory of human communication.

I. *All human speech communication exhibits common elements.* Berlo synthesizes the thinking of many in the communication area by identifying the following elements in any human communication situation: (1) source (sender); (2) encoding action; (3) message; (4) channel (medium); (5) decoding action; (6) receiver (3). One additional element is necessary when considering speech communication: (7) feedback (4). A closer look at each of these elements may be beneficial. A "source" is an individual who consciously and intentionally seeks to affect the behavior of at least one other human being through communication. To accomplish his purpose, the source must engage in some form of "encoding action" which will translate his ideas into symbols that may be combined or arranged and expressed in some form of "message." The form the message will take depends upon a host of variables, such as source self-concept, educational level, image of the receiver, status relationships, etc. This message travels to the receiver by means of a "channel." In human speech communication the two channels most commonly used—usually simultaneously—are the vocal and the visual. The receiver initiates "decoding action" in response to the message, hoping to produce approximately the same ideas encoded by the sender. It is because distortion is so probable that the last common element of human communication, called "feedback," is so important. Feedback in human communication consists of the signals sent back to the original sender by the receiver, in response to the original message (5). These signals are the primary means by which the original sender may gage the effect of his message on the receiver, and know to make the adjustments required to clarify, elaborate, or otherwise alter subsequent messages.

II. *Human attention is highly selective.* People are constantly screening available stimuli in any situation, and consciously and unconsciously select some stimuli to which they will respond while at the same time ignoring others (6). Through this selection process, and the emphasis of some details at the expense of others, "we may change the whole meaning of a complex pattern of stimuli" (7). In addition to his neurological limitations, man has his perceptual or attentive faculty influenced by technological, attitudinal, conceptual, and social factors (8). Hartley and Hartley observe that "In addition to the general social directives internalized by the individual, there are many idiosyncratic pressures, internal patterns of needs and preoccupations, that emerge from the interaction between the individual's biological drives and the ways these drives are handled by his particular social group. These pressures may be seen . . . as particularized sensitivities to specific stimuli or tendencies to avoid the recognition of certain stimuli. . . . In general, people will notice things that interest them and in some way affect their own welfare. They will delegate to the background items of no direct relevance to their own needs and interests" (9). Newcomb, Turner, and Converse agree that the receiver's "pre-message motives and attitudes selectively lower certain of his thresholds. . . ." (10). It seems clear that human attention is not the result of random and incidental factors at work within the individual.

III. *Man actively seeks consistency between his self-image, his behavior, and perceived information.* The self-image referred to here is equivalent to the "self-concept" of Tannenbaum, Weschler, and Massarik (11). It is a kind of psychological "base of operations" (12). Mead identifies it as characteristically being an object of itself (13). And Carl Rogers describes the self-structure as an "organized configuration of perceptions of the self which are admissable to awareness" (14). It is composed of such elements as the perception of one's characteristics and abilities, the percepts and concepts of the self in relation to others and the environment, and the value qualities which are perceived as associated with experiences and objects (15). Whether one refers to the self-image as man's "conscious identity" (16), as does Allen Wheelis, or prefers Burke's reference to it as the "first person addressed by a man's consciousness" (17), there seems to be consensual agreement as to the central role of the self-image in man's attempt to communicate. Given this central role, it is not surprising that individual man seeks to behave in ways which do not threaten his self-image. Possibly more unexpected is the conclusion of research surveyed by Berelson and Steiner which states that people "tend to see and hear communications that are favorable or congenial to their predispositions; they are more likely to see and hear congenial communications than neutral or hostile ones" (18). Brown explains this phenomenon as the principle of "cognitive consistency," supporting the tendency of the human mind to seek consistency between an individual's frame of reference and available information (19). At least three major treatments of this theme are well known in psychology: (1) congruity-incongruity (Osgood and Tannenbaum), (2) balance-imbalance

(Abelson and Rosenberg), and (3) consonance-dissonance (Festinger) (20).

IV. *Man maintains perceptual consistency by distorting information or by avoiding data he cannot alter.* Not only does man seek consistency, as indicated by the preceding principle, but he will alter reality to maintain desired consistency. Another way of saying this is to suggest that man's psychological frame of reference determines what is perceived and how it is perceived (21). Krech and Crutchfield contend that the ego or self has a role of unparalleled significance in the structuring of the perceptual field: "Some of the most potent of all needs and the most effective of all goals have to do with defense of the self, i.e., with the adjustment of the field in such a way as to enhance feelings of self-esteem, self-regard, etc., or to remove threats to self-esteem and self-regard" (22). S.I. Hayakawa summarizes confirming studies of Cantril, Kilpatrick, and others, when he asserts that the "self-concept is the fundamental determinant of our perceptions, and therefore of our behavior. As John Dewey said, 'A stimulus becomes a stimulus by virtue of what the organism was already preoccupied with'" (23). Sherif, Sherif, and Nebergall report that an individual's own position on an issue is the *basic determinant* of whether or not he will accept a message on that issue, completely ignore the message, debunk the message, distort the message, reinforce his own position, etc. (24). Certainly the well-known work of Hovland, Janis, and Kelly affirms the importance of predispositional factors in perception and attitude change (25). There seems little question in relevant literature that people tend to perceive information in accordance with their own predisposition, their own ego-image, and will achieve psychological consistency even though it requires them to distort or evade the true nature of the message.

V. *Active participation in the communication act by the receiver tends to produce better retention of information and tends to more surely induce changes in the receiver's behavior.* Speculating that ego-involvement may be the clue as to why this principle is true, Sherif, Sherif, and Nebergall maintain that experimental literature suggests that if a person is required to give a speech or write an essay or in some way physically perform a task involving information, then that information will be better retained and more completely accepted than if the person is only passively involved as a listener (26). Active participation "tends to augment the effectiveness of persuasive communications" (27). Berelson and Steiner agree that techniques which involve people actively in dealing with information, such as discussion (as opposed to lecture), are much more effective in involving the ego and in changing attitudes and behavior (28). The implication of this principle for communication seems obvious: communication acts which require overt use of message information will be more likely to be accepted and remembered by the receiver.

VI. *Social roles and status systems define communication patterns within any social organization.* In expressing this principle the authors assume Ralph Linton's conception of a social role, since it is undoubtedly the most widely known and influential in the social sciences (29). In Linton's view the role is the living performance of a position (a status in a particular social organization), while a "status" is a collection of rights and duties distinct from the individual who occupies the position to which those rights and duties accrue (30). For practical purposes, role and status are inseparable and may be thought of as organized patterns of expectancies related to the tasks, attitudes, behaviors, and relationships operant within a specific group (31). Utilizing this conception of role and status, principle six expresses a well-established finding in social psychology: that social systems significantly affect how, why, to and from whom, and with what effects communication occurs (32). Social organization limits the number of contacts, establishes the frequency of messages sent and received, and partially determines what kinds of messages will be transmitted to whom and from whom (33). Most importantly, the status system or role organization greatly affects the manner in which members regard or perceive their messages.

VII. *Speech communication is a symbolic process.* Spoken words, as well as gestural, postural, facial expressions, etc., make up the "socially institutionalized sign system" used in speech communication activity (34). Use of this sign system is a highly complex and elaborate human symbolic activity. John Carroll suggests a useful framework for discussion of this principle. He notes that any language possesses three essential properties: (1) it consists of a finite set of discrete signs, (2) those signs fulfill a reference function, and (3) the sign system is arbitrary. It is important to observe that the identifying characteristic of a sign is its use as a symbol; that is, the word or gesture serves to represent something other than itself. In so serving, the sign fulfills the second necessary property of a language, that of possessing a reference function. The sign is only a reference pointer to the thing for which it stands, and it is this referencing or pointing which is the heart of principle seven. Once this reference function is understood, it is obvious that any given linguistic-gestural system is essentially arbitrary. From a functional point of view there is no difference between "dog," "chien," "hund," or "perro"; the referent is the same. The difference in each case is only the symbol. There is no reason, other than a historical one, why "pin" stands for a small pointed object instead of a storage receptacle (35).

It seems apparent, then, that language is an essentially arbitrary collection of signs, discrete and referencial, to which the using community has assigned particular elements of human experience (referents) (36). As Mario Pei says it: "A language is essentially an array of words, each of which is accepted by the social group as conveying a given meaning or meanings (37). The critical point is that the assignment of "meaning" to a specific sign is a culturally local function; a task of the particular using community, and hence, an arbitrary assignment. Carroll's three properties are present, then, in the oral-aural-gestural symbol system utilized in speech communication. Speech communication is a symbolic process.

VIII. *Human communication occurs only through the use of a shared symbol system.* To communicate with one another, members of the using community must use identical symbols and use them in relatively the same way (38). The folly of attempting communication through use of uncommon symbols is apparent to anyone who has traveled abroad without a facility in the appropriate language. Yet it is not necessary to travel abroad to discover communication failures due to differing interpretation of symbols. Consider the problems inherent in the use of such symbols as "black power," "civil rights," "the free world," "conservative point of view." Although all within the family of a common language, these symbols are regarded frequently as connotative or affective; that is, the referent (object) to which they refer is not universally shared. The difference between denotation and connotation seems only a question of the extent of common agreement of the users on the symbol-to-referent relationship. Fortunately a sufficient portion of English is denotative enough to permit its users to accomplish essential "practical" daily communication.

IX. *No symbol has a fixed referent.* Because a large part of daily communication is accomplished through use of a restricted number of "familiar" words, many people develop the idea that the object to which a word refers is always the same; that the word's meaning is fixed and unchanging. This fallacy of "fixed referent" causes much difficulty in human communication. Ogden and Richards suggest that the "theory of direct meaning relationship between words and things is the source of almost all the difficulty which thought encounters . . ." (39). Neither the speaker nor the listener can communicate effectively if he ignores that fact that words stand for nothing but the ideas in the mind of him who utters them. Some authorities consider it impossible to measure the meaning of linguistic elements of a message (40). Others, such as Osgood and his associates at Illinois, believe that an instrument like the semantic differential is at least a beginning in the development of means to evaluate connotative words (41).

X. *Symbolic "meaning" is a relationship of the symbols used, the object referred to, the sender, and the receiver of the message* (42). The symbols of a message are chosen by the sender because he assumes that *he and* the receiver share approximately the same understanding of the "meaning" of those symbols. Communication is doomed if this assumption is incorrect. And there is much room for error. Both the sender and receiver confront a referent with their individual and differing backgrounds of information and attitudes. They both make assumptions about one another's information and attitudes toward themselves and the referent (43). From the presented message the receiver selectively perceives those elements most relevant to his needs, a selection determined by his existing motives and predispositions (44). Depending upon the congruence of the new information and the receiver's existing attitudes, he will accept, distort, or reject the substance of the message. Commenting on the complexity of attaining meaning fidelity in human communication, F.J. Roethlisberger suggests that "due to differences of background, experience, and motivation, it seems . . . extraordinary that any two persons can ever understand each other (45). In such an abstruse, subtly varying four-fold relationship, small wonder that the symbols used, the referent, the sender, and the receiver combine only occasionally to create clear symbolic meaning.

XI. *All referents, references, and symbols are abstractions.* The general semanticists make a major point of the idea that all human knowledge is the result of the process of faulty human perception (46). They use the word "abstract" as an active verb referring to the selective and organizing nature of human perception. (47). In addition to the psychological factors involved in perception, some of which have been discussed, the general semanticist is concerned with the physiological limitations of the human neurological system (48). The manner in which humans perceive with vision, touch, etc., is the result of the peculiar qualities of the individual person's nervous system, and it follows that "There are 'sights' we cannot see, and, as even children know today with their high-frequency dog whistles, 'sounds' that we cannot hear" (49). According to the general semanticist, it is not rational to suggest that human beings ever perceive anything "as it really is" (50).

In addition to using "abstraction" as a verb, the general semanticist also uses the term as a noun, to refer to "sense impressions" of a given referent at any one of four levels of abstraction (verb) (51). Four separate levels of the abstraction process may be identified: (1) the event, or submicroscopic physical-chemical processes, (2) the ordinary object manufactured from the event by the lower nervous centers, (3) the psychological "picture" manufactured by the higher centers, and (4) the verbal label or term (52). It may now be apparent that according to general semantics usage, one could use a term (abstraction-noun) the referent of which was identifiable at any one of the four levels of abstraction (process-verb). As the selectivity becomes more stringent, the number of characteristics remaining lessens, and the level of abstraction (process) is said to become "higher" (53).

It is clear at this point that the general semanticist sees the entire world of the human being as a series of abstractions (noun), which are the products of selective perception. If the general semanticist's thinking is valid, then all referents, all references, and all symbols are abstractions.

XII. *Non-verbal language contributes significantly to human communication.* Acknowledged on a superficial level for centuries by rhetoricians, this fundamental insight gains in importance when applied to a less restrictive setting than the speaking platform. This importance is based upon the obvious fact that what a receiver sees guides his understanding of what he hears (54). From the sender's viewpoint, visual feedback clues sent by the receiver provide an invaluable index to the effect of the message. Whichever viewpoint, however, it is true that the continuous, analogic, visual cues which accompany the discrete verbal symbols are often believed when words are not. This point gathers additional credibility when we accept the generalization that visual gestures and facial movements are "adaptive movements of the organism responding to all internal and external stimuli at once" (55). Weaver and Strausbaugh maintain that because the perception of visual language affords almost simultaneous stimulation of the brain, glands, and muscles, whereas spoken language involves discrete stimuli (words in linear presentation), visual language may have more immediate impact (56). The visual cues which accompany spoken messages are said by Ruesch and Kees to constitute "specific instructions given by a sender about the way messages ought to be interpreted . . ." (57). They maintain that "the nature of interpersonal communication necessitates that these coincide in time . . ." (58). If both the information content of the message and the visual clues as to how the receiver should interpret the message do coincide, then the referential aspects of the statement may be clear. "But when action codifications contradict verbal codifications, then confusion is almost certain to result" (59). It appears certain that to obtain satisfactory speech communication fidelity, both the verbal and the visual messages must coincide in interpreted meaning.

The preceding pages have summarized the twelve principles felt by the authors to be basic in any consideration of interpersonal communication theory. It would be presumptuous to presume that the listing was definitive, for one might argue that the discussion should have included *all* pertinent findings of psychology, sociology, language, rhetoric, and so on. There is merit in such a position, perhaps; yet this brief summary has focused not on all elements which could be included in theory building, but on those which *must* be included. The precepts discussed warrant maximum priority in any serious theory of human interpersonal communication.

NOTES

1. "Human interpersonal communication" is used herein to refer to a process of human interaction which psychologist Carl Hovland describes as one by which "an individual (the communicator) transmits stimuli (usually verbal symbols) to modify the behavior of other individuals (communicatees)." See Carl Hovland, "Social Communication," *Proceedings of the American Philosophical Society,* XCII (November, 1948), 371.

2. Frank E.X. Dance, ed. *Human Communication Theory: Original Essays* (New York, 1967), pp. vii–viii; Floyd W. Matson and Ashley Montagu, eds. *The Human Dialogue: Perspectives on Communication* (New York, 1967), pp. viii–ix; Alfred G. Smith, ed. *Communication and Culture: Readings in the Codes of Human Interaction* (New York, 1966), p. v.

3. David K. Berlo, *The Process of Communication: an Introduction to Theory and Practice* (New York, 1960), pp. 30–32.

4. Norbert Wiener, *Cybernetics: or Control and Communication in the Animal and the Machine* (Massachusetts, 1948), pp. 95–115.

5. Ibid.

6. Eugene L. Hartley and Ruth E. Hartley, *Fundamentals of Social Psychology* (New York, 1958), p. 54.

7. Ibid., p. 53.

8. Ibid., p. 132.

9. Ibid., pp. 54–55.

10. Theodore M. Newcomb, Ralph H. Turner, and Phillip E. Converse, *Social Psychology, the Study of Human Interaction* (New York: 1965), pp. 206–207.

11. Robert Tannenbaum, Irving R. Weschler, and Fred Massarik, "The Process of Understanding People," in *Interpersonal Dynamics: Essays and Readings of Human Interaction*, eds. Warren G. Bennis et al. (Homewood, Illinois, 1964), p. 732.

12. Ibid.

13. George H. Mead, *Mind, Self and Society* (Chicago, 1934), p. 136.

14. Carl R. Rogers, *Client-Centered Therapy: Its Current Practice, Implications, and Theory* (Boston, 1951), p. 501.

15. Ibid.

16. Allen Wheelis, *The Quest for Identity* (New York, 1958), p. 19.

17. Kenneth Burke, *A Rhetoric of Motives* (New York, 1955), pp. 38–39.

18. Bernard Berelson and Gary A. Steiner, *Human Behavior: an Inventory of Scientific Findings* (New York, 1964), pp. 529–530.

19. Roger Brown, *Social Psychology* (New York, 1965), pp. 557–609.

20. Charles E. Osgood and Percy H. Tannenbaum, "The Principle of Congruity in the Prediction of Attitude Change," *Psychological Review*, LXII (1955), 42–55; R.P. Abelson and M.J. Rosenberg, "Symbolic Psychologic: a Model of Attitudinal Cognition," *Behavioral Science*, III (1958), 1–13; Leon Festinger, *A Theory of Cognitive Dissonance* (Stanford, California, 1957).

21. David Krech and Richard S. Crutchfield, *Theory and Problems of Social Psychology* (New York, 1948), p. 94.

22. Ibid., p. 69.

23. S.I. Hayakawa, *Symbol, Status and Personality* (New York, 1950), p. 38.

24. Carolyn W. Sherif, Muzafer Sherif, and Roger E. Nebergall, *Attitude and Attitude Change: the Social Judgment-Involvement Approach* (Philadelphia, 1965), pp. 219–246.

25. Carl L. Hovland, Irving L. Janis, and Harold H. Kelly, *Communication and Persuasion: Psychological Studies of Opinion Change* (New Haven, Connecticut, 1953), pp. 175–214.

26. Sherif, Sherif, and Nebergall, op. cit., p. 197.

27. Hovland, Janis, and Kelly, op. cit., p. 228.

28. Berelson and Steiner, op. cit., pp. 547–548.

29. Lionel J. Neuman and James W. Hughes, 'The Problem of the Concept of Role—a Survey of the Literature," *Social Forces*, XXX (December, 1951), 149.

30. Ralph Linton, *The Study of Man* (New York, 1936), pp. 113–114.

31. Carl H. Weaver and Warren L. Strausbaugh, *Fundamentals of Speech Communication* (New York, 1964), p. 187.

32. Berlo, op. cit., pp. 147–152; Weaver and Strausbaugh, op. cit., pp. 215–221; Bruce J. Riddle and Edwin J. Thomas, eds. *Role Theory: Concepts and Research* (New York, 1966), pp. 64–102; Newcomb, Turner, and Converse, op. cit., pp. 341–345; Hartley and Hartley, op. cit., pp. 148–154.

33. Berlo, op. cit., p. 148.

34. John B. Carroll, *Language and Thought* (New Jersey, 1964), pp. 3–8.

35. Ibid., p. 6.

36. Edward Sapir, *Language: An Introduction to the Study of Speech* (New York, 1921), p. 11.

37. Mario Pei, *The Story of Language* (New York, 1949), p. 123.

38. Stephen Ullmann, "Signs and Symbols," *Introductory Readings on Language*, eds. Wallace L. Anderson and Norman C. Stageberg (New York, 1962), pp. 198–201.

39. C.K. Ogden and I. A. Richards, *The Meaning of Meaning* (New York, 1923), pp. 12–15.

40. Carl H. Weaver and Garry L. Weaver, "Information Theory and the Measurement of Meaning," *Speech Monographs*, XXXII (November, 1965), 447.

41. Charles E. Osgood, George J. Suci, and Percy H. Tannenbaum, *The Measurement of Meaning* (Urbana, Illinois, 1957), pp. 18–25.

42. Robert Benjamin, *Semantics* (San Diego, 1965), p. 10.

43. Hartley and Hartley, op. cit., pp. 36–91.

44. Berelson and Steiner, op. cit., pp. 536–540.

45. F.J. Roethlisberger, "Barriers to Communication Between Men," *The Use and Misuse of Language*, ed. S.I. Hayakawa (Greenwich, Connecticut, 1943), p. 41.

46. John C. Condon, Jr., *Semantics and Communication* (New York, 1966), pp. 11–23.

47. Ibid., p. 19.

48. Alfred Korzybski, *Science and Sanity: An Introduction to Non-Aristotelian Systems and General Semantics* (Lakeville, Connecticut, 1933), pp. 371–385.

49. S.I. Hayakawa, *Language in Thought and Action*, 2nd ed. (New York, 1939), p. 176.

50. Ibid., p. 177.

51. Korzybski, op. cit., p. 384.

52. Ibid.

53. Hayakawa, op. cit., pp. 177–178.

54. Weaver and Strausbaugh, op. cit., p. 260.

55. Ibid., p. 261.

56. Ibid.

57. Jurgen Ruesch and Weldon Kees, *Nonverbal Communication: Notes on the Visual Perception of Human Relations* (Berkeley, 1956), p. 7.

58. Ibid., p. 193.

59. Ibid.

1. What influence does the amount of shared experience have upon interpersonal communication?
2. How does our perception of the other communicator affect communication?
3. What factors affect the image we have of ourselves and others when communicating?

▶◀ Persuasion and Interpersonal Relations

JAMES H. CAMPBELL AND HAL W. HEPLER

Let's begin by setting up a communication situation that is as elementary as we can imagine. Suppose that you are a jet pilot forced to parachute from your aircraft over central Australia. You descend safely and disentangle yourself from your parachute. You look up and see loping toward you across the plain an Austrialian aborigine. He is naked except for a spear. He approaches you and stops about twenty feet away.

The situation is now fairly clear. You must communicate with this man, and you must be able to understand and deal with his efforts to communicate with you. You must make some effort to shape his behavior so that it will be of some benefit to you, and you must endeavor to present yourself to him in such a way that he will be favorably impressed by your actions. You, of course, do not know his language, and he does not know yours. His culture is as foreign to you as yours is to him. The need to communicate with him is urgent and the penalty for failing to communicate may lead him merely to trot off and forget about you, or it may lead him to use his spear if he perceives you as some sort of threat (1).

The situation then stands with the aviator hoping that he can elicit a favorable reaction from the aborigine and with the aborigine hoping that he can elicit a favorable reaction from the aviator. Where can they start? The aborigine has never seen an aviator. The aviator has never seen an aborigine. They have no language in common. They have no cultural elements in common. What, then, do they hold in common? Their humanness. They both must eat and drink and rest and be protected in some way from the elements.

If we focus our attention upon the aviator, we can perhaps decide upon some actions that he might wish to avoid and some actions that might have a fairly good probability of eliciting a positive reaction. For example, it would probably be unwise for the aviator to stride toward the native and abruptly thrust forth his hand in the typically American gesture of greeting. It is entirely possible that the native, not having any experience with hand-shaking as a code, might interpret this as an unfriendly and threatening act and use his spear. The aviator might, however, rub his stomach and make small groaning sounds, and this might remind the native that this strange creature from the skies was a man much like himself in *some* ways and capable of being hungry.

We are dealing here with the relationships that exist between two men in a situation foreign in many ways to both. This communication situation is much like those that all of us face. In some ways it is more difficult than most of our communicative situations and in other ways it is far easier.

We can use a pair of circles as a model for this situation. Let each circle represent a man, and let the amount of overlap of the circles represent the knowledge, information, facts, language skills, etc. that the two men hold in common. In the present situation we could draw two circles that just barely touch each other. This will indicate that the two men have in common only very few elements, the most basic being their membership in the same species (see Figure 3–4).

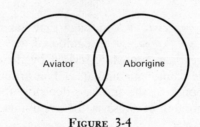

FIGURE 3-4

Very few of us will ever have so little in common with the person with whom we must communicate. Most people we communicate with share with us a common language and culture. However, overlap varies greatly. Total overlap never occurs, but what would be the situation with the most complete overlap? It probably comes closest to occurring in the case of identical twins reared together in a *similar* environment. Identical twins often are able to anticipate each other's words and emotions, but not always. Even here the two organisms are not identical in every respect. Environments *can* be similar, but they cannot be *identical* for any two humans—not even twins (see Figure 3–5).

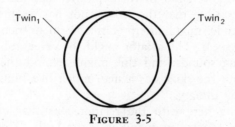

Twin₁   Twin₂

FIGURE 3-5

What happens when the amount of overlap between two people is not as complete as for identical twins and not as incomplete as for the aviator and the aborigine? We make predictions (judgments, guesses, or estimates) about the effect our behavior will have upon the behavior of other people. Those who consistently make accurate predictions are often called "effective communicators" or "good salesmen" or "good teachers" or something equally complimentary.

We generalize from our interpersonal relationships to classes of such relationships. That is, we decide how valuable, to us, some given message is on the basis of our experience with other messages from similar sources in the past.

Is it possible to conceive of a message that has no source? Even government documents, we know, were composed by some one individual somewhere. They were then, probably, revised by many. But one man was the source; two people cannot manipulate a typewriter simultaneously. The point is that our response to the message depends upon many things, and one of the more important of these is the credibility that this source has for this particular message.

Credibility is a curious thing. It does not rest wholly upon either emotion or logic. A source may be credible for us because he is our friend or relative. Or he may be credible because he is neither. Much depends upon our own personalities. But most important is the way our personality interacts with that of the other person (or persons) in a communication situation.

There are a lot of different ways of looking at a communication situation. One way can be called *an analytic model of the interaction process.*

Let us suppose that two men come into each other's presence for the first time. Let's call them Bob and Bill. As they enter each other's presence, they have notions about what they themselves are like; they think of themselves as having certain vices and virtues. These self-evaluations are unevenly accurate from person to person, but we have all made these evaluations and are making more all the time.

Within a very few seconds of their first contact, Bob and Bill have formed some more or less durable impression of each other. That is, they each have added to their notions of themselves a set of notions about the other. Where Bob had a notion of what he himself was like before (a Bob's Bob), he now has also a Bob's Bill. He now has made some more or less reliable decisions about the character and personality of the other person in this communication situation. Bill, of course, has done the same.

Another quick mutual evaluation is the one about what the other fellow thinks of *him*. Bob becomes concerned about what Bill thinks Bob is like. But can Bob know what Bill thinks? No. Bob can only update his previous estimate of the character and personality of Bill. Bob probably says something like this to himself: "Given that I believe Bill to have X characteristics and that I think myself to be of Y personality, then what will someone like Bill think of someone like me?" Remember that the best way to know how someone thinks of you is to interact with him and observe what he does, and what you do, when you are in each other's company. As we all do before we have had enough time together to be very certain of our evaluations. Bob is making predictions based on his past experience. But that is not all his predictions are based upon. He also has the evidence of his present encounter, and this form of evidence grows in importance as it increases in quantity.

Figure 3–6 illustrates three categories of evidence stemming from the encounter. Descriptive labels that might be attached to each of these categories are: gross acts, linguistic acts, and minimal cues.

You can hardly miss noticing gross acts in human behavior. They are things like a punch in the nose; or the fact that Mr. Z always moves out of a group that you join; or the friendship of someone who walks beside you as you move among groups at a large party. These things are all gross, grand, large-scale acts. However, they can be misleading. They can be shammed. They are sometimes used to announce a dramatic shift in the nature of a relationship.

Minimal cues are at the opposite pole in terms of ease of detection. These are often indetectable unless there has already been considerable contact and interaction between the people involved. The study of the small acts that reveal internal states is called kinesics by Ray Birdwhistell (2). His attempt to categorize posture and facial expressions, among other things, is the beginning of the work that will hopefully lead to some system for

FIGURE 3-6. The square boxes are ideas that Bob and Bill carry with them all the time. The balloon shapes indicate ideas formed as a direct result of the interaction. Keep in mind that the notions in the balloons are also based on the past experiences of Bob and Bill.

increasing the accuracy of predictions about attitudes of others toward ourselves and what we say.

We all know the stereotyped facial expressions used by actors and comedians to convey attitudes or emotional states. But we seldom mistake the comedians' version for the actors' version. And we do not often mistake the actors' version for the real thing. (Remember that the "real thing" may be a carefully contrived demonstration designed to cause us to think what someone else wants us to think.) The way in which the individual uses these expressions and gestures and the way in which he personally modifies them and makes them his own tells us a good deal about him and helps us predict his future responses.

Last, but certainly far from least, let's take a look at linguistic acts. There are several levels on which these may be approached. First of all, what sort of subject does the other fellow choose to bring up and pursue in your presence? Americans seem to be willing to discuss baseball with anyone. They will not talk about their moral values at all except under certain very special circumstances and only with certain very special people.

Secondly, given some particular topic, how does a person talk? Is he condescending and impatient as a listener, and dogmatic as a speaker? If so, then you certainly can conclude that he thinks little of your understanding of the subject, and perhaps of any subject. One of the better clues we have to the attitude of a speaker is the intonation patterns he imposes on sentences or utterances. For instance, how many ways can you think of to say "fine"? It is possible to say "fine" so that it sounds as though you mean anything *but* fine. You can say "fine" in such a way that the listener still cannot decide what your attitude is toward some particular object, event, or person. Modifications of meaning are, of course, also present in even the most complex messages, as well as in this short one-word utterance.

Now that the categories of evidence are somewhat more fully explained, let's go back to Bob and Bill and see what they have been up to since we left them. Isn't it quite likely that each will now have begun to wonder what the other fellow thinks he has decided about him? That is, Bob, in addition to having a Bob's Bob, a Bob's Bill, and a Bob's Bill's Bob, may have generated a Bob's Bill's Bob's Bill.

We are approaching the limit, schematically, of this model. If we wish to pursue it further, we will need some pseudomathematical symbols to prevent the tongue twisting into which the Bob and Bill labels quickly lead us. Certain it is that, so far, this analysis is unrealistic because it is so very incomplete. In human encounters, many more evaluations are made than the few we have suggested here.

Not only are the numbers of evaluations greater than we have suggested in the two-person situation, but consider the complexities introduced when a third person, John, is added. John now needs to make estimates of what Bob thinks Bill has decided about John. And John must remember that the Bob whose decisions about Bill's decisions about John are important to John is a Bob who exists only within John's head; it is the Bob whose characteristics are assigned by John to Bob on the basis of estimates and inferences. Further, John must remember that Bob knows that these estimates and inferences are being made and that therefore Bob may have taken steps to hide his true attitudes and thereby cause John to think Bob has none. Or Bob may want John to think Bob's attitudes are the exact opposite of the ones which Bob does, in fact, hold.

Finally, these face-to-face personal encounters are the basis for the ways in which we interpret messages that are not delivered face to face. We recall, when interpreting a written message, the intonation patterns we have heard this particular writer use, the facial expressions we have seen associated with these intonation patterns, and the body posture customary to the individual, as well as a great many other factors. On the basis of these memories we infer the mannerisms that the source might have exhibited if he had delivered the message in person; from these inferences we make predictions about the meaning of the message. That is, we *interpret* the message. If we have no personal knowledge of the source of a written message, then we interpret the message on other bases.

We can consider the magazine, journal, or paper in which it appears. We can note the style in which it is written. We can even apply a sort of "stereotype" notion about the source which we have to use when we have no other kinds of information.

The next big question becomes: "What factors contribute to the views that we hold of ourselves and of others?" This is, obviously, a question that cannot be dealt with in a short essay, but some lines of thought may be indicated. It seems clear that most of our values, beliefs, and attitudes are derived from the groups that we come into contact with and that we belong to. Some of these groups we have no choice about joining and others we do. We have no choice about the family that we are born into, or about the cultural or ethnic groups of which we are a part. As children, we have almost nothing to say about the schools and other groups of which we are a part, or about the town we live in or the church we attend. As we grow older we have, in theory at least, some choice about the groups that we join voluntarily. You appear to be free to become a member of Alpha Beta Gamma or of the Loyal and Intense Order of the Aardvark. But even here the pressures that have moulded you throughout your life will bear heavily upon your decisions. All of the groups with which you have associated will contribute to the expectations you will have of other humans, and will contribute to the roles you will play in your life.

What do we mean by expectations or mutual expectations? These mutual expectations consist of the modes of behavior that we expect from those that we come to associate with and know. For example, if we know that Egbert Kranz is, among other things, a citizen of the United States, Caucasian, Protestant, and a native of a city of 2,300 people in the Middle Western state of Iowa we can roughly predict his behavior. But we may be completely mistaken.

A concept that parallels the notion of mutual expectations is one termed "role" or "role behavior." We daily play a number of roles that are largely determined by the groups of which we are and have been members. If you are a college student, you can play a number of roles if you wish. You may play the role of "campus intellectual" and cultivate the groups that further this image. You may frequent certain places, carry certain books, and enroll in the classes that will further the role that you have chosen to play. If the role of "intellectual" does not appeal to you, there are countless other roles and combinations of roles that you may assume or attempt to assume. You may decide to play the role of "campus politician," "campus playboy," or "campus athlete." Each of these roles will require that you behave in certain fairly well prescribed manners.

An objection that is often raised to the concept of role playing is: "I'm not going to play *any* role. I'm just going to be myself." This implies two things. One is that role playing is somehow bad or dishonest. The other implication is that we can avoid role playing. This essay maintains that we all play roles to a greater or lesser extent and those who play roles consciously will be more effective in shaping the behavior of others than will those not conscious of their image or of the influence it has on others.

What are other ways of shaping behavior? What can we do to influence the behavior of the people with whom we interact?

It seems clear that much of our behavior is to some extent under the control of others. If we can consider that many of our actions are randomly emitted, then it seems reasonable that we will tend to continue to do those things that get approval from our contemporaries and associates. In this sense, then, we can say that our role behavior is determined, to an extent, by the reactions of those with whom we associate.

In summary, we have made the following points:

1. All communicative activity is directed to changing behavior.
2. The amount of *knowledge* held in common by two interacting communicators will determine in large part the manner in which they will interact.
3. There are many levels of interaction.
4. Much of our interaction will depend on the mutual expectations that assist us in determining the roles played by the communicators.
5. The effective communicator/persuader will be conscious of the part played by expectations and roles and will be aware of what he is doing when he communicates.
6. Our roles, and the roles we expect others to take, are determined by the groups to which we belong and by the behavior of others toward us in interaction.

NOTES

1. There was an incident paralleling this hypothetical one some years ago involving missionaries and Indians in South America. The missionaries evidently misevaluated the effects of their communicative efforts and were killed by the Indians. Most of our day-to-day communication, happily, does not involve such directly unpleasant and final results!

2. Ray L. Birdwhistell, *Introduction to Kinesics: An Annotation System for Analysis of Body Motion and Gesture* (Washington, D.C.: Foreign Service Institute, Department of State, 1952).

STUDY GUIDE
QUESTIONS
1. What are the characteristics of each of the three ego states existing in all of us?
2. How can an analysis of the type of transaction occurring help us avoid communication breakdowns?
3. What communicative characteristics can be thought to reside within the "adult" ego state?
4. What communicative characteristics can be thought to reside within the "parent" ego state?

▶◀ Transactional Analysis: A Different Perspective of Communication

RICHARD D. CARROLL

INTRODUCTION

According to Smith, there are three principal traditions in communication theory: "the mathematical; the social psychological; and the linguistic" (Smith, 13). Although it is doubtful that the second tradition—the social psychological—is meant to include the entire field of psychology or the area of psychotherapy in particular, there is a branch of psychotherapy, known as Transactional Analysis, that does seem to lend itself to this tradition. Transactional Analysis is a theory of social intercourse developed by Eric Berne (Keltner, 13).

Although Transactional Analysis was developed specifically for use in psychotherapy, it lends itself to a discussion of communication theory and there may be contributions that it can make to that field. This article deals with two things: first, a discussion of Transactional Analysis, and, second, a discussion of the applications of Transactional Analysis to communication theory.

"Transactional Analysis: A Different Perspective of Communication," by Richard D. Carroll. Reprinted with permission of the author. This original essay appears here in print for the first time.

148

TRANSACTIONAL ANALYSIS

Before discussing Transactional Analysis, a note of clarification seems warranted. The field of communication theory contains some references to the concept of *transactions*. Authors such as Barnlund, Sereno and Mortensen, and Toch and MacLean make references to this term in various ways that may persuade the casual reader that Transactional Analysis is already being utilized in some form by communication theorists. However, upon closer examination of these writers, this author believes that the only real similarity exists in the usage of the same word—*transaction*—to represent a communicative event. Transactional Analysis as a school of thought founded by Berne is not the same as the transactional considerations that the previously mentioned authors undertake.

In order to understand Transactional Analysis, it is necessary to consider both the basic concepts upon which it is based and the way in which it attempts to view the process of human interaction.

Motivation for Transactions

The core of Berne's theory rests upon the concept of *stroking*. According to him:

By an extension of meaning, "stroking" may be employed colloquially to denote any act implying recognition of another's presence. Hence a stroke may be used as the fundamental unit of social action. An exchange of strokes constitutes a transaction which is the basic unit of social intercourse (Berne, 1964, 15).

Keltner further shows the importance of this concept to speech-communication. "Thus the reciprocal bond, which is at the heart of speech-communication, may begin with the need for strokes, as Berne uses the term" (Keltner, 14). Berne feels that recognition-hunger—the adult's need to be recognized or stroked—is a result of a partial transformation of the infantile stimulus-hunger—the infant's need to be held, stroked, loved and so on (Berne, 1964, 14).

After stimulus-hunger and recognition-hunger comes structure-hunger —how to structure your waking hours. Structure-hunger can be satisfied in three ways:

1. Material programming—essentially based on data processing. An example would be building a boat. This involves the use of materials in a certain way to achieve a desired product or result.
2. Social programming—this results in traditional ritualistic or semiritualistic interchanges. An example of this can be seen in courting or mourning rituals.
3. Individual programming—according to Berne, "as people become better

acquainted, more and more individual programming creeps in, so that 'incidents' begin to occur." (Berne, 1964, 17)

Structural Analysis

Thus we have the motivation for stroking and transactions. Yet before discussing Transactional Analysis in detail, one further area needs to be considered—Structural Analysis. Berne used the term *Structural Analysis* to describe the structure of the human mind. He believes it is necessary to understand Structural Analysis before attempting to discuss Transactional Analysis. According to Berne, Structural Analysis is concerned with the segregation and analysis of ego states (Berne, 1964, 22).

An ego state is defined as a system of feelings accompanied by a related set of behavior patterns (Berne, 1964, 23). There are three categories of ego states that all humans possess. Berne claims that these ego states are observable and can be determined through a person's actions and certain verbal cues or language patterns. These are not roles but psychological constructs. These ego states are usually separate, distinct, and often inconsistent with one another. The following are the three categories of ego states described by Berne.

I. *Parent (exteropsychic)*—These are ego states that resemble parental figures. The Parent is exhibited in two forms, direct and indirect: as an active ego state and as an influence. Berne states that, "When directly active, the person responds as his own father (or mother) actually responded . . . when it is an indirect influence, he responds the way they wanted him to respond" (Berne, 1964, 26).

Harris further clarifies this ego state.

The Parent is a huge collection of recordings in the brain of unquestioned or imposed external events perceived by a person in his early years, a period which we have designated roughly as the first five years of life . . . the name Parent is most descriptive of this data inasmuch as the most significant "tapes" are those provided by the example and pronouncements of his own real parents or parent substitutes (Harris, 18–19).

The Parent has two main functions: first, it enables the individual to act as the parent of actual children; second, it makes many responses automatic, which conserves a great deal of time and energy (Berne, 1964, 27).

II. *Child (archaeopsychic)*—These are the ego states that represent archaic relics, still-active ego states that were fixated in early childhood. The Child is exhibited in two forms.

1. Adapted Child—the one who modifies his behavior under the Parental influence—he behaves as his parents wanted him to behave. "Thus the Parental influence is the cause and the adapted Child is the effect" (Berne, 1964, 26).

2. Natural Child—spontaneous expression. "In the Child reside intuition, creativity, and spontaneous drive and enjoyment" (Berne, 1964, 27).

Harris further illustrates the Child.

While external events are being recorded as that body of data we call the Parent, there is another recording being made simultaneously. This is the recording of internal events, the responses of the little person to what he sees and hears (this is known as the Child) (Harris, 24).

III. *Adult (neopsychic)*—These are those ego states that are autonomously directed toward objective appraisal of reality. The Adult processes data and computes the probabilities that are necessary for dealing effectively with the world. The Adult also regulates the activities of the Parent and Child and mediates between them. Berne defines a "mature" person as one who is able to keep the Adult in control most of the time (Berne, 1964, 30). Harris describes in detail how the Adult functions.

The Adult is a data-processing computer, which grinds out decisions after computing the information from three sources: the Parent, the Child, and the data which the Adult has gathered and is gathering. One of the important functions of the Adult is to examine the data in the Parent, to see whether or not it is true and still applicable today, and then to accept it or reject it; and to examine the Child to see whether or not the feelings there are appropriate to the present or are archaic and in response to archaic Parent data. The goal is not to do away with the Parent and Child but to be free to examine these bodies of data (Harris, 30).

These three ego states exist within each of us. Each time we perform in a transaction, we are dealing from one of our ego states to one of the ego states within the other person. Most of the time the Adult should be in control, but under stress the functioning of the Adult can be impaired. As Harris states, "The boundaries between Parent, Adult, and Child are fragile, sometimes indistinct, and vulnerable to incoming signals which tend to overload the Adult capacity" (Harris, 33). Thus we can see the way stress can affect the individual and thereby affect his communication.

Transactional Analysis

Transactional Analysis, then, is concerned with diagnosing or determining which ego state implemented the transactional stimulus and which one executed the transactional response (Berne, 1964, 29). According to Harris, "Transactional Analysis also is the method of systematizing the information derived from analyzing these transactions in words which have the same meaning, by definition, for everyone who is using them (Harris, 13). If this claim is true, this type of analysis overcomes many of the problems that plague psychoanalysis resulting from vagueness and uncertainty as to what is being observed or dealt with. This problem is not unique to psychoanalysis, as anyone in communication theory is acutely aware. If this claim of clarity of terms and better understanding is true, then perhaps whatever aspects of Transactional Analysis that may be borrowed by communication theory might help clear up much of the confusion and disagreement that presently exists within the field and thereby bring about more uniformity as well as better understanding on the part of laymen who are exposed to our concepts. Being better understood by those both within and without our area of expertise is indeed a worthwhile undertaking.

According to the theory, there are two basic divisions of transactions. The first division consists of complementary transactions. In this type, the person responding does so in the same ego state as that which the original stroke or communication is aimed at. For example, Mr. A speaks in his Parent directed toward Mr. B's Child. The transaction is complementary if Mr. B responds in his Child directed toward Mr. A's Parent.

The second division is crossed transactions. In this case Mr. A might speak from his Parent to Mr. B's Child but Mr. B responds in his Parent directed at Mr. A's Child.

Berne sums up how these two major divisions affect communication.

Communication will proceed smoothly as long as transactions are complementary (the response is appropriate and expected). This is independent of the nature and content of the transactions. . . . Communication is broken off when a crossed transaction occurs. It remains broken until the vectors can be realigned (complementary transactions occur) (Berne, 1964, 30).

A complete illustration of all possible transactions appears in Figure 3-7. This figure represents what Berne calls a relationship diagram. According to Berne,

Complementary transactions between "psychological equals" are represented by $(1-1)^2$, $(5-5)^2$, and $(9-9)^2$. There are three other complementary transactions: $(2-4)(4-2)$, $(3-7)(7-3)$, and $(6-8)(8-6)$. All other combinations form crossed transactions, and in most cases these show up as crossings in the diagram (Berne, 1964, 32).

In addition, transactions may be either simple or ulterior. A simple transaction consists of two ego states. Ulterior transactions involve more than two ego states and may be either angular or duplex. Angular transactions involve three ego states—stroke initiated in one ego state seems aimed at another but is actually aimed at a third. Duplex transactions involve four ego states—actually a dual level transaction. Ulterior transactions are the "games" that Berne discusses in his book and are discussed later in this article (Berne, 1964, 29–34).

Although each line in Figure 3-7 represents a transaction, it is important to note that transactions usually proceed in series, these series, according to

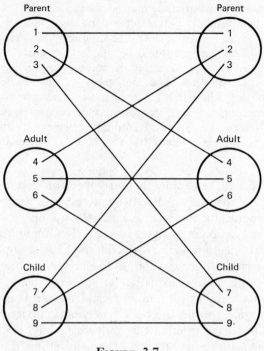

FIGURE 3-7

Berne, "are not random but programmed" (Berne, 1964, 35). There are four basic types of transaction programs.

1. Procedures—A procedure is a series of simple complementary Adult transactions directed toward the manipulation of reality. An example might be piloting an airplane or removing an appendix.
2. Rituals—There are stereotyped series of simple complementary transactions programmed by external social forces. An example of these might be social leave-taking (informal ritual) or Roman Catholic Mass (formal ritual). The form of a ritual is basically Parentally determined by tradition.

Berne discusses the similarities and differences between procedures and rituals in the following:

The essential and similar feature of both procedures and rituals is that they are stereotyped. Once the first transaction has been initiated, the whole series follows a predetermined course. . . . The difference between them lies in the origin of the predetermination: procedures are programmed by the Adult and rituals are Parentally patterned. Individuals who are not comfortable or adept with rituals sometimes evade them by substituting procedures (Berne, 1964, 39–40).

3. Pastimes—A simple pastime may be defined as "a series of semi-ritualistic, simple, complementary transactions arranged around a single field of material, whose primary object is to structure an interval of time" (Berne, 1964, 41). An example would be simple "chit-chat."
4. Games—"A game is a series of complementary ulterior transactions progressing to a well-defined predictable outcome." (Berne, 1964, 48) It should be noted here that games have a concealed motivation. They differ from procedures, rituals, or pastimes in two ways: first, their ulterior quality; second, the payoff. According to Berne, "Every game is basically dishonest, and the outcome has a dramatic . . . quality." (Berne, 1964, 48)

It should be evident by now that an important feature of Transactional Analysis is to view the individual not alone, existing within a vacuum, but rather as a communicator interacting with others. This viewpoint makes the link between Transactional Analysis and speech-communication quite vivid. The transactional orientation is perhaps the single most important thing that this type of psychoanalysis can bring to speech-communication. Possible applications to group process in particular seem especially likely. These and other applications are discussed in more detail later in this article.

Harris has gone beyond the basic tenets of Transactional Analysis laid down by Berne and has suggested that individuals hold one of the following four life positions with respect to themselves and others. These positions not only determine to some extent which ego state the person is in but also how he functions with that ego state.

1. I'm not OK—You're OK—This is the universal position of early childhood.
2. I'm not OK—You're not OK—Because of experiences during the first year, the child may experience insufficient stroking and develop this outlook. In this position the Adult stops developing.
3. I'm OK—You're not OK—This position Harris calls the criminal position. According to Harris.
    The person in the I'm OK—You're not OK position suffers from stroking deprivation and yet in this position there are no OK strokes. He seeks strokes but distrusts them and looks upon them as despicable (Harris, 49).
4. I'm OK—You're OK—Harris explains the difference between this position and the preceding three.
    There is a qualitative difference between this position and the preceding three. The first three are unconscious, having been made in early life. I'm not OK—You're OK came first and persists for most people throughout life. For certain extremely unfortunate children this position was changed to positions two and three. . . . The fourth position, I'm OK—You're OK, because it is a conscious and verbal decision, can include not only an infinitely greater amount of information about the

individual and others, but also the incorporation of not-yet-experienced possibilities which exist in the abstractions of philosophy and religion. The first three positions are based on feelings, the fourth is based on thought, faith, and the wager of action (Harris, 50).

To change positions, especially to assume the fourth position, requires conscious effort.

The relationship between these positions and other tenets of Transactional Analysis can be seen in the fact that most people deal with the position of I'm not OK—You're OK, the one most of us are in, by playing games. Harris comments on games in the following way, "most games cause trouble . . . they are relationship wreckers and the misery producers . . ." (Harris, 119). The position of I'm OK—You're OK functions generally when a person communicates from his Adult to another's Adult. To maximize the Adult ego state while allowing the person freedom of choice in his responses, and to allow the person to accept the position of I'm OK—You're OK is the goal of Transactional Analysis.

Harris feels that there are two functional problems that can occur between ego states and can thereby affect the transactions.

1. Contamination—This occurs when the ego states overlap. The results can be as follows:
   a. when the Parent overlaps with the Adult, dated, unexamined Parent data is externalized as true and prejudice results. This may be an alternate explanation for the communication concept of dogmatism.
   b. when Adult and Child overlap, feelings or archaic experiences are inappropriately externalized in the present. This can result in delusions or hallucinations.
2. Exclusion—According to Berne,
   Exclusion is manifested by a stereotyped, predictable attitude which is steadfastly maintained as long as possible in the face of any threatening situation. The constant Parent, the constant Adult, and the constant Child all result primarily from defensive exclusion of the two complementary aspects in each case (Berne, 1961, 100).

These psychotherapeutic explanations provide greater insight into many of the problems we encounter in communicating both interpersonally and intrapersonally. They provide us with a different way of looking at communication. But is it a better viewpoint than any that communication theorists presently possess?

APPLICATIONS TO COMMUNICATION THEORY

From the discussion thus far, it should be obvious that Transactional Analysis has many applications to communication theory. The applications about to be discussed here are not presented as the only possible ones. They are, however, the more obvious and basic ones that seem apparent to this author.

Transactional Viewpoint

As was mentioned earlier in this article, Transactional Analysis offers a different viewpoint of how people interact with one another. This process-oriented view seems both more macroscopic and realistic. Although the concept of process is a much discussed topic within the field of communication theory, Transactional Analysis not only adds increased emphasis to process-orientation but also provides a possible framework to enable us to consider more the interrelationships between the many aspects of communication. This transactional viewpoint, which is people-oriented rather than variable-oriented, would give us a clearer picture of human communication.

There is an old parable about six blind men who went to see an elephant. Each blind man felt a different part of the elephant and each had a different perception of what the elephant looked like. Many of us in communication suffer from the same problem. Our emphasis upon individual variables or perhaps the interrelationship of two or three may indeed warp our perspective. This is not to say that emphasis upon variables is of no useful purpose in the study of communication. Much of our experimental work in the field is completely dependent upon the isolation of variables. However, this emphasis should be tempered and balanced by a perspective of communication that realizes that each time individuals interact, or *transact*, the resulting communication is more than the sum of the parts or variables of which it is comprised. This transactional viewpoint would look upon communication as a unique, dynamic interaction between human beings. Such a viewpoint would allow us to remove at least some of the blindfolds and thereby permit us to obtain a clearer picture of what we are studying. This viewpoint might then, in turn, enable us to discover new variables and interrelationships.

Parent Communicative Characteristics

In addition to the general perspective that a transactional viewpoint provides, an examination of the Parent and Adult ego states offers insight into certain communicative characteristics discussed by many communication theorists. Such an insight might enable us to pull together seemingly unrelated concepts into a unified theory.

According to Transactional Analysis, the Parent is the judgmental, authoritarian part of each of us. The Parent reacts internally on the basis of previously made judgments and conclusions. The Parent is thus a nonprocess, more rigid ego state than the Adult. This tendency to react internally on the basis of previously made judgments without bothering to test their veracity is what general semanticists have long called an *intensional* orientation. It is this orientation, the general semanticists say, that creates so many of our communication problems. This intensional orientation tends to disregard the changing environment and thus ignores the concept of process. In short, we react to people and situations as we have reacted to them in the past. We interact with people on the basis of stereotypes and fixed judgments. We label people and events without bothering to evaluate the correctness of the label and without realizing that all labels distort to some degree our perception of what is being labeled.

The Parent is the authoritarian part of our personality. Berne tells us that we can expect trouble when communicating from our Parent if the other person will not assume the Child ego state, since this kind of transaction bond is so strong. This concept lends support for what communication theorists tell us about authoritarianism. Gibb, for example, tells us that perceived authoritarian communication (communication from the Parent) is often less effective. According to Gibb, "arousing defensiveness interferes with communication and thus makes it difficult . . . for anyone to convey ideas clearly. . . ." (Cathcart and Samovar, 306–307).

From this discussion we can see that some of the Parent characteristics can often inhibit rather than enhance effective communication. General semanticists tell us we should avoid an intensional orientation; Gibb tells us we should avoid authoritarian communication; Berne tells us that communicating from the Parent often causes crossed transactions. This correlation tends to suggest that the Parent is a rather poor communicator and that these characteristics exhibited by the Parent ego state should be avoided. Once again, Transactional Analysis gives us a different perspective in viewing and explaining concepts in communication. We not only have an explanation of intensional orientation and authoritarianism but also a possible rationale for why they exist.

Adult Communicative Characteristics

Just as the Parent exhibited certain communication characteristics, so does the Adult. However, within the Adult reside the characteristics generally associated with more effective communication.

The Adult is the problem-solver, the discoverer, that part of us which questions, observes, and verifies. In other words, it is within the Adult that a process orientation resides. Unlike the Parent state that reacts on the basis of past judgments, the Adult state seeks to gather data from the environment to confirm or deny the judgments existing within the Parent state. The normal functioning Adult state constantly seeks additional information. When functioning within this ego state, we react to people more as individuals, as they really are. We tend to be nonauthoritarian and more conscious of our ever-changing environment.

These characteristics of the Adult state are associated with what general semanticists refer to as an extensional orientation. According to general semantics, an extensional orientation allows us to maintain a process orientation while communicating. In short, an extensional orientation can make us more effective communicators.

Thus in the Adult ego state we are extensionally oriented, nonauthoritarian communicators, whereas in the Parent ego state we are intensionally oriented, authoritarian communicators. In light of what general semanticists have said about the importance of an extensional orientation and in addition to what Gibb has suggested about defensiveness, one can readily see why communicating from our Adult ego state should be the general rule. This is not to suggest that communicating from the Parent is always bad, nor that communicating from one's Child state is never appropriate. However, as Harris has suggested, the Adult ego state should remain in control and permit us to move between any and all three of the ego states when and where appropriate. With the Adult in control, we are careful to watch for possible communication breakdowns and are able to analyze the problem and take corrective steps.

Additionally, the Adult state is associated with the life position of I'm OK—You're OK. Harris has pointed out that such a life position permits better understanding and tolerance between individuals. This increased understanding and tolerance in turn can encourage increased openness and trust between individuals. This atmosphere results in what Gibb calls a supportive communication climate. Such a climate, according to Gibb, enhances communication and eliminates breakdowns.

The Adult would seem to be the best communicative state. Utilizing the concepts from Transactional Analysis and trying to communicate from our Adult ego state would therefore improve our communication habits and result in better interpersonal communication.

Prescriptive Clarity

Prescriptive clarity is another major value of Transactional Analysis. Many of the explanations it offers are much clearer than those offered by many communication theorists. For this reason they are more readily understood by the layman. Many times even communication theorists have difficulty understanding their own concepts. Since our goal is to improve communication, the clarity of the suggestions offered is of paramount importance. Whether the explanations offered by Berne and Harris are overly simplistic or not, following their suggestions would seem to enable people to become better communicators. The Adult ego state makes a better communicator, and since a well-developed and utilized Adult state is what Berne and Harris are after, the goals of both fields, communication theory as well as psychotherapy, are the same.

If our major concern is to improve communication habits, then the method we use is less important as long as the desired results are obtained. Transactional Analysis, like general semantics, offers prescriptive suggestions to all the layman to understand and apply the concepts of effective communication to his everyday life. The basic points of Transactional Analysis can also provide the framework around which we may group many of the previously seemingly diverse theories and concepts of communication theory. In this sense, Transactional Analysis can be viewed as a rallying point for the study of human communication that has yet to be fully realized.

As was stated earlier, this discussion should not be considered a complete, final statement as to the applications of Transactional Analysis to communication theory. It is up to the student of communication to determine for himself the usefulness of the applications suggested here. Many additional applications and interrelationships have yet to be discovered. One thing, however, does appear certain, whether or not man actually functions the way Berne and Harris suggest seems of less importance if, through following their suggestions, we can improve our communication habits.

REFERENCES

Barnlund, Dean C. (ed.). *Interpersonal Communication: Survey and Studies.* Boston: Houghton Mifflin Company, 1968.
———. *Foundations of Communication Theory.* Edited by Kenneth K. Sereno and C. David Mortensen. New York: Harper & Row, Publishers, Inc., 1970.
Berne, Eric. *Transactional Analysis in Psychotherapy.* New York: Grove Press, 1961.
———. *Games People Play.* New York: Grove Press, Inc., 1964.
———. *Small Group Communication.* Edited by Robert S. Cathcart and Larry A. Samovar. Dubuque, Iowa: William C. Brown, Company, Publishers, 1970.
Gibb, Jack R. *Small Group Communication.* Edited by Robert S. Cathcart and Larry A. Samovar. Dubuque, Iowa: William C. Brown Company, Publishers, 1970.
Giffin, Kim and Bobby R. Patton (eds.). *Basic Readings in Interpersonal Communication.* New York: Harper & Row, Publishers, Inc., 1971.
Harris, Thomas A. *I'm OK—You're OK.* New York: Harper & Row Publishers, Inc., 1967.
Keltner, John W. *Interpersonal Speech-Communication Elements and Structures.* Belmont, Calif.: Wadsworth Publishing Co., Inc., 1970.

Laing, Ronald D., Herbert Phillipson, and A. Russell Lee. *Basic Readings in Interpersonal Communication*. Edited by Kim Giffin and Bobby R. Patton. New York: Harper & Row, Publishers, Inc., 1971.

Toch, Hans and Malcolm S. MacLean, Jr. *Foundations of Communication Theory*. Edited by Kenneth K. Sereno and C. David Mortensen. New York: Harper & Row, Publishers, Inc., 1970.

Smith, Alfred G. (ed.). *Communication and Culture*. New York: Holt, Rinehart and Winston, Inc., 1966.

IV Group Communication

We might begin by remembering all the communication situations we were involved in during the past twenty-four hours. Consider how many of these situations involved two or more other individuals. We should not be surprised to discover that the majority of our communicative efforts took place in a group environment.

We belong to many groups both large and small. We participate in informal conversations with friends; we join groups for political, professional, and social reasons; we are appointed or volunteer for committees at school or on the job; we join groups for fun, prestige, or work. We live in a world formed by and functioning in a group structure. Groups are part of our everyday existence. Most of our day-to-day communicative behavior involves interaction in small groups.

What is a group? Unfortunately, what seems a simple question has a complex answer. However, we attempt to provide what may be interpreted by some as an overly simplistic definition of the group. A group is composed of two or more *interdependent* members; interdependent because they *influence* one another. Group members share *common goals* or *purposes*, for example, sharing information, solving problems, implementing tasks, or providing social support. As group members interact they tend to create rules for member behavior that we call *norms*. If the norms refer to the behavior expected of a specific individual, they make up his *role*. Some people play leadership roles, whereas others feel easier being jokesters or working within the group structure. However, we have not listed the most crucial characteristic of the group—*communication*.

Communication unites the group members when they interact to fulfill a common goal. Communication assists the group in resolving internal and external pressures when the group attempts to meet that goal. Communication allows group members to appraise their functions, roles, and norms within the group; members need to evaluate their abilities, learn what others believe, modify their opinions and behaviors, and try to change the beliefs of others.

Joseph Luft's *The Johari Window: A Graphic Model of Awareness in Interpersonal Relations* bridges our study of interpersonal and group communication. The Johari Window provides a graphic model for illustrating the communicative relationships between individuals in a group or groups of individuals. It illustrates human relationships in terms of human awareness. Communication is crucial to human awareness because only by communication (verbal and nonverbal) can we determine the reasons for individual and group behavior.

In *Nonverbal Behavior and Small Group Interaction* by Lawrence B. Rosenfeld we discover that nonverbal behaviors in which members of a group engage offer a great deal of information. Nonverbal behaviors may accurately reveal both the physical and emotional states of the other members. The correct interpretation of these cues should help group members maintain good relations with each other, and good interpersonal relations should, in turn, help the group achieve its task.

Leon Festinger's *Informal Social Communication* differentiates the types of communication that give rise to tendencies for group members to communicate and "laws" of communication that stem from these sources. A series of interrelated hypotheses are presented to account for the sources of pressures to communicate in groups.

Groupthink by Irving L. Janis delves into the drive for consensus and the suppression of dissent in groups. Groupthink involves nondeliberate suppression of critical thoughts as a result of internalization of group norms. The symptoms of groupthink are explained with reference to contemporary political and military group decisions. Solutions to groupthink are discussed and criticized.

The Role of Conflict in Discussion by John L. Petelle examines conflict as a force in groups, to determine what, if any, positive functions it may have and to determine the role of conflict in discussion. It is pointed out that conflict can become a valuable criterion to help us evaluate the process of group discussion.

Ronald L. Applbaum and Karl W. E. Anatol's *The Role of Communication in Small Group Choice Shift* examines the interaction processes during small group choice shift. The first part of the article reviews the previous major theoretic orientations toward choice shift and the second part explores an informational approach to choice shifts.

Conceptual and Methodological Approaches to the Study of Leadership by Dennis S. Gouran discusses four discernible approaches to the study of leadership; trait, stylistic, situational, and functional. The strengths and weaknesses of each approach are examined. A new analytical system for future leadership research is suggested. In addition, it is suggested that more leadership research should be investigatory rather than experimental.

Intercultural Communication in the Group Setting by Richard E. Porter explores the effects of culture upon communication and group processes. Four variables influencing the communication and group processes are investigated: (1) attitudes; (2) patterns of thought; (3) roles and role prescriptions; and (4) nonverbal expression.

1. What is the purpose of the Johari Window?
2. What are the components or quadrants composing the Johari Window?
3. How can we explain communication between group members using the Johari Window?
4. How can we explain communication between groups using the Johari Window?
5. Can the Johari Window be used to explain intrapersonal communication?

◄ The Johari Window: A Graphic Model of Awareness in Interpersonal Relations

JOSEPH LUFT

Like the happy centipede, many people get along fine working with others without thinking about which foot to put forward. But when there are difficulties, when the usual methods do not work, when we want to learn more—there is no alternative but to examine our own behavior in relation to others. One trouble is that it is so hard to find ways of thinking about such matters, particularly for people who have no extensive backgrounds in the social sciences.

When Luft and Ingham (1955) first presented the Johari Window to illustrate relationships in terms of awareness, they were surprised to find so many people, academicians and nonprofessionals alike, using and tinkering with the model. It seems to lend itself as a heuristic device to speculating about human relations. It is simple to visualize the four quadrants of the model (Figure 4-1).

Quadrant 1 the area of free activity, or open area, refers to behavior motivation known to self and known to others.

Quadrant 2 the blind area, is where others can see things in ourselves of which we are unaware (1).

Reprinted from GROUP PROCESSES: *An Introduction to Group Dynamics*, by Joseph Luft, by permission of National Press Books. Copyright © 1963, 1970, Joseph Luft, 2nd ed., 1970.

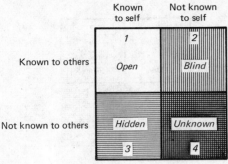

FIGURE 4-1.
The Johari Window.

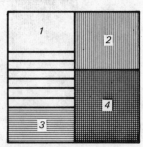

FIGURE 4-2.
Degrees of openness.

Quadrant 3 the avoided or hidden area, represents things we know but do not reveal to others (e.g., a hidden agenda or matters about which we have sensitive feelings). (See Figure 4-2).

Quadrant 4 the area of unknown activity, points to the area where neither the individual nor others are aware of certain behaviors or motives. Yet we can assume their existence because eventually some of these things become known, and we then realize that these unknown behaviors and motives were influencing relationships all along. (See Figure 4-3).

In a new group, Q1 is very small; there is not much free and spontaneous interaction. As the group grows and matures, Q1 expands in size, and this usually means we are freer to be more like ourselves and to preceive things as they really are. Quadrant 3 shrinks in area as Q1 grows larger. We find it less necessary to hide or deny things we know or feel. In an atmosphere of growing mutual trust, there is less need for hiding pertinent thoughts or feelings. It takes longer for Q2 to reduce in size because usually there are "good" reasons of a psychological nature to blind ourselves to certain things we feel or do. Quadrant 4 changes somewhat during a learning laboratory, but we can assume that such changes occur even more slowly than shifts in Q2. At any rate, Q4 is undoubtedly far larger and more influential in an individual's relationships than the hypothetical sketch illustrates (Figure 4-4).

The Johari Window may be applied to *intergroup* relations. Quadrant 1 then means behavior and motivation known to the group and also known to other groups. Quadrant 2 signifies an area of behavior to which a group is blind, but other groups are aware of the behavior, e.g., cultism or prejudice. Quadrant 3, the hidden area, refers to things a group knows about itself, but which are kept from other groups. Quadrant 4, the unknown area, means a group is unaware of some aspects of its own behavior, and other groups are

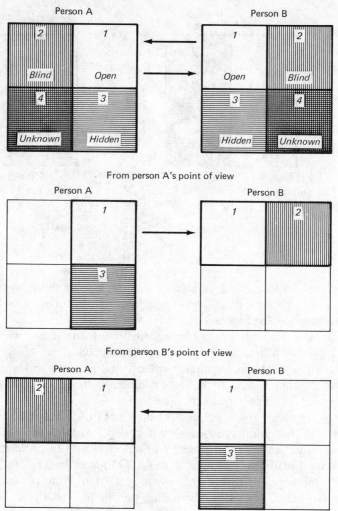

FIGURE 4-3. Interaction between two persons.

also unaware of this behavior. Later, as the group learns new things about itself, there is a shift from Q4 to one of the other quadrants.

Principles of Change

1. A change in any one quadrant will affect all other quadrants.
2. It takes energy to hide, deny, or be blind to behavior which is involved in interaction.

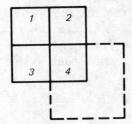

FIGURE 4-4. The relative size of Q4.

3. Threat tends to decrease awareness; mutual trust tends to increase awareness.
4. Forced awareness (exposure) is undesirable and usually ineffective.
5. Interpersonal learning means a change has taken place so that Q1 is larger and one or more of the other quadrants has grown smaller.
6. Working with others is facilitated by a large enough area of free activity. An increased Q1 means more of the resources and skills in the membership can be applied to a task.
7. The smaller the first quadrant, the poorer the communication.
8. There is universal curiosity about the unknown area, but this is held in check by custom, social training, and diverse fears.
9. Sensitivity means appreciating the covert aspects of behavior, in quadrants 2, 3, and 4, and respecting the desire of others to keep them so.
10. Learning about group processes as they are being experienced helps to increase awareness (enlarge Q1) for the group as a whole as well as for individual members.
11. The value system of a group and its membership may be noted in the way *unknowns* in the life of the group are confronted.
12. A centipede may be perfectly happy without awareness, but after all, he restricts himself to crawling under rocks.

Having familiarized himself with this outline, a group member might learn to use it to help himself to a clearer understanding of the significant events in a group. Futhermore, the outline is sufficiently broad and loose so that it may have heuristic value in stimulating the identification and elaboration of problems in new ways. Several illustrations of different kinds of intergroup and intragroup behavior are given below.

The Objectives of a Group Dynamics Laboratory

Using the model we may illustrate one of the general objectives of the laboratory, namely, to increase the area of free activity (Q1) so that more of the relationships in the group are free and open (2). It follows, therefore, that the work of the laboratory is to increase the area of Q1 while reducing the area of quadrants 2, 3, and 4. The largest reduction in area would be in Q3, then Q2 and the smallest reduction would be Q4 (see Figure 4-5).

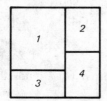

FIGURE 4-5.
Laboratory objectives.

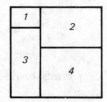

FIGURE 4-6.
Beginning interaction in a new group.

An enlarged area of free activity among the group members implies less threat of fear and greater probability that the skills and resources of group members can be brought to bear on the work of the group. The enlarged area suggests greater openness to information, opinions, and new ideas about each member as well as about specific group processes. Since the hidden or avoided area, Q3, is reduced, less energy is tied up in defending this area. Since more of one's needs are unbound, there is greater likelihood of satisfaction with the work and more involvement with what the group is doing.

The Initial Phase of Group Interaction

Applying the model to a typical meeting of most groups, we can recognize that interaction is relatively superficial, that anxiety or threat is fairly large, that interchange is stilted and unspontaneous. We also may note that ideas or suggestions are not followed through and are usually left undeveloped, that individuals seem to hear and see relatively little of what is really going on.

The Model May Depict Intergroup Processes As Well As Intragroup Processes

The group may be treated as an entity or unit. Cattell (1956), for instance, uses the term "syntality" to mean the quality of a group analogous to the personality of an individual. Lewin conceives of the group as an organized field of forces, a structured whole. In this model, a group may relate to other groups in a manner similar to the relationship between

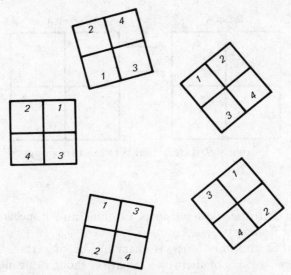

FIGURE 4-7. One way of looking at a group.

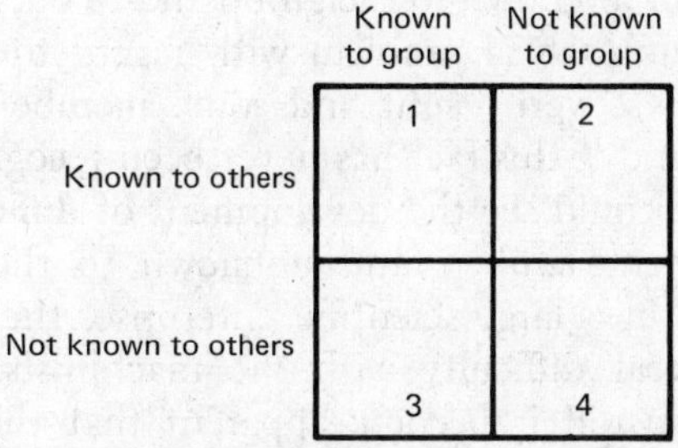

	Known to group	Not known to group
Known to others	1	2
Not known to others	3	4

FIGURE 4-8. A group as a whole.

individuals. The first quadrant (Figure 4-8) represents behavior and motivation of a group which is known to group members and also known to others. A college seminar, for instance, may share certain knowledge and behavior about itself with other classes on campus, such as requirements for the course, subject matter of the seminar, or the amount of work it sets out to do. However, many things occur in a seminar that are known to its members, but not known to outside groups (quadrant 3).

An illustration of an area of avoided behavior might be the students' feeling that their seminar is very special or quite superior to other classes. Or they might feel the course is a waste of time, but for some reason they

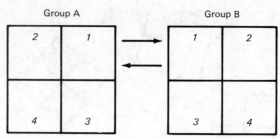

FIGURE 4-9. Interaction between two groups.

do not share this attitude with outsiders. Or sometimes a special event occurs, and this is kept from outsiders.

Quadrant 2, the blind area, is characteristic of certain cults that are unaware of some aspects of their own behavior, though outsiders are able to discern the cultish qualities. Or the prejudices of a certain group may be perfectly apparent to outsiders but not to the group members themselves.

Quadrant 4 applies to attitudes and behavior that exist in the group but for some reason remain unknown to the group and to outsiders. An illustration of this might be an unresolved problem with regard to over-all goals of the group. If the group is covertly split and some members want to go off in different directions—and if this fact has never been recognized or brought out in the open—then we could see the development of difficulties which remain unknown to the group members and unknown to the members of other groups. For example, in a large scientific enterprise, the physicists and engineers were having great difficulty with the machinists. Only after a long period of investigation did it become apparent that the question of status and privilege was producing bitter feelings between groups, yet the members of the various groups were unaware of the ramifications of this problem.

Representations of Interaction

Another way of representing a relationship is shown in Figure 4-10, where all the information bearing on the relationship is contained in the matrix. Each person in the relationship has blind spots in areas open to the other person, and both are blind or lack awareness with respect to certain aspects of their relationship, as represented by quadrant 4. A critical factor in the relationship is the manner in which the unknowns are dealt with; recurring interaction patterns establish the style or quality of the interpersonal tie. Every relationship can be characterized by the constraint inherent in the relationship.

	Known to supervisor	Not known to supervisor
Known to employee	1 Open area	2 Employee aware Supervisor is blind
Not known to employee	Supervisor aware Employee is blind 3	Both unaware 4

FIGURE 4-10. A model of person-to-person interaction: employee-supervisor.

The persons represented are interdependent in Q1, and each is both independent and dependent in Q2 and Q3. Independence is defined here as awareness which is exclusive; the dependent one lacks awareness of an interpersonally relevant matter of which the other *is* aware. Withholding information or feelings which are interpersonally relevant is therefore a way of controlling or manipulating the other. Both persons are dependent where both are unaware, in Q4.

The representation lends itself to consideration of a variety of questions. Regarding Figure 4-10, for instance, what kinds of information or feelings are apt to be found in Q2? In Q3? In Q4? What happens when information flows from Q2 to Q1 or Q3 to Q1 or from Q4 to Q1? Or, regarding Figure 4-11, what kinds of interaction help to enlarge the open area? Similar questions might be raised for Figures 4-12, 4-13, and 4-14.

	Known to student	Not known to student
Known to teacher	1 Open area	2 Teacher aware Student is blind
Not known to teacher	Student aware Teacher is blind 3	Both unaware 4

FIGURE 4-11. A model of person-to-person interaction: student-teacher.

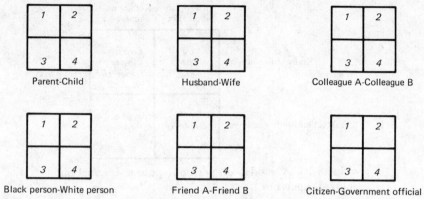

FIGURE 4-12. Other kinds of person-to-person interaction.

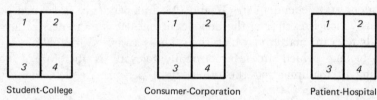

FIGURE 4-13. Interaction between individuals and organizations.

FIGURE 4-14. Interaction between organizations or groups.

NOTES

1. "Undoubtedly you know much of what goes on in your mind and can report it. Undoubtedly you have private evidence that bears on the current activity of your mind. Thus, in important respects, your knowledge of yourself is more complete and reliable than the knowledge others may have. Yet it is clear that this knowledge must be inferential and theoretical—at least in part. A second person may be better able than you to evaluate your present mental state and predict your behavior. In principle self-knowledge may depend on the same kinds of inference that knowledge of another depends on" (Hebb, 1969, p. 55).

2. "The fact that others know reality is something which we never doubt;

communication puts the 'world in their reach' within our reach, too. A crucial prototype of this process occurs in person-to-person interaction. Here, in the direct communication between two people who attend to each other fully and speak the same language, the shared vivid present of the 'We' establishes shared reality" (Holzner, 1968, p. 8).

STUDY GUIDE
QUESTIONS

1. What are some of the considerations that must be made when attempting to define *nonverbal communication?*
2. What are some of the key distinctions between verbal and nonverbal communication?
3. Why are nonverbal cues of particular importance for individuals in a group?
4. Before interacting with other members of a group, what nonverbal cues do you receive from them?
5. How do nonverbal cues relating to physical appearance affect how you respond to group members?
6. What cues reveal what an individual's status is in the group?
7. How do the internal and external contexts in which you interact affect how you interpret the nonverbal behavior you observe?
8. What is the relationship among the various nonverbal cues?

▸◀ Nonverbal Behavior and Small Group Interaction

LAWRENCE B. ROSENFELD

Within a few seconds after you enter a group you are ready to pass judgments on the other members of the group. You are ready to predict which members will be friends, which will be hard workers, and which will be troublemakers. But if someone dared to ask how you made these judgments, you would probably be hard put to provide an articulate answer. You would repeat how

---

"Nonverbal Behavior and Small Group Interaction," by Lawrence B. Rosenfeld. Reprinted with permission of the author. This original essay appears here in print for the first time.

you felt, but never really tell why. Is it the clothes they wore? The shape and smell of their bodies? How they combed their hair? Maybe it is the way they sat, or where they sat, or how they moved their bodies when they turned to look at you? Maybe it was the way they said "Hello," or "Hi," or "I hope this will be a great group"? The basis for your judgments may not be so obvious as to be found in the other members. It is possible that the room "turned you off." The shape, size, color, and decorations of the room may have made you feel uneasy. You may have transferred your uneasy feeling to the other members of the group, saying, "*They* are making me feel uneasy, so this must be a rotten group." Maybe the answer is even more subtle: you may have been out of step, "walking to the beat of a different drummer," when you entered the group. Was it an off day for you? Were you feeling down or blue? Did you get a good night's sleep the night before?

The predictions you made about the other members of your group may be explained by the answer to any one of these questions, but it is more likely that there are several answers, all interacting to produce an explanation that is so subtle and complex that it is difficult, almost impossible, to articulate. Because the nonverbal behaviors that we encounter may not be as "obvious" as the verbal behaviors or may not be as consciously sent (encoded) or received (decoded), we may be unaware of them. Nevertheless, these are cues to which we are continually responding.

Given the difficulty we have recognizing nonverbal cues, it is not surprising that there are a variety of definitions of nonverbal communication. They range from "all the cues that are not words" (1) to definitions that restrict nonverbal communication to those messages that are consciously intended by the senders (2). The more effort spent in attempting to define nonverbal communication, the clearer it becomes that the problem will not be solved to everyone's satisfaction. Should we define it from the point of view of the receiver (e.g., if a receiver interprets "it" then "it" qualifies as an act of nonverbal communication), the sender (e.g., if a sender intended "it" to communicate, "it" qualifies as an act of nonverbal communication), or according to the absence or presence of words either spoken or written? Must we confine ourselves to human senders and receivers, or can we claim that architecture "communicates" (3)? Harrison (4) and Knapp (5) agree that, given the research being conducted under the rubric of "nonverbal communication," it is best to define the area broadly: nonverbal communication applies to those events in which words are neither spoken nor written.

What is important to note is that there *are* differences between verbal and nonverbal communication. They do not provide the same kinds of information, nor do they seem to operate in similar fashion. Although the differences are not absolute, there are several distinct continua on which we can make our differentiations. Brooks (6) has charted some of these continua, the most salient of which seem to be the following:

(1) Verbal communication has as its basic element the word, composed of letters and sounds that have discrete beginnings and ends; non-verbal communication is based on continuous functions with no beginnings and ends, but rather messages that seem to come in pulses.

(2) Understanding verbal messages is based on prior verbal agreement (the words we assign to objects are arbitrary); understanding non-verbal messages is based on empathy, the sharing of similar feelings.

(3) Verbal communication is consciously taught; nonverbal communication is learned earlier in life on a more intuitive basis.

(4) Verbal communication, because of the way it is learned and the nature of its elements, is primarily intellectual; nonverbal communication is primarily emotional.

The differences between verbal and nonverbal communication point to differences in functions. Nonverbal communication, according to Applbaum et al. (7), transmits "feelings, emotions, likings, personal meaning, and preferences." However, nonverbal behaviors do not exist in an emotional vacuum; they also accompany verbal communication and play an important role in how verbal communication is decoded. Nonverbal behaviors can either reinforce, contradict, accent, or even substitute for verbal messages. Pounding your fist on the table while presenting an argument may serve to emphasize a point, whereas saying "I love you" in a monotone, with no eye contact, and following it with a yawn, serves to contradict your verbal message. When there is a contradiction, it is likely that the nonverbal message, and not the verbal one, will be interpreted and believed. Your yawn (so far as the other person was concerned) said, "I don't love you—you bore me." Actions speak louder than words, as Eliza Doolittle sings, "Don't talk of stars burning above, if you're in love show me" (8).

As I stated elsewhere (9), research in nonverbal communication, except that concerned with seating arrangements and other aspects of small group ecology, rarely focuses on the impact of nonverbal communication in the small group. But this does not make nonverbal communication any less important in the small group setting. In fact, because of the uniqueness of the situation, nonverbal behaviors become more important since they are essential for ensuring good interpersonal relationships. Individuals in groups must receive and correctly interpret nonverbal cues to help them maintain good feelings, solidarity, cohesiveness, and, finally, allow successful task completion.

Our examination of nonverbal communication in the small group, and our application of research done in other settings to the small group setting, is best divided into three parts, based loosely on the order in which we appear to receive various types of nonverbal cues. First, we are confronted with the *physical appearance* of the other group members, what they are wearing, their shape, and their smell. Then we engage in *interaction*, during which we become aware of how they use the space around them, what territory they lay claim to, how they move, and how they sound both when they talk and when they are silent. Finally, we realize that we interact in two *contexts*, an outside and an inside one: there is the physical environment, with its colors, shapes, and temperatures, and there is our own body, with its special rhythms that dictate, in part, how we feel and respond.

Each one of these topics is large enough to warrant its own book, let alone space in a short article. To solve the problem this creates, what follows is little more than an overview of each area, with less space being given to topics covered extensively in a variety of sources, and more being provided those that usually receive little attention. But! be forewarned: the references may indeed be the real meat of this article.

PHYSICAL APPEARANCE

Clothing

The impact of what others wear is a function of how well we know them. The clothing of strangers provides important clues for us, whereas clothing worn by individuals we know provides us with little information (10). Because we consciously select what we wear, others take our clothing very seriously—something we may learn painfully.

Too Poor for New Dress—So Didn't Graduate
Clifton, Ariz. (AP)—A teen-age girl whose parents said they were too poor to buy her a new dress was sent home in tears from her eighth grade graduation ceremony because her clothing did not conform with school rules. . . .

"Sure it hurt her feelings," [school principal] McDowell said. "But we wanted it to be a formal affair and not have many different kinds of dresses. Long before the graduation, I sent three other girls home to change their dresses, and I felt the only alternative was not to allow her to participate.". . .

William Blair, board president, said . . . "But we had 66 graduates, and we couldn't have everybody different. She was defying authority" (11).

As well as symbols of defiance, clothes and jewelry often serve as symbols of status and position. We tell others that we are policemen, bankers, "hip" and "together" students, conservatives or liberals (12). Several studies also revealed that the clothes we select reflect certain of our personality characteristics. Aiken (13) found that undergraduate women who liked decoration in their dress were best characterized by such traits as conformity and nonintellectualism. Comfort in dress went along with extroversion, whereas interest in dress went along with social conscientiousness. Economy in dress seemed indicative of intelligence and efficiency.

A study by Andersen, Jensen and King (14) provided evidence that speakers dressed in the same fashion as members of the audience were perceived as more credible than speakers dressed in a dissimilar fashion. Although hair style was also examined, no relationship was found, i.e., whether the speakers' hair style was similar to the audience members or not was irrelevant to the task of judging the speakers' credibility.

Keeping up with the new trends in dress, Hamilton and Hunter (15) conducted a study to measure the effects of bralessness. They found that large-breasted, less attractive women were perceived as being more sociable and of better character when they were braless. No effect was found for large-breasted, attractive women, or small-breasted women.

What others wear not only affects our judgments of them but also affects our behavior directly. Lefkowitz, Blake, and Mouton (16) found that pedestrians were more likely to violate a pedestrian "wait" signal by following a well-dressed individual than a poorly dressed one.

Body Shape and Smell

We are attracted by what we consider to be well-formed and pleasant looking, and repelled by what we consider to be ugly. Given the machinations we go through each day, including shaving, showering, brushing our teeth, and gargling with mouthwash to name but a few, it is obvious that we want to make ourselves beautiful for the world (17). It is also extremely rare to encounter an individual who is *not* trying to change his shape. Whether ectomorphs (frail and thin) or endomorphs (fat and flabby), we try our best to become mesomorphs (muscular and athletic). But there is good reason for all the activity: ectomorphs are perceived as tense, nervous, and less masculine; endomorphs are perceived as old, ugly, and sloppy; whereas mesomorphs are perceived as strong, masculine, and good-looking (18).

Stanley Keleman, in an interview for *Psychology Today*, talked about how he interpreted physical characteristics of different parts of the body. "The lower half of the body gives me clues about how a person relates to the instinctual world. Sexuality and excretion reflect the relation to the private instinctual world and the legs and feet show how a person feels about independence and grounding. The upper body represents the way a person lives in a social world. By noticing the arms, hands, chest, and face I get an idea of how a person reaches out to manipulate and love the world" (19).

We do not seem to mind talking about how we look (or would like to look), but a sure way to stop any conversation is to raise the topic of how we smell. The giant in *Jack and the Beanstalk* was aware that individuals have bodily odors, and he put that information to good use, given his repetitions of "Fee, fie, foh, fum, I smell the blood of an Englishman." But besides serving up cues to start the giant's mouth watering, body odors also play a part in racial stereotyping (20). Stereotypes based on smells, however, are best attributed to olfactory hallucinations given the lack of empirical support for them.

The olfactory environment in which we were raised affects how we interact with others, or so we may conclude from studies conducted with mice (and, as we all know, psychological studies done with mice may be generalized to freshmen in college, and studies done with freshmen may be generalized to mice, if so desired). Stark and Huzett found that "mice raised in the complex olfactory environments [with the smells of other mice] are more aggressive . . . or mice raised in less complex environments are more fearful when in the presence of strange [olfactory] stimuli" (21). Mice raised with the smells of other mice initiated 90 per cent of the interactions!

Some smells "turn us on" (I am particularly fond of Shalimar perfume, myself), and some "turn us off." Some smells even affect the two sexes differently (22). Regardless, when we enter a group we are bombarded with a host of different smells, and, depending upon the environment in which we were raised and the smells we are used to, we will differentially evaluate the other individuals in the group.

INTERACTION

Personal Space and Seating Arrangement

Personal space is the space you place between yourself and others: an invisible boundary that is difficult to realize exists until it is broken. The space, however, is not fixed, but varies according to both the context in which we interact and the people with whom we are engaged. Hall (23) describes four distinct distances we use. The first, intimate distance, is about eighteen inches or less and is used when we make love, fight, or get shoved in a crowded elevator. If our personal space is violated, we respond by pulling ourselves in, tightening our muscles, and avoiding eye contact. The second type of distance, personal distance, represents the area from one and one-half to four feet away. This distance, used for close friends and most interpersonal encounters, often requires a comfortable atmosphere. It also varies from culture to culture: whereas for Americans it varies from one and one-half to four feet, it is much less for Arabs and members of other contact cultures (cultures that encourage closeness, such as prolonged eye contact). Recent investigations revealed that subcultures also vary according to their personal distance (24). The third type of distance Hall refers to as social distance, the area from four to twelve feet away. This is the distance used for most business transactions and interaction at an informal party. This distance may represent a psychological "distance" when used by a group member to separate himself from other members of the group. The fourth and last type of distance used Hall calls public distance, the area from twelve to about twenty-five feet away. This distance is used by lecturers and other speakers, individuals who want to set themselves apart from those whom they address. It is the most formal distance one may attain—being further than twenty-five feet usually means a complete loss of contact.

Comfortable and intimate situations call for a smaller personal space than situations that are uncomfortable and threatening. The closer we feel to a person psychologically, the closer we move physically. Conversely, as relationships strain, physical distance increases (25). Results of research conducted on standing individuals closely parallels the results from research done with groups seated at rectangular and round tables.

Russo (26) examined seating arrangements at rectangular tables and found that, generally, larger distances indicated less acquaintance, friendliness, and talkativeness. Individuals seated next to each other on the same side of a table were the most friendly, whereas those seated at opposite ends were the most hostile. But the effects of seating arrangement are not unaffected by eye contact: Lott and Sommer (27), Strodtbeck and Hook (28), and Russo in the study already cited found that eye contact was a major stimulus for interaction.

Cultural influences affect how we respond to various seating positions. The head of the table is, indeed, perceived as the leadership position. This may be a function of the greater accessibility this position has to the other group members, both in terms of eye contact and the availability of lines of communication. Strodtbeck and Hook, and Hare and Bales (29), also found that individuals who were likely to assume the role of leader frequently chose the seat at the head of the table.

Sommer (30) found that for casual groups the preference was for corner seating (i.e., the seats next to each other round a corner of a table). The explanation given was that this seating arrangement allowed good eye contact and close proximity. Cooperating groups chose either the corner seating arrangement or the side-by-side arrangement. Those preferring the former stressed ease of conversing, those who preferred the latter stressed ease of sharing things. Co-acting groups (individuals who are part of a group, but need not work together) preferred a distant arrangement, emphasizing the need to be apart, yet feel together. Finally, competing groups preferred opposite, distant-opposite, and distant seating. Opposite seating arrangements, which allowed for face-to-face contact, stimulated competition.

Seating preferences at round tables closely parallel those at rectangular tables. Cooperating individuals sit side-by-side, co-acting ones prefer one seat between them, and those in competition prefer to sit opposite each other, face-to-face. Individuals who dislike each other prefer to sit far apart, but opposite. The goal seems to be both distance and decreased eye contact.

Studies conducted on the affects of seating arrangements on interaction, particularly in the school setting, indicate that where individuals sit, and how they arrange themselves in relation to others, determines to a large extent the degree to which they interact (31). Whether individuals who place themselves outside the interaction arena do so to avoid interacting, or whether the position itself exerts the greatest influence, is difficult to determine. Evidence exists, however, that the position, irrespective of the individual occupying it and his or her desires, exerts a great deal of influence (32).

Territoriality

Scene: My brother Allan arrives back at Fort Dix after a night of drinking in Philadelphia. He finds another soldier curled up in his bunk, asleep—obviously trying to avoid the hangover he will, like my brother, experience in the morning.

"What the hell do you think you're doing?!" my brother yells.

"Huh?" the sodden soldier replies.

"What the hell are you doing sleepin' in my bunk?!"

"Huh?" the sodden soldier manages to say again.

The sergeant moves in to check what the noise is, arriving in time to watch my brother dump his bunk over in an effort to regain it. The sergeant is mildly amused.

"Hey, Allan, who the hell do you think you are? The Papa Bear? Come off it, that ain't Goldilocks! So what if he's in your bunk? Take his."

Allan opens his mouth to explain, but nothing comes out (33).

My brother laid claim to, and was protecting, "his" territory. Territoriality is characterized by the assumption of proprietary rights toward some geographical area, with the realization that there is no legal basis for those rights (34). What could my brother explain to his sergeant? The bunk is, indeed, not "his," but rather the property of the United States Army. Why did he behave as he did? The liquor? Probably not. The bunk is his because he sleeps on it, because he changes its sheets, and because he has occupied it for several months. It is *his* bunk because he *feels* as if it is his, and that's that!

Territoriality has been studied more extensively in animals than in humans (35), and there is even the question of whether such a drive as territoriality exists in humans at all (36). Nevertheless, we do seem to engage in behaviors that may best be labeled as territorial in nature: we have "our" seat in each classroom; we have "our" place at the dinner table; and we have "our" place on the floor for group meetings.

The territory we lay claim to, the method by which we protect it, and the method by which we invade the territory of others, all may be indicative of our status in our group (37). As our status increases, our territory is likely to increase—we may get a larger work area, a room of our own, or an exclusive key to the executive bathroom. As our territory increases, it is likely also to be more desirable; more centrally located, with better lighting, furniture, and so on. Also, as our status increases, our territory is better protected—other members of the group are less likely to come onto our territory without first clearing it with us (a cough, perhaps, to warn of their intended invasion). Finally, as our status increases we have more freedom to invade the territory of others. For example, we can look over the shoulders of the other members to check on their work, but they would avoid this behavior with us.

One other aspect of territoriality deserves mention: the territory to which we lay claim may be indicative of the position we seek in the group, as well as that which we occupy. De Long (38) found that individuals in a small seminar setting grouped themselves according to their rank or status in the group. Individuals desiring high status, therefore, may best select a place next to those who already possess it. Move close to the power source and it is possible, just possible, that some of it will rub off in your direction.

Facial Expression

"The eyes have it!" a friend of mine liked to exclaim. The eyes reveal mood, depth of feeling (Does she love me?), and a multitude of other things. McCroskey, Larson, and Knapp (39), summarizing the findings of studies focusing on eye contact, found that people use eye contact when they seek feedback, want to signal that they may be communicated with, want to convey the need for involvement, and want to produce anxiety in others. People avoid eye contact when they want to hide their feelings, when they are tense, when they are interacting with someone they dislike, or when they are attempting to cut off social contact.

We convey a great deal with other features of our face. Our facial gestures express our emotions (40), as well as our level of interest (41). But facial expressions, including eye contact and pupil size, are often context bound. Cline (42) found that whether a face was viewed in or out of context determined how it was perceived. For example, Cline found that a face perceived as glum when alone was perceived as "defeated, jealous, or embarrassed" when paired with a smiling face. When paired with a frowning face, the glum face was perceived as "aloof, independent, or cool." Along the same lines, Secord (43) found that both the cues we attend to and how we interpret them are dictated, in part, by our culture. Isolating a cue from its context, or thinking that one interpretation is *the* interpretation, are pitfalls that must be avoided if we want to increase the effectiveness of our interaction.

Body Movements

Can you look at a newly married couple and tell whether or not they are happy?

Two psychologists at the University of Utah, Ernst Beier and Daniel Sternberg, say yes. They maintain that the happiness or unhappiness of newlyweds is reflected in their "body language."

Happily married couples subconsciously sit closer together than those who are unhappily married. They touch and look at each other more frequently, converse for longer periods of time . . .

Touch, eye contact, open and closed sitting positions, initiative in conversing —these are some of the clues that psychologists Beier and Sternberg describe as "prognostic and might help us make a reasonable prediction as to which marriages are likely to fail" (44).

Individuals in a small group may not be overly concerned with the future happiness of Beier and Sternberg's newlyweds, but the point is well taken: we convey how we feel by the way we position and move our bodies. Group members who engage in a great many extraneous movements, or who constantly change their postural positions, may convey to the others that they are nervous or tense (45). Mehrabian and Friar (46) found that a positive attitude is conveyed by a small backward lean of the torso, close distance, and great eye contact.

Specific gestures consciously employed are often culture-bound. What serves as an obscene gesture in one culture may be either meaningless or mean something entirely different in another culture (47). I had the opportunity during the summer of 1973 to discuss this with my class in Nonverbal Communication. Luckily, there was a sampling of individuals from all over the United States, as well as some from Japan. We found that the so-called "usual" hand gesture used to convey sexual intercourse was not "usual" at all! In fact, whether you came from Long Island, The Bronx, Albuquerque, Sacramento, or Tokyo determined the gesture you used (if you used any at all). Like facial gestures, body movements and gestures are often culture-bound, and so must be interpreted with care.

Vocal Cues

Think back to the time you first asked your father for the family car and he said no. You probably said something in response that, seemingly, should have been okay, that is, it should not have generated too much hostility. But, slam!, his verbal abuse came flying out at you, and you ran for cover. You stammered a series of "but's," as he yelled, "It's not *what* you said, but *how* you said it!" And the odds are your father was correct. Vocal cues provide a great deal of information, and often *how* we say something, and not the words we use, conveys our true meaning.

Our voice conveys personal attributes, emotional states, and personality characteristics. A number of studies found that on the basis of vocal cues alone, listeners agree on the characteristics they ascribe to a speaker. Some of these characteristics are age, height, overall appearance, intelligence, vocation, extraversion, introversion, degree of sociability, and hypertension. Other correctly identified characteristics include ethnic group, level of education attained, and dialect region (48).

Davitz and Davitz (49) identified several voice qualities with different emotional states. A loud voice, high pitch, blaring timbre, and fast rate were associated with active feelings. Passive feelings were associated with a quiet voice, low pitch, resonant timbre, and slow rate.

A number of researchers have concentrated on the vocal cues that indicate anxiety (50). Generally, anxiety relates positively to the number of nonfluencies interjected into a conversation. Nonfluencies include such things as "uh," and "um," stuttering, repetitions, sentence corrections, and hesitations.

As with territoriality, vocal cues also convey status, an important variable affecting human interaction. Harms (51) found that subjects, regardless of their own status, could differentiate among speakers according to their status. These distinctions were verified by the Hollingshead status measure that considers occupation and education. Ellis (52) found that status is conveyed by vocal cues even when a speaker tries to fake his vocal qualities.

It would seem that the best way to avoid revealing anything about yourself is to remain silent. But that won't work either. Silence can be as deafening as speech noises. We use silences for a variety of reasons. For example, we are silent when we are too angry to speak, attentively listening to someone or something, contemplating, in a state of grief, or when staring down an opponent, daring him to make the first move.

Silence can also convey respect or defiance. Consider being silent both at a wild, swinging party and at a funeral. It may be appropriate to the latter, but not to the former. Offering silence when a teacher asks for an answer to his question is often more expressive than stuttering, stammering, or giving the correct response (53). Bruneau (54), in his summary article, describes many of the functions of silence. Silence serves speakers, listeners, and individuals engaged in interpersonal communication ("interactive silences"). The uses of silence are also idiosyncratic; each culture has its own use that may be so indicative of the culture that a speaker's background may be unwittingly revealed.

CONTEXT

Environment

We do not meet and deal with each other in a vacuum. Our interaction takes place in an environment that affects how we feel and behave. Some buildings and rooms encourage us to engage one another, whereas others are designed to keep us apart. Notice how the chairs are arranged in your library, and compare this arrangement to one found in a small conference room. Libraries are arranged to discourage interaction: chairs are usually far apart, face away from each other, and are surrounded with book racks or desks. Conference rooms usually have their chairs close together, facing each other, with no obstacles in the way—all of which encourage interaction.

Sommer (55) found that room size affects interaction: the larger the room, the closer individuals sit, thus increasing interaction; the smaller the room, the further apart individuals sit, thus decreasing interaction. In general, Sommer found that eight feet was a comfortable distance for conducting conversations.

The aesthetic qualities of a room also affect how we behave. Maslow and Mintz (56) had subjects rate pictures of faces in a beautiful, an ugly, and an average room. Subjects in the beautiful room gave significantly higher ratings to the pictures than subjects in either of the other two rooms. In a follow-up study, Mintz (57) focused upon the prolonged effects of occupying a beautiful or an ugly room. He noted that subjects in the ugly room had such reactions as monotony, fatigue, headaches, irritability, and hostility, whereas those in the beautiful room had feelings of comfort, pleasure, enjoyment, and energy.

Colors also affect us. Reds and oranges are usually perceived as bright and alive, deep blues and shades of gray are usually considered dull and drab (58). There is a story (I do not know how true it is, but the point is worth noting) about a football coach who painted his own team's locker room red-orange, and the opposing team's locker room deep blue, all in an effort to spur his men on while slowing down the "enemy." And it worked!

Architecture can create moods, set moods, and establish a style. Interaction in a church is different from interaction at a back lawn party, possibly because churches seem to convey a definite message: be quiet, still, reverent. Tall buildings are responded to differently than short ones. I can remember showing friends around New York City and learning that the residual message, what they remembered when the trip was over, was the feeling of smallness that overcame them when confronted with one skyscraper after the other (59).

Body Rhythms

"From the moment of conception until death rhythm is as much a part of our structure as our flesh and bones. Most of us are dimly aware that we fluctuate in energy, mood, well-being, and performance each day, and that there are longer, more subtle behavioral alterations each week, each month, season, and year" (60).

Ask yourself the following questions: (61) Do you rise slowly and reluctantly, or do you work best in the morning? Do you have up days and down days? When does food taste best to you? When do you hear best? At what hour do you defecate? Do drugs affect you differently at different times? When do you prefer to make love? If you keep a diary of your answers, you should uncover some of our own rhythms. Although life may seem a series of random changes, it is not: the rhythms that exist are evident—all we have to do is look for them (62).

Lane (63), in a review of some of the effects of circadian rhythms ("around a day") found that members of a group synchronize with each other: removal of an individual from his group may cause changes in his sodium, potassium, and calcium levels in his urine, as well as variations in his body temperature.

Dreiske (64) believes that we have three overriding biological rhythms or cycles: a physical cycle, a sensitivity cycle, and an intellectual cycle. He reports that several companies in Japan make good use of the information provided by each worker's physical cycle, a twenty-three-day cycle with critical days occurring on the first, the 11½, and the twenty-third day of the cycle, to help curb accidents (see Dreiske for instruction on how to chart the three cycles). A critical day indicates a change in the direction of the cycle from below to above, or above to below, the median line. This is an unstable period when chances of an accident increase. Investigations in these Japanese companies revealed that most accidents occurred to individuals who, on the day of their accident, were experiencing a critical period in their physical cycle. The solution adopted was simple: each employee's physical cycle was charted, and warnings went out automatically when a critical period was about to occur. Although there are other feasible explanations for why accidents decreased in each factory (e.g., workers, in general, became more aware of safety procedures by receiving a reminder slip every eleven days), the point is that they did decrease by half.

The next time you fail a test or have a fight with one of your friends, check your chart and see if it is a critical day for you. Then try to explain it to the teacher or the friend. And good luck!

Although the area of nonverbal communication has been broken down into what may be presumed to be its essential component parts, it should be clear that the process of analysis is an artificial one. As we deal with the other members in our groups, the nonverbal cues we receive are synthesized into a coherent message. We are simultaneously confronted by clothing, shapes and smells, patterns of interaction, including the use of space and territory. We see faces and watch bodies move, and when mouths open and sounds come out, we are bombarded with still more cues that have to be interpreted. Yet still more cues jolt us: we exist in an external and internal environment that forms the context in which we do our interpreting.

All of these cues must be received and processed immediately, for we have to react and interact with the other members of our group. It is not an individual cue we respond to, but rather a synthesis of many cues, each interacting with the others to produce affects that are unpredictable by looking at only one cue at a time.

The complexity of the situation is overwhelming, especially in light of the other elements of the communication barrage we must contend with: verbal and nonverbal communication immerse us in a total communication situation where cues are simultaneously and constantly sent and received. And the fact that nonverbal communication is difficult to define and even harder to explain does not seem to matter as we effectively respond to "a secret code that is nowhere, known by none, and understood by all" (65).

NOTES

1. John Wenburg and William Wilmot, *The Personal Communication Process* (New York: John Wiley & Sons, Inc., 1973), p. 97.
Also see: Abne Eisenberg and Ralph Smith, *Nonverbal Communication* (New York: The Bobbs-Merrill, Co., Inc., 1971); and Albert Mehrabian, *Silent Messages* (Belmont, Calif.: Wadsworth Publishing Co., Inc., 1971).
2. For a review of definitions, see: Randall Harrison, "Nonverbal Behavior: An Approach to Human Communication," *Approaches to Human Communication*, R. Rudd and B. Ruben, eds. (New York: Spartan Books, 1972), pp. 253–268.
3. For a discussion of the problems in separating nonverbal *behavior* from nonverbal *communication*, see: Morton Wiener, Shannon Devoe, Stuart Rubinow, and Jesse Geller, "Nonverbal Behavior and Nonverbal Communication," *Psychological Review*, 79 (1972), pp. 185–214.
4. Harrison, op. cit.
5. Mark Knapp, *Nonverbal Communication in Human Interaction* (New York: Holt, Rinehart and Winston, Inc., 1972).
6. William Brooks, *Speech Communication* (Dubuque, Iowa: William C. Brown Company, Publishers, 1971), pp. 101–118.
7. Ronald Applbaum, Karl Anatol, Ellis Hays, Owen Jenson, Richard Porter, and Jerry Mandel, *Fundamental Concepts in Human Communication* (San Francisco: Canfield Press, 1973), p. 109.
8. A. Lerner and F. Lowe, *My Fair Lady*, 1956.
9. Lawrence Rosenfeld, *Human Interaction in the Small Group Setting* (Columbus, Ohio: Charles E. Merrill, Publishers, 1973), pp. 183–184.
10. R. Hoult, "Experimental Measurement of Clothing As a Factor in Some Social Ratings of Selected American Men," *American Sociological Review*, 19 (1954), pp. 324–328.
11. *Albuquerque Tribune*, June 14, 1973, p. 1.
12. See: K. Gibbons, "Communication Aspects of Women's Clothes and Their Relation to Fashionability," *British Journal of Social and Clinical Psy-*

chology, 8 (1969), pp. 301–312; J. Kelley and S. Star, "Dress and Ideology: The Nonverbal Communication of Political Attitudes," paper presented to the Annual Meeting of the American Sociological Association, 1971; W. McKeachie, "Lipstick As a Determiner of First Impressions of Personality: An Experiment for the General Psychology Course," *Journal of Social Psychology*, 36 (1952), pp. 241–244; J. Schwartz, "Men's Clothing and the Negro," *Phylon*, 24 (1963), pp. 224–231.

13. L. Aiken, "Relationships of Dress to Selected Measures of Personality in Undergraduate Women," *Journal of Social Psychology*, 59 (1963), pp. 119–128.

14. Peter Andersen, Thomas Jensen, and Lyle King, "The Effects of Homophilous Dress and Hair Styles on Credibility and Comprehension," paper presented to the International Communication Association Annual Convention, 1972.

15. Paul Hamilton and Richard Hunter, "The Effects of Bralessness on Perception of Communication Sources." Paper presented to the International Communication Association Annual Convention, 1972.

16. M. Lefkowitz, R. Blake, and J. Mouton, "Status Factors in Pedestrian Violation of Traffic Signals," *Journal of Abnormal and Social Psychology*, 51 (1955), pp. 704–706.

17. See: J. Mills and E. Aronson, "Opinion Change As a Function of the Communicator's Attractiveness and Desire to Influence," *Journal of Personality and Social Psychology*, 1 (1965), pp. 73–77; R. Widgery and B. Webster, "The Effects of Physical Attractiveness Upon Perceived Initial Credibility," *Michigan Speech Association Journal*, 4 (1969).

18. W. Wells and B. Siegel, "Stereotyped Somatypes," *Psychological Reports*, 8 (1961), pp. 77–78.

19. Sam Keen, "We Do Not *Have* Bodies, We *Are* Our Bodies', A Conversation with Stanley Keleman about Bioenergetics and the Language of the Body," *Psychology Today*, 7 (September 1973), p. 65.

20. B. Bettelheim and M. Janowitz, *Social Change and Prejudice* (New York: The Free Press, 1964), p. 143.

21. B. Stark and B. Huzlett, "Effects of Olfactory Experience on Aggression in Mus Musculus and Peromyscus Maniculatus," *Behavioral Biology*, 7 (1972), pp. 268–269.

22. Eric Berne, *Sex in Human Loving* (New York: Pocket Books, 1972), pp. 105–106.

23. Edward Hall, *The Hidden Dimension* (Garden City, N. Y.: Anchor Books, 1969), pp. 113–130.

24. See: S. Jones, "A Comparative Proxemics Analysis of Dyadic Interaction in Selected Subcultures of New York City," *Journal of Social Psychology*, 84 (1971), pp. 35–44; S. Jones and J. Aiello, "The Acquisition of Proxemic Norms of Behavior: A Study of Lower-Class Black and Middle-Class White Children at Three Grade Levels," unpublished paper, 1972.

25. See: K. Little, Personal Space," *Journal of Experimental Social Psychology*, 1 (1965), pp. 237–247; M. Justice, *Field Dependency, Intimacy of Topic and Interaction Distance*, diss., University of Florida, Gainesville, 1969; F. Willis, Initial Speaking Distance As a Function of the Speaker's Relationship," *Psychonomic Science*, 5 (1966), pp. 221–222.

26. Nancy Russo, "Connotation of Seating Arrangement," *Cornell Journal of Social Relations*, 2 (1967), pp. 37–44.

27. D. Lott and R. Sommer, "Seating Arrangements and Status," *Journal of Personality and Social Psychology*, 7 (1967), pp. 90–94.

188   GROUP COMMUNICATION

28. F. Strodtbeck and L. Hook, "The Social Dimensions of a Twelve Man Jury Table," *Sociometry*, 24 (1961), pp. 397–415.

29. A. Hare and R. Bales, "Seating Position and Small Group Interaction," *Sociometry*, 26 (1963), pp. 480–486.

30. R. Sommer, "Further Studies of Small Group Ecology," *Sociometry*, 28 (1965), pp. 337–348.

31. See: Raymond Adams, "Location As a Feature of Instructional Interaction," *Merrill-Palmer Quarterly*, 15 (1969), pp. 309–321; Raymond Adams and B. Biddle, *Realities of Teaching: Explorations with Video Tape* (New York: Holt, Rinehart and Winston, Inc., 1970); Donn Byrne, "The Influence of Propinquity and Opportunities for Interaction on Classroom Relationships," *Human Relations*, 14 (1961), pp. 63–70; J. Getzels, "A Social Psychology of Education," *Handbook of Social Psychology*, 2nd ed., G. Lindzey and E. Aronson, eds. (Reading, Mass.: Addison-Wesley Publishing Co., Inc., 1969), pp. 459–537, esp. 502–519; Herbert Walbert, "Physical and Psychological Distance in the Classroom," *School Review*, 77 (1969), pp. 64–70.

32. R. Sommer, *Personal Space* (Englewood Cliffs, N. J.: Prentice-Hall, Inc., 1969), p. 110ff.

33. As related to me by my brother on a weekend trip to The Bronx.

34. Lawrence Rosenfeld, op. cit., p. 196.

35. See: Robert Ardrey, *The Territorial Imperative* (New York: Atheneum Publishers, 1967); Robert Ardrey, *The Social Contract* (New York: Atheneum Publishers, 1970); Edward Hall, *The Hidden Dimension* (Garden City, N. Y.: Anchor Books, 1969); F. Mowat, *Never Cry Wolf* (New York: Dell Publishing Co., Inc., 1963).

36. Alexander Alland, *The Human Imperative* (New York: Columbia University Press, 1972).

37. Gerald Goldhaber, *Organizational Communication* (Dubuque, Iowa: William C. Brown Company, Publishers, 1974).

38. A. De Long, "Dominance—Territorial Relations in a Small Group," *Environment and Behavior*, 2 (1970), pp. 170–191.

39. James McCroskey, Carl Larson, and Mark Knapp, *An Introduction to Interpersonal Communication* (Englewood Cliffs, N. J.: Prentice-Hall, Inc., 1971), pp. 110–114.

40. See: C. Osgood, "Dimensionality of the Semantic Space for Communication Via Facial Expressions," *Scandinavian Journal of Psychology*, 7 (1966), pp. 1–30; J. Shapiro, "Responsivity to Facial and Linguistic Cues," *Journal of Communication*, 18 (1968), pp. 11–17; J. Shapiro, C. Foster, and T. Powell, "Facial and Bodily Cues of Genuineness, Empathy, and Warmth," *Journal of Clinical Psychology*, 24 (1968), pp. 233–236.

41. E. Hess, "Attitude and Pupil Size," *Scientific American*, 212 (1965), pp. 46–54.

42. M. Cline, "The Influence of Social Context on the Perception of Faces," *Journal of Personality*, 25 (1956), pp. 142–158.

43. P. Secord, "Facial Features and Inference Processes in Interpersonal Perception," *Person Perception and Interpersonal Behavior*, R. Tagiuri and L. Petrullo, eds. (Stanford: University of California Press, 1958), pp. 300–316.

44. *Albuquerque Journal*, April 8, *Parade Magazine* (section), p. 6.

45. E. Davis, *The Elementary School Child and His Posture Patterns* (New York: Appleton-Century-Crofts, 1958).

46. A. Mehrabian and J. Friar, "Encoding of Attitude by a Seated Com-

municator Via Posture and Positional Cues," *Journal of Consulting and Clinical Psychology*, 33 (1969), p. 330–336.

47. Harrison, op. cit.

48. See: D. Addington, "The Effect of Selected Vocal Characteristics to Personality Perception, *Speech Monographs*, 35 (1968), p. 498; E. Kramer, "Judgment of Personal Characteristics and Emotions from Nonverbal Properties of Speech," *Psychological Bulletin*, 60 (1963), pp. 408–420; E. Kramer, "Personality Stereotypes in Voice: A Reconsideration of the Data," *Journal of Social Psychology*, 62 (1964), pp. 247–251; G. Nerbonne, *The Identification of Speaker Characteristics on the Basis of Aural Cues*, diss., Michigan State University, 1967; W. Pearce and R. Conklin, "Nonverbal Vocalic Communication and Perceptions of a Speaker," *Speech Monographs*, 38 (1961), pp. 235–241; J. Starkweather, "Vocal Communication of Personality and Human Feelings," *Journal of Communication*, 11 (1961), pp. 63–72.

49. J. Davitz and L. Davitz, "Nonverbal Vocal Communication of Feelings," *Journal of Communication*, 11 (1961), pp. 81–86.

50. See: Gerald Goldhaber, *The Effect of 'Ego-Involvement' on Selected Dimensions of Speech Production*, diss., Purdue University, 1970; Frieda Goldman-Eisler, "Speech Analysis and Mental Processes," *Language and Speech*, 1 (1958), pp. 59–75; G. Mahl, "Disturbances and Silences in the Patient's Speech in Psychotherapy," *Journal of Abnormal and Social Psychology*, 53 (1956), pp. 1–15; G. Mahl, "Some Observations about Research on Vocal Behavior," *Disorders of Communication*, 42 (1964), pp. 466–483.

51. L. Harms, "Listener Judgments of Status Cues in Content Free Speech," *Quarterly Journal of Speech*, 47 (1961), pp. 164–168.

52. D. Ellis, "Speech and Social Status in America," *Social Forces*, 14 (1967), pp. 431–437.

53. Gail Myers and Michele Myers, *The Dynamics of Human Communication* (New York: McGraw-Hill, Inc, 1973), pp. 167–171.

54. Thomas Bruneau, "Communicative Silences: Forms and Functions," *Journal of Communication*, 23 (1973), pp. 17–46.

55. R. Sommer, "The Distance for Comfortable Conversation: A Further Study," *Sociometry*, 25 (1962), pp. 111–116.

56. A. Maslow and N. Mintz, "Effects of Esthetic Surroundings: Initial Effects of These Esthetic Surroundings Upon Perceiving 'Energy' and 'Well-Being' in Faces," *Journal of Psychology*, 41 (1956), pp. 247–254.

57. N. Mintz, "Effects of Esthetic Surroundings: II. Prolonged and Repeated Experience in a 'Beautiful' and an 'Ugly' Room," *Journal of Psychology*, 41 (1956), pp. 459–466.

58. Max Lüscher, *The Lüscher Color Test*, trans. by Ian Scott (New York: Random House, Inc., 1969).

59. Dean Barnlund, ed., *Interpersonal Communication: Survey and Studies* (Boston: Houghton Mifflin Company, 1968), pp. 511–542.

60. Bertram Brown, "Foreword," *Biological Rhythms in Psychiatry and Medicine*, G. Luce (Washington, D.C.: National Institute of Mental Health, 1970), p. iv.

61. Gay Gaer Luce, "Understanding Body Time in the Twenty-Four Hour City," *New York* (November 15, 1971), pp. 38–43.

62. For a comprehensive and readable survey of the literature pertaining to body rhythms, see: Gay Gaer Luce, *Biological Rhythms in Psychiatry and Medicine* (Washington, D.C.: National Institute of Mental Health, 1970).

63. Leroy Lane, "Communicative Behavior and Biological Rhythms," *Speech Teacher*, **20** (1971), pp. 16–20.

64. Paul Dreiske, "Are There Strange Forces in Our Lives?," *Family Safety*, **31** (1972), pp. 15–16, 23.

65. E. Sapir, Quoted in Mark Knapp, op. cit., p. 91.

STUDY GUIDE
QUESTIONS

1. What are the three sources of pressure for informal social communication?
2. What are the two major sources of pressure toward uniformity among group members?
3. What do we mean by "instrumental" communication?
4. What sources act on members to locomote in the group or to move from one group to another?
5. What role does emotional expression play in producing forces to communicate?

◄ Informal Social Communication

LEON FESTINGER

The importance of strict theory in developing and guiding programs of research is becoming more and more recognized today. Yet there is considerable disagreement about exactly how strict and precise a theoretical formulation must be at various stages in the development of a body of knowledge. Certainly there are many who feel that some "theorizing" is too vague and indefinite to be of much use. It is also argued that such vague and broad "theorizing" may actually hinder the empirical development of an area of knowledge.

On the other hand there are many who express dissatisfaction with instances of very precise theories which do exist here and there, for somehow or other a precise and specific theory seems to them to leave out the "real" psychological problem. These persons seem to be more concerned with those aspects of the problem which the precise theory has not yet touched. From this point of view it is argued that too precise and too strict theorizing may also hinder the empirical development of an area of knowledge.

Leon Festinger, "Informal Social Communication," *Psychological Review*, **57** (1950), 271–282. Copyright © 1950 by the American Psychological Association. Reprinted by permission.

It is probably correct that if a theory becomes too precise too early it can have tendencies to become sterile. It is also probably correct that if a theory stays too vague and ambiguous for too long it can be harmful in that nothing can be done to disprove or change it. This probably means that theories, when vague, should at least be stated in a form which makes the adding of precision possible as knowledge increases. It also probably means that theory should run ahead, but not too far ahead, of the data so that the trap of premature precision can be avoided. It certainly means that theories, whether vague or precise, must be in such a form that empirical data can influence them.

This article is a statement of the theoretical formulations which have been developed in the process of conducting a program of empirical and experimental research in informal social communication. It has grown out of our findings thus far and is in turn guiding the future course of the research program (1). This program of research concerns itself with finding and explaining the facts concerning informal, spontaneous communication among persons and the consequences of the process of communication. It would seem that a better understanding of the dynamics of such communication would in turn lead to a better understanding of various kinds of group functioning. The theories and hypotheses presented below vary considerably in precision, specificity and the degree to which corroborating data exist. Whatever the state of precision, however, the theories are empirically oriented and capable of being tested.

Since we are concerned with the spontaneous process of communication which goes on during the functioning of groups we must first differentiate the variety of types of communication which occur according to the theoretical conditions which give rise to tendencies to communicate. It is plausible to assume that separating the sources or origins of pressures to communicate that may act on a member of a group will give us fruitful areas to study. This type of differentiation or classification is, of course, adequate only if it leads to the separation of conceptually clear areas of investigation within which communication can be organized into statable theoretical and empirical laws.

We shall here deal with those few of the many possible sources of pressures to communicate in which we have thus far been able to make theoretical and empirical progress. We shall elaborate on the theory for regarding them as giving rise to pressures to communicate and on specific hypotheses concerning the laws of communication which stem from these sources.

I. Pressures Toward Uniformity in a Group

One major source of forces to communicate is the pressure toward uniformity which may exist within a group. These are pressures which, for one reason or another, act toward making members of a group agree concerning some issue or conform with respect to some behavior pattern. It is stating the obvious, of course, to say that these pressures must be exerted by means of a process of communication among the members of the group. One must also specify the conditions under which such pressures toward uniformity arise, both on a conceptual and an operational level so that in any specific situation it is possible to say whether or not such pressures exist. We shall, in the following discussion, elaborate on two major sources of pressures toward uniformity among people, namely, social reality and group locomotion.

1. *Social reality:* Opinions, attitudes, and beliefs which people hold must have some basis upon which they rest for their validity. Let us as a start abstract from the many kinds of bases for the subjective validity of such opinions, attitudes, and beliefs one continuum along which they may be said to lie. This continuum we may call a scale of degree of physical reality. At one end of this continuum, namely, complete dependence upon physical reality, we might have an example such as this: A person looking at a surface might think that the surface is fragile or he might think that the surface is unbreakable. He can very easily take a hammer, hit the surface, and quickly be convinced as to whether the opinion he holds is correct or incorrect. After he has broken the surface with a hammer it will probably make little dent upon his opinion if another person should tell him that the surface is unbreakable. It would thus seem that where there is a high degree of dependence upon physical reality for the subjective validity of one's beliefs or opinions the dependence upon other people for the confidence one has in these opinions or beliefs is very low.

At the other end of the continuum where the dependence upon physical reality is low or zero, we might have an example such as this: A person looking at the results of a national election feels that if the loser had won, things would be in some ways much better than they are. Upon what does the subjective validity of this belief depend? It depends to a large degree on whether or not other people share his opinion and feel the same way he does. If there are other people around him who believe the same thing, then his opinion is, to him, valid. If there are not others who believe the same thing, then his opinion is, in the same sense, not valid. Thus where the dependence upon physical reality is low the dependence upon social reality is correspondingly high. An opinion, a belief, an attitude is "correct," "valid," and "proper" to the extent that it is anchored in a group of people with similar beliefs, opinions, and attitudes.

This statement, however, cannot be generalized completely. It is clearly not necessary for the validity of someone's opinion that everyone else in the world think the way he does. It is only necessary that the members of that group to which he refers this opinion or attitude think the way he does. It is not necessary for a Ku Klux Klanner that some northern liberal agree with him in his attitude toward Negroes, but it is eminently necessary that there be other people who also are Ku Klux Klanners and who do agree with him. The person who does not agree with him is seen as different from him and not an adequate referent for his opinion. The problem of independently defining which groups are and which groups are not appropriate reference groups for a particular individual and for a particular opinion or attitude is a difficult one. It is to some extent inherently circular since an appropriate reference group tends to be a group which does share a person's opinions and attitudes, and people tend to locomote *into* such groups and *out of* groups which do not agree with them.

From the preceding discussion it would seem that if a discrepancy in opinion, attitude, or belief exists among persons who are members of an appropriate reference group, forces to communicate will arise. It also follows that the less "physical reality" there is to validate the opinion or belief, the greater will be the importance of the social referent, the group, and the greater will be the forces to communicate.

2. *Group locomotion:* Pressures toward uniformity among members of a group may arise because such uniformity is desirable or necessary in order for the group to move toward some goal. Under such circumstances there are a number of things one can say about the magnitude of pressures toward uniformity.

(a) They will be greater to the extent that the members perceive that group movement would be facilitated by uniformity.

(b) The pressures toward uniformity will also be greater, the more dependent the various members are on the group in order to reach their goals. The degree to which other groups are substitutable as a means toward individual or group goals would be one of the determinants of the dependence of the member on the group.

We have elaborated on two sources of pressure toward uniformity among members of groups. The same empirical laws should apply to communications which result from pressures toward uniformity irrespective of the particular reasons for the existence of the pressures. We shall now proceed to enumerate a set of hypotheses concerning communication which results from pressures toward uniformity.

II. Hypotheses About Communication Resulting from Pressures toward Uniformity

Communications which arise from pressures toward uniformity in a group may be seen as "instrumental" communications. That is, the communication is not an end in itself but rather is a means by which the communicator hopes to influence the person he addresses in such a way as to reduce the discrepancy that exists between them. Thus we should examine the determinants of: (1) when a member communicates, (2) to whom he communicates and (3) the reactions of the recipient of the communication.

(1) Determinants of the magnitude of pressure to communicate:

Hypothesis 1a: *The pressure on members to communicate to others in the group concerning "item x" increases monotonically with increase in the perceived discrepancy in opinion concerning "item x" among members of the group.*

Remembering that we are considering only communication that results from pressures toward uniformity, it is clear that if there are no discrepancies in opinion, that is, uniformity already exists in the group, there will be no forces to communicate. It would be plausible to expect the force to communicate to increase rapidly from zero as the state of affairs departs from uniformity.

Hypothesis 1b: *The pressure on a member to communicate to others in the group concerning "item x" increases monotonically with increase in the degree of relevance of "item x" to the functioning of the group.*

If "item x" is unimportant to the group in the sense of not being associated with any of the values or activities which are the basis for the existence of the group, or if it is more or less inconsequential for group locomotion, then there should be few or no forces to communicate even when there are perceived discrepancies in opinion. As "item x" becomes more important for the group (more relevant), the forces to communicate when any given magnitude of perceived discrepancy exists, should increase.

Corroborative evidence for this hypothesis is found in an experiment by Schachter (8) where discussion of the same issue was experimentally made relevant for some groups and largely irrelevant for others. It is clear from the data that where the discussion was relevant to the functioning of the group there existed stronger forces to communicate and to influence the other members. Where the issue is a relevant one the members make longer individual contributions to the discussion and there are many fewer prolonged pauses in the discussion.

Hypothesis 1c: *The pressure on members to communicate to others in the group concerning "item x" increases monotonically with increase in the cohesiveness of the group.*

Cohesiveness of a group is here defined as the resultant of all the forces acting on the members to remain in the group. These forces may depend on the attractiveness or unattractiveness of either the prestige of the group, members in the group, or the activities in which the group engages. If the total attraction toward the group is zero, no forces to communicate should arise; the members may as easily leave the group as stay in it. As the forces to remain in the group increase (given perceived discrepancies in opinion and given a certain relevance of the item to the functioning of the group) the pressures to communicate will increase.

Data from an experiment by Back (1) support this hypothesis. In this experiment groups of high and low cohesiveness were experimentally created using three different sources of attraction to the group, namely, liking the members, prestige attached to belonging, and possibility of getting a reward for performance in the group activity. For each of the three types of attraction to the group the more cohesive groups were rated as proceeding at a more intense rate in the discussion than the corresponding less cohesive groups. In addition, except for the groups where the attraction was the possibility of reward (perhaps due to wanting to finish and get the reward) there was more total amount of attempted exertion of influence in the highly cohesive groups than in the less cohesive groups. In short, highly cohesive groups, having stronger pressures to communicate, discussed the issue at a more rapid pace and attempted to exert more influence.

(2) Determinants of choice of recipient for communications:

Hypothesis 2a: *The force to communicate about "item x" to* A PAR-TICULAR MEMBER *of the group will increase as the discrepancy in opinion between that member and the communicator increases.*

We have already stated in Hypothesis 1a that the pressure to communicate in general will increase as the perceived non-uniformity in the group increases. In addition the force to communicate will be strongest toward those whose opinions are most different from one's own and will, of course, be zero towards those in the group who at the time hold the same opinion as the communicator. In other words, people will tend to communicate to those within the group whose opinions are most different from their own.

There is a clear corroboration of this hypothesis from a number of studies. In the previously mentioned experiment by Schachter (8) the distribution of opinions expressed in the group was always as follows: Most of the members' opinions clustered within a narrow range of each other while one member, the deviate, held and maintained an extremely divergent point of view. About five times as many communications were addressed to the holder of the divergent point of view as were addressed to the others.

In an experiment by Festinger and Thibaut (5) the discussion situation was set up so that members' opinions on the issue spread over a considerable range. Invariably 70 to 90 per cent of the communications were addressed to those who held opinions at the extremes of the distribution. The curve of number of communications received falls off very rapidly as the opinion of the recipient moves away from the extreme of the distribution. The hypothesis would seem to be well substantiated.

Hypothesis 2b: *The force to communicate about "item x" to* A PAR-TICULAR PERSON *will decrease to the extent that he is perceived as not a member of the group or to the extent that he is not wanted as a member of the group.*

From the previous hypothesis it follows that communications will tend to be addressed mainly toward those with extreme opinions within the group. This does not hold, however, for any arbitrarily defined group. The present hypothesis, in effect, states that such relationships will apply only within *psychological* groups, that is, collections of people that exist as groups psychologically for the members. Communications will tend not to be addressed towards those who are not members of the group.

The study by Schachter (8) and the study by Festinger and Thibaut (5) both substantiate this hypothesis. In Schachter's experiment those group members who do not want the person holding the extremely divergent point of view to remain in the group tend to stop communicating to him towards the end of the discussion. In the experiment by Festinger and Thibaut, when the subjects have the perception that the persons present include different kinds of people with a great variety of interests, there tends to be less communication toward the extremes in the last half of the discussion after the rejection process has had time to develop. In short, communication towards those with different opinions decreases if they are seen as not members of the *psychological* group.

Hypothesis 2c: *The force to communicate "item x" to a particular member will increase the more it is perceived that the communication will change that member's opinion in the desired direction.*

A communication which arises because of the existence of pressures toward uniformity is made in order to exert a force on the recipient in a particular direction, that is, to push him to change his opinion so that he will agree more closely with the communicator. If a member is perceived as very resistant to changing his opinion, the force to communicate to him decreases. If it seems that a particular member will be changed as the result of a communication so as to increase the discrepancy between him and the communicator, there will exist a force not to communicate to him. Thus under such conditions there will be tendencies *not* to communicate this particular item to that member.

There is some corroboration for this hypothesis. In a face to face verbal discussion where a range of opinion exists, the factors which this hypothesis points to would be particularly important for those members whose opinions were near the middle of the range. A communication which might influence the member at one extreme to come closer to the middle might at the same time influence the member at the other extreme to move farther away from the middle. We might then expect from this hypothesis that those holding opinions in the middle of the existing range would communicate less (because of the conflict) and would address fewer communications to the whole group (attempting to influence only one person at a time).

A number of observations were conducted to check these derivations. Existing groups of clinical psychologists who were engaging in discussions to reconcile their differences in ratings of applicants were observed. Altogether,

147 such discussions were observed in which at least one member's opinion was in the middle of the existing range. While those with extreme opinions made an average of 3.16 units of communication (number of communications weighted by length of the communication), those with middle opinions made an average of only 2.6 units of communication. While those with extreme opinions addressed 38 per cent of their communications to the whole group, those with middle opinions addressed only 29 per cent of their communications to everyone.

(3) Determinants of change in the recipient of a communication:

Hypothesis 3a: *The amount of change in opinion resulting from receiving a communication will increase as the pressure towards uniformity in the group increases.*

There are two separate factors which contribute to the effect stated in the hypothesis. The greater the pressure towards uniformity, the greater will be the amount of influence exerted by the communications and, consequently, the greater the magnitude of change that may be expected. But the existence of pressures toward uniformity will not only show itself in increased attempts to change the opinions of others. Pressures toward uniformity will also produce greater readiness to change in the members of the group. In other words, uniformity may be achieved by changing the opinions of others and/or by changing one's own opinions. Thus we may expect that with increasing pressure towards uniformity there will be less resistance to change on the part of the members. Both of these factors will contribute to produce greater change in opinion when the pressure toward uniformity is greater.

There is evidence corroborating this hypothesis from the experiment by Festinger and Thibaut (5). In this experiment three degrees of pressure towards uniformity were experimentally induced in different groups. Irrespective of which of two problems were discussed by the group and irrespective of whether they perceived the group to be homogeneously or heterogeneously composed, the results consistently show that high pressure groups change most, medium pressure groups change next most, and low pressure groups change least in the direction of uniformity. While the two factors which contribute to this effect cannot be separated in the data, their joint effect is clear and unmistakable.

Hypothesis 3b: *The amount of change in opinion resulting from receiving a communication will increase as the strength of the resultant force to remain in the group increases for the recipient.*

To the extent that a member wishes to remain in the group, the group has power over that member. By power we mean here the ability to produce real change in opinions and attitudes and not simply change in overt behavior which can also be produced by means of overt threat. If a person is unable to leave a group because of restraints from the outside, the group can then use threats to change overt behavior. Covert changes in opinions and attitudes, however, can only be produced by a group by virtue of forces acting on the member to remain in the group. Clearly the maximum force which the group can successfully induce on a member counter to his own forces can not be greater than the sum of the forces acting on that member to remain in the group. The greater the resultant force to remain in the group, the more effective will be the attempts to influence the member.

This hypothesis is corroborated by two separate studies. Festinger, Schachter and Back (4) investigated the relationship between the cohesiveness of social groups in a housing project (how attractive the group was for its members) and how effectively a group standard relevant to the functioning of the group was maintained. A correlation of .72 was obtained between these two variables. In other words, the greater the attractiveness of the group for the members, the greater was the amount of influence which the group could successfully exert on its members with the result that there existed greater conformity in attitudes and behavior in the more cohesive groups.

Back (1) did a laboratory experiment specifically designed to test this hypothesis. By means of plausible instructions to the subjects he experimentally created groups of high and low cohesiveness, that is, conditions in which the members were strongly attracted to the group and those in which the attraction to the group was relatively weak. The subjects, starting with different interpretations of the same material, were given an opportunity to discuss the matter. Irrespective of the source of the attraction to the group (Back used three different types of attraction in both high and low cohesive conditions) the subjects in the high cohesive groups influenced each other's opinions more than the subjects in the low cohesive groups. In short, the greater the degree of attraction to the group, the greater the amount of influence actually accomplished.

Hypothesis 3c: *The amount of change in opinion resulting from receiving a communication concerning "item x" will decrease with increase in the degree to which the opinions and attitudes involved are anchored in other group memberships or serve important need satisfying functions for the person.*

If the opinion that a person has formed on some issue is supported in some other group than the one which is at present attempting to influence him, he will be more resistant to the attempted influence. Other sources of resistance to being influenced undoubtedly come from personality factors, ego needs and the like.

Specific evidence supporting this hypothesis is rather fragmentary. In the study of social groups in a housing project by Festinger, Schachter and Back (4), the residents were asked whether their social life was mainly outside the project or not. Of those who conformed to the standards of their social groups within the project about 85 per cent reported that their social life was centered mainly within the project. Less than 50 per cent of those who did not conform to the standards of the project social group, however, reported that their social life was centered mainly in the project. It is likely that they were able to resist the influences from within the project when their opinions and attitudes were supported in outside groups.

The experiments by Schachter (8) and by Festinger and Thibaut (5) used the same discussion problem in slightly different situations. In the former experiment subjects identified themselves and verbally supported their opinions in face-to-face discussion. In the latter experiment the subjects were anonymous, communicating only by written messages on which the sender of the message was not identified. Under these latter conditions many more changes in opinion were observed than under the open verbal discussion situation even though less time was spent in discussion when they wrote notes. This difference in amount of change in opinion is probably due to the ego defensive reactions aroused by openly committing oneself and supporting one's opinions in a face-to-face group.

(4) Determinants of change in relationship among members:

Hypothesis 4a: *The tendency to change the composition of the psychological group (pushing members out of the group) increases as the perceived discrepancy in opinion increases.*

We have already discussed two of the responses which members of groups make to pressures toward uniformity, namely, attempting to influence others and being more ready to be influenced. There is still a third response which serves to move toward uniformity. By rejecting those whose opinions diverge from the group and thus redefining who is and who is not in the psychological group, uniformity can be accomplished. The greater the discrepancy between a person's opinion and the opinion of another, the stronger are the tendencies to exclude the other person from the psychological group.

There is evidence that members of groups do tend to reject those whose opinions are divergent. In the study of social groups within a housing project Festinger, Schachter and Back (4) found that those who did not conform to the standards of their social group were underchosen on a sociometric test, that is, they mentioned more persons as friends of theirs than they received in return. Schachter (8) did an experiment specifically to test whether or not members of groups would be rejected simply for disagreeing on an issue. Paid participants in the groups voiced divergent or agreeing opinions as instructed. In all groups the paid participant who voiced divergent opinion on an issue was rejected on a postmeeting questionnaire concerning whom they wanted to have remain in the group. The same paid participants, when voicing conforming opinions in other groups, were not rejected.

Hypothesis 4b: *When non-conformity exists, the tendency to change the composition of the psychological group increases as the cohesiveness of the group increases and as the relevance of the issue to the group increases.*

We have previously discussed the increase in forces to communicate with increase in cohesiveness and relevance of issue. Similarly, these two variables affect the tendency to reject persons from the group for non-conformity. Theoretically we should expect any variable which affected the force to communicate (which stems from pressures toward uniformity) to affect also the tendency to reject non-conformers in a similar manner. In other words, increases in the force to communicate concerning an item will go along with increased tendency to reject persons who disagree concerning that item.

The previously mentioned experiment by Schachter (8) was designed to test this hypothesis by experimentally varying cohesiveness and relevance in club groups. In this experiment the more cohesive groups do reject the non-conformer more than the less cohesive groups and the groups where the issue is relevant reject the non-conformer more than groups where the issue is not very relevant to the group functioning. Those groups where cohesiveness was low and the issue was not very relevant show little, if any, tendency to reject the deviate.

III. Forces to Change One's Position in a Group

Another important source of forces to communicate are the forces which act on members of groups to locomote (change their position) in the group, or to move from one group to another. Such forces to locomote may stem from the attractiveness of activities associated with a different position in the group or from the status of that position or the like. Thus a new member of a group may wish to become more central in the group, a member of an organization may wish to rise in the status hierarchy, a member of a business firm may want to be promoted or a member of a minority group may desire acceptance by the majority group. These are all instances of forces to locomote in a social structure.

It is plausible that the existence of a force acting on a person in a specific direction produces behavior in that direction. Where locomotion in the desired direction is not possible, at least temporarily, there will exist a force to communicate in that direction. The existence of a force in a specific direction will produce behavior in that direction. One such kind of behavior is communication. This hypothesis is not very different from the hypothesis advanced by Lewin (6) to account for the superior recall of interrupted activities.

An experiment by Thibaut (9) tends to corroborate this theoretical analysis. In his experiment he created two groups, one of high status and privileged, the other of low status and under-privileged. These two groups, equated in other respects, functioned together so that the members of the high status group could play an attractive game. The low status group functioned merely as servants. It was clear that forces were acting on the members of the low status group to move into the other group. As the privilege position of the high status group became clearer and clearer the amount of communication from the low status team to the high status group increased. The number of communications from members of the high status group to the low status group correspondingly decreased. When, in some groups, the status and privilege relationship between the two teams was reversed toward the end of the experimental session, thus reducing the forces to locomote into the other group, the number of communications to that other group correspondingly decreased.

Further corroboration is found in a preliminary experiment, mainly methodologically oriented, conducted by Back et al. (2). In this experiment new items of information were planted with persons at various levels in the hierarchy of a functioning organization. Data on transmission of each of the items of information were obtained through cooperators within the organization who were chosen so as to give adequate coverage of all levels and all sections within it. These cooperators recorded all instances of communication that came to their attention. Of seventeen acts of communication recorded in this manner, eleven were directed upwards in the hierarchy, four toward someone on the same level and only two were directed downwards. The existence of forces to move upward in such a hierarchical organization may be taken for granted. The great bulk of the communications recorded went in the same direction as these forces to locomote.

In considering communication among members of differentiated social structures it is important also to take into account restraints against communication.

Infrequent contact in the ordinary course of events tends to erect restraints against communication. It is undoubtedly easier to communicate a given item to a person whom one sees frequently or to a person to whom one has communicated similar items in the past. The structuring of groups into hierarchies, social clusters, or the like, undoubtedly tends to restrict the amount and type of contact between members of certain different parts or levels of the group and also undoubtedly restricts the content of the communication that goes on between such levels in the ordinary course of events. These restrictions erect restraints against certain types of communication.

There are some data which tend to specify some of the restraints against communication which exist. In the study of the communication of a spontaneous rumor in a community by Festinger, Cartwright et al. (3) it was found that intimacy of friendship tended to increase ease of communication. Persons with more friends in the project heard the rumor more often than those with only acquaintances. Those who had few friends or acquaintances heard the rumor least often. At the same time this factor of intimacy of friendship was not related to how frequently they relayed the rumor to others.

In other words, it was not related to forces to communicate but seemed to function only as a restraint against communicating where friendship did not exist.

There is also some evidence that the mere perception of the existence of a hierarchy sets up restraints against communication between levels. Kelley (7) experimentally created a two-level hierarchy engaging in a problem-solving task during which they could and did communicate within levels and between levels. Control groups were also run with the same task situation but with no status differential involved between the two subgroups. There was more communication between subgroups under these control conditions than where there was a status differential involved.

It seems that, in a hierarchy, there are also restraints against communicating hostility upwards when the hostility is about those on upper levels. In the same experiment by Kelley there was much criticism of the *other group* expressed by both high status and low status members. The proportion of these critical expressions which are directed upward by the low status group is much less, however, than the proportion directed downward by the high status groups.

IV. EMOTIONAL EXPRESSION

An important variety of communications undoubtedly results from the existence of an emotional state in the communicator. The existence of joy, anger, hostility and the like seems to produce forces to communicate. It seems that communications resulting from the existence of an emotional state are consummatory rather than instrumental.

By an instrumental communication we mean one in which the reduction of the force to communicate depends upon the effect of the communication on the recipient. Thus in communication resulting from pressures toward uniformity in a group, the mere fact that a communication is made does not affect the force to communicate. If the effect has been to change the recipient so that he now agrees more closely with the communicator, the force to communicate will be reduced. If the recipient changes in the opposite direction, the force to communicate to him will be increased.

By a consummatory communication we mean one in which the reduction of the force to communicate occurs as a result of the expression and does not depend upon the effect it has on the recipient. Certainly in the case of such communications the reaction of the recipient may introduce new elements into the situation which will affect the force to communicate, but the essence of a consummatory communication is that the simple expression does reduce the force.

Specifically with regard to the communication of hostility and aggression, much has been said regarding its consummatory nature. The psychoanalytic theories of catharsis, in particular, develop the notion that the expression of hostility reduces the emotional state of the person. There has, however, been very little experimental work done on the problem. The previously mentioned experiment by Thibaut in which he created a "privileged-underprivileged" relationship between two equated groups has some data on the point. There is evidence that those members of the "underprivileged" groups who expressed their hostility toward the "privileged" groups showed less residual hostility toward them in post-experimental questionnaires. There is, however, no control over the reactions of the recipients of the hostile communications nor over the perceptions of the communicators of what these reactions were. An experiment is now in progress which will attempt to clarify some of these relationships with both negative and positive emotional states.

V. SUMMARY

A series of interrelated hypotheses has been presented to account for data on informal social communication collected in the course of a number of studies. The data come from field studies and from laboratory experiments specifically designed to test the hypotheses.

Three sources of pressures to communicate have been considered:

1. Communication arising from pressures toward uniformity in a group. Here we considered determinants of magnitude of the force to communicate, choice of recipient for the communication, magnitude of change in recipient and magnitude of tendencies to reject nonconformers.

2. Communications arising from forces to locomote in a social structure. Here we considered communications in the direction of a blocked locomotion and restraints against communication arising in differentiated social structures.

3. Communications arising from the existence of emotional states. In this area data are almost completely lacking. Some theoretical distinctions were made and an experiment which is now in progress in this area was outlined.

NOTE

1. This research program consists of a number of coordinated and integrated studies, both in the laboratory and in the field. It is being carried out by the Research Center for Group Dynamics under contract N6onr–23212 NR 151–698 with the Office of Naval Research.

REFERENCES

1. Back, K. The exertion of influence through social communication. *J. abn. soc. Psychol.*, 1950 (in press).
2. ———, Festinger, L., Hymovitch, B., Kelley, H. H., Schachter, S., & Thibaut,

J. The methodological problems of studying rumor transmission. *Human Relations,* 1950 (in press).

3. Festinger, L., Cartwright, D., *et al.* A study of a rumor: its origin and spread. *Human Relations,* 1948, 1, 464–486.

4. ———, Schachter, S., & Back, K. *Social pressures in informal groups: a study of a housing project.* New York: Harper & Bros., 1950.

5. ———, & Thibaut, J. Interpersonal communication in small groups. *J. abn. soc. Psychol.* (in press).

6. Lewin, K. Formalization and progress in psychology. In *Studies in Topological and Vector Psychology I., Univ. Ia. Stud. Child Welf.,* 1940, 16, No. 3.

7. Kelley, H. H. Communication in experimentally created hierarchies. *Human Relations* (in press).

8. Schachter, S. Deviation, rejection, and communication. *J. abn. soc. Psychol.* (in press).

9. Thibaut, J. An experimental study of the cohesiveness of underprivileged groups. *Human Relations,* 1950, 3.

STUDY GUIDE   1. What is Groupthink?

QUESTIONS   2. What are the symptoms of Groupthink?

            3. Why does Groupthink occur?

            4. What examples of Groupthink can you discover that have occurred within the past three years?

            5. How can we guard against Groupthink?

◄ Groupthink

IRVING L. JANIS

"How could we have been so stupid?" President John F. Kennedy asked after he and a close group of advisers had blundered into the Bay of Pigs invasion. For the last two years I have been studying that question, as it applied not only to the Bay of Pigs decision-makers but also to those who led the United States into such other major fiascos as the failure to be prepared for the attack on Pearl Harbor, the Korean War stalemate and the escalation of the Vietnam War.

Stupidity certainly is not the explanation. The men who participated in

"Groupthink," by Irving L. Janis. Reprinted from *PSYCHOLOGY TODAY* Magazine, November, 1971. Copyright © Communication/Research/Machines, Inc.

making the Bay of Pigs decision, for instance, comprised one of the greatest arrays of intellectual talent in the history of American Government—Dean Rusk, Robert McNamara, Douglas Dillon, Robert Kennedy, McGeorge Bundy, Arthur Schlesinger Jr., Allen Dulles and others.

It also seemed to me that explanations were incomplete if they concentrated only on disturbances in the behavior of each individual within a decision-making body: temporary emotional states of elation, fear, or anger that reduce a man's mental efficiency, for example, or chronic blind spots arising from a man's social prejudices or idiosyncratic biases.

I preferred to broaden the picture by looking at the fiascos from the standpoint of group dynamics as it has been explored over the past three decades, first by the great social psychologist Kurt Lewin and later in many experimental situations by myself and other behavioral scientists. My conclusion after poring over hundreds of relevant documents—historical reports about formal group meetings and informal conversations among the members —is that the groups that committed the fiascos were victims of what I call "groupthink."

"Groupy"   In each case study, I was surprised to discover the extent to which each group displayed the typical phenomena of social conformity that are regularly encountered in studies of group dynamics among ordinary citizens. For example, some of the phenomena appear to be completely in line with findings from social-psychological experiments showing that powerful social pressures are brought to bear by the members of a cohesive group whenever a dissident begins to voice his objections to a group consensus. Other phenomena are reminiscent of the shared illusions observed in encounter groups and friendship cliques when the members simultaneously reach a peak of "groupy" feelings.

Above all, there are numerous indications pointing to the development of group norms that bolster morale at the expense of critical thinking. One of the most common norms appears to be that of remaining loyal to the group by sticking with the policies to which the group has already committed itself, even when those policies are obviously working out badly and have unintended consequences that disturb the conscience of each member. This is one of the key characteristics of groupthink.

1984   I use the term groupthink as a quick and easy way to refer to the mode of thinking that persons engage in when *concurrence-seeking* becomes so dominant in a cohesive ingroup that it tends to override realistic appraisal of alternative courses of action. Groupthink is a term of the same order as the words in the newspeak vocabulary George Orwell used in his dismaying world of 1984. In that context, groupthink takes on an invidious connotation. Exactly such a connotation is intended, since the term refers to a deterioration in mental efficiency, reality testing and moral judgments as a result of group pressures.

The symptoms of groupthink arise when the members of decision-making groups become motivated to avoid being too harsh in their judgments of their leaders' or their colleagues' ideas. They adopt a soft line of criticism, even in their own thinking. At their meetings, all the members are amiable and seek complete concurrence on every important issue, with no bickering or conflict to spoil the cozy, "we-feeling" atmosphere.

Kill Paradoxically, soft-headed groups are often hard-hearted when it comes to dealing with outgroups or enemies. They find it relatively easy to resort to dehumanizing solutions—they will readily authorize bombing attacks that kill large numbers of civilians in the name of the noble cause of persuading an unfriendly government to negotiate at the peace table. They are unlikely to pursue the more difficult and controversial issues that arise when alternatives to a harsh military solution come up for discussion. Nor are they inclined to raise ethical issues that carry the implication that *this fine group of ours, with its humanitarianism and its high-minded principles, might be capable of adopting a course of action that is inhumane and immoral.*

Norms There is evidence from a number of social-psychological studies that as the members of a group feel more accepted by the others, which is a central feature of increased group cohesiveness, they display less overt conformity to group norms. Thus we would expect that the more cohesive a group becomes, the less the members will feel constrained to censor what they say out of fear of being socially punished for antagonizing the leader or any of their fellow members.

In contrast, the groupthink type of conformity tends to increase as group cohesiveness increases. Groupthink involves nondeliberate suppression of critical thoughts as a result of internalization of the group's norms, which is quite different from deliberate suppression on the basis of external threats of social punishment. The more cohesive the group, the greater the inner compulsion on the part of each member to avoid creating disunity, which inclines him to believe in the soundness of whatever proposals are promoted by the leader or by a majority of the group's members.

In a cohesive group, the danger is not so much that each individual will fail to reveal his objections to what the others propose but that he will think the proposal is a good one, without attempting to carry out a careful, critical scrutiny of the pros and cons of the alternatives. When groupthink becomes dominant, there also is considerable suppression of deviant thoughts, but it takes the form of each person's deciding that his misgivings are not relevant and should be set aside, that the benefit of the doubt regarding any lingering uncertainties should be given to the group consensus.

Stress I do not mean to imply that all cohesive groups necessarily suffer from groupthink. All ingroups may have a mild tendency toward groupthink, displaying one or another of the symptoms from time to time, but it need not be so dominant as to influence the quality of the group's final decision. Neither do I mean to imply that there is anything necessarily inefficient or harmful about group decisions in general. On the contrary, a group whose members have properly defined roles, with traditions concerning the procedures to follow in pursuing a critical inquiry, probably is capable of making better decisions than any individual group member working alone.

The problem is that the advantages of having decisions made by groups are often lost because of powerful psychological pressures that arise when the members work closely together, share the same set of values and, above all, face a crisis situation that puts everyone under intense stress.

The main principle of groupthink, which I offer in the spirit of Parkinson's Law, is this: *The more amiability and esprit de corps there is among the members of a policy-making ingroup, the greater the danger that independent critical thinking will be replaced by groupthink, which is likely to result in irrational and dehumanizing actions directed against outgroups.*

Symptoms   In my studies of high-level governmental decision-makers, both civilian and military, I have found eight main symptoms of groupthink.

1. *Invulnerability.* Most or all of the members of the ingroup share an *illusion* of invulnerability that provides for them some degree of reassurance about obvious dangers and leads them to become overoptimistic and willing to take extraordinary risks. It also causes them to fail to respond to clear warnings of danger.

The Kennedy ingroup, which uncritically accepted the Central Intelligence Agency's disastrous Bay of Pigs plan, operated on the false assumption that they could keep secret the fact that the United States was responsible for the invasion of Cuba. Even after news of the plan began to leak out, their belief remained unshaken. They failed even to consider the danger that awaited them: a worldwide revulsion against the U.S.

A similar attitude appeared among the members of President Lyndon B. Johnson's ingroup, the "Tuesday Cabinet," which kept escalating the Vietnam War despite repeated setbacks and failures. "There was a belief," Bill Moyers commented after he resigned, "that if we indicated a willingness to use our power, they [the North Vietnamese] would get the message and back away from an all-out confrontation. . . . There was a confidence—it was never bragged about, it was just there—that when the chips were really down, the other people would fold."

A most poignant example of an illusion of invulnerability involves the ingroup around Admiral H. E. Kimmel, which failed to prepare for the possibility of a Japanese attack on Pearl Harbor despite repeated warnings. Informed by his intelligence chief that radio contact with Japanese aircraft carriers had been lost, Kimmel joked about it: "What, you don't know where the carriers are? Do you mean to say that they could be rounding Diamond Head (at Honolulu) and you wouldn't know it?" The carriers were in fact moving full-steam toward Kimmel's command post at the time. Laughing together about a danger signal, which labels it as a purely laughing matter, is a characteristic manifestation of groupthink.

2. *Rationale.* As we see, victims of groupthink ignore warnings; they

also collectively construct rationalizations in order to discount warnings and other forms of negative feedback that, taken seriously, might lead the group members to reconsider their assumptions each time they recommit themselves to past decisions. Why did the Johnson ingroup avoid reconsidering its escalation policy when time and again the expectations on which they based their decisions turned out to be wrong? James C. Thompson Jr., a Harvard historian who spent five years as an observing participant in both the State Department and the White House, tells us that the policymakers avoided critical discussion of their prior decisions and continually invented new rationalizations so that they could sincerely recommit themselves to defeating the North Vietnamese.

In the fall of 1964, before the bombing of North Vietnam began, some of the policymakers predicted that six weeks of air strikes would induce the North Vietnamese to seek peace talks. When someone asked, "What if they don't?" the answer was that another four weeks certainly would do the trick.

Later, after each setback, the ingroup agreed that by investing just a bit more effort (by stepping up the bomb tonnage a bit, for instance), their course of action would prove to be right. *The Pentagon Papers* bear out these observations.

In *The Limits of Intervention*, Townsend Hoopes, who was acting Secretary of the Air Force under Johnson, says that Walt W. Rostow in particular showed a remarkable capacity for what has been called "instant rationalization." According to Hoopes, Rostow buttressed the group's optimism about being on the road to victory by culling selected scraps of evidence from news reports or, if necessary, by inventing "plausible" forecasts that had no basis in evidence at all.

Admiral Kimmel's group rationalized away their warnings, too. Right up to December 7, 1941, they convinced themselves that the Japanese would never dare attempt a full-scale surprise assault against Hawaii because Japan's leaders would realize that it would precipitate an all-out war which the United States would surely win. They made no attempt to look at the situation through the eyes of the Japanese leaders—another manifestation of groupthink.

3. *Morality.* Victims of groupthink believe unquestioningly in the inherent morality of their ingroup; this belief inclines the members to ignore the ethical or moral consequences of their decisions.

Evidence that this symptom is at work usually is of a negative kind— the things that are left unsaid in group meetings. At least two influential persons had doubts about the morality of the Bay of Pigs adventure. One of them, Arthur Schlesinger Jr., presented his strong objections in a memorandum to President Kennedy and Secretary of State Rusk but suppressed them when he attended meetings of the Kennedy team. The other, Senator J. William Fulbright, was not a member of the group, but the President invited him to express his misgivings in a speech to the policymakers. However, when Fulbright finished speaking the President moved on to other agenda items without asking for reactions of the group.

David Kraslow and Stuart H. Loory, in *The Secret Search for Peace in Vietnam,* report that during 1966 President Johnson's ingroup was concerned primarily with selecting bomb targets in North Vietnam. They based their selections on four factors—the military advantage, the risk to American aircraft and pilots, the danger of forcing other countries into the fighting, and the danger of heavy civilian casualties. At their regular Tuesday luncheons, they weighed these factors the way school teachers grade examination papers, averaging them out. Though evidence on this point is scant, I suspect that the group's ritualistic adherence to a standardized procedure induced the members to feel morally justified in their destructive way of dealing with the Vietnamese people—after all, the danger of heavy civilian casualties from U.S. air strikes was taken into account on their checklists.

4. *Stereotypes.* Victims of groupthink hold stereotyped views of the leaders of enemy groups: they are so evil that genuine attempts at negotiating differences with them are unwarranted, or they are too weak or too stupid to deal effectively with whatever attempts the ingroup makes to defeat their purposes, no matter how risky the attempts are.

Kennedy's groupthinkers believed that Premier Fidel Castro's air force was so ineffectual that obsolete B-26s could knock it out completely in a surprise attack before the invasion began. They also believed that Castro's army was so weak that a small Cuban-exile brigade could establish a well-protected beachhead at the Bay of Pigs. In addition, they believed that Castro was not smart enough to put down any possible internal uprisings in support of the exiles. They were wrong on all three assumptions. Though much of the blame was attributable to faulty intelligence, the point is that none of Kennedy's advisers even questioned the CIA planners about these assumptions.

The Johnson advisers' sloganistic thinking about "the Communist apparatus" that was "working all around the world" (as Dean Rusk put it) led them to overlook the powerful nationalistic strivings of the North Vietnamese government and its efforts to ward off Chinese domination. The crudest of all stereotypes used by Johnson's inner circle to justify their policies was the domino theory ("If we don't stop the Reds in South Vietnam, tomorrow they will be in Hawaii and next week they will be in San Francisco," Johnson once said). The group so firmly accepted this stereotype that it became almost impossible for any adviser to introduce a more sophisticated viewpoint.

In the documents on Pearl Harbor, it is clear to see that the Navy commanders stationed in Hawaii had a naive image of Japan as a midget that would not dare to strike a blow against a powerful giant.

5. *Pressure.* Victims of groupthink apply direct pressure to any indi-

vidual who momentarily expresses doubts about any of the group's shared illusions or who questions the validity of the arguments supporting a policy alternative favored by the majority. This gambit reinforces the concurrence-seeking norm that loyal members are expected to maintain.

President Kennedy probably was more active than anyone else in raising skeptical questions during the Bay of Pigs meetings, and yet he seems to have encouraged the group's docile, uncritical acceptance of defective arguments in favor of the CIA's plan. At every meeting, he allowed the CIA representatives to dominate the discussion. He permitted them to give their immediate refutations in response to each tentative doubt that one of the others expressed, instead of asking whether anyone shared the doubt or wanted to pursue the implications of the new worrisome issue that had just been raised. And at the most crucial meeting, when he was calling on each member to give his vote for or against the plan, he did not call on Arthur Schlesinger, the one man there who was known by the President to have serious misgivings.

Historian Thompson informs us that whenever a member of Johnson's ingroup began to express doubts, the group used subtle social pressures to "domesticate" him. To start with, the dissenter was made to feel at home, provided that he lived up to two restrictions: 1) that he did not voice his doubts to outsiders, which would play into the hands of the opposition; and 2) that he kept his criticisms within the bounds of acceptable deviation, which meant not challenging any of the fundamental assumptions that went into the group's prior commitments. One such "domesticated dissenter" was Bill Moyers. When Moyers arrived at a meeting, Thompson tells us, the President greeted him with, "Well, here comes Mr. Stop-the-Bombing."

6. *Self-censorship*. Victims of groupthink avoid deviating from what appears to be group consensus; they keep silent about their misgivings and even minimize to themselves the importance of their doubts.

As we have seen, Schlesinger was not at all hesitant about presenting his strong objections to the Bay of Pigs plan in a memorandum to the President and the Secretary of State. But he became keenly aware of his tendency to suppress objections at the White House meetings. "In the months after the Bay of Pigs I bitterly reproached myself for having kept so silent during those crucial discussions in the cabinet room," Schlesinger writes in *A Thousand Days*. "I can only explain my failure to do more than raise a few timid questions by reporting that one's impulse to blow the whistle on this nonsense was simply undone by the circumstances of the discussion."

7. *Unanimity*. Victims of groupthink share an illusion of unanimity within the group concerning almost all judgments expressed by members who speak in favor of the majority view. This symptom results partly from the preceding one, whose effects are augmented by the false assumption that any individual who remains silent during any part of the discussion is in full accord with what the others are saying.

When a group of persons who respect each other's opinions arrives at a unanimous view, each member is likely to feel that the belief must be true. This reliance on consensual validation within the group tends to replace individual critical thinking and reality testing, unless there are clear-cut disagreements among the members. In contemplating a course of action such as the invasion of Cuba, it is painful for the members to confront disagreements within their group, particularly if it becomes apparent that there are widely divergent views about whether the preferred course of action is too risky to undertake at all. Such disagreements are likely to arouse anxieties about making a serious error. Once the sense of unanimity is shattered, the members no longer can feel complacently confident about the decision they are inclined to make. Each man must then face the annoying realization that there are troublesome uncertainties and he must diligently seek out the best information he can get in order to decide for himself exactly how serious the risks might be. This is one of the unpleasant consequences of being in a group of hardheaded, critical thinkers.

To avoid such an unpleasant state, the members often become inclined, without quite realizing it, to prevent latent disagreements from surfacing when they are about to initiate a risky course of action. The group leader and the members support each other in playing up the areas of convergence in their thinking, at the expense of fully exploring divergencies that might reveal unsettled issues.

"Our meetings took place in a curious atmosphere of assumed consensus," Schlesinger writes. His additional comments clearly show that, curiously, the consensus was an illusion—an illusion that could be maintained only because the major participants did not reveal their own reasoning or discuss their idiosyncratic assumptions and vague reservations. Evidence from several sources makes it clear that even the three principals—President Kennedy, Rusk and McNamara—had widely differing assumptions about the invasion plan.

8. *Mindguards*. Victims of groupthink sometimes appoint themselves as mindguards to protect the leader and fellow members from adverse information that might break the complacency they shared about the effectiveness and morality of past decisions. At a large birthday party for his wife, Attorney General Robert F. Kennedy, who had been constantly informed about the Cuban invasion plan, took Schlesinger aside and asked him why he was opposed. Kennedy listened coldly and said, "You may be right or you may be wrong, but the President has made his mind up. Don't push it any further. Now is the time for everyone to help him all they can."

Rusk also functioned as a highly effective mindguard by failing to transmit to the group the strong objections of three "outsiders" who had learned of the invasion plan—Undersecretary of State Chester Bowles, USIA Director Edward R. Murrow, and Rusk's intelligence chief, Roger Hilsman. Had Rusk done so, their warnings might have reinforced Schlesinger's memorandum and jolted some of Kennedy's ingroup, if not the President himself, into reconsidering the decision.

Products   When a group of executives frequently displays most or all of these interrelated symptoms, a detailed study of their deliberations is likely to reveal a number of immediate consequences. These consequences are, in effect, products of poor decision-making practices because they lead to inadequate solutions to the problems under discussion.

First, the group limits its discussions to a few alternative courses of action (often only two) without an initial survey of all the alternatives that might be worthy of consideration.

Second, the group fails to reexamine the course of action initially preferred by the majority after they learn of risks and drawbacks they had not considered originally.

Third, the members spend little or no time discussing whether there are nonobvious gains they may have overlooked or ways of reducing the seemingly prohibitive costs that made rejected alternatives appear undesirable to them.

Fourth, members make little or no attempt to obtain information from experts within their own organizations who might be able to supply more precise estimates of potential losses and gains.

Fifth, members show positive interest in facts and opinions that support their preferred policy; they tend to ignore facts and opinions that do not.

Sixth, members spend little time deliberating about how the chosen policy might be hindered by bureaucratic inertia, sabotaged by political opponents, or temporarily derailed by common accidents. Consequently, they fail to work out contingency plans to cope with foreseeable setbacks that could endanger the overall success of their chosen course.

Support   The search for an explanation of why groupthink occurs has led me through a quagmire of complicated theoretical issues in the murky area of human motivation. My belief, based on recent social psychological research, is that we can best understand the various symptoms of groupthink as a mutual effort among the group members to maintain self-esteem and emotional equanimity by providing social support to each other, especially at times when they share responsibility for making vital decisions.

Even when no important decision is pending, the typical administrator will begin to doubt the wisdom and morality of his past decisions each time he receives information about setbacks, particularly if the information is accompanied by negative feedback from prominent men who originally had been his supporters. It should not be surprising, therefore, to find that individual members strive to develop unanimity and esprit de corps that will help bolster each other's morale, to create an optimistic outlook about the success of pending decisions, and to reaffirm the positive value of past policies to which all of them are committed.

Pride   Shared illusions of invulnerability, for example, can reduce anxiety about taking risks. Rationalizations help members believe that the risks are really not so bad after all. The assumption of inherent morality helps the members to avoid feelings of shame or guilt. Negative stereotypes function as stress-reducing devices to enhance a sense of moral righteousness as well as pride in a lofty mission.

The mutual enhancement of self-esteem and morale may have functional value in enabling the members to maintain their capacity to take action, but it has maladaptive consequences insofar as concurrence-seeking tendencies interfere with critical, rational capacities and lead to serious errors of judgment.

While I have limited my study to decision-making bodies in Government, groupthink symptoms appear in business, industry and any other field where small, cohesive groups make the decisions. It is vital, then, for all sorts of people—and especially group leaders—to know what steps they can take to prevent groupthink.

Remedies   To counterpoint my case studies of the major fiascos, I have also investigated two highly successful group enterprises, the formulation of the Marshall Plan in the Truman Administration and the handling of the Cuban missile crisis by President Kennedy and his advisers. I have found it instructive to examine the steps Kennedy took to change his group's decision-making processes. These changes ensured that the mistakes made by his Bay of Pigs ingroup were not repeated by the missile-crisis ingroup, even though the membership of both groups was essentially the same.

The following recommendations for preventing groupthink incorporate many of the good practices I discovered to be characteristic of the Marshall Plan and missile-crisis groups.

1. The leader of a policy-forming group should assign the role of critical evaluator to each member, encouraging the group to give high priority to open airing of objections and doubts. This practice needs to be reinforced by the leader's acceptance of criticism of his own judgments in order to discourage members from soft-pedaling their disagreements and from allowing their striving for concurrence to inhibit critical thinking.

2. When the key members of a hierarchy assign a policy-planning mission to any group within their organization, they should adopt an impartial stance instead of stating preferences and expectations at the beginning. This will encourage open inquiry and impartial probing of a wide range of policy alternatives.

3. The organization routinely should set up several outside policy-planning and evaluation groups to work on the same policy question, each deliberating under a different leader. This can prevent the insulation of an ingroup.

4. At intervals before the group reaches a final consensus, the leader

should require each member to discuss the group's deliberations with associates in his own unit of the organization—assuming that those associates can be trusted to adhere to the same security regulations that govern the policymakers—and then to report back their reactions to the group.

5. The group should invite one or more outside experts to each meeting on a staggered basis and encourage the experts to challenge the views of the core members.

6. At every general meeting of the group, whenever the agenda calls for an evaluation of policy alternatives, at least one member should play devil's advocate, functioning as a good lawyer in challenging the testimony of those who advocate the majority position.

7. Whenever the policy issue involves relations with a rival nation or organization, the group should devote a sizable block of time, perhaps an entire session, to a survey of all warning signals from the rivals and should write alternative scenarios on the rivals' intentions.

8. When the group is surveying policy alternatives for feasibility and effectiveness, it should from time to time divide into two or more subgroups to meet separately, under different chairmen, and then come back together to hammer out differences.

9. After reaching a preliminary consensus about what seems to be the best policy, the group should hold a "second-chance" meeting at which every member expresses as vividly as he can all his residual doubts, and rethinks the entire issue before making a definitive choice.

How   These recommendations have their disadvantages. To encourage the open airing of objections, for instance, might lead to prolonged and costly debates when a rapidly growing crisis requires immediate solution. It also could cause rejection, depression and anger. A leader's failure to set a norm might create cleavage between leader and members that could develop into a disruptive power struggle if the leader looks on the emerging consensus as anathema. Setting up outside evaluation groups might increase the risk of security leakage. Still, inventive executives who know their way around the organizational maze probably can figure out how to apply one or another of the prescriptions successfully, without harmful side effects.

They also could benefit from the advice of outside experts in the administrative and behavioral sciences. Though these experts have much to offer, they have had few chances to work on policy-making machinery within large organizations. As matters now stand, executives innovate only when they need new procedures to avoid repeating serious errors that have deflated their self-images.

In this era of atomic warheads, urban disorganization and ecocatastrophes, it seems to me that policymakers should collaborate with behavioral scientists and give top priority to preventing groupthink and its attendant fiascos.

1. What role does conflict play in society?
2. What are the positive functions of conflict?
3. What is the role of conflict in small group communication?
4. How can conflict be beneficial to the group communication process?
5. How can conflict be harmful to the group communication process?

▶◀ The Role of Conflict in Discussion

JOHN L. PETELLE

The place of cooperation in group discussion has long been stressed by those persons interested in the discussion process. Definitions of discussion such as ". . . the conversation that results when members of a group gather to share their information and opinions on a topic or to think through a common problem . . ." (1) indicate the cooperative effort. Statements regarding the importance of "cooperative investigation" (2) and concepts such as discussion is primarily a "cooperation-enlisting" (3) process, illustrate the role of cooperation in discussion. At the same time, however, the majority of persons describing discussion also admit the need for conflict. Howell and Smith, for example, point out that "Good discussion is born in conflict and thrives on conflict. But the conflict must be one of ideas rather than personalities" (4). Ewbank and Auer maintain that there ". . . is a need for differences of opinion" (5). Harnack and Fest acknowledge that:

Cooperative groups are obviously preferable to competitive groups, yet cooperation does not mean absence of conflict, as some believe. It does mean absence of conflict to *block individuals* and the vigorous presence of conflict intended to explore ideas (6).

Although many persons agree that conflict as well as cooperation is needed in the discussion process, little attention has been given to the role of conflict. It is my position that the presence of conflict may be a positive force in intercommunication.

While most of us in the field of speech agree upon the importance of understanding the process of communication in small groups probably

"The Role of Conflict in Discussion," by John L. Petelle, from *Speaker and Gavel*, Vol. 2, No. 1, pp. 24–28.

few of us would embark upon identical or perhaps even similar courses of action in carrying out such an objective. I would submit that such deviation of thought, conflict, if you will, serves as a positive force in aiding us to achieve a greater and more comprehensive understanding of what this process is. It is not, however, the purpose of this article to examine what this course of action might be. Rather, it is my intention to examine conflict as a common operating force in society, to determine what, if any positive functions it may have, and then to determine the role of conflict in the discussion process.

The presence of conflict in today's society is quite apparent. A scanning of the headlines, a twist of the radio dial, a flick of the TV switch brings to us only all too readily, the element of conflict. Types of conflict and situations where conflict occurs are so numerous it would be impossible to consider them all within the scope of this article. Broadly speaking, we may cite two general categories of conflict; conflict of force and conflict of ideas. Although admittedly the two may, and indeed often do, occur together, and while one is often the cause of the other, let us limit ourselves to that category of conflict which manifests itself most commonly in small group communication; the conflict of ideas.

I believe we may accept as our initial premise, that conflict is a common element in society. As we consider conflict I would like to think of it as being a continuum, ranging from a deviant thought to overt physical force. In this context we can see that conflict must, at some point on the continuum, always exist whenever people interact. Thus, as the German sociologist Georg Simmel pointed out, conflict must be considered as a form of socialization (7). Granting then, that conflict is a common operating force in society, our immediate concern is whether this force may ever exist in a positive nature.

Since the beginning of civilization, conflict has been a vital force in the progress of man. From the conflict of force which drove the Piltdown man toward the creation of new weapons for survival, to the twentieth century's conflict of multi-ideologies, conflict has operated not only as a destructive element which has separated men, but also as a positive force which has stimulated advancement. Edward A. Ross in *Principles of Sociology*, pointed out that "The good side of opposition is that it stimulates" (8). And indeed, there have been few, if any, forward steps in man's progress which did not have their origin in point and counterpoint.

Perhaps one of the most advanced as well as thorough theories of conflict is the product of Georg Simmel. In his treatise, *Conflict*, Simmel outlines his philosophy of the nature of conflict. In examining this work one can hardly help but observe that Simmel accords a number of positive functions to conflict. In considering what I believe to be some of the major positive functions of conflict as they relate to the small group communicative process, I am heavily indebted to Simmel's theories.

According to Simmel, one of the positive functions of conflict, as it relates to the group is that conflict tends to create order within the group (9). That is, as a result of conflict either from within the group or from an outside origin, the group begins to structure itself into some form of an organized hierarchy. This does not mean to imply that structure is dependent upon conflict but rather that conflict often aids the ordering process.

Another positive function of conflict, according to Simmel, is that it acts as a cohesive agent upon the group. A state of conflict tends to ". . . pull the members so tightly together and subject them to such a uniform impulse that they either must completely get along with or completely repel one another" (10). In addition to this, conflict not only acts as a cohesive force in uniting the group but it may also be the prime agent which brings groups or individuals together. Thus, conflict may establish communication where before there was none. Again turning to Simmel, he remarks:

Conflict may not only heighten the concentration of an existing unit, radically eliminating all elements which might blur the distinctness of its boundaries against the enemy; it may also bring persons and groups together which have otherwise nothing to do with each other (11).

Finally, Simmel contends that conflict is an indication of group stability (12). That is, the more intimate and secure the group, the more intense the conflict and the greater its frequency. Our individual experiences bear out, I believe, this particular aspect of Simmel's theory inasmuch as each of us tends to be less patient, more direct, more openly hostile in situations we feel confident in and in groups we know. Much more tact and reserve, for example, is often accorded a stranger than is given a wife, a brother, or even a close friend.

In relating these concepts of conflict to small group communication, or anything else for that matter, I feel no matter how obvious it would seem, that a note of caution should be injected. That is, one cannot conclude from these propositions that such will always be the case. As long as we deal with human behavior we must ever keep in mind the element of probability.

Thus far we have determined that conflict is a common force in our society and that it does possess certain positive functions. At this point then, let us try to correlate the positive elements of conflict with the role of conflict in small group communication.

The discussion or small group communicative situation is obviously in its very essence, a social function. Inasmuch as conflict is an inherent element in almost all social interactions we might expect to find conflict present in group discussions. As has been pointed out by any number of discussion textbooks, the basic purpose of discussion is a problem-solving activity and as such has as its main objective to serve as a testing ground whereby through cooperational effort ideas and information may be exchanged and evaluated. Now as was pointed out earlier, while discussion textbooks deal with the element of cooperation as requisite to a successful group discussion, little seems to have been done regarding the necessity for the presence of conflict, or in fact, what one may tell about the group after observing group conflict in operation (13). It is my contention that the presence of conflict in group discussion may be just as requisite and valuable as cooperation. Indeed, I would argue, as did Cooley, that "The more one thinks of it the more he will see that conflict and cooperation are not separable things, but phases of one process which always involves something of both" (14). Granted then, the presence of conflict in discussion, let us return to our definition of conflict. That is, a continuum ranging from deviant thought to overt force. Considering discussion as a problem-solving activity in which there is an exchange and evaluation of ideas we must recognize that to some extent conflict must be present in this communicative interaction. It would be difficult to imagine any "exchange and evaluation" without some disagreement. In fact, one might very well question the effectiveness of a problem-solving activity devoid of different ideas and thinking. If the group were unanimous in ideas and action little, in most cases, would be achieved toward the solution of a problem. And if a solution were reached through unanimous thought and action the progress and success of the group interaction could at best be representative of the weaker elements of the group.

If the real aim of discussion is to make progress in a problem area then perhaps we should recognize and encourage the presence of conflict as a stimulant to group interaction. Naturally, however, we do not want conflict merely for the sake of conflict. Nor do we want just any kind of conflict. Lewis A. Coser in *The Functions of Social Conflict* (15) identifies two kinds of conflict; realistic and non-realistic (16). Realistic conflict, according to Coser, is that conflict which is the result of frustration in attempting to achieve a goal. It is a means toward a specific result and in such conflict, one may find functional alternatives as to the desired means. Non-realistic conflict, on the other hand, is conflict which is a result of a lack of a release of tension and in such conflict there exists only functional alternatives as to objects. Groups, of any type, form for a variety of reasons. Certainly one of the reasons for the formation of a discussion group is the recognition of a common problem or goal. The need for the interaction of ideas would imply that among individuals there exists a frustration of how to reach a goal or solve a problem. Once such a problem or goal is recognized a means is required by which to achieve or solve it. It would seem then, that realistic conflict, the conflict arising from frustration or inability to select the proper means, is one conflict which may have been the result of a dialectical *intracommunicative* process which might be observed and indeed encouraged in the group's interaction, for out of the expression of such frustrations, real forward progress may be made.

The presence of conflict in discussion, then, is perhaps requisite to group progress. Using this conflict, however, as a tool in furthering the group requires caution and knowledge; caution in exercising control of it, in that it must be allowed to flourish but not dominate, and knowledge in being able to recognize it in its form and when possible, its origin and purpose.

It would seem that the proper role or function of conflict in discussion is to encourage inquiry, to promote objectivity, and to sharpen analysis. From this we might contend that conflict exists as a positive functioning element in the dialectical interchange between and among individuals.

But internal conflict in a discussion group is more than just a force to encourage inquiry. It is also a criteria by which we may make certain value judgments concerning both individuals and the group. To begin with, we may observe that a group which experiences a conflict of ideas is one in which overt interest and concern is being manifested. Keeping Simmel's theories of conflict in mind, we may relate the presence of conflict to group structure and hierarchal order. From this we may also consider the relationship of conflict to lines of communication. We might also relate the presence of conflict with the emergence of ingroups and outgroups within the primary group. Another way in which conflict might be used as a group measurement is to relate it to group cohesiveness and stability. And finally, we might relate the presence of conflict as a stimulus to group productivity and success in reaching desired ends.

The presence of conflict in society may be stated with certainty. The positive force of conflict may be stated with almost equal certainty. The role or function of conflict in discussion, or the use of conflict as a criterion in the measurement and evaluation of discussion, however, is quite something else. As a point of departure in analyzing the role of conflict or in utilizing conflict as a measuring device of small group communication we might begin with certain of Simmel's, Ross's, and Cooley's postulates. We may observe conflict as a stimulus in discussion and observe certain responses and reactions to it; we may even observe arising in the presence of conflict, the same pattern of behavior mentioned by Simmel, Ross, and Cooley. But to establish the causal relationship between group conflict and group communicative behavior, we need more investigation, more study, more experimentation. It has not been my intention in this article to argue at this time that conflict is a "must" in effective group discussion, or that it "is" a useful criterion in measuring small group communication. Rather, I am suggesting a point of view that it is quite possible that conflict could become a valuable criterion to help us further evaluate the process of group discussion. It would seem that such a force, operational in practically all social interaction, is worthy of more experimentation by those interested in understanding and evaluating small group communication.

NOTES

1. Henry L. Ewbank and J. Jeffery Auer, *Discussion & Debate*, New York: F.S. Crofts & Co., 1946, p. 289.
2. Ibid., p. 300.
3. Laura Crowell, *Discussion: Method of Democracy*, Chicago: Scott, Foresman, & Co., 1963, p. 10.
4. William S. Howell and Donald K. Smith, *Discussion*, New York: Macmillan Publishing Co., Inc., 1956, p. 256.
5. Ewbank and Auer, op. cit., p. 295.
6. Victor Harnack and Thorrel B. Fest, *Group Discussion, Theory and Technique*, New York: Appleton-Century-Crofts, 1964, p. 176.
7. Georg Simmel, *Conflict*, trans. by Kurt H. Wolff, Illinois: The Free Press, 1955, p. 13.
8. Edward A. Ross, *The Principles of Sociology*, New York: The Century Co., 1920, p. 167.
9. Simmel, op. cit., pp. 87–91.
10. Ibid., pp. 92–93.
11. Ibid., pp. 98–99.
12. Ibid., pp. 43–49.
13. Although not elaborated upon in great detail, categories 10 and 12 of Bales' interaction chart in his *Process Analysis* at least recognizes the possibility of utilizing conflict in this manner.
14. Charles H. Cooley, *Social Process*, New York: Charles Scribner's Sons, 1918, p. 39.
15. Lewis A. Coser, *The Functions of Social Conflict*, New York: The Free Press, 1956, pp. 49–50.
16. Ibid.

◄ The Role of Communication In Small Group Choice Shift

RONALD L. APPLBAUM AND KARL W. E. ANATOL

Until rather recently, it was believed that there was, inherent in the process of group discussion, an influence that caused individuals to privately recommend greater degrees of risk after group discussion than these same individuals would have privately recommended before group discussion. In other words, it was believed that groups take more risk than individuals in making decisions. The stimulus for this assumption originated with Stoner's discovery that group decisions were more risky than individual decisions (1). Marquis, who confirmed Stoner's findings, comments that the results were "contrary to common belief that committees are typically cautious, compromising, and conservative" (2).

According to Dean Pruitt, the belief that group decisions always tend to reflect risky alternatives must, at least in part, be abandoned (3). Some groups move or shift toward a riskier decision, whereas others move toward a cautious decision following group discussion. This process of group decision-making called the choice shift phenomenon seems to constitute a major determinant of the quality of group consensus, judgment, or solutions. It seems incumbent upon us, therefore, to examine the essential characteristics of this process.

"The Role of Communication in Small Group Choice Shift" by Ronald L. Applbaum and Karl W. E. Anatol. Reprinted with permission of the authors. This original essay appears here in print for the first time. The research was supported in part by LBSU Grant No. 212F–144.

REVIEW OF LITERATURE

Four basic theoretic orientations have been suggested by researchers to account for the choice shift: (1) diffusion of responsibility; (2) familiarization; (3) leadership; and (4) values.

Diffusion of Responsibility Theory

According to the diffusion of responsibility theory, greater risk-taking in group discussion occurs because group members diffuse the responsibility for their decisions to the group as a whole. An individual can shift the responsibility for negative consequences of a particular decision from himself to the other group members. The diffusion of responsibility reduces the anxiety caused by his selection of a risky decision. Evidence shows that the more anxious an individual, the greater is his shift toward risk (4). If we assume that the greater the anxiety the more is the concern about negative outcomes, group members will be more affected by anxiety reduction when they have a chance to diffuse responsibility.

An early study of risk-taking found that group discussion produces a greater shift toward risk when success or failure of the decision affects the welfare of the entire group rather than when it affects only a single group member (5). This might suggest that group members feel more responsible when the decision affects the entire group and hence the idea of "responsibility diffusion." Studies support the hypothesis that emotional bonds among group members encourage the risky shift. It has been found that an attenuated risky shift occurs with groups of people whose personalities cause them to be aloof or fearful of interpersonal bonds (6). In addition, one study found that the greater the group cohesiveness the greater was the size of risky shift (7).

Despite some evidence in support of this theory, conflicting evidence casts serious doubts on the theory's validity. One study found that highly anxious, low defensive individuals do not move toward greater risky shift. Risky shifts have been observed even when individuals merely observed, watched, or listened to a discussion. Even the mere aspect of listening to a recorded discussion has, at times, tended to induce a risky shift. It is difficult to imagine individuals placing the blame of decision outcomes on people whom they have never met nor interacted with.

Familiarization Theory

Familiarization theory is based on the assumption that increasing a group member's familiarity with a problem increases the group member's riskiness in decision making. Replications of a familiarization technique have failed to produce familiarization effect in a number of studies (8). In fact, a study by Stokes found that familiarization produced a slight shift in a direction opposite to the orientation (toward risk or caution) of the problem (9). It may be significant that upon examining the interaction between group members, Stokes found that the arguments during the discussion were contrary to the orientation of the problem. It is possible that group members were persuaded to take positions opposite to the problem's orientation.

The two previous theories both lack an important ingredient in theory construction, i.e., parsimony. Neither theory accounts for the shift toward caution, but only the shift toward risk, and, therefore, some other mechanism must be used to explain the shifts toward caution.

Leadership Theory

The basic assumption of leadership theory is that high risk takers are more persuasive in those group discussions that produce a risky shift. Conversely, cautious individuals are more persuasive in discussions that produce a cautious shift. This position suggests that high risk or cautious individuals are perceived by group members as having been more influential in the discussion. However, an alternative interpretation may be that individuals shift toward a specific position, for example, risk or caution, and in the process cause individuals who hold their new position to appear influential when in fact they may not have been really influential.

Leadership theory states that people making decisions involving high risk are more confident of their position. This confidence is transformed into greater assertiveness and influence during group discussion. The evidence concerning a possible relationship between confidence and risk-taking is inconsistent (10).

Teger and Pruitt found that risky shifts occurred even when members merely exchanged information by holding up cards rather than freely discussing a problem (11). One could argue that the information-exchange condition did not provide a format for leadership. On the other hand, one could argue that the information-exchange-only condition did entail face-to-face interaction, and, thus, permitted nonverbal communication that could be a vehicle for leadership. It is important to note that the shift toward risk in the information-exchange condition was less than the shift occurring in full group discussion. This would be consistent with leadership theory since a combination of verbal and nonverbal communication provided by a group discussion would permit more effective leadership and more risky shift. One study, for example, found a full risky shift when individuals watched and listened to a group discussion, but only a partial shift when individuals only listened to a group discussion. The absence of certain forms of nonverbal communication might reduce the risky shift.

Recently a number of writers have attempted to provide comprehensive reviews of the risky-shift literature (12). All agree that the group shifts do not seem attributable, to any great extent, to the diffusion of responsibility via the development of affective bonds among group members, nor to the reduction of uncertainty resulting from more exposure to stimulus materials, nor to a relationship between leadership ability and a propensity to take risks.

Value Theory

The Teger and Pruitt study suggests that two processes may be involved in the choice-shift phenomenon. First, the choice-shift seems to be enforced by the proliferation of an underlying value for risk or caution. Second, the choice-shift may be influenced by the communication that occurs during group discussion.

Under the terms of "value theory," we are subsuming a number of closely related theories that share the common assumption that groups shift in a direction toward which most members of the group are already attracted as individuals. Roger Brown suggests that riskiness is a culturally prescribed value or ego ideal that demands of an individual to want to be at least as risky in his behavior as other people similar to him (13).

Two value theories appear to offer plausible explanations for the totality of the choice shift phenomenon. The first suggests that individuals seek social comparison with fellow group members and that this comparison leads to a drive for achieving parity in ideas, suggestions, and group solutions. The assumptions of the "social comparison theory" imply that more exposure to the initial decision of others is the necessary and sufficient condition for eliciting shift on the part of group members (14). The second theory is concerned with the effect of the arguments proposed during discussion upon group members. It is suggested that the dominant value or values of a decision problem tend to elicit persuasive arguments in group discussion that convince group members to "move further in the direction of their initial values" (15). The major assumption underlying both value theories is that group interaction serves to enhance the initially dominant value.

The remainder of the review of research focuses on the previously identified role that communication plays in choice shifts. Accordingly, the dimensions of what we label an "informational influence approach" are explored.

INFORMATIONAL INFLUENCE APPROACH TO CHOICE-SHIFTS

Brown recognized the possibility that a prevailing value will influence the flow of information so that more relevant information will be elicited supporting the value than opposing it. No single member of a group is likely to possess all the information that objectively bears on the decision and the discussion will give each group member some new reasons for moving toward the value (16). Vinokar refines the relevant arguments explanation by postulating that maximum shift is expected where there is a preponderance of persuasive arguments for one alternative and probability is only moderate that an average subject will possess most of these arguments. This maximizes the likelihood that new persuasive information will be made available to subjects during discussion, enabling them to move toward the response they would tend to adopt if they possessed all the relevant information (17).

Because only a few research projects have been concerned with caution shifts, the research that we describe is oriented toward the influence of communication during the risky shift. It is concluded by researchers that group discussion provides the necessary and sufficient conditions for generating a risky-shift effect (18). Group members are less willing to accept risk in the absence of discussion (19). These results are consistent for male and female subjects, groups of varied sizes, varied ages, and whether the person taking the risk plays a role or is indeed a real member of a group (20). Studies using restricted information conditions have obtained either no risky shift or a smaller risky shift than that which occurred in full discussion conditions (21). This suggests that the risky-shift effect in groups is dependent upon discussion explicitly focused on risk-taking. Mere discussion, regardless of content is not a sufficient condition for the risky-shift phenomenon (22).

Observing a group discussion without participating also elicits response shifts, although observers tend to shift less than do participants (23). According to Lamm, this finding is to be expected since nonparticipants were still privileged to the information exchange that, according to Brown, is the primary source of risky shift (24). It might be suggested that when subjects only listen to a discussion, the shift is less because subjects have a smaller degree of comprehension, no chance to rehearse arguments as in active discussion, and have no opportunity for seeking clarification of ambiguous points. This exchange of information can only occur in an interactive context. A mere reading of group discussion must provide both information regarding the social value of risk and the physical presence of the other group members before a complete risky shift can take place (25).

Vinokar comments that risky items are unambiguous and elicit a number of arguments that may convince group members of their validity.

When these persuasive arguments are elicited in group discussion, they influence the more conservative members to shift their opinion and accept greater risk. The influence exerted, then, is the result of persuasiveness of the arguments. It results in covert change of opinion and acceptance of a new group decision (26).

Nørdhoy observed that risk-supporting arguments predominated in group discussions. His interpretation was that the shift toward risk was related to the justification provided by the arguments (27). St. Jean postulated that specific arguments, rather than specific risk levels, pull a group member in the direction of the shift (28). It appears that the crucial information transmitted in the group discussion is not the risk level of others but information specific to the item being discussed. Discussing certain problems does not affect responses to undiscussed problems (29). The discussion must be relevant to the problem on which a decision will be made for the shift to occur. This is consistent with the observation that shifts do not occur when judgments without discussion are made, and, thus, it is the arguments that induce the shifting process (30).

Wallach and Mabli found that conservative group members are influenced by the character of the arguments that are brought up in discussion regardless of the majority or minority status of the arguments or opinions (31). There is an indication then, that risk taking is not an enforcement that is brought about by conformity pressures. Since most problems used in the studies are risk-oriented, they tend to arouse arguments supporting a risky position. If an individual initially advocates a relatively risky stand and is provided through discussion with additional risky arguments by other group members, the individual becomes willing to advocate an even riskier stand. This effect will occur whether the individual receives the argument alone or along with the presence of interacting others. However, should others be present the arguments take on additional salience and the result is a stronger shift to risk. Thus, specific arguments combined with an interactional context tend to produce a greater shift toward risk.

Because individuals are generally more conservative in their initial decision, the information provided by the arguments in a discussion concerning the others' initial position induces a greater shift. There would appear to be a strong support for the argument that initial responses are an operational index of a subject's prediscussion value or to the direction of arguments in the informational repertoire (32). However, it should be pointed out that the initial risk does not predict, to any great extent, the amount of shift that the group is going to experience. In fact, Myers, Wong, and Murdoch found that the significant shifts can occur without the group members knowing exactly the initial positions of the other group members (33). Listening to and participating in discussion of arguments appears to provide subtle but unequivocal information about each member's choice.

There is still some question as to whether the persuasive arguments are persuasive by dint of their appeal to cultural values of risk or whether they are persuasive merely because they bring information that bears upon the desirability of various outcomes in a situation (34). According to Brown's information exchange hypothesis, when group members are told the initial position of other group members this information will subsequently lead to greater risky shift (35). Evidence does not support this contention. The difference between a group member's riskiness and the perceived riskiness of others is not related to the shift scores (36). Myers and Murdoch, when correlating the proportion of talking time contributed by group members with initial extremity, found no support for the hypothesis that group shift occurred because extreme individuals were disproportionately influential (37). The risky and cautious shifts result from the pooling of discussion arguments that disproportionately support a position.

Silverthorne found clear evidence to support the contention that group shift is influenced by the arguments that proliferate during the group discussion (38). Silverthorne's study leads to four major conclusions that relate to the effect of information provided during the group discussion. First, the content of the group discussion, i.e., the protocols, inputs, inductions, and so on, seems to reflect the gradual emergence toward the shift. Items that engendered a risky shift were in the ratio of 12.5 risky arguments to 1 cautious argument. Second, the group shift does not seem to be the antecedent condition that enforced the presentation or providing of information; rather it was the providing of information that influenced the shift. Thus the group shift represented a consequent action; information or arguments constitute the necessary antecedent condition. Third, the interaction processes within the group affect the essential first step by intensifying the motivation of members to offer contributions. The interaction process may serve to facilitate or inhibit the flow of contributions and also, in certain circumstances, to encourage certain kinds of contributions while discouraging others. Fourth, whereas initial group member responses indicate that group members lean toward a specific course of action, the group discussion increases commitment to that course of action.

Myers and Bishop support Silverthorne's last conclusion when they found that arguments tend to favor the predominant initial response tendency. They found a high proportion (3 to 1) of arguments favoring the dominant direction and the magnitude of shift in the direction (39). Applbaum and Anatol found that risk arguments are predominant with risk-oriented problems, but caution-oriented problems do not always elicit primarily caution arguments (40). These results support in part Brown and Vinokar's suggestions that shift effects are partly the result of an enhancement of the prevailing value by discussion arguments (41).

It might be argued that these prevailing arguments lead to group norms resulting in a preselection of appropriate group member contributions. This might explain acceptance of unethical risk-taking behavior by individuals (42). Unethical behavior is reinforced by group members, thereby making such risk-taking socially desirable. Chandler and Rabow have previously suggested that norms play a role in the group decision-making and that these norms are critical to the actual shift and direction of shift (43). The norms provide support for the person who exercises caution or risk. The support is related to the circumstances involved or specifically to the problem under discussion. The group discussion would allow the group members to contribute information that supports the socially favored norm (44).

Although research has shown that the type of argument provided within the context of the group discussion will influence the risky shift, it also appears that the amount of information provided during the discussion period also will have direct bearing on the decision-making process. Streufert and Streufert found that between ten and twelve independent items of information (arguments) by decision-makers per half hour provides the interactive context within which the riskiest decisions are made (45).

The composition of the group in respect to initial responses to an item will also affect the shifting process in the group discussion. The more diversity among initial responses to an item the greater is the shift occurring in the group. Although shifts do occur in homogeneous groups (members having the same initial response), a greater shift occurs in heterogeneous groups (members having different initial responses). It is possible that the diversity among group members promotes a more active exchange of communication in order to reconcile differences and this discussion then produces the greater shifting within the group (46).

If after responding to the choice dilemma item, subjects are asked to guess how the average peer would respond and what response they admire most, subjects tend to estimate that the group average is less in the valued direction than their own ideal response (47). According to "relevant-arguments" theory, the group member has personal arguments and if the information predominately favors one alternative he responds accordingly. However, he has not considered how others might respond when he makes his initial decision. When asked to determine the group average, the group member not knowing where others stand or whether they have considered the same arguments, assumes an average response of lesser extremity than his own. The fact that subjective estimates of relative risk tend to be veridical (the riskier his response, the more a subject considers himself to be riskier than others) is consistent with his interpretation (48).

The informational influence approach may also explain these additional processes operating when the group shift occurs. First, group members tend to change as well as shift following discussion (49). This shift, for example, by the conservative group member to a more risky position, may be a convergence toward a rational choice following a pooling of informational resources. Second, group-induced shifts persist for several weeks following group discussion and decision (50). The permanence of change may be a result of a genuine cognitive effect of informational influence on subjects' attitudes. Third, the magnitude of shift tends to grow with group size up to five members, at least with male subjects. This could derive from greater informational resources of a larger number of individuals in the group (51).

A construct within leadership theory called the "rhetoric-of-risk" may relate more to the informational influence approach to the choice shift phenomenon than to leadership. Unlike the relevant-arguments theory, which looks at arguments as the major units in the influencing process, the "rhetoric-of-risk" identifies the language structure of arguments as the influencing factor. The language of arguments for risk are more "dramatic" and hence more persuasive than arguments for caution. Thus, shift toward risk will occur more frequently than shifts toward caution. However, the approach does not explain the reason why shifts toward caution do in fact occur (52).

SUMMARY

On the basis of prior analysis of the communication process within terms of choice shift, researchers have been able to isolate the argument as a principal influencing agent. These findings have identified the proportion of arguments in groups making specific choice shifts. However, none of the communication analysis has attempted to identify the verbal components of the process of communication taking place in the decision-making groups. We have investigated the impact of communication in small group choice shift. Researchers have suggested that communication among group members plays an important part in group decision-making. The arguments used by group members may be the principal influencing agent in choice-shift behavior. When the preponderance of arguments support an orientation (risk or caution), the group choice shift generally reflects this informational exchange. For example, if a group shifts toward greater risk, the majority of the preceding arguments will be risk-oriented. The impact of group communication extends to individuals merely observing the group discussion. However, the amount of choice shift is less for observers than for participants. The question still remains as to whether the choice shift results from the argument's persuasive nature, the individual's gain of new information, or the argument's support of previously held values.

NOTES

1. J. A. F. Stoner, "Comparison of Individual and Group Decisions Involving Risk," Unpublished Master's thesis, MIT, 1961.
2. D. G. Marquis, "Individual Responsibility and Group Decisions Involving Risk," *Industrial Management Review*, 3 (1962), 8–23.
3. D. G. Pruitt, "Choice Shifts in Group Discussion: An Introductory Review," *Journal of Personality and Social Psychology*, 20 (1971), 339–359.
4. N. Kogan and M. A. Wallach, "The Risky-Shift Phenomena in Small Decision Making Groups: A Test of the Information Exchange Hypothesis," *Journal of Experimental Social Psychology*, 3 (1967), 75–84.
5. M. A. Wallach, N. Kogan, and D. J. Bem, "Diffusion of Responsibility and Level of Risk Taking in Groups," *Journal of Abnormal and Social Psychology*, 68 (1964), 263–274.
6. Kogan and Wallach, loc. cit.
7. D. G. Pruitt and A. I. Teger, "The Risky Shift in Group Betting," *Journal of Experimental Social Psychology*, 5 (1969), 115–126.
8. R. St. Jean, "A Reformulation of the Value Hypothesis in Group Risk-Taking," Proceedings of the 78th Annual Convention of the American Psychological Association, 5 (1970), 339–340; K. L. Dion, R. S. Baron, and N. Miller, "Why Do Groups Make Riskier Decisions Than Individuals?" in L. Berkowitz, ed., *Advances in Experimental Social Psychology*, Vol. 5 (New York, 1970), pp. 306–377; P. R. Bell and B. Jamison, "Publicity of Initial Decisions and the Risky-Shift Phenomenon," *Journal of Experimental Social Psychology*, 6 (1970), 329–345.
9. Stokes, "Effects of Familiarization and Knowledge of Others' Choices on Shifts to Risk and Caution," *Journal of Personality and Social Psychology*, 20 (1971).
10. E. Burnstein, "An Analysis of Group Decisions Involving Risk ("The Risky Shift")," *Human Relations*, 22 (1969), 381–395; G. Clausen, "Risk Taking in Small Groups," unpublished Ph.D. dissertation, University of Michigan, 1965; Stoner, loc. cit.; N. Kogan and M. A. Wallach, "Risk-Taking As a Function of the Situation, the Person, and the Group," in *New Directions in Psychology III*, New York (1967), pp. 224–226; A. I. Teger and D. G. Pruitt, "Components of Group Risk-Taking," *Journal of Experimental Social Psychology*, 3 (1967), 189–205.
11. Teger and Pruitt, ibid.
12. Dion, et al., loc. cit.; Pruitt, loc. cit.; R. Brown, *Social Psychology* (New York, 1965); R. D. Clark, III, "Group Induced Shift Toward Risk: A Critical Appraisal," *Psychological Bulletin*, 20 (1971), 360–372; A. Vinokar, "Review and Theoretical Analysis of the Effects of Group Processes Upon Individuals and Group Decisions Involving Risk," *Psychological Bulletin*, 76 (1971), 231–249.
13. Brown, ibid.
14. Pruitt, loc. cit.; J. M. Jellison and J. Riskind, "A Social Comparison of Abilities Interpretation of Risk Taking Behavior," *Journal of Personality and Social Psychology*, 15 (1970), 375–390; G. Levinger and D. J. Schneider, "A Test of the

'Risk Is a Value' Hypothesis," *Journal of Personality and Social Psychology*, **18** (1969), 165–169; Brown, loc. cit.

15. Pruitt, loc. cit.

16. Brown, loc. cit.

17. Vinokar, loc. cit.

18. Marquis, loc. cit.; M. A. Wallach and N. Kogan, "The Role of Information, Discussion, and Consensus in Group Risk-Taking," *Journal of Experimental Social Psychology*, **1** (1965), 1–19.

19. Wallach and Kogan, loc. cit.; Kogan and Wallach, loc. cit.

20. Clark, loc. cit.; Bell and Jamison, loc. cit.; R. D. Clark, III, W. H. Crockett, and R. L. Archer, "The Relationship Between Perception of Self, Others, and the Risky," *Journal of Personality and Social Psychology*, **20** (1971), 425–429; S. Chandler and J. Rabow, "Ethnicity and Acquaintance As Variables in Risk-Taking," *Journal of Social Psychology*, **77** (1969), 221–229; H. A. Alker, and N. Kogan, "Effects of Norm-Oriented Group Discussion on Individual Verbal Risk-Taking and Conservatism," *Human Relations*, **21** (1968), 393–405; Chandler and Rabow, loc. cit.

21. Alker and Kogan, loc. cit.; Wallach and Kogan, loc. cit.; Teger and Pruitt, loc. cit.

22. Bell and Jamison, loc. cit.

23. Bell and Jamison, ibid.; Kogan and Wallach, loc. cit.; St. Jean, loc. cit.; H. Lamm, "Will an Isolated Individual Advise Higher Risk Taking After Hearing a Discussion of the Decision Problem?" *Journal of Personality and Social Psychology*, **16** (1967), 467–471; H. Lamm, "Will an Observer Advise Higher Risk Taking After Hearing a Discussion of the Decision Problem?" *Journal of Personality and Social Psychology*, **19** (1970), 467–471.

24. Lamm, ibid.

25. S. Rettig and S. J. Turoff, "Exposure to Group Discussion and Predicted Ethical Risk Taking," *Journal of Personality and Social Psychology*, **7** (1970), 177–180.

26. Vinokar, 231–249, loc. cit.

27. F. NØrdhoy, "Group Interaction in Decision-Making Under Risk," Unpublished Master's thesis, School of Industrial Management, MIT, 1962.

28. St. Jean, loc. cit.

29. G. R. Madaras and D. J. Bem, "Risk and Conservatism in Group Decision-Making," *Journal of Experimental Social Psychology*, **4** (1968), 350–365.

30. P. Murdoch and D. G. Myers, "Information Effects on Cautious and Risky-Shift Items," *Psychonomic Science*, **20** (1970), 97–98.

31. M. A. Wallach and J. Mabli, "Information Versus Conformity in the Effects of Group Discussion on Risk-Taking," *Journal of Personality and Social Psychology*, **19** (1970), 149–156.

32. D. G. Myers and S. J. Arenson, "Enhancement of Initial Risk Tendencies in Group Discussion," Unpublished manuscript, Hope College, 1971.

33. D. G. Myers, D. W. Wong, and P. Murdoch, "Discussion Arguments, Information about Others' Responses, and Risky Shift," *Psychonomic Science*, **24** (1971), 81–83.

34. Brown, loc. cit.; Wallach and Mabli, loc. cit.

35. Brown, ibid.

36. Myers, Wong, Murdoch, loc. cit.

37. D. G. Myers and P. Murdoch, "Is Risky Shift Due to Disproportionate

Influence by Extreme Group Members?" *British Journal of Social and Clinical Psychology,* in press.

38. C. Silverthorne, "Information, Input and the Group Shift Phenomenon in Risk Taking," *Journal of Personality and Social Psychology,* **20** (1971), 456–461.

39. D. G. Myers and G. D. Bishop, "The Enhancement of Dominant Attitudes in Group Discussion," *Journal of Personality and Social Psychology,* **20** (1971), 386–391.

40. R. L. Applbaum and K. W. E. Anatol, "Communication in Small Group Choice Shift," unpublished research report, CSULB, February 1972, p. 18.

41. A. Vinokar, "Distribution of Initial Risk Levels and Group Decisions Involving Risk," *Journal of Personality and Social Psychology,* **18** (1969), 207–214; Brown, loc. cit.

42. S. Rettig, "Group Discussion and Predicted Ethical Risk Taking," *Journal of Personality and Social Psychology,* **15** (1966), 629–633.

43. Chandler and Rabow, loc. cit.

44. J. Rabow et al., "The Role of Social Norms and Leadership in Risk-Taking," *Sociometry,* **29** (1966), 16–27.

45. S. Streufert and S. Streufert, "Information Load, Time Spent, and Risk-Taking in Complex Decision Making," *Psychonomic Science,* **13** (1968), 327–328.

46. H. D. Ellis, C. P. Spencer, and H. Oldfield-Box, "Matched Groups and the Risky Shift Phenomenon: A Defense of the Extreme Member Hypothesis," *British Journal of Social and Clinical Psychology,* 8 (1969), 333–339; G. D. Bishop and D. G. Myers, "The Influence of Persuasive Arguments in Group Discussion," manuscript in preparation, Hope College, 1971; M. Hermann and N. Kogan, "Negotiation in Leader and Delegate Groups," *Journal of Conflict Resolution,* **12** (1968), 332–334; G. C. Hoyt and J. A. F. Stoner, "Leadership and Group Decisions Involving Risk," *Journal of Experimental Social Psychology,* 4 (1968), 275–284; E. P. Willens and R. D. Clark, III, "Dependence on the Risky Shift on Instructions; a Replication," *Psychological Reports,* 25 (1969), 811–814.

47. D. A. Ferguson and N. Vidmar, "Effects of Group Discussion on Estimates of Culturally Appropriate Risk Levels," *Journal of Personality and Social Psychology,* **20** (1971), 436–445; C. Fraser, C. Gouge, and N. Billig, "Risky Shifts, Cautious Shifts, and Group Polarization," *European Journal of Social Psychology,* in press; H. Lamm, E. Schaude, and G. Trommsdorff, "Risky Shift As a Function of Group Members' Value of Risk and the Need for Approval," *Journal of Personality and Social Psychology,* **20** (1971), 430–435.

48. Myers and Murdoch, loc. cit.

49. Hermann and Kogan, loc. cit.; G. R. McCauley, Jr., "Risk and Attitude Shifts Under Group Discussion." Unpublished Ph.D. dissertation, University of Pennsylvania, 1970.

50. M. A. Wallach, N. Kogan, and D. J. Bem, "Group Influence on Individual Risk Taking," *Journal of Abnormal and Social Psychology,* 65 (1962), 76–86; L. Johnston, Jr., "The Immediate and Short-Term Effects of Group Discussion and Individual Study on Risk Levels." Unpublished Ph.D. dissertation, Florida State University, 1968.

51. N. Vidmar and T. C. Burdeny, "Interaction Effects of Group Size and Relation Risk Position with Item Type in the Group Shift Phenomenon," *Research Bulletin,* No. 128, University of Western Ontario, 1969; D. G. Pruitt, "Conclusion: Toward an Understanding of Choice Shifts in Group Discussion," *Journal*

of Personality and Social Psychology, **20** (1971), 495–510; Myers and Arenson, loc. cit.

    52. Pruitt, 339–359; Pruitt, 495–510.

STUDY GUIDE   1. What are the four basic approaches used to study leadership?
QUESTIONS   2. What are the advantages and disadvantages of each approach?
                  3. Which approach has the greatest promise for providing significant information about leadership in the future?
                  4. What role should the study of communication play in the investigation of leadership in the group?

▶◀ Conceptual and Methodological Approaches to the Study of Leadership

DENNIS S. GOURAN

Despite the voluminous amount of research on leadership, empirical findings to date have not contained as much of interest for communication specialists as some would like. The purpose of this article is to discuss conceptual and methodological perspectives for leadership research that hopefully will yield more of the kind of information that is relevant to the interests of our discipline than much of the existing research has.

    Examining the scholarly literature on leadership, one rather quickly discovers four discernible approaches to study of the phenomenon, including what have been described as the trait, stylistic, situational, and functional approaches. Since many of the studies emanating from these research approaches have been summarized by Bormann (1), Cartwright and Zander (2), and Hollander (3), the following discussion of previous contributions will be comparatively brief. The emphasis rather will be on the relative

---

Dennis S. Gouran, "Conceptual and Methodological Approaches to the Study of Leadership," *Central States Speech Journal,* **XXI** (Winter, 1970), 217–223. By permission.

strengths and weaknesses of each approach as exemplified by particular studies.

Research based on the trait approach has frequently grown out of the long held assumption that leaders are born, not made. Apparently accepting the validity of this assumption, some early social psychologists attempted to study leadership by simply identifying the personality variables which theoretically would distinguish leaders from non-leaders. What for centuries had been a commonly held assumption, however, began to be rejected as research findings accumulated. Bird, for example, found in his survey of research designed to identify the unique traits of leaders that only five per cent of those discovered were common to four or more investigations (4).

Borgatta, Couch, and Bales conducted a study (5), which is frequently cited in support of the trait approach. These investigators found that individuals rated high by other group members on task ability, individual assertiveness, and social acceptability after participation in a problem-solving discussion continued to emerge and be recognized as leaders in subsequent sessions. After one carefully examines the study, however, these results seem to be less impressive. Close scrutiny reveals that of the original 126 subjects, only eleven met the investigators' criterion of leadership, and only seven of these remained leaders throughout as many as three group sessions. More importantly, the tasks in every work session in which the leaders participated were highly similar. This similarity in task from one trial to another, of course, did not allow for a very rigorous test of the generalizability of leadership from situation to situation.

Perhaps the most encouraging support for the trait approach is the conclusion reached by Stogdill. His review of leadership research indicated that leaders generally excel non-leaders in intelligence, scholarship, dependability and responsibility, activity and social participation, and socio-economic status (6). In spite of the findings reported by Stogdill, Hollander (7), Cartwright and Zander (8), and Gouldner (9), suggest that the approach has fallen into disfavor and in recent years has been largely abandoned.

Among all of the studies of leadership traits, the one having possibly the greatest interest for communication scholars is Geier's (10). In an investigation of leadership emergence, he identified five negative traits associated with failure to achieve the position of leader in small group discussions. These traits included being uninformed, non-participation, extreme rigidity, authoritarian behavior, and offensive verbalization. With more concentration on communication traits and less on personality variables, the genre of trait research could once again become fashionable.

A second approach to the study of leadership was given impetus by the new classic investigations of White and Lippitt (11). Focusing on what leaders do rather than on their personalities, White and Lippitt studied leadership in three different social climates. The styles of leadership behavior examined included what the investigators labelled authoritarian, democratic, and *laissez-faire*. The democratic style proved to be superior to the others in a number of respects, including the level of group cohesiveness developed, the amount of independent behavior exhibited by the subjects, and the degree of satisfaction with group activities.

Other investigators, while often using terminology different from White and Lippitt's, have studied leadership styles and have generally found the democratic style to be superior in terms of its relative effects on certain dependent variables of interest. Berkowitz, for example, discovered that groups having more permissive leaders developed higher levels of cohesiveness than groups with less permissive leadership (12). In a similar study, Hare reported finding participatory leadership superior to supervisory leadership in producing opinion change (13). Finally, in a non-laboratory setting, Coch and French discovered that employee participation in some decision-making activities in the Harwood Manufacturing Corporation had a significant effect in reducing resistance to change in working conditions (14).

Careful scrutiny of research growing out of the stylistic approach reveals two fairly common tendencies. First, the democratic and participatory styles at their best are frequently studied in relation to more autocratic styles at their worst. This tendency is particularly evident in the White and Lippitt study. The title of the book in which they report their research is *Democracy and Autocracy*, yet what they actually studied was democratic behavior versus authoritarian behavior (15). While authoritarianism may be a characteristic of many autocrats, it is far from being a necessary characteristic. For example, one can retain complete responsibility for making a decision that will be binding on the members of the group, but the exercise of such control would not necessitate prohibiting expressions of others' opinions.

A second tendency evident in this body of research involves the investigators' confusion over what is meant by participation and democratic behavior. In some studies, it includes a role for non-leaders in decision-making activities. In others, it involves no opportunity to exert influence, but only token participation. The confusion is perhaps best exemplified in the Coch and French study (16). What they called "total participation" amounted to the Harwood employees approving or disapproving a plan which the management had proposed. No formal decision, however, was reached by the group, nor were any of the employees permitted to participate in the development of the plan.

Perhaps some of the questionable aspects of stylistic research on leadership could be overcome by more careful manipulations of the various styles investigated. A recent study by Sargent and Miller (17) may have significant implications in this respect. Comparing leaders who preferred the autocratic style with others who preferred the democratic, they found the two types differed along a number of communication dimensions. Autocratic leaders' statements were more task-oriented, more concerned with achievement of their own preferred outcomes, and less favorably disposed to other member participation than democratic leaders'. These fiindings could be the basis for development of a set of criteria for manipulating leadership styles, thereby allowing for more rigorous tests of the effects of different styles on group outcomes.

Despite improvements in the quality of stylistic research which a study like Sargent and Miller's may permit, it is unlikely that we will ever discover one style of leadership to be consistently more effective than others. Korten has argued that the style which is most appropriate for the achievement of a specific set of objectives will depend on a number of situational variables (18). For example, when group goals are more important than individual goals and when ambiguities obscure the paths to achieving such goals, authoritarian leadership will be sought. When ambiguities are not stress-inducing, however, and the attainment of group goals is perceived as unnecessary for the attainment of individual goals, more democratic forms of leadership will be sought.

While the stylistic approach to leadership has indeed been more fruitful than the trait approach, the position developed by Korten reflects what seems to be the major inadequacy in the study of leadership styles. As a result, leadership research has increasingly become a product of the situational approach. In a sense, this approach combines the best features of both of the previous ones. According to Bormann, its underlying assumption is that leadership is "a function of the traits (personality variables) of the members, the purpose of the group, the internal and external pressures on the group, and the *inter-actions of the members*" (19).

Perhaps the most well known exponent of the situational school is Fiedler (20). His years of research with groups performing diverse tasks in a variety of social settings revealed that the successful exercise of leadership is not uniformly related to a particular style or personality type. On the contrary, Fiedler reports having found successful leadership to be the result of individuals in key positions employing a style demanded by the situation and the degree of psychological distance between them and other group members. Other studies by Burke (21), Mulder and Stemerding (22), and Shaw and Blum (23) have produced similar findings.

As Haiman notes, one can easily form the impression from research based on the situational approach that leadership effectiveness depends so heavily on specific situational factors that no general principles can be discovered (24). More important, however, is the general failure of investigators to specify the critical behavior factors in the exercise of influence as they vary from situation to situation. For example, Fiedler found that psychologically close leaders experience greater success in extremely favorable and unfavorable situations while psychologically distant leaders enjoy greater success in only moderately favorable situations (25). His explanation for this difference is that psychologically distant leaders, being more task-oriented, can function better under circumstances which do not create a need for dealing with inter-personal problems. Conversely, psychologically close leaders can function better in those situations which demand attention to interpersonal problems. This explanation, however, does not help one to identify what specific differences in the behavior of close and distant leaders exist and, more important, which behaviors contribute most to these respective types of leaders' success.

A final approach to leadership research involves the identification of group functions which promote the achievement of specific objectives. Cattell was one of the earliest theorists to espouse the functional position. He argues that any group member exerts leadership if the properties (syntality) of the group are modified by his presence (26). More recently, Bavelas, in defense of the functional approach, has asserted that we need to define the leadership functions that must be performed in various situations and "regard as leadership those acts which perform them" (27).

The major problem with the functional approach so far has been that it has not yielded a set of functions that are uniquely related to leadership, nor has it identified those behaviors which most consistently contribute to the achievement of group goals. As Cartwright and Zander point out, the trend in this body of research has been simply "to identify the various group functions, without deciding finally whether or not to label each specifically as a function of leadership" (28). This tendency is particularly evident in the pioneering research efforts reported by Krech and Crutchfield (29) and Shartle (30). Within the last few years, however, a new trend has begun to emerge with scholars attempting to discover what determines the development of group functions, their allocation, and the consequences resulting from their execution (31).

Of the four approaches to leadership research just reviewed, the functional approach appears to have the greatest promise for significant developments in future research. Despite the differences among the trait, stylistic, and situational approaches, they seem to have two things in common which, in this writer's judgment, render them relatively less useful than the functional approach. First, they focus on individuals as leaders as they affect group behavior rather than on leadership as a total process of achieving goals. Second, because of the centrality of particular individuals in these approaches, the research which has grown out of them provides at best only limited information about the ways in which group goals are achieved; that is, we learn about the behavior and contributions of only one or two group members, but not much about other contributions which may be at least as important as those made by the so-called leaders.

Most of the research growing out of the functional approach has been more concerned with the distribution and execution of many different kinds of activities in groups and organizations than with communication acts exclusively. In addition, many of the functions studied have been defined in terms of variables that are too global to be of much interest in communication research. Two of the functions sometimes studied, for example, are planning and maintenance. More emphasis should be placed on the statements which group members make and, more particularly, on the measurable properties of those kinds of statements which seem to be in evidence whenever a group achieves one of its goals and absent when it does not.

The notion of studying statements in leadership research is, of course, by no means a new one, nor is the functional approach the only one of the four reviewed which is amenable to such a methodological strategy. The earlier mentioned studies by Geier (32) and by Sargent and Miller (33) rather clearly focused on the kinds of statements made by leaders. The emphasis in these studies, however, was not on the characteristics of statements related to the achievement of group goals.

To focus on the statement as the unit of interest in leadership research will necessitate developing a meaningful set of descriptive characteristics with which to make evaluations. One system which already exists is Bales' Interaction Process Analysis (34). Because of its availability and because of the considerable amount of research that has employed it, IPA would obviously be useful in the type of research being proposed. There are some problems associated with Bales' system of analysis, however, which have led some people to believe that new methodological approaches and strategies need to be developed in order to move our research substantially forward. The author has argued elsewhere that IPA suffers in at least two important respects (35). First, the categories are mutually exclusive, which precludes looking at the same statement from more than one perspective. Many statements made in a discussion, however, serve several functions and could be classified in more than one way. Second, the system does not lend itself to precise statistical analysis. One is limited to comparing the relative proportions of certain kinds of statements emanating from different groups.

Unfortunately, it is not possible at present to offer as well a defined system of analysis with which to replace Bales' as might be desirable. However, some promising methodological research has been completed recently which might eventually lead to the development of a more useful analytical system than Interaction Process Analysis. In separate studies, Taylor (36), Russell (37), and Gouran (38) have had judges rate discussion statements on a substantial number of variables. In each case the task

of the judges was to determine the extent to which the statements exhibited each of several different properties, such as opinionatedness, clarity,
provocativeness, and informativeness. These data were then factor analyzed,
and subsequent examination of the results in the separate studies has revealed the emergence of three rather stable factors which could be called
goal facilitation, social-emotional behavior, and communication skills. Each
of these factors was common to at least two of the studies. The first dimension was characterized by such variables as orientation, cooperativeness,
and objectivity; the second by emotionality, defensivenesss, and argumen-
tativeness; and the third by clarity, informativeness, and clarification.

The three factors and related variables just described could form the
basis of a new analytical system for use in future leadership research. Over
time, such a system would undoubtedly undergo considerable revision and
refinement as investigators continue to tap more of the dimensions of group
processes, better define the variables which represent them, and improve
the methods of detecting their presence in discussion statements. Until a
more refined system does evolve, however, considerable headway in leadership research can still be made. The remainder of this discussion will explain and exemplify the form which this research might take.

For the immediate future, perhaps more of our leadership research
should be investigatory than experimental. At present, we do not have
sound bases for making the kinds of predictive statements demanded in
experimental research. Well designed and carefully executed investigations
could provide the kind of information with which it would be possible to
generate research hypotheses which subsequently could be experimentally
tested.

The question which naturally arises is, "What type of investigatory
research should be done?" Perhaps initially, the most fruitful strategy is to
compare groups which have achieved their goals with those which have
failed to achieve them in terms of the kinds of communication variables
previously mentioned. For example, if problem-solving were a goal of interest, one might try to discover if groups which are successful in this activity
make statements which are consistently clearer, more objective, and more
informative than groups which are unsuccessful. Discovering differences, of
course, could be coincidental, but one would at least have some basis for
making an intelligent prediction about the effects of certain kinds of communication behavior on the achievement of a group goal.

An actual example of the success of this proposed strategy might help
to make it more acceptable. In an investigation of variables related to consensus, the author discovered that the statements of consensus groups manifested generally higher levels of orientation than those of non-consensus
groups (39). As a result, in a subsequent experiment, Knutson had a basis
for predicting that groups having high orientation statements deliberately

injected into their discussions would come closer to consensus on a question of policy than groups without such statements (40).

The characteristics of the communication behaviors associated with the achievement of consensus on questions of policy, of course, are not the only ones of interest. Those related to the achievement of other kinds of goals, such as the development of cohesiveness, conciliation, increased sensitivity, accuracy of communication, and information gain, would also be worthy of study. The purpose of this article, however, has not been to indicate specific studies which need to be undertaken. Rather, it has been to encourage a particular way of looking at leadership and to develop a general methodological strategy for research. The precise features of leadership that should be examined, of course, will depend on the judgment of individual researchers and the uses to which they wish to put the knowledge they might uncover.

While much remains to be learned about the phenomenon of leadership, hopefully the focus which has been suggested and the strategy which has been outlined will help achieve this end. The knowledge that might be obtained from this kind of approach would be valuable in the development of a fruitful theory of group communication and would have significant practical implications as well.

NOTES

1. Ernest G. Bormann, *Discussion and Group Methods: Theory and Practice* (New York: Harper & Row, 1969), pp. 244–248.

2. Dorwin Cartwright and Alvin Zander, eds., *Group Dynamics: Research and Theory*, 3rd ed. (New York: Harper & Row, 1968), pp. 301–315.

3. Edwin P. Hollander, *Leaders, Groups, and Influence* (New York: Oxford University Press, 1964), pp. 3–15.

4. Cartwright and Zander, p. 303.

5. Edgar Borgatta et al., "Some Findings Relevant to the Great Man Theory of Leadership." *American Sociological Review*, XIX (1954), 755–759.

6. Ralph Stodgill, "Personal Factors Associated with Leadership: A Survey of the Literature," *Journal of Psychology*, XXV (1948), 1–14.

7. Hollander, p. 4.

8. Cartwright and Zander, pp. 302–304.

9. A. W. Gouldner, ed., *Studies in Leadership* (New York: Harper & Row, 1950), pp. 23–45.

10. John G. Geier, "A Trait Approach to the Study of Leadership in Small Groups," *Journal of Communication*, XVII (1967), 316–323.

11. Ralph White and Ronald Lippitt, *Autocracy and Democracy* (New York: Harper & Row, 1960).

12. Leonard Berkowitz, "Sharing Leadership in Small Decision-Making Groups," *Journal of Abnormal and Social Psychology*, XLVIII (1953), 231–238.

13. A. Paul Hare, "Small Group Discussions with Participatory and Supervisory Leadership," *Journal of Abnormal and Social Psychology*, XLVIII (1953), 273–275.

14. Lester Coch and John R. French, Jr., "Overcoming Resistance to Change," *Human Relations*, XI (1948), 512–532.

15. White and Lippitt.

16. Coch and French.

17. James F. Sargent and Gerald R. Miller, "Some Differences in the Communication Behaviors of Autocratic and Democratic Group Leaders." (Paper presented at the Speech Association of America Convention, December 28, 1969, New York.)

18. David G. Korten, "Situational Determinants of Leadership Structure," *Journal of Conflict Resolution*, VI (1962), 222–235.

19. Bormann, p. 246.

20. Fred E. Fiedler, "Personality and Situational Determinants of Leadership Effectiveness," in Cartwright and Zander, pp. 362–380.

21. W. Warner Burke, "Leadership Behavior as a Function of the Leader, the Follower, and the Situation," *Journal of Personality*, XXXIII (1965), 60–81.

22. Mauk Mulder and Ad Stemerding, "Threat, Attraction to Group, and Need for Strong Leadership," *Human Relations*, XVI (1963), 317–334.

23. Marvin E. Shaw and Michael J. Blum, "Effects of Leadership Style upon Group Performance as a Function of Task Structure," *Journal of Personality and Social Psychology*, III (1966), 238–242.

24. Franklyn Haiman, *Group Leadership and Democratic Action* (Boston: Houghton Mifflin, 1951), pp. 10–11.

25. Fiedler, p. 375.

26. Raymond Cattell, "New Concepts for Measuring Leadership in Terms of Group Syntality," *Human Relations*, IV (1951), 378–383.

27. Alex Bavelas, "Leadership: Man and Function," *Administrative Science Quarterly*, IV (1960), p. 494.

28. Cartwright and Zander.

29. David Krech and Richard S. Crutchfield, *Theories and Problems of Social Psychology* (New York: McGraw-Hill, 1948), cited in Cartwright and Zander, p. 305.

30. C. L. Shartle, *Executive Performance and Leadership* (Englewood Cliffs, N.J.: Prentice-Hall, 1956), cited in Cartwright and Zander, p. 305.

31. Cartwright and Zander, p. 305.

32. Geier.

33. Sargent and Miller.

34. For the most recent version of Interaction Process Analysis Techniques, see Robert F. Bales, *Personality and Interpersonal Behavior* (New York: Holt, Rinehart and Winston, 1970).

35. Dennis S. Gouran, *An Investigation to Identify the Critical Variables Related to Consensus in Group Discussions of Questions of Policy* (Washington, D.C.: Educational Research Information Center, 1969), p. 6.

36. K. Phillip Taylor, "An Investigation of Majority Verbal Behavior Toward Opinions of Deviant Members in Group Discussions of Policy (Ph.D. dissertation, Indiana University, 1969), pp. 37–62.

37. Hugh C. Russell, "An Investigation of Leadership Maintenance Behavior" (Ph.D. dissertation, Indiana University, 1970), pp. 30–61.

38. Gouran, pp. 9–14.

39. Ibid., pp. 63–64.

40. Thomas J. Knutson, "An Experimental Study of the Effects of Statements Giving Orientation on the Probability of Reaching Consensus on Group Discussion of Questions of Policy" (Ph.D. dissertation, Indiana University 1970).

1. What is intercultural communication?
2. What variables in the communication process are acutely influenced by culture?
3. What is the role of intercultural communication within groups?

▶◀ Intercultural Communication in the Group Setting

RICHARD E. PORTER

During the past twenty years, foreign and domestic events have focused our attention on an area of human interaction called intercultural communication. Racial and ethnic minorities have left the barrio or ghetto and demanded a place in the mainstream of modern American life. Sometimes these demands have been reasoned and peaceful; at other times they have been wild and violent. Advances in transportation and communication have caused hundreds of thousands of us to travel abroad or to be exposed to other cultures in our living rooms. These new contacts have often resulted in communication failures and our development of unfavorable or hostile attitudes toward "those other people."

What has happened is that many of us have been forced into communication events for which we were not prepared. We were communicating interculturally using habits and techniques that were only suitable for intracultural communication.

WHAT IS INTERCULTURAL COMMUNICATION?

Literally, intercultural means between cultures, and intercultural communication occurs whenever a message is produced in one culture and consumed in another. In other words, whenever a person who is a member of one culture sends a message—whether it be verbal or nonverbal, spoken or written—to someone who is a member of another culture, both are communicating interculturally.

"Intercultural Communication in the Group Setting," by Richard E. Porter. Reprinted with permission of the author. This original essay appears here for the first time.

Since intercultural communication is that which takes place between cultures, you may rightly be asking what cultures are. What are these things between which this communication occurs? After all, cultures are not people, cultures cannot speak, read, write, or express themselves. Or can they? Let us take a look at cultures.

In the traditional anthropological sense, culture is the sum deposit of experiences, beliefs, values, attitudes, perceptions, ways of doing things, ways of living, religion, habits, modes of dress, uses of space, conceptualization of time, and social organization shared by a geographically bound group of people over generations. This view of culture is still valid, but in order to understand the problems of contemporary intercultural communication, we must modify it to a degree. The major modification of our view of culture is in the time required for a culture to develop. In times past cultures were highly stable; changes came about slowly because of the limiting constraints of travel and transportation. Prior to World War II, few of us ever ventured beyond our own county. There might have been a once-in-a-lifetime vacation to California or New York, but most of us were born, lived, and died in our community. There was little opportunity for change to be introduced or for us to gain knowledge of other ways of life. We essentially lived in isolation.

World War II, Korea, Vietnam, television, and jet airplanes have changed all this. Today we are a highly mobile society. We move about freely, live in different parts of the country, visit foreign countries, and have other cultures enter our living room via the television tube. Consequently, we are exposed to many new ideas and ways of life. And, as we are adaptive animals, we tend to take for ourselves those elements of culture we find most satisfying. As a result, new cultures—or subcultures if you wish— develop at a rate not envisioned in the traditional view of culture. Granted many of these "new cultures" may be short-lived and not survive. But, during their existence we may find need to communicate with their members. We cannot ignore their presence merely because they may disappear within the decade.

Today, in the United States we find many cultures. Some are based on race: black, Chicano, Oriental, and the original American—the Indian. Others are based on ethnic differences: Jew, Italian, German, Pole, Irish, and Greek are but a few of the many ethnic cultures we find in the United States. There are also cultures based on socioeconomic differences. The world of the Rockefellers or the Kennedys is vastly different from that of the third-generation welfare families of Denver. And, finally, cultures develop around ways of life and value systems. Members of the drug culture share perceptions of the world that are vastly different from those shared by, for example, members of the John Birch Society or the Ku Klux Klan.

If we choose to venture beyond our national boundaries, we can find vastly greater differences in cultures. Religious, philosophical, political, economic, and social-role views may be greatly different from our own as may be communities, modes of life, forms of work, degrees of industrialization, and social organizations. In these cases, people are noticeably different from ourselves in their ways of life, customs, and traditions.

CULTURE AND COMMUNICATION

Many variables in the communication process are determined or influenced by culture. These variables help influence the way meaning is attached to the messages we receive (or for that matter the way in which we form messages). If our perception of a message is incorrect, we will attach the wrong meaning to it and misunderstanding will occur. Among the many variables in the communication process four are acutely influenced by culture: (1) attitudes, (2) patterns of thought, (3) roles and role prescriptions, and (4) nonverbal expression. We examine these variables to develop a basic knowledge and understanding of cultural factors and their influence on group interaction.

Attitudes

Attitudes are psychological states derived from our beliefs and values that predispose us to behave in specific manners when we come in contact with various social events or objects. Attitudes influence both our overt behaviors and our perceptions. They lead us to interpret events so that they are in accord with our beliefs and values. We sometimes tend to see things as we wish them to be rather than as they are. Four forms of attitudes exert the greatest influence on intercultural communication.

The first form of attitude is *ethnocentrism*. This is a tendency for us to view others by using ourselves as the standard for all judgments. We place ourselves at the center of the universe and rate all others accordingly. The greater their similarity the nearer we place them; the greater the dissimilarity, the farther away they are. We rank one group above another, one element of society above another, and one country above another. We see our own groups, our own country, and our own culture as the best. Ethnocentrism demands our first loyalty and carried to extremes it produces acts such as Watergate.

When we allow ethnocentrism to interfere with our social perception, the effectiveness of our intercultural communication is reduced because we cannot view another culture objectively. The degree to which ethnocentrism reduces communication effectiveness cannot be predicted because of the variety of circumstances under which it manifests itself. We do know, however, that it is strongest in moral and religious contexts, where emotion may overshadow rationality and promote the hostility that prevents effective communication. Finally, at the extreme, ethnocentrism can take from us the willingness or desire to communicate interculturally.

World view is the second form of attitude. How we view the world in which we live is a function of our culture. We as Americans tend to have a man-centered world view. Our world is a vast space on which we may carry out our desires. We build what we wish, we seek to control nature, and when displeased, we tear it all down and start again. Projects such as urban renewal are but just one result of this view.

Other cultures view the world differently. Orientals are apt to view the man-cosmos relationship as one of balance in which man shares a place between heaven and earth. Each thing that we do has some effect on the balance of that relationship. We must act carefully so as not to upset the balance because it is the nature of the universe to tend toward harmony.

World view gives us a perspective from which we shape and form our attitudes. As we encounter people with differing world views, our communicative behavior may be hampered because we view events differently; we use frames of reference that may seem vague or obscure to others, just as theirs may seem to us. Our perceptions become clouded and our attitudes interfere with our ability to share perceptions with others.

The third form of attitude is *absolute values*. These are closely related to and are often derived from ethnocentrism and world view. Absolute values are culturally derived notions we have of right and wrong, good and bad, beautiful and ugly, true and false, positive and negative, and so on. They influence our social perception by providing us with a set of basic precepts from which we judge the behavior and beliefs of others. We take these notions to be absolute—to be "truth"—and do not or cannot realize that these "absolutes" are not absolute but are subject to cultural variation. An absolute value or concept is meaningful to us only in the relative sense of what is accepted or believed within a given culture.

The fourth form of attitude is *stereotypes and prejudices*. Stereotypes are attitudinal sets in which we assign attributes to another person solely on the basis of the class or category to which that person belongs. Stereotyping might lead us to believe, for example, that all Irish are quick-tempered and redheaded; that all Japanese are short, buck-toothed, and sly; that all Jews are shrewd and grasping; or that all blacks are superstitious and lazy. Although these generalizations are commonly held stereotypes, they are untrue! Prejudices, on the other hand, are attitudinal sets that predispose us to behave in certain ways toward people solely on the basis of their membership in some group. For example, because a person is an Oriental, a Jew, or a black, we may deny him membership in a country club, force him to live in a ghetto or barrio, or restrict him to low-paying jobs and the performance of menial tasks. Stereotypes and prejudices are closely interrelated.

The effect of prejudice and stereotypes on our impressions of others is illustrated by Secord and Backman:

A prejudiced person perceives selectively certain aspects of the behavior of the Negro: those that fit in with his preconceived ideas concerning the Negro. Thus he observes and notes behavior incidents that demonstrate stupidity, laziness, irresponsibility, or superstition; he overlooks other incidents that might contradict his prevailing ideas. The behavior of the Negro as he observes it thus supports his prejudicial beliefs. (p. 15)

Stereotypes and prejudices work in various ways to affect our communication. By predisposing us to behave in specific ways when confronted by a particular stimulus and by causing us to attach generalized attributes to people whom we encounter, we allow stereotypes and prejudices to interfere with our communicative experiences and to limit their effectiveness. We spend our time looking for whatever reinforces our prejudices and stereotypes and ignore what is contradictory.

Patterns of Thought

The form of reasoning prevalent in a culture influences intercultural communication. Pribram has suggested:

Mutual understanding and peaceful relations among the peoples of the earth have been impeded not only by the multiplicity of languages but to an even greater degree by differences in patterns of thought—that is, by differences in the methods adopted for defining the source of knowledge, and for organizing coherent thinking. . . . The most striking differences among philosophical doctrines are attributable to deep-seated divergencies in the methods of forming fundamental concepts and of deriving the functions of Reason—that is, the cognitive power of the human mind and the extent and validity of that power. (p. 1)

Oliver has suggested that a major difficulty in intercultural communication is the differences between Aristotelian modes of reasoning that are prevalent in our Western culture and the non-Aristotelian systems of the Orient. The Aristotelian system was developed for men who were presumed to be free and having the right to cast ballots; it views man as a rational being who is available to factual and sound reasoning.

Our Western assumptions are not universal. There are many modes of thinking, many standards of value, many ways in which we conceive of our relationship to the universe. In the Taoist view, men are not rational beings, nor is truth to be conceived in terms of reason and logic. Tao states that human life is conditioned and unfree, and only when we recognize this limitation and make ourselves dependent on the harmonious forces of the universe do we achieve success. Tao holds that truth is most likely to emerge when we wait for it, when we accept it as it comes rather than setting forth along a preconceived path in a predetermined manner to define a preconceived truth. Tao teaches the wisdom of being foolish, the success of failure, the strength of weakness, and the futility of contending for power.

If we are to improve our intercultural communication abilities, we must determine what effect differences in reasoning patterns have on communicative behavior. We must also learn how to communicate with those whose reasoning is different from our own. We must learn to recognize that a system that teaches the futility of contending for power assumes that power rightly comes to those who deserve it; it need not be sought.

Roles and Role Prescriptions

Roles and role prescriptions are important in intercultural communication because they vary culturally. If we encounter members of other cultures and their behavior seems strange to us, it could very well be a matter of different role prescriptions. And, although we might wish to argue the value of a particular role prescription, we must realize—if we are to succeed in our task of communication—that, for members of the culture with which we are in contact, their behaviors are completely natural, normal, and moral.

An example of cultural differences in role prescriptions and the effect it had on intercultural relations comes to us from England during World War II. British women came to see American servicemen stationed in England as immoral and lustful. Simultaneously, American servicemen found English girls to be wanton and without morals. This was not the general case! Cultural differences in the role of sex-behavior moderator caused the misunderstanding. In America, this responsibility is prescribed for the female role; in England, this responsibility was a male role behavior. Thus, American servicemen, who were used to being told "no" by American women, suddenly found themselves dating English women who had never learned to say "no" because their culture did not require it of them. And, English women, who were used to men not making advances unless they were seriously intended, found themselves dating American servicemen who were used to making sexual advances until told to stop.

We cannot assume that the rest of the world should and does share the same role behaviors as we do. We must remember that what seems strange and perhaps wrong to us is completely natural and normal for others. And, our customs and behaviors probably seem just as strange to others.

Nonverbal Expression

Nonverbal expression is the last major variable in the communication process affected by culture that we discuss.

It is a common experience among people who travel to find that it is difficult to interpret the facial expressions of peoples of cultures other than their own. This difficulty has frequently been voiced with reference to Oriental people whose modes of expression are bound to differ from those of Caucasians. (Vinacke, p. 407)

The form that nonverbal messages take as well as the circumstances calling for their expression and the amount of expression permitted is culturally determined. Klineberg has pointed out:

We find that cultures differ widely from one another in the amount of emotional expression which is permitted. We speak, for example, of the imperturbability of the American Indian, the inscrutability of the Oriental, the reserve of the Englishman, and at the other extreme of the expressiveness of the Negro or the Sicilian. Although there is always some exaggeration in such clichés, it is probable that they do correspond to an accepted cultural pattern, at least to some degree. (p. 174)

The Japanese smile is a law of etiquette that has been elaborated and cultivated from early times; it is not necessarily a spontaneous expression of amusement. This smile is a silent language that is often inexplicable to Westerners. The Japanese child is taught to smile as a social duty so he will always show an appearance of happiness and avoid inflicting sorrow upon his friends.

The problem as it affects intercultural communication can be seen in the following anecdote. A Japanese woman servant smilingly asked her Western mistress if she might go to her husband's funeral. Later she returned with his ashes in a vase, and, actually laughing, said, "Here is my husband." Her mistress regarded her as a cynical creature, although her smile and laughter may have been reflective of pure heroism.

There are cultural variations even in what may be considered a more basic form of expression—the nonverbal expressions of what we call verbal statements. In our culture, we often express the verbal statement "no" nonverbally by moving our heads from side to side. Yet, an Abyssinian is apt to express "no" by jerking the head to the right shoulder; a Dyand of Borneo may express it by contracting the eyebrows slightly; and Sicilians express "no" by raising the head and chin. Among the Ainu of northern Japan our particular head noddings are unknown; "no" is expressed by a movement of the right hand and affirmation by a simultaneous movement of both hands.

There is much for us to learn about how people from other cultures use nonverbal cues to express themselves. Until we gain this knowledge we are going to encounter trouble whenever we communicate with people from other cultures. Nonverbal aspects of intercultural communication are probably among the most difficult because of the reliance we place on the interpretation of nonverbal cues in the decoding of verbal cues.

This discussion of the relationships between culture and communication has only been a brief introduction. The variables we have discussed were merely highlighted, and not all have been mentioned. One reason is the obvious lack of space. Another is that our knowledge of the effect of culture on communication is woefully inadequate.

INTERCULTURAL COMMUNICATION WITHIN GROUPS

The emphasis we have given to describing culture and its influence on the communication process was necessary in order to show how we come to possess different backgrounds and experiences that are not necessarily available to or known by others with whom we may wish to communicate. Our ability to decode and understand a message requires knowledge of the culture in which it was encoded. Ignorance of this knowledge can result in our misinterpreting and misunderstanding, which can lead us to inappropriate responses. Sometimes the consequences are negligible; at other times they can be fatal. Sitaram has suggested: "What is an effective communication symbol in one culture could be an obscene gesture in another culture. The communication technique that makes a person successful in New York could kill him in New Delhi" (p. 19).

Intercultural communication is often a factor in group communication settings. This comes about when a group is composed of people from various cultural backgrounds. We find this in international settings when people from various countries meet to discuss and solve international problems. Or we find it in domestic areas when students representing various ethnic and racial cultures attempt to guide their school policies and actions. And, we frequently find intercultural group situations when civic bodies or panels are formed. In this case an often first effort is to empanel as members a priest, a minister, and a rabbi, a black, an Oriental, and a Chicano, as well as women and representatives of other diverse groups within the community. However admirable this may be in terms of democratic institutions, it often results in groups whose composition defies many rules of group dynamics. This is especially so in the area of shared values, beliefs, and attitudes. Whereas a natural group—one formed through the ongoing process of group dynamics—is composed of members who share similar relevant values, beliefs, and attitudes, artificial groups—those we form by administrative action—may be composed of members who have dissimilar value systems and who distrust and even dislike the cultural systems each other represents. Tolerance may be practiced, but it does not overcome differences in basic beliefs and values that influence the outcomes of group interaction.

An example of how cultural influence on attitudes affected communication in the group situation can be seen in the description of an interaction exchange between participants in an intercultural communication workshop. A discussion between black and white students about black-white relationships had been ongoing for about thirty minutes. The general trend of the discussion was that blacks did not trust or believe whites. Finally, a frustrated white student, who could not understand why this attitude prevailed, asked a black woman if he came to her and said that he would like to help the blacks achieve equality, how would she respond! She responded by saying, "I wouldn't believe you." When she was asked to explain why she wouldn't believe him, she outlined the history of the white man's relationship with the American Indian in which promises and treaties were made and later broken when it was to the advantage of the whites. After citing numerous instances of whites having broken promises and treaties and generally mistreating minorities, she queried the white student with, "Why should I believe you?"

One cannot argue that our past behavior toward racial and ethnic minorities has been one that would result in a minority distrust of the majority. What must be recognized, however, by both the minorities and the majority is that each individual cannot be judged by the behaviors of the group from which he comes. There are very good grounds for blacks and other minorities to distrust some or many whites, but not all of them. Only through intercultural communication can we learn who can and who cannot be trusted. And, the white who hopes to successfully interact with minorities must be prepared to show—even to prove—that he is worthy of trust and belief.

Other aspects of culture can also effect intercultural communication within groups. Differences in the way people view problem solving and the basic philosophy upon which it is based can contribute to misunderstanding and group failure. Several years ago representatives of countries from the Far East met in the Philippines to discuss economic self-help. The conference goal was to find how these countries could develop economically without having to be dependent on the Western world for economic assistance. After several days of conferring and trying to establish a way in which the "have" nations could help the "have not" countries, a Chinese delegate, who had been educated in the West and who was a Christian, offered the traditional charitable Christian view that it is better to give than it is to receive. That remark was responded to by another Chinese who had been raised and educated in the Taoist tradition, who said that he agreed it is better to give than to receive, but it is even better not to give at all. The result of this exchange was the dissolution of the conference.

What went wrong? Granted many factors could have been and quite likely were at work. However, one major difference between the two delegates was their cultural backgrounds and the influence these backgrounds had on their approaches to problem solving. Western philosophy is more directed to the world as it exists than is Oriental philosophy. Tao stresses a concern with the world as it ought to be rather than with how it actually is. This difference also affects approaches to problem solving. Consequently, when the Western-educated Christian delegate spoke of giving he was speaking from his own frame of reference and toward the immediate problem. On the other hand, the Taoist delegate's comments reflected his background and a solution for a world as it ought to be. If the world were as it ought to be, there would be no "have" nations and no "have not" nations, and consequently there would be no need for giving. So from his point of view, a better state would be the one in which giving was not necessary.

As stated earlier, there were undoubtedly many other factors at work, such as economic considerations. But, the inability of the delegates to continue their conference following that particular dialogue suggests cultural variance in ways of viewing the world and its problems was a major influence in the outcomes of that intercultural communication event.

A final example of cultural influence in group communication comes from a group discussion class. In this instance, the group formed at the beginning of the semester to discuss the common interest problem of divorce in the United States. For several weeks everything went well. During the initial phases of the discussion, agreement was easily reached on the nature of the problem, its extent, its effects, and even its causes. But, when the solution phase of the discussion began, difficulty developed. One member of the group was a deeply devout Catholic. To him the only possible solution was to make divorce illegal because it was an immoral act that should not be permitted. This was his only position and he was adamantly against any other possible solution. The result of this was an initial attempt by the other six members of the group to communicate with him and attempt to have him modify his position or at least listen to alternatives that could be available to non-Catholics. This effort met with no success, and when it became evident that the Catholic would not alter his position or even listen to other views, he was essentially banished from the group. He became a mere observer of the group to which he had once been an active member. And after a short time, he began to miss the group discussions altogether. Here was a case where the prevailing belief-value system of the group was too different from his and it soon became more rewarding for him not to be a member of the group than to continue his group membership. Consequently, he dropped out of the group.

This event was an extreme example. But, it is the type of situation that can easily crop up when we form groups to represent all views and interests. Some views are just not compatible with others as some interests are not compatible with others. When we force these to interact, the outcome may be a very large CRUNCH.

Here we have taken the approach that the chief barriers to intercultural communication come from errors in the interpretation of messages. For there to be successful intercultural communication within groups, we must be aware of the cultural factors affecting communication in both our own culture and the culture of others. We need to understand not only cultural differences but also cultural similarities. Understanding differences will help us know where problems lie, but understanding similarities may help us become closer.

REFERENCES

Klineberg, O. *Social Psychology*, rev. ed. New York: Holt, Rinehart and Winston, Inc., 1954.
Oliver, R. T. *Culture and Communication*, Springfield, Ill.: Charles C Thomas, Publishers, 1962.
Pribram, K. *Conflicting Patterns of Thought*. Washington, D.C.: Public Affairs Press, 1949.
Secord, P. F., and C. W. Backman. *Social Psychology*. New York: McGraw-Hill, Inc., 1964.
Siteram, K. S. "What Is Intercultural Communication?" *Intercultural Communication: A Reader*, edited by L. A. Samovar and R. E. Porter. Belmont, Calif.: Wadsworth Publishing Co., Inc., 1972.
Vinacke, E. W. "The Judgment of Facial Expressions by Three National-Racial Groups in Hawaii: I. Caucasian Faces." *Journal of Personality*, 17 (1949), 407–429.

V Strategies of Communication

How important is speech communication? In the past three sections of the text we have seen the pervasive role of speech communication in intrapersonal, interpersonal, and group communication. However, we have been dealing with the general processes of human communication. We have not dealt with the situational role of speech communication, that is, the environmental context in which it occurs and how the situation affects the speech communication process.

Business, industry, social agencies, and governmental operations are particularly interested in the individual's ability to communicate effectively. Industrial firms, for example, General Motors, have established speech communication training programs for employees, potential managers, and corporate executives. These firms recognize a relationship between an individual's ability to communicate and that individual's job effectiveness. Managers complain that they feel "left out." They are frustrated because their orders, instructions, and directions are lost or misinterpreted. Rank-and-file workers complain that upward communication is ineffective. Communication is censored and important items are deleted. Feedback is inadequate and not dependable. These beliefs are evidenced by low morale and inefficient work.

Sound business practices require that a manufacturer produce products that potential consumers want. The manufacturer must see to it that prospective buyers are informed about their products. As a result, the manufacturer attempts to make potential buyers aware of and stimulate their desires for more goods and services. Advertising communication serves the function of creating a demand for goods and services. It is designed to add to the number of people consuming a product; to induce buyers to increase their consumption; to reach individuals who will influence others who actually do the buying; to dispel existing prejudices; and to help shape the tastes, habits, and customs of consumers.

Most Americans listen to, or are at least in the presence of a radio or television, several hours a day. Mass media exposes us to experiences from around the world. We are now attending to messages we might have missed or even ignored in the past—foreign wars, riots in the streets, political corruption, and the development and fragmentation of the American family. In addition, the electronic media has become the greatest huckster in our society. It has been said somewhat sarcastically that a television show is actually twelve commercials interrupted by doctors, detectives, and cowboys; curing the uncurable, solving the unsolvable, and protecting the unprotectable.

From our experience with television, the courtroom is a situation involving communicative gamesmenship between lawyers, judges, witnesses, and juries. An intelligent viewer realizes that discrepancies exist between the fantasy of law performed for the media and the reality of the existing legal system. However, effective communication is a requisite to the efficient functioning of the legal system. In the courtroom, lawyers must command the knowledge and ability to utilize persuasive strategies. Judges and juries must be able to evaluate the credibility of witnesses, their testimony, and the evidence. Judges must be able to communicate the legal rules to the jury and lawyers.

Since our representative democracy requires the popular election of most governmental, city, and country officials, we are bombarded with information attempting to influence our voting behavior. We are confronted with television, radio, newspapers, pamphlets, and door-to-door canvassers selling the candidate for office. The candidate's public communications have become performances staged for the benefit of the listening audience, the potential voter.

The articles in this section examine the role of communication in a number of different situations. *Organizational Communication: An "Unconventional" Perspective* by Gary M. Richetto examines the field of organizational communication. Richetto describes a framework for analyzing and understanding communication behavior in organizations. This framework conceives of human communication as an intervening variable between "causes" and "end-results." He also suggests a direction for future research in organizational communication springing from this conceptual framework.

Joseph T. Plummer, in A *Theoretical View of Advertising Communication*, presents a four-level model of the communication process operating in television advertising: (1) unconscious level, (2) immediate perceptual level, (3) retention or learning level, and (4) behavioral level. Each level is examined and its role in the total communication process is explored.

Robert F. Forston, in *Communication Perspectives in the Legal Process*, explores the role of communication in legal settings. The communication involved in legal disputes leading to trial are investigated on five levels:

(1) negotiation between attorneys; (2) pleadings and motions; (3) motions for preliminary relief and trial advantage; (4) the trial; and (5) posttrial motions and appeals. The communication roles of lawyers, witnesses, judges, and juries are examined separately.

Communication and the Media by Robert K. Avery utilizes our knowledge of interpersonal communication as a stepping-stone in developing an awareness of media, first by calling attention to the differences between interpersonal and mass communication and second by describing how these forms interface to complete the mass communication process. Following a brief review of the research tradition in mass communication, the reader is confronted with the task of resolving the conflicting statements of concerned critics and research reports.

Karl W. E. Anatol, in *Communication Perspectives in Political Campaigns*, investigates the major factors that constitute the communication perspectives in the political campaign process. He describes (1) the facets of the campaign staff; (2) the importance of image, themes, and slogans; (3) the effects of various channels and the types of audiences drawn to them; (4) the audience and its attitudes toward the party and the issues; and (5) the context surrounding the campaign.

William B. Lashbrook and Michael D. Scott, in *Man-Machine Communication: The Strategy of the Future,* view the evolution of communication into an information science. Man the communicator is to be viewed as an information processing system. Mechanistic innovations in the present and future will intensify the demands placed on the information-processing capabilities of the individual and bring added stress to his relationship with the environment. This will require an understanding of technologically assisted information processing for purposes of adaptation and control.

1. What is the surveyfeedback approach to organizational analysis?
2. How can communication be viewed within the organization?
3. How can we view communication as "causal" or "end-result" variables?
4. How does communication act as an intervening variable in organizations?

◄ Organizational Communication: An "Unconventional" Perspective

GARY M. RICHETTO

A department supervisor sits down with one of his employees to conduct the annual "appraisal interview."

A junior accountant begins the report to his boss with the familiar "per your request . . ."

The General Manager of Production Control and the General Manager of Production disagree about schedules for the new model.

A "ninth-level" executive steps off the eighteenth green, having lost the $5 "Nassau" to his "tenth-level" opponent, but having gained "confidential" information about the company's pending reorganization.

A group of employees drink coffee in the cafeteria and discuss the latest "shake-up" in personnel.

A rank-and-file employee pushes on the door marked MEN, only to find that this particular rest room requires a key that only "certain level" personnel possess.

What do each of these activities share? First, they involve human communication. They, therefore, share components and characteristics with which the reader is already familiar: "source," "message," "channel," "receiver," "feedback." It would be misusing time and energy to further describe these to the reader. However, one characteristic of these communication systems should be amplified, for it will play an important role in what is to follow. This characteristic is the *interdependence* between and among the variables composing these systems. That is, each variable interacts simultaneously with one or more of the other system variables. A change in one variable, therefore,

"Organizational Communication: An 'Unconventional' Perspective," by Gary M. Richetto. Reprinted with permission of the author. This original essay appears here for the first time.

256

will effect change in one or more of the others. "Messages," for example, cannot be viewed apart from their "antecedents" (source systems) or from their "effects" (response systems of intended or unintended receivers).

Second, each of these communication systems functions within a unique environment—a formal organization. This means that if we are to better understand the communication behavior in these systems, we must consider characteristics *beyond* the systems themselves. We must include relevant characteristics of the *organizations* within which they function. In this context, we could list any number of factors, but the most relevant of these have been cited already by W. Charles Redding (1972):

Organizational Characteristics Bearing Upon Communication
1. There is interdependence, or interlocking, of activities; in other words, an organization is a system . . .
2. Members of the organization occupy positions, and these positions typically carry with them 'role specifications'; in other words, persons occupying certain positions are expected to behave—and to communicate—in ways appropriate for those positions.
3. These prescribed ways of behaving reflect in large part some kind of division of labor, which in turn implies varying degrees of job specialization . . .
4. Regardless of individual variations, the organization reveals some kind of status hierarchy, which exists as a coordinating and controlling mechanism. In other words, there are 'superiors' and 'subordinates' even though these terms may not be expressly used, and even though there may exist fluid arrangements whereby superior and subordinate roles may be reversible (pp. 17–18).

Such characteristics have led us to focus on organizational communication in terms of "direction" (e.g., "upward," "downward," "horizontal," "diagonal") as well as in the broader terms of "verbal" and "nonverbal" (the latter a relatively "untapped" area of organizational communication research, incidently), "intentional" and "unintentional," and the like. In fact, most writers have dealt with introductions to organizational communication in precisely that fashion—placing subject matter into "directional" compartments.

The Organizational Communication Specialist

As the reader may well imagine, those working in the field of organizational communication must become conversant with research and theory that supersedes "communication" *per se*. Relevant theory and research derived from a variety of behavioral, social, and administrative sciences must be explored for their contributions to the field. But despite the research

demands upon organizational communication specialists (perhaps by definition "generalists" would be the better term), the field seems to be a rapidly
growing one (Goldhaber, 1974).

Researchers who study communication in organizations carry with them
"frameworks" or "perspectives" for both the communication process and for
its role in formal organizations. Although these frameworks, of course, vary
from researcher to researcher, they are based upon two primary factors: (1) the
organizational communication specialist's personal research and consulting
experiences in organizations and (2) his interpretation of relevant literature
in his and related disciplines. Being no exception, such a framework for
organizational communication is employed as a way of focusing on human
communication within the organizations in which I conduct research and
consulting activities.

The primary purpose here is to introduce the reader to the field of
organizational communication, in as "personal" a fashion as possible, by sharing with you the framework within which I presently view communication in
organizations.

An Organizational Communication Framework

The framework that presently guides my thinking about (and studying
of) organizational communication has grown from my consulting experience
with various organizations and from my academic endeavors as a faculty
member of the Department of Communication and Organizational Behavior
at General Motors Institute (GMI). The former activity has forced me to
describe communication variables in contexts that "make sense" to my clients.
The latter activity has taken me on research projects with industrial psychologists in the "hybrid" science of "organization development" (OD).

Our present work in OD has been greatly influenced by the surveyfeedback approach to organizational analysis developed by Rensis Likert
(formerly Director of the Institute for Social Research at the University of
Michigan). A thorough explanation of Likert's work can be found in his
text, *The Human Organization* (1961). Those aspects of his research that are
useful in understanding the "framework" for organizational communication
are now described.

Likert has developed a "model" that describes organizational variables
(and their relationships) that appear to account for "effective" or "ineffective"
organizational performance. His model focuses on what he terms "causal,"
"intervening," and "end-result" variables. Causal variables are those such as
"leadership style" and "organizational climate" that "cause" certain behaviors
among intervening variables. Intervening variables include such things as
"motivation," "communication," "coordination"—variables operating between

the causal and end-result variables, and thus affecting each of those to some degree. Finally, end-result variables are those such as "productivity," "absenteeism," and "job satisfaction" that result from combinations of causal and intervening variables. A graphic form of Likert's model appears in Figure 5-1.

Now, as with any "model," Likert's is incomplete in the sense that it cannot possibly account for all of the variables that can affect organizations and it does not fully capture the "interdependent" nature of those variables upon which it focuses. Tony Hain (1972), a colleague at GMI, has "extended" Likert's original model significantly by adding the variables depicted in Figure 5-2.

The strength of Hain's additions to the original model are obvious: (1) he indicates the necessity of taking into account what he terms "external" causal variables—influences operating outside of the organization itself, over which the organization has minimal or no control, but nonetheless having significant impact upon events within the organization, (2) he indicates the "dual" nature of some variables ("absenteeism," for example) that can function in end-result *or* intervening capacities, depending upon one's level of analysis, and (3) he has stressed the importance of "time" (also treated in Likert's original work) as a variable that must be considered in any organizational analysis. Hain, in fact, contends that this "time" variable may account for some of the "contradictory" findings in such areas as the relationship between "performance" and "job satisfaction" or "morale" (1972). (Low correlations that have frequently been found between these factors may be greatly affected by the duration of time in which the employee's "morale" or "job satisfaction" has been low before our measurements of his feelings. Thus, measuring the same variables among the same employees *across time* may yield far different findings than taking those measurements on a "one shot" basis.)

As one with an interest in organizational communication, however, I would extend Hain's "extended" model even further. Two conceptual contributions appear to me to strengthen the model from a communication vantage point. First, it would seem that if, in fact, external causal variables impact upon internal causal variables as Hain suggests, there must be some mechanism by which they penetrate the organization in question. In other words, there must exist intervening variables between external causal and internal causal variables. My assumption is that chief among these is, of course, communication. (Moreover, this assumption focuses attention on another area of organizational communication research that has not been sufficiently explored—the study of the mechanisms by which organizations interface effectively or ineffectively with their environments.)

Second, I believe that the model can be strengthened by indicating the reciprocal, interdependent nature of variables as well as their linear relationships. Thus, I would conceive of an end-result variable ("absenteeism," for

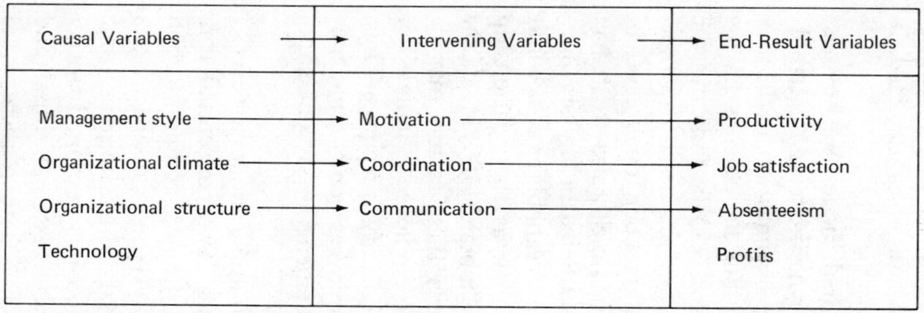

Causal Variables	Intervening Variables	End-Result Variables
Management style	Motivation	Productivity
Organizational climate	Coordination	Job satisfaction
Organizational structure	Communication	Absenteeism
Technology		Profits

FIGURE 5-1. The relationship of causal, intervening, and end-result variables. (Adapted from Likert, 1961.)

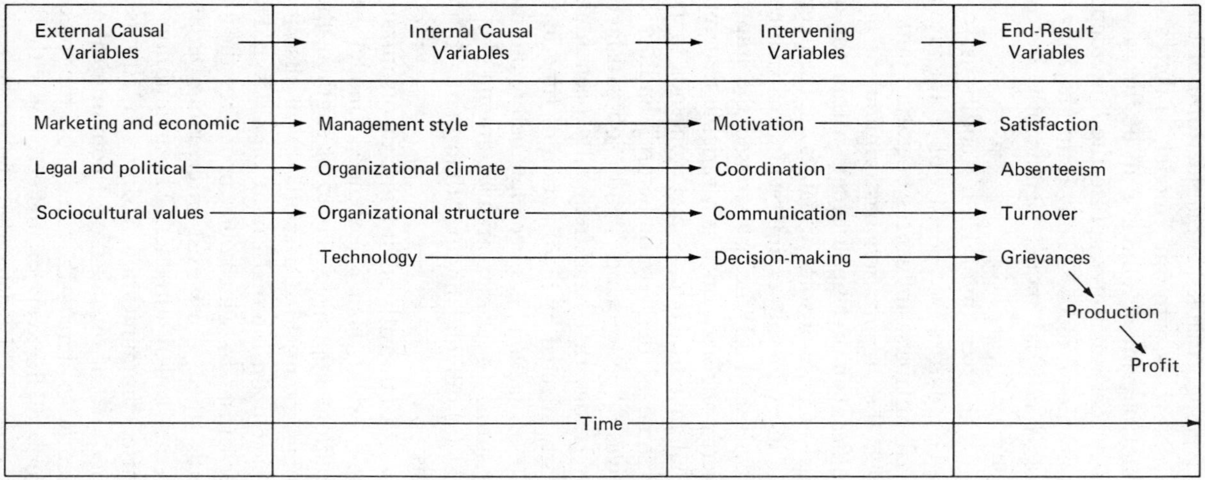

External Causal Variables	Internal Causal Variables	Intervening Variables	End-Result Variables
Marketing and economic	Management style	Motivation	Satisfaction
Legal and political	Organizational climate	Coordination	Absenteeism
Sociocultural values	Organizational structure	Communication	Turnover
	Technology	Decision-making	Grievances
			Production
			Profit

Time

FIGURE 5-2. The Hain Model (1972).

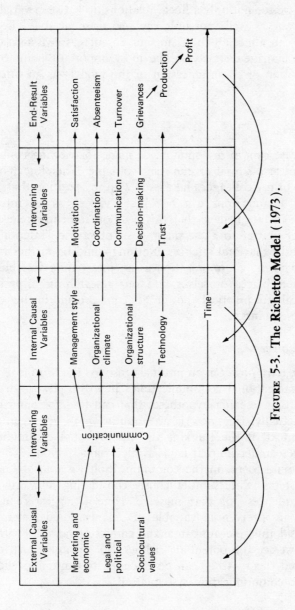

FIGURE 5-3. The Richetto Model (1973).

External Causal Variables	Intervening Variables	Internal Causal Variables	Intervening Variables	End-Result Variables
Marketing and economic		Management style	Motivation	Satisfaction
Legal and political	Communication	Organizational climate	Coordination	Absenteeism
Sociocultural values		Organizational structure	Communication	Turnover
		Technology	Decision-making	Grievances
			Trust	Production
				Profit

Time

example) feeding back to one or more intervening variables ("communication," for example), and these to the causal variables ("leadership," for example). Thus, what I would consider a more "complete" model appears in Figure 5-3. Here we see not only a linear relationship between variables but an interdependent one as well: not only can management style affect communication, which can affect absenteeism, but absenteeism vis-à-vis communication can affect management style. The most important point to grasp, however, is the position of communication in the model—as an *intervening* variable.

FRAMEWORK RATIONALE

A legitimate case can, in my opinion, be made for viewing communication in organizations as a causal or end-result variable. Therefore it will not surprise me if some of my colleagues take issue with my position that, overall, communication in organizations can be "best" viewed as an intervening variable. Some may in fact believe that this position somehow relegates our discipline or subject matter to a "secondary" or otherwise "inferior" status among the social and behavioral sciences. Nothing could be further from my intent. I feel that viewing communication as an intervening variable in the complex organization places ourselves and our research in a position of significant theoretical and practical "power." Let me provide further clarification on both of these points.

Theoretical Power

I am using the term *power* in an unusual sense. As the term is used here, I have in mind organizational communication's heuristic power—that is, its potential for generating research hypotheses that can lead to sound and far-reaching theory. Actually, this view is an application in an organizational communication context of the thinking in "interpersonal communication" proposed by some researchers in that field (Kibler, Barker, 1968). Their argument is that we should focus on the communication variable of "message" in interpersonal systems while simultaneously considering relevant "antecedents" and "consequences" of that message. Here I suggest focusing on communication as an intervening variable in organizational systems while simultaneously considering relevant causal and end-result variables with which it is linked. Thus, we see the potential "richness" of organizational communication research and theory—they can be extended to cause and effect variables outside of the communication system itself.

Practical Power

Viewing communication as an intervening variable in organizations has "practical power" in terms of consultation. I have found that organizations will let me "in the door" to study "communication" far more readily than they will let me in to study, say, "managerial style" or "employee motivation" or "organizational effectiveness." Because of most managers' static (in some cases naïve) view of communication, this area of research seems "safe" to them. I have yet to meet a manager who does not desire "better communication" among his goals. In this day of "enlightened management," believing in "good communication" is analogous to being for motherhood and against sin.

Further, although most of us will not readily admit that we are "poor" leaders, "ineffective" decision-makers, or "minimal" risk-takers, even the most vain among us will admit to an occasional "communication breakdown" with superiors and subordinates. "Communication" seems somehow abstract, something outside of us; we can talk about a communication problem without feeling a critical part of the problem. Thus, the same manager who would balk at the idea of my investigating his organization's "psychological climate" will welcome my help in solving the "communication problem around here." Little does he expect (even though I insist upon putting his "communication problem" into the framework I have described before the consultation begins) that I must also gather data concerning the causal and end-result variables that appear to be linked by the intervening variable of communication. After I am finished, the client frequently finds that his "communication problem" is symptomatic, rather than causal; that the "real" problem lies behind the communication failure.

I have found that this approach places the manager in what Jack Gibb (1964) calls a "problem-solving" posture in which he:

tends to see communication primarily as a symptom or indicator of more basic organizational or managerial inadequacy. Information about communicative distortion is used as diagnostic data which will guide the manager in taking new managerial actions, re-organizing work patterns, or achieving new attitudes toward the organization or the people in it.

Practically speaking, then, the "power" of viewing communication as an intervening organizational variable for consulting purposes is that it (1) makes us more readily acceptable to the client, (2) permits us to feed back to him "gutsy" data in a "nonthreatening" or at least "minimally threatening" fashion, and (3) educates him toward the important role of communication as a link between causal and end-result variables in his organization.

FRAMEWORK POTENTIAL

Generally speaking, formalized research on communication is relatively new to the organizational scene. There are several reasons for the "lag" in communication research in organizations, in contrast to research in other areas such as leadership, structure, and technology. Perhaps the greatest reason is the complex, "process" nature of the subject. As Redding (1972) has noted:

(paraphrasing Guetzkow) perhaps a part of the blame may be attributed to the highly complex and 'contingent' nature of the data; for example, some communication variables, such as direction of message flow, sometimes do and sometimes do not seem to be associated with the size of the organization. Human communication behavior is frustratingly difficult to capture and pin down; it is composed of millions upon millions of constantly shifting bits, interacting both among themselves and with the organizational environment in which the behavior takes place. (pp. 8–9)

Our attempts to "capture and pin down" this process have led us to focus on organizational communication in terms of its "directional" flow. In fact, prior to Redding's 1972 publication, major reviews of our literature have been organized under the headings of "downward," "upward," "horizontal," and "diagonal," along with the more general area of "informal" communication (Carter, 1972; Tompkins, 1967).

In our efforts to "get a handle" on the role of communication in organizations, we have committed the same conceptual error we are now beginning to see in reviews of the research on interpersonal communication. That is, giving "lip service" to communication as a *process* and then researching it as a directional, linear activity (Smith, 1972). As Mark Knapp (1969) has noted: "The dynamics of communication activities . . . are not within the confines of the 'up-down-across' system. Generally, this classification system does not adequately describe the range of activities in this field" (p. 37). An important advantage of focusing on communication in organizations as an intervening variable is that it forces us to deal with its dynamic, "process" nature—both within the communication systems themselves and between causes and effects linked together by these systems.

A New Direction for Organizational Communication Research

It seems plausible that viewing communication in organizations as an intervening variable may take us in "new" directions of research. These are directions, which, frankly, I presently do not comprehend fully, because they lie in the future and will grow out of the combined efforts of interdisciplinary research teams composed of communication, computer, and open-systems specialists. This "marriage" will rely not only upon the merging of theory from a number of sciences but upon a more "sophisticated" use of the computer as a simulation tool in our research. This sophistication will likely result from our finding that, as Forrester (1971) contends, we tend to use computers for things that could best be done by man and to use man for things that could best be done by computers.

Jay W. Forrester's (1971) efforts to analyze the nature of social systems has led him to the conclusion that these systems behave "counterintuitively"; that is, they behave in ways that are difficult for the human mind to follow through what he calls "multi-loop, nonlinear feedback." What is more, "positive" changes in these systems can be misleading in that their effects are often hidden, because of the complex way in which the systems function across time. The computer, however, can be programmed to "follow" these long-range "cause-effect" relationships. An example from Forrester's simulation work in "urban dynamics" will serve to exemplify this "counterintuitive" quality:

In fact, it emerges that the fundamental cause of depressed areas in the cities comes from *excess* housing in the low-income category rather than the commonly presumed housing shortage. The legal and tax structures have combined to give incentives for keeping old buildings in place. As residential buildings age, they are used by lower-income groups who are forced to use them at a higher population density. Therefore, jobs decline and population rises while buildings age. Housing, at the higher population densities, accommodates more low-income urban population than can find jobs. A social trap is created where excess low-cost housing beckons low-income people inward because of the available housing. . . . (Forrester, p. 57).

What is the point of all this? It seems possible to me that we have perhaps been so busy focusing on organizational communication in terms of downward, upward, horizontal, and diagonal systems that we have failed to investigate the ways in which these systems may *relate to one another*. Does an improvement in one communication system (such as "downward") have a "positive" or "negative" effect on another system (such as "horizontal")? Can any one of our systems be "too good" in the sense that reliance upon it stifles motivation for using others? Is it possible that each directional communication system in an organization has a "utility curve"—that each has a point at which "improvements" within itself adversely affect the other systems? I can conceive of an organization, for example, in which downward communication is so "effective," so well-distributed across units that the motivation to develop "horizontal" or "diagonal" communication systems is minimal.

My point is that the multiple, overlapping, and interdependent communication systems in complex organizations may, like those systems studied by Forrester, behave counterintuitively.

If, in fact, organizational communication research begins to move in the direction of computer simulation, we may be at the threshold of a new breakthrough in our science. The result may be a "contingency theory of organizational communication." We may discover "optimum blends" of communication systems that are "organization-specific," depending upon climate, leadership, resources, and environment of the organization in which they function. Just as "contingency theory" (Fiedler, 1965) has made significant contributions to the study of leadership, we may find contingency approaches of considerable value in designing communication systems. Briefly,

Fiedler's theory is an "it depends" one—he suggests that there exists a number of contingencies available to a manager in selecting a leadership style. Unlike other "one best way" leadership theories, Fiedler contends that one's leadership style should emerge from the blend of three factors operating in the situation: (1) leader-member relations (the extent to which leaders and members like and trust one another); (2) task structure (the explicitness with which the task is defined); and (3) position power (the "legitimate," rather than personal authority of the leader).

May we not one day develop organizational communication systems along "contingency" lines? Once we know, for example, the relationship between communication systems across time, we may begin to identify "factors" similar to Fiedler's, which, blended together, yield the most optimum combination of directional communication systems for the organization and environment in question. We are at present a long way from such knowledge, of course, but I find the concept an exciting one.

Summary

In introducing the reader to the field of organizational communication, I have described a "framework" within which I feel human communication behavior in organizations can best be analyzed and understood. This framework conceives of human communication as an intervening variable between "causes" and "end results." I have suggested that viewing organizational communication in this context places the field and its researchers in an "optimal" position—a position for the field that facilitates broad theory-building—and a position for its researchers as resources to organizations who can provide knowledge not only in terms of communication systems *per se* but in terms of the causal and end-result variables that these systems link together.

Finally, I have described a direction for future research in organizational communication that springs from this conceptual framework. This new research area would draw upon the combined talents of communication, computer, and general systems specialists, and focus upon the interdependence of organizational communication systems through the technique of computer simulation.

Essentially, I have attempted to provide an alternative to "conventional" perspectives on organizational communication, for I wholeheartedly agree with Redding (1972) that perhaps: "the conventional analysis of organizational communication in terms of up, down and horizontal is not the most appropriate for yielding valuable insights" (p. 489).

REFERENCES

Carter, Robert M. *Communication in Organizations: An Annotated Bibliography and Sourcebook.* Detroit, Mich.: Gale Research Company, 1972.

Fiedler, F. "Engineering the Job to Fit the Manager." *Harvard Business Review* (September–October 1965), pp. 113–122.

Forrester, Jay W. "Counterintuitive Behavior of Social Systems." *Technology Review*, **73**, 3 (January 1971), Alumni Association of the Massachusetts Institute of Technology, 52–68.

Gibb, Jack R. "Communication and Productivity." *Personnel Administration* (January–February 1964), pp. 485–487.

Goldhaber, Gerald. *Organizational Communication.* Dubuque, Iowa: William C. Brown Company, Publishers, 1974.

Hain, Tony. *Organizational Change Patterns.* General Motors Institute, 1972.

Kibler, R. J., and L. L. Barker (eds.). *Conceptual Frontiers in Speech-Communication.* Report of the New Orleans Conference on Research and Instructional Development, February 1968. New York: Speech Communication Association, 1969.

Knapp, Mark L. "A Taxonomic Approach to Organizational Communication." *Journal of Business Communication*, 7 (1969), 37–46.

Likert, Rensis. *The Human Organization.* New York: McGraw-Hill, Inc., 1967.

Redding, W. Charles. *Communication Within the Organization: An Interpretive Review of Theory and Research.* New York: Industrial Communication Council, Inc., 1972.

Smith, David H. "Communication Research and the Idea of Process." *Speech Monographs*, **39**, 3 (1972), 174–182.

Tompkins, Phillip K. "Organizational Communication: A State-of-the-Art Review," in G. M. Richetto (ed.). *Conference on Organizational Communication*, August 8–11, 1967, George C. Marshall Space Flight Center, National Aeronautics and Space Administration (NASA), 1967, pp. 4–26.

1. What are the characteristics of most formalized models of advertising communication in television?
2. What three elements of advertising should be recognized in a model of advertising communication?
3. How may we define the process of advertising communication?
4. What are the four levels of viewer response?
5. Which level do you feel is the most important in the advertising communication process?

▶◀ A Theoretical View of Advertising Communication

JOSEPH T. PLUMMER

Abstract

It is proposed that advertising research be based less on one-way transmission models of communication and more on multivariate studies with emphasis on receivers' contributions to communication outcomes. A four-level model of the process is presented and several dimensions within each level are identified, based upon recent research on TV commercial effects. The four levels described are (1) the unconscious level, (2) the immediate perceptual level, (3) the retention or learning level, and (4) the behavior level. Research at each level is discussed.

Most concepts or formalized models of advertising communication have implicitly stated some expression of a unidimensional, one-way, stimulus-response theory. Probably the most current model of advertising communications states that an effective television commercial should:

a. attract and hold the attention of the target audience,
b. communicate a message, explicitly or implicitly, about the brand,
c. favorably affect attitudes toward the brand.

There can be little argument about the logic or the usefulness of this model for decision-makers intent upon evaluating the job accomplished by the communication stimuli. At the same time, this model does little to shed insights into the role of the receiver, except that he perform specific tasks. It places emphasis on what the communication does to people and has placed

"A Theoretical View of Advertising Communication," by Joseph T. Plummer, Jr., from *The Journal of Communication*, Vol. 21, No. 4 (December 1971), pp. 315–325.

little emphasis on what people do to the communication. The purpose of this paper is to challenge this conception and to present an alternate view using as support some recent research conducted by the author and some of his colleagues.

Before presenting an alternate view, a few observations should be made on the model stated earlier and on another even simpler concept that "advertising builds sales." The sales effect notion and the three-step model are goals of advertising. But the true effect of advertising on sales is not known. Advertising helps, but in what ways and to what degrees have not been demonstrated empirically, except that advertising can increase brand awareness through manipulation of spending levels and that there is some correlation between basic measures of advertising—such as recall or pre-post scores— and sales. There is no clear picture of how the three-step model relates to sales, nor do we have very clear notions of the interrelationships of the three steps among themselves.

Factor analytic studies of commercial testing data show that recall measures and attitude measures seldom vary together and that they seldom rank order commercials in the same way [5, 13]. Finally, these are the goals and the related measurements made on a single commercial, at a single point in time. Overlooked are the effects of repeated exposures over time interspersed with actual experience with the product by consumers.

In order to understand how advertising works as communication between source and receiver, it is necessary to examine *the process* of advertising communication. It is the purpose of this paper to propose one way of thinking about advertising as a communication process between visual and aural stimuli and the people experiencing these stimuli.

It will help to first consider the place of advertising in the total communications spectrum. At one end of the spectrum there is person-to-person communication. Farther along the spectrum is person-to-group communication and at the opposite end is mass communication—a message delivered to an unseen audience. Without discussing all the differences and similarities between the various forms of communication, it is important to the understanding of mass communications to state that immediate, observable feedback or "feed forward" is difficult to obtain in most mass communications except through research of some kind. Unlike a participant in person-to-person communication (in which it is difficult enough), the creator or sender of the mass media message has little or no opportunity to observe or get a sense of what hearers and viewers are understanding, structuring, accepting, rejecting, enjoying, intending to do, etc., except through some form of audience research. This makes the task of communicating rather difficult because the sender does not have firsthand knowledge of whom he is reaching or how this unknown receiver is reacting. This lack of feedback has made the gaining of real insights into the process of advertising communication very difficult.

There are three unique aspects of advertising as a form of communication that need to be recognized in a model of advertising communication. The first aspect is the *repetitive nature of advertising over time*. It is this aspect, technically called "wearout," into which research has shed very little understanding up to now. There have been a few research studies on the repetition aspect from the perspective of learning [7]. Another special aspect of advertising is the highly competitive nature of the environment where advertising messages exist. This competitive environment has been called "clutter" as it relates to television. In just four years, the average number of different network commercials per month increased from 1,990 in 1964 to 3,022 in 1968 [6]. Whether it is "clutter" or not, advertisers have seen day-after recall scores slowly declining over the past five years. Television advertising is very short—many messages are less than 30 seconds—which has given rise to the clutter. In order to get through this clutter then, television advertising needs to be more than straight transmission of hard product information unless the sender is saying something like "the product now costs five cents."

The third unique aspect of advertising communication is the role it plays in our culture. Because advertising has become an accepted part of our popular culture, things can be shown or said that outside of advertising would be rejected as absurd. As a result of this cultural role and the "addictive" nature of television, people probably "see" most television advertising, but the degrees of their interest, involvement, comprehension, retention, and responses vary significantly.

Given the above perspective, it is proposed that advertising communication be viewed as *a process that incorporates both the messages and the receivers, with major emphasis on the viewers' perspectives*. One way to think about the advertising communication process is to theorize that there are several dimensions within each of four levels of viewer response. These four levels are (a) the unconscious level, (b) the immediate perceptual level, (c) the retention or learning level, and (d) the behavior level.

The first level, unconscious response, is the most difficult to conceptualize, measure, and illustrate; but there is evidence that it probably does exist. One indication that unconscious responses to advertising communication take place may be seen in the physiological responses, such as galvanic skin response and heart beat rate, that have been measured in the laboratory. The present knowledge in this area is that reliable differences between stimuli effects can be measured. However, what the various differences mean are still equivocal.

A second level of response is seen in the immediate cognitive responses that a viewer has while viewing the commercial. This level relates to the feelings, emotions, personal experiences and attitudes the commercial arouses in the viewer. It has to do with how people perceive and affectively interpret what they see and hear. Laughter, stimulation, empathy, dislike, etc., are the kinds of responses that make up this level of the communication process.

The third level of response is the level of learning that takes place as a result of experiencing the commercial. It is best conceptualized as the "filing" of elements from the communication experience in ones "filing system." Recall of specific elements or product claims is part of the retention process, but so are the attitudes and images stored and retrieved at a later time. This level of retention has been indicated by years of delayed recall research in advertising at varying time-delays, the most common being twenty-four hours. It appears that the amount a person is able to recall or play back is a function of many variables such as the interviewing time, the number of cues provided to aid recall, the interest of the person in the product category, etc. But there can be little question that retention and recall do take place and constitute a major response mode to advertising communication.

The final level of response is the action or behavior that takes place as a result of the communication experience. In most cases of advertising communication, this level of response is less traceable to a particular commercial and is farthest removed in time. Immediate behavior can take place as when a person goes to his refrigerator and gets a beer after experiencing a beer commercial. The primary behavior advertisers are interested in is product purchase, but there are other types of behavior, such as information seeking, that may be linked to the advertising communication. Another link is through a "two-step flow" in which people who view a commercial influence others to buy the product. Clearly, much purchase behavior is not just the result of a single commercial experience, but of many factors in addition, such as previous experience with the product, other promotional activity, and availability.

Each level of response by the viewer has some relationship to the other levels and to the various dimensions of the message presented to them. The important thing to keep in mind is that understanding how a commercial is communicating requires consideration of all levels of response.

The present understanding of the level of unconscious response as measured by physiological dimensions centers on two concepts: arousal and potential wearout. Neither of these concepts has been definitely proven, but accumulating evidence does suggest some validity for these concepts [2, 4]. Significant pupil and skin responses occur when the commercials present stimulating action, or extreme changes in the mood, tempo or volume of the commercial, or when there is some sexy event in the commercial. Further research and experience with this level of response—often overlooked—is clearly needed in advertising communication research.

In the last two years a great deal of research effort at the Leo Burnett Company has gone into the investigation of the second level of response—the immediate cognitive response to the commercial. Adjectives and descriptive sentences have been used to allow viewers to rate commercials immediately after exposure. Rating data from over four thousand respondents and over a hundred different commercials have been factor analyzed a number of times using principal components analysis and an orthogonal rotation procedure. In general, the results are quite similar with a few factors unique to the adjective data and a few factors unique to the sentence data. In-depth discussions of both procedures and the research development of them can be found in recent reports [12]. The factor analysis results indicate that the immediate cognitive response level is multidimensional and not merely a general evaluation.

A brief description of the various dimensions that emerged from the research and the kinds of commercials that relate to the responses on each dimension may provide an understanding of this response level. Seven independent dimensions emerged, accounting for over seventy percent of the total variance.

The dimension that accounted for the most variance might be called .*entertainment* or *stimulation*. This dimension appears to measure the extent to which viewers enjoy and are positively stimulated by a commercial. Humorous ads often score high on this dimension as do those that portray warm, charming people. Among the ads that score high are those which feature well-liked characters, such as the Pillsbury "Doughboy" and the Green Giant elves, or which star popular entertainers. Another type of commercial that is seen as entertaining and stimulating is the contemporary, "swinging" commercial. In short, this dimension differentiates those commercials which are pleasureable and stimulating to watch and listen to and those which are not. A second dimension that appears to be the opposite response from the first dimension, but which does not co-vary with it, may be called *irritation*. This suggests that viewers are making a judgment of annoyance independent of an ad's stimulation. This dimension appears to relate to viewers' perceptions of ads as farfetched, untrue in their implications, or insulting in manner. The negative feelings people have toward the characters or situations, particularly anxiety-producing ones, also seem to be reflected in this dimension.

The third dimension, which may be called *familiarity*, appears to measure the viewers' perception of ads as being familiar to them or being very unique and novel in their presentations. Very few commercials are perceived by respondents to be truly unique or novel. This response seems to relate to the total execution of the commercial rather than some specific element.

The fourth dimension seems to indicate the degree to which viewers say, in effect, "I am like or wish I were like" the people portrayed in the ads. One might call this dimension *empathy* or *gratifying involvement* as the commercials that score high on this dimension show attractive characters, cute children, warm family situations, beautiful spots like Hawaii, or meaningful adult social interactions that viewers can identify with or get involved with in an idealized fashion.

The fifth dimension, extent of *confusion*, relates to the degree to which viewers feel confused by a commercial. Respondents perceive most commercials to be relatively clear, but this does not mean that they truly understand everything nor that they grasp the point that the copywriter is trying to make. There are a few commercials that viewers do perceive to be more confusing than most, however. Commercials that utilize disconnected quick-cuts, that lack audio-video congruence or those that include distracting or obscurely related elements are likely to be perceived as less comprehensible.

The sixth dimension might be called *informativeness* or *personal relevance*. This dimension does not measure the content of the information, but only the extent to which something in the commercial was of interest and importance to viewers. It also appears to be a measure of the viewers' impression that the commercial was informative in nature. Most ads for new products perform at the high end of this dimension, as one would expect. The judgment of "how important, how relevant to me and my interest in this product was the information in the commercial?" is one of the major responses viewers make to commercials.

The final dimension might be called *brand reinforcement*. It relates to the degree to which respondents' brand attitudes and images are reinforced by the ad. It is important to note that viewers do respond to commercials in terms of pre-determined brand attitudes and images, yet few researchers try to measure this elusive dimension. However it did emerge from the research reviewed here and can be useful in spotting commercials that present an image deviant from the one that viewers bring to the commercial. It appears that the more similar the commercial's execution is to previous commercials, the more likely that brand reinforcement will take place.

These seven factors of response comprise the immediate cognitive response level in the proposed model. These dimensions provide insight into advertising communication experiences, which have been overlooked in advertising research.

Historically, emphasis in research has been on the third level in the model, the retention level. Most television commercial testing services operate on the level of retention and are of two basic types of measurement systems—24-hour proved recall and pre-post attitude shifting measures. Several correlational studies of the two types of measurement systems and several factor analytic studies of systems that include both of these measures indicate that commercials vary on proved recall effects independently of pre-post brand attitude shift measures. These data suggest that a commercial or elements of a commercial can be recalled without an accompanying "effect" on attitudes or choices of the advertised brand and vice versa. Clearly, there is some minimal recall required for some brand response, but the two do not go hand in hand. Nor does either measure alone provide an understanding of this third level of response.

Factor analytic studies [13] suggest three or possibly four dimensions in this retention response level. These dimensions are (1) *proved awareness of the commercial* in general, (2) *specific awareness of the intended message*, (3) *attitude toward the advertised brand*, and (4) *attitude toward the commercial*. The first dimension is a measure of the proportion of viewers who remember seeing the commercial when it was shown in a normal environment 24 hours earlier. The second dimension indicates the proportion of viewers aware of the commercial who retained the important product message. Often a highly memorable character or personality can create high awareness, yet lead few people to retain what it was the character or personality was trying to say about the brand. The third dimension indicates how many viewers retained over time a positive or negative attitude attributed to the commercial. This attitude retention could be in the form of a reminder of previous attitudes, or creation of new attitudes. The fourth dimension appears less stable than the other three, but general liking or disliking of a commercial does appear to account for some of the variance.

This third level of response appears to be related to the extent and kind of learning (or forgetting) that takes place as a result of the advertising communication. Work by Leavitt [9] suggests that the major underlying construct operating on this third level is meaningfulness based upon organizational structure. Although rats can learn to recognize nonsense stimuli via conditioning, Leavitt's notion was that organized, meaningful stimuli which are relevant to viewers of advertising communication are recognized most quickly. This underlying construct of structure as an indication of meaningfulness does appear to relate to the three major dimensions in the retention level of viewer response. Experience with structure has generated some useful concepts about the kinds of communication variables that enhance retention.

In many cases, the inherent structure of the commercial is very similar to the structure viewers impose upon it. There are times, however, when viewers have trouble structuring or organizing the commercial either because it has little inherent structure or because the structure is too complex and meaningless. It is in these instances that very little information is retained over time. Such principles as shape in a commercial or the building and reduction of tension, congruence of audio and video, integration of the product into the storyline as high points of interest rather than at random, and visual dramatization of the product claim rather than mere statement of it, appear to enhance learning significantly. Some recent research [1] has indicated that commercials which viewers can organize easily around the product are retained by more people and deliver more specific information than those commercials which viewers cannot organize in their minds.

Another important construct that relates to this retention level is "the needs of the viewer." A person who has no need for nor interest in the product is much less likely to be aware of or to retain something from the commercial. In order to enhance learning it would seem best to start with some need or knowledge already shared by the viewer and build upon that rather than an abstract approach remote from the world of the viewer.

The final level of response, action, is extremely difficult to attribute solely to the communication. Part of the difficulty arises from the fact that the communication is received in the home while purchasing action occurs outside the home at a later time. Purchasing action is the result of many interacting variables or influences which challenge conceptualization and research. Very little conclusive work has been done on the subject of immediate or delayed action as it relates to advertising communication. Yet, this level is the most central to the question of communication effectiveness. Perhaps as more large-scale experiments are conducted and the relationships of the levels of the model presented here are further explored, advances will be made in understanding of all kinds of communication and their relationships to behavior.

These advances will depend upon the abilities of people from all communication-related disciplines to join in their thinking and research. Leo Bogart [3] articulated the challenge very well when he stated, "The twilight areas of advertising research are precisely those of social psychology in general: (1) the relation between emotional arousal or affect and the transmittal of information; (2) the relation between learning information on a subject and acquiring certain opinions about it; (3) the conditions under which favorable opinions are translated into overt behavior."

It seems clear that a narrow view of the communication process or the manipulation of a single message variable offers little promise of new information about advertising communication. Through application of a conceptual model of various multidimensional levels, such as the four-level model presented here, some new insights into key questions may emerge.

Note

1. Reported by Fred Schlinger in a presentation on Structural Analysis in 1968.

References

1. Agres, Stuart. "The Use of Skin Conductance in Predicting Commercial Effectiveness." In house report. Leo Burnett Company, Inc., January 1968.
2. ———. "The Effect of Repeated Stimulus Exposure on the Structure of Verbal Responses." Working paper. Leo Burnett Company, Inc., 1969.
3. Bogart, Leo. "Where Does Advertising Research Go From Here?" *Journal of Advertising Research*, 9:3–15, 1969.
4. Cloverdale, Herbert L., Jr. "Pupil Response, GSR and Novelty: A Pilot Study." Unpublished report. Illinois Institute of Technology, September, 1968.

5. Cage, C., and J. Plummer. "A Look at Leo Burnett Commercial Test." In house report. Leo Burnett Company, Inc., 1968.
6. Gould, Jack. "Why Viewers Tune Out, or Plugged to Death." *New York Times*, January 4, 1971, p. D17.
7. Crass, R. C. "The Use of Research to Forecast the Effectiveness of Television Advertising." Paper presented to the Winter Regional Conference of the Division of Consumer Psychology, American Psychological Association, at West Point, New York, March 12, 1970.
8. Hess, E. H. "Attitude and Pupil Size." *Scientific American*, 212:46–54, 1965.
9. Leavitt, C. "Response Structure: A Determinant of Recall." *Journal of Advertising Research*, 8:3–6, 1968.
10. ———. "Notes on Communication #2." Working paper. Leo Burnett Company, Inc., 1970.
11. ———. "A Multidimensional Set of Rating Scales for Television Commercials." *Journal of Applied Psychology*, 54:427–429, 1970.
12. ———, M. McCinville and W. D. Wells. "A Reaction Profile for TV Commercials." *Journal of Advertising Research* (in press).
13. Plummer, J. "A Systematic Approach to Commercial Testing Evaluation." Working paper. Leo Burnett Company, Inc., 1970.
14. ——— and M. J. Schlinger. "Viewer Response Profile." Working paper. Leo Burnett Company, Inc., 1970.

1. What is entailed in a sustained legal persuasive campaign?
2. What is the communication role of the lawyer in the legal process?
3. What is the role of witnesses in the legal communicative process?
4. What is the communication role of the judge in the legal process?
5. What is the communication role of juries in the legal process?

▶◀ Communication Perspectives in the Legal Process

R O B E R T   F .   F O R S T O N

The successful lawyer has been pictured in numerous films and television series as a skillful, witty individual interrogating hostile witnesses and as a golden tongued orator making an eloquent closing appeal to the jury. In actuality, the trial attorney does little public speaking as compared to the other forms of communication in which he engages. The art of expression through interpersonal and small-group communication accounts for far more of the lawyer's success than does his public speaking skill. Much of a lawyer's time is spent in the negotiation process before hearings, in civil litigation, in divorce cases (child custody and property settlement), in immunity bargaining (from being prosecuted for one's criminal activities) in return for testimony about other's criminal activities (1), or in plea bargaining for a lesser criminal charge in return for a guilty plea by the defendant (2). Interviewing skills are also important for interviewing clients and witnesses. The art of interrogation is vital for the jury selection process and for the examination of witnesses.

Another view of the communication process in legal settings is that a client comes to an attorney because he seeks some kind of action. Illustrations of four actions follow. The client's leg has been broken as a result of someone's negligence and he wants a court to order the other party to *accept* responsibility and compensate him for medical treatment, lost wages, and pain and anguish. Another client's building contractor has walked off

"Communication Perspectives in the Legal Process," by Robert F. Forston. Reprinted with permission of the author. This original essay appears here for the first time.

the construction site and he wants a court to order the contractor to *continue* the work. Still another's private wildlife preserve is being threatened by a proposed highway project and he seeks a court order *deterring* its construction. And another's values are being destroyed by billboard advertisements of pornographic literature on the roof of a neighborhood bookstore and he wants a court to force the *discontinuance* of the displays.

The attorney knows that legal action in each of these cases will involve the exercise of persuasion. He must weigh the merits of each client's case against the standards of persuasion that must be met in order to achieve the legal goals that each client seeks. The law, of course, divides each of these four actions into more specific and technical motions.

An even more in-depth analysis of the communication involved in a legal dispute leading to a trial is that lawyers may work on at least five levels of a sustained persuasive campaign. These sustained campaign levels include (1) negotiation between attorneys; (2) pleadings and motions; (3) motions for preliminary relief and trial advantage; (4) the trial; and (5) posttrial motions and appeals (see Figure 5–4). The lawsuit and the sustained persuasion campaign may be likened to a war. Its theaters are set down in the rules of legal procedure. In each theater, a different persuasive campaign is fought. Success in any theater may conclude the war. More realistically, however, is that success in each previous campaign is instrumental in obtaining success in the next—and finally in the war itself.

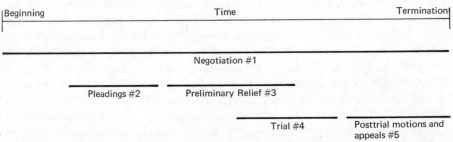

| Beginning | Time | Termination |

Negotiation #1

Pleadings #2   Preliminary Relief #3

Trial #4   Posttrial motions and appeals #5

FIGURE 5-4. Sustained campaign in a legal dispute.

LEVEL 1—NEGOTIATION BETWEEN ATTORNEYS

Negotiation or bargaining between parties often begins before the attorneys are contacted. If satisfactory terms are not reached, the next step in the persuasion process is for the parties to show the seriousness of their dispute by contacting their attorney. The attorneys always attempt to settle the dispute without going to trial. The pretrial stage of the negotiation offers the most viable opportunity for the parties to employ persuasion to reach an acceptable zone of agreement. Here the negotiators employ a number of persuasive techniques first to discover how little or how much the other party is willing to give. If the parties find that they are not within an acceptable zone of agreement, the next stage is to show determination of one's seriousness by making arrangements for a trial. However, if the parties discover that they can come to an agreement, each attorney employs a variety of strategies to gain the best possible agreement within the zone. These strategies include a threat to go to court, "take it or leave it—final offer," mutual balanced concessions (compromise), and rationalizations as to why a particular offer should be acceptable for the other party. Other advanced stages of bluffing or calling a bluff in negotiation occur when the parties go to the pretrial conference with the judge or when the trial actually starts. Of course, negotiations can and do continue concurrently with and after the trial. It is not unheard of for the litigants to settle out of court when the trial is nearly completed.

Consider the dispute over the secret White House tapes that pertained to the Watergate crisis. Archibald Cox, special prosecutor for the Watergate issue negotiated with President Nixon's legal counsel over access to the tapes. At some point in the negotiations, Cox subpoenaed the tapes. After Judge John Sirica ordered the President to relinquish the secret tapes for a private hearing by the judge himself, negotiations once again commenced seriously with the encouragement of the U.S. Court of Appeals. Hence, the court itself often encourages out-of-court settlements.

Level 2—The Pleadings

The second theater of a dispute involves the filing of pleadings and motions for dismissal and summary judgment (an immediate judgment based upon summaries of the pleadings). This portion of the dispute is carried on before a judge, whereas previous discussions were between the parties or between their legal counsel. The weapons of this battle include briefs, affidavits, and sometimes oral arguments. Success or failure at this point could end the dispute or it could simply alter positions for the next level of the persuasive legal campaign.

The pleadings filed by the plaintiff set out the acts of the defendant that allegedly breached his rights and the damages that proximately resulted from the acts. The defendant usually files an answer denying one or more of the acts. But he may instead file a motion to dismiss the complaint or a motion for a judgment on the pleadings. In so doing he would be saying to the judge, "Suppose I committed those acts. So what? They did not breach any of his legal rights." A battle over the law of the case ensues— a battle calling for effective persuasion.

In such a persuasive campaign, the advocate usually files a brief of his argument with the judge. The filing of this brief will make the judge at least aware of the advocate's interpretation of the law. In the contents of the brief and in the oral argument, each side attempts to nurture acceptance of his position and interpretation of the law by citing authorities and legal precedents.

Alternatively, an attorney may file a motion for summary judgment. This motion differs from a dismissal motion in that it can be accompanied by evidence in the form of affidavits. With this motion the plaintiff can win an unconditional victory before beginning the trial. The affidavits are another set of weapons in the persuasive campaign. They can reveal the cruelty of the injury and indicate the hardship of the client and thus help to induce further in the judge the desire to support that advocate's position.

A lawyer seeking to win at this stage must be aware that he carries a heavier burden of persuasion or proof. The law dictates that even a scintilla of material evidence contrary to the allegation made in the counsel's motion or the existence of a genuine factual issue will prevent a dismissal or summary judgment and will send the case through further stages in the legal process.

LEVEL 3—MOTIONS FOR PRELIMINARY RELIEF AND BETTER TRIAL ADVANTAGE

The next theater of the persuasive campaign involves a variety of pretrial motions heard by the judge. The motions are not the kind that dispose of the case but can be highly instrumental for success later on.

An attorney who fears that the property of the defendant will be sold or moved outside the state may seek a temporary remedy of attachment of that property. One who fears that his client's position will be irreparably harmed if the defendant is allowed to take certain actions may seek a temporary restraining order. These types of temporary orders are often granted after only an ex parte (one-sided) hearing in which one party informally makes his case to the judge and then hands the judge the order, neatly typed, ready for his signature. The Supreme Court has tended to frown on the practice of ex parte hearings, particularly in cases against debtors. The adversary hearing is becoming more common. At adversary hearings the plaintiff's attorney may have an easier time succeeding because the goal that he seeks is essentially the continuance of things as they were in order to prevent a change that could devalue his final remedy.

At this stage of the legal process, an attorney will begin to prepare his case for trial and will seek out the evidence that is in the possession of the other side. Modern discovery rules generally allow him to meet and interrogate the other party's witnesses and obtain important documents from them. However, it is not uncommon for one party to refuse to cooperate and to seek a protective order on some grounds of privilege. A hearing then is often held where one attorney will attempt to persuade the judge to allow concealment, whereas the other attorney will try to persuade the judge to allow disclosure. The attorney seeking to deter discovery may have a more difficult burden than the other in light of the clear public policy behind the discovery rules—access to all relevant evidence and avoidance of tricks and surprises at trial.

Just prior to a jury trial an attorney also has the opportunity to seek an order barring the presentation of a piece of inadmissible evidence at trial for fear the jury will be improperly influenced if the controversy over its admissibility takes place during the proceedings. Here again the judge may call for oral arguments where the party seeking to deter the attempted offer of evidence will have to bear the additional burden of overcoming the judge's likely preference for regular trial procedure in which evidence is considered for admissibility in its context.

Another practice of attorneys that does not involve judicial hearings is the witness conference. This conference is also important in the sustained campaign. Just prior to the trial, an attorney may ask all of his witnesses to meet together. In this conference, he explains the trial process so the witnesses know what to expect, explains how each individual's testimony is important to the overall case, and generally tries to build self-confidence for the witnesses' courtroom appearance.

LEVEL 4—THE TRIAL

The trial itself involves the most significant campaign in the war—the lawsuit. Here the attorney attempts to persuade the jury and judge (the judge has the power to direct—to overturn—the jury's verdict) by seeking a series of instrumental effects. In this fourth level of the campaign, six stages are involved: *voir dire*, opening arguments, examination of witnesses, objections, closing arguments, and judge's instructions.

The persuasion process in the courtroom begins well before the opening statements. The attorneys begin influencing potential jurors immediately by making each aware of the outline and basic appeals of the case in the questions he asks during the *voir dire* (jury selection) examination. The lawyers then carefully observe the potential juror's verbal response and the general demeanor—attitude, tone of voice, intelligence, and facial expression. From this perceptive analysis of the potential jurors, each attorney tries to select those jurors he thinks will be empathic to his appeals and strikes those he believes will be more empathic to the appeals of the opposing counsel (3). Those jurors who are clearly prejudiced will be dismissed for cause by the judge.

The vital importance of this *voir dire* process is illustrated by the apocryphal story:

An English barrister advised an American lawyer that a trial in England begins when the jury is accepted by counsel and sworn to try the case. The American Lawyer replied, "Hell, in the United States the trial is all over by that time!" (4)

In his opening statement, the attorney attempts to nurture acceptance of his case by introducing his client, by describing the accident and the injuries sustained by the client in a case involving personal injury, and by outlining what he hopes to prove during the trial. Later each attorney tries to guide the jurors to a preference for his client by calling self-assured witnesses who support his client's story. He also attempts to destroy the self-assuredness of the witnesses from the opposing side in the cross-examination. Making appropriate objections to certain lines of questions and responses to questions is also vital in the persuasion process in keeping certain information from the jury. In the closing argument, the attorney continues his influence appeal by summarizing all the evidence presented and by making logical inferences as to what the overall evidence presented should mean to the jury.

Even after the closing argument, the lawyer's persuasive campaign continues. Many judges provide the attorneys an opportunity to suggest instructions that will be given to the jury prior to entering the jury room. An attorney may even be allowed to argue the merits of his suggested instructions or object to the proposed instructions of the opposing counsel in the judge's chambers. Hence, each attorney again attempts to persuade the judge of the validity of his interpretation of the law.

LEVEL 5—POSTTRIAL MOTIONS AND APPEALS

After the jury has returned its verdict, another series of battles begin before the trial judge or appellate judges. The losing party will probably move immediately for judgment notwithstanding the verdict. The judge usually overrules this motion. In a few cases he may consider it, and even call an adversary hearing where the movant will have to bear the burden of persuading the judge that no reasonable jury could have decided the case the way this one did. If the losing attorney fails on this motion, he will usually move for a new trial. He will then have to convince the judge that he, the judge, committed an error in the trial or that the verdict was against the clear weight of the evidence. Failing here, the losing attorney may appeal to a higher court on the basis of the judge's (not, except in an extreme case, the jury's) errors at trial. In some appellate courts, for example the United States Supreme Court, accepting the appeal will be discretionary with the appellate court. Thus in putting together the appeal, the lawyer must make every attempt to gain the attention of the appellate judges or their clerks and give them the impression that the legal question raised is one that needs to be decided. Once the appeal is accepted for consideration, the attorneys file written briefs and are later called to appear at a hearing before the appellate court to state their respective positions in about a thirty-minute oral argument, during which the attorney is often required to respond to questions from the appellate judges challenging his position. The main thrust of this argument is to convince the appellate court judges that the law is or should be different than the trial judge ruled it was. To be effective in persuading them, the advocate should deemphasize his own case and emphasize instead the merits of adopting his position for the benefit of citizens who may in the future be in the same situation as his client.

Thus far, the reader has viewed the legal process from a communication perspective in terms of the different communication skills necessary for the successful lawyer and in terms of the concurrent sustained persuasive campaign on five levels that frequently occurs. The remainder of this reading focuses on the communicative behaviors of the trial functionaries: the attorneys, the witnesses, the judge, and the jury.

ATTORNEYS

Much lawyer folklore and some questionable research (5) substantiate the common axiom that juries try the lawyer rather than the client (6). If the jury likes one lawyer better than the opposing counsel, the probability is good that the jury will return a favorable verdict. However, recent research reveals startling evidence to the contrary.

In the videotaped content analysis study of jury deliberations, Forston found that actual county jurors who had participated in live trials (7) made references that pertained to the attorneys less than 0.2 per cent of the deliberation time. When comments about the attorneys were examined in detail, the statements were found to be general rather than referring to specific attorneys. In one trial plaintiff's attorney was a tall, dynamic Irishman who was colorful in his demeanor and who had won sixty-seven consecutive cases. Even in this situation where a second jury had been called, the percentage of the jury's comments in general about attorneys was only 0.4 per cent, and only two of the comments referred specifically to him or the opposing counsel. These comments did not appear to be crucial kinds of statements (8). On the other hand, the jurors did discuss the credibility of the witnesses in quite specific terms—over 11.2 per cent of the deliberation time (9).

Obviously the attorneys are the most visible and vocal trial participants. The trial lawyer has considerable opportunities to influence judge and jury in the various parts of the trial. The forensics of the trial can be most dynamic. The trial offers the opportunity for the use of a variety of persuasive ploys, semantics, and nonverbal ploys that make lawyers famous and glamorous.

For example, Max Wildman, a Chicago defense lawyer, uses his knowledge of semantics. "Take the word accident; which is the bedrock of all tort (personal injury) litigation," he once explained. "To a lawyer it means an occurrence, while to the layman sitting on a jury it means a mishap where no one is at fault. I can't tell you how many cases I've won exploiting that confusion in meaning" (10). The San Francisco attorney Melvin Belli is famous for his expert art of demonstrative evidence. One story tells of his trying a case while a long, large object wrapped in white butcher paper lay on the table. During the closing argument, he unwrapped the object to reveal an artificial leg that his client would have to wear for the remainder of his life. Other lawyers use a variety of techniques calculated to create certain impressions with jurors.

The nonverbal facial expressions, physical gestures, mannerisms, and paralanguage—the vocal qualities that accompany the spoken word or even silence itself—are often more important than what the lawyer actually says. Other ploys include the attorney's eating in the courthouse cafeteria with the jurors; having a young, attractive secretary ask the opposing client (if he is a middle-aged businessman) an innocent question, smile, and pat his hand; or jumping up to solicitously offer a handkerchief to the opposing lawyer's client, when she bursts into tears.

The *primacy effect* (creating a good first impression) is most critical to trial attorneys in the jury selection process and in the closing arguments. The results of several empirical investigations indicate that early initial commitment, even when tentative and private, tend to influence the final verdict of jurors (11).

On the other hand, the *recency effect* (the final impression) plays a lesser but, nevertheless, important part in the closing argument. Contrary to popular notions, trials are not usually won by eloquent appeals in the final minutes of the trial. The main function of the closing argument is to provide jurors with reasonable arguments to support their preference in the deliberation process. It is during this last stage that the lawyer can urge the jurors to not merely support his client but to become an active advocate for justice in the jury room. Another function of the closing statement for plaintiff attorneys is to reveal and justify the amount of the award (called the *prayer*) that he is asking for his client. The prayer for permanent disabilities of the loss of a leg or an eye, or a pretty teenage girl's anguish over a disfigured face and torso caused by the defendant's negligence, may be justified by an itemized procedure. The attorney tries to justify a large prayer by breaking it down into smaller segments such as medical costs, loss of wages, future loss of wages, or pain and anguish to be suffered during the remainder of the plaintiff's life. For example, a figure of nearly $110,000 might be explained for the pain and anguish part alone. By telling the jurors that although there is no way of putting a dollar amount on pain, $110,000 is a conservative award if one views the pain and anguish at $.50 an hour for twelve hours a day. Some attorneys ask the jurors if they would be willing to assume the client's pain and anguish for $.50 an hour or $6 a day. The daily figure is then multiplied by 365 days for a yearly sum of $2,190. The yearly sum is multiplied times fifty years, the life expectancy of the plaintiff, for a total of $109,500.

Witnesses

The major role of a witness is to provide the most objective, accurate firsthand description of events relevant to a case that is available. Witness *perception*, *memory* (time lapse), and *coaching* are all factors that impede the primary function of a witness.

Perception of an event is dependent upon a host of variable personal influences including motives, expectations, background, and the unique pressures of the situation. Memory is subject to similar kinds of selection and change as perception (12). Delayed recall or delayed testimony distorts since the delayed recall is more selective and less detailed as time passes. The language symbols that are chosen to describe the event produce an additional selection process. The distortion patterns of condensation, leveling, sharpening, and assimilation occur naturally. Witnesses reduce the event to a few easily remembered details. This reduction process is done through leveling or systematically omitting details of the event that do not conform to the stereotypes of the witness. Sharpening stresses the details of the description of the occurrence that remain in a familiar pattern, whereas assimilation adapts the event to the most reasonable explanation as a result of one's frame of reference and personal experiences. None of these influences presume dishonest motivation or the conscious effort to act in selfish self-interest.

A legal practice that frequently encourages biased or slanted testimony from witnesses is placing the witness in a position of commitment to either the prosecution (plaintiff) or defense prior to his court appearance. The decision to present the witness for a particular side is, of course, planned. His potential testimony is heard, reheard, and "coached" prior to his appearance. "Coaching" is too strong a word to use in context of overt instruction, but hardly too strong a word in the context of the kinds of refinements in testimony that can result from carefully repeating a story under a lawyer's guidance.

Sometimes a witness conference is held for all the witnesses on one side to become familiar with how the different testimony fits into the trial plan. By the time this process is finished, the witness has established a helping relationship with one attorney, who will be a friendly attorney and to whom he has some commitment as well as to whom he can turn for security if he finds the actual trial a threatening experience. Since witnesses have stage fright too, the need for a friend under trial circumstances is strong. The witness also has a clear role relationship with the opposing counsel— a hostile (defensive) relationship (13).

Regarding the credibility of witness testimony, Forston found that jurors employ several standards in testing the believability:

1. Was the witness in a *position* to see (hear) and understand the event?
2. Did the witness have a *reason* for observing the event at the precise time that it occurred?
3. Did the witness make any *overt action* to warn, stop, or help the accident or situation at the precise time that the event was occurring?
4. Was the general *demeanor* of the witness during the testimony consistent with what he said? (14)

These four standards are used to test the testimony of the witnesses independently of other witnesses. A fifth comparison standard is:

5. Did the testimony of the others substantiate any part of this witness' testimony?

Hence, a witness who tells how he was sitting on his balcony as he saw an accident below is probably in a good position to see and hear what happened. But if he can provide a definite reason for noticing the event or the people involved, his credibility will increase. Therefore, if the balcony witness tells how he was watching a little girl playing in the empty parking lot below and that she reminded him of his granddaughter, he provides a definite reason for observing the accident prior to and during the accident. If the witness then testifies that he saw an automobile approaching the entrance of the parking lot and could tell that the driver might hit the girl, he yelled to the girl "watch out—jump to the curb." This overt action also increases the believability of the witness.

THE JUDGE

In addition to the judge's decision-making on the law itself, one of his primary functions in the courtroom is to regulate the communication of the lawyers and witnesses. Regulation of trial communication is essential for enhancing justice and creating an atmosphere of dignity and decorum in which a fair trial may be held. The judge's regulation consists of prohibiting communication, intervening and ceasing communication, altering communication, and eliciting communication.

By sustaining objections by one attorney, the judge *prohibits* or *keeps* the opposing counsel from presenting certain kinds of evidence and exhibits that may improperly influence the jury. He also rules on objections to certain kinds of testimony (e.g., personal opinions by nonexpert witnesses) and questions (e.g., leading questions), which are being stated; hence, he has the power to *cease* or to approve the continuance of such statements by sustaining or overruling the objections. He, of course, need not wait for objections from an attorney to act but may intervene on his own behalf regarding a concern about certain testimony that is inappropriate for the jury to consider. The judge may on his own initiative *intervene* to *cease* or to *alter* the communication approach by a lawyer or witness. He may also ask a lawyer or witness to speak louder or to repeat a statement. To maintain the dignity and decorum of the courtroom, the judge occasionally deals with outbursts in the courtroom such as Judge Hoffman did in the Chicago Seven conspiracy trial when he ordered defendant Bobby Seale bound and gagged after repeatedly warning him to cease outbursts during the trial. Another way that a judge occasionally regulates trial communication is by *eliciting* further testimony in order to clarify the disputed issue so that the jury might better understand the testimony. Eliciting additional testimony may also be requested in order to serve justice for the larger community such as Judge Sirica did in the first Watergate trial when he asked for further information from the defendants in order to uncover more of the Watergate scandal.

Still another way in which a judge regulates trial communication is through his instructions to the jury. He instructs the jury from time to time on how to consider the statements of attorneys and the testimony of witnesses. Likewise, the judge warns jurors about trial publicity outside the courtroom. Regarding testimony, the judge sometimes instructs the jury to disregard entirely certain evidence that was heard, or he may attempt to limit the manner in which a jury may consider certain evidence. Sometimes the judge chooses to keep the jury out of the courtroom while lengthy arguments over an objection are being heard. All of these forms of regulation of trial communication by the judge are presumed to be important to ensure a fair trial.

Most of the judge's instructions come at the end of the trial, prior to jury deliberation and presumably before the juror has made up his mind. These instructions are about points of law that are not at issue so that the jury can make a judgment about points of fact that are at issue. The instructions tell the jury how to apply the law to the facts as they find them. The importance of the judge's charge to the jury is frequently discounted by legal scholars (15). This discounting is unwarranted. Forston found in his content analysis of jury deliberations that nearly 10 per cent of the jury's deliberation time was spent discussing some aspect of the instructions—either clarifying them or applying them to the facts as found. This percentage was the second highest category of time spent next to the actual substantive issue of determining liability in a civil case (16). Forston's research also revealed that when the jury was given both oral and written instructions, the discussion of the instructions increased to 14 per cent of the deliberation time. In viewing the videotapes of these deliberations, the merits of instructions, especially the written charge, were dramatic in the effects of helping the jury reach a quality decision.

The judge's charge to the jury was once described by a judge like "being doused with a kettleful of law which would stagger a third-year law student." If this statement is even partially valid, it is unfortunate, for jurors have no legal training to comprehend the technical language of the law. Moreover, since the jury system is founded upon the premise that jurors do, in fact, *understand* and *apply* the rules of law as given by a judge, the crucial question arises: What kind of justice do we obtain if jurors do not comprehend the charge as given?

The concern over judicial instructions is not new, for legal and communication researchers have been investigating this problem since the 1930's. The findings of most of these studies concur that the typical juror neither understands nor applies the rules of law adequately (17).

The problem of jury confusion over the charge to the jury was recently given nationwide attention in the Harrisburg Seven trial. The jury in this trial deliberated longer than any other federal jury in history—more than fifty hours over seven days. The result was a deadlocked jury confused over the issues and the instructions. The jury tried to solve some of its problems by requesting a written copy of the two-hour instructions, but the request was denied.

That the Harrisburg Seven jury was confused was hardly a revelation to communication scholars. The jury had the overwhelming task of evaluating the testimony of sixty-four witnesses given during a fifty-six-day trial and then relating the judge's instructions to each of seven defendants who were accused of ten different charges.

The enormity of this decision-making task becomes clearer when one realizes that more than one thousand possible decision combinations of guilty or not guilty existed for just *one defendant* on the ten charges. When one considers the combinations of decisions for all seven defendants together, he finds that several million exist. This immense number of possible decisions is a mind-staggering task for any group of human beings.

Recent experimental studies in three cities of the Midwest have demonstrated that jury confusion over instructions is a serious problem for even the *simplest* of *trials* (18).

The testing of the jurors' comprehension of judges' instructions was conducted under almost ideal conditions: the jurors were experienced, nearing the end of the two-to-four-week service; the instructions were very short (none more than twenty minutes in length); the instructions were read orally during the morning while the jurors were mentally alert; the cases involved relatively ordinary issues rather than complex issues; and the comprehension test measured immediate rather than delayed comprehension. The instructions were read in some cases after the jurors heard testimony in simulated trials and in other cases after they were given a summary of testimony that would have been presented in an actual trial.

The results revealed an average comprehension level as low as 46 per cent for civil personal injury cases and 53 per cent for criminal cases. The comprehension level was as low as 15 to 25 per cent on some of the crucial legal concepts such as proximate cause, proof of guilt, evidence, and contributory negligence.

The jurors were then given a second chance at answering the same comprehension test. They were divided into face-to-face deliberating juries to reach a consensus of their understanding of the rules of law. Even under these ideal conditions of immediate recall and group interaction, *four-fifths of the juries misunderstood the concepts of evidence and proof of guilt.* One-half of the juries had difficulties in accurately understanding other crucial elements of the instructions (19).

It should be noted that this research was conducted in ideal conditions, but jurors rarely received their charge under such ideal conditions. Frequently the instructions are considerably longer, and the forgetting curve has had an opportunity to take its toll in deliberations, since juries do not need to recall or apply specific rules of law until several hours or even days later in the deliberation process.

The answer to this problem is not to dispense with the jury system, as some argue, for it is our way of administering justice and our safeguard against official tyranny. The essential point is that jurors ought not be hindered with lengthy technical instructions, much of which is incomprehensible to lawmen or perhaps even to senior law students.

Clearly, the trial judges need to give more attention to the phrasing of instructions in layman's terms rather than relying so heavily on highly technical and abstract legal language. However, if trial judges are expected to employ less legal jargon, higher court justices must lend their positive support by upholding instructions that deviate from the present standardized legal language.

Moreover, rather than including the vast majority of the instructions after the trial, a significant amount of the instructions could be provided during various parts of the trial to help the juror define his role more gradually and more consistently as the testimony is presented. Repetition of these instructions at the end of the trial through oral and written instructions should facilitate the juror's understanding of the charge.

The Jury

The mystique of the jury has been developed by decades of lawyer folklore. No one—neither attorney, bailiff, nor judge—is permitted to enter or eavesdrop on the jury deliberations. Nor are the jurors required to justify their verdict. Myths result from this vacuum of knowledge. Two major research projects have shed some light upon the shadows of juror behavior: the University of Chicago Jury Project, which is thoroughly described in Kalven and Zeisel's book, *The American Jury* (20); and Forston's research mentioned previously (21). Both studies were careful to simulate trials and to employ actual jurors. Some of Forston's jurors thought that their verdict was legally binding.

The foreman myth is one of the most interesting jury theories to consider. This myth claims that one person—the foreman of a jury is like a lion among sheep. Be kind to the lion (foreman) and he will handle the sheep (other jurors) for you (22). The best way to expose this myth is to describe the foreman and his role with the other jurors. Not much thought goes into the selection of the foreman. Forston's research revealed that the mean time for selecting the foreman in 96 per cent of the juries was only thirty-two seconds (23). Typically, no democratic election or even a nomination process was held. Usually the first person who spoke or indicated that he wanted the role of foreman was allowed to be foreman. The title foreman did not automatically make that person one of the leaders of the jury. Approximately one-half of the time someone else in the jury was considered to be more influential and important than the foreman. In some cases the foreman was only a nominal leader.

Both the University of Chicago Project and Forston found no evidence to support the one-man jury theory (24). Instead they found that five to seven jurors in a twelve-member jury normally controlled the deliberation process. This discovery led to the detailed analysis of what was called the "Central Work Group," composed of jurors who were perceived by other jurors as the most active and influential participants in reaching a verdict, and the "Peripheral Observers," consisting of the residual jurors who were perceived as noninfluential and usually inactive participants in the deliberation process.

Analyzing the communication of the jurors who comprised the Central Work Group revealed that an average of 6.1 jurors accounted for over 85 per cent of the deliberation time, whereas the Peripheral Observers accounted for the remainder of the time. Closer analysis of the Peripheral Observers' communication showed that even this small contribution was not particularly helpful to the jury in terms of reaching a verdict. Hence, the jury is not a "one-person jury" but a jury dominated by a group of about six jurors.

The social dimensions of the twelve-member jury table also have significant implications. As can be seen in Figure 5–5, the jury table has four different types of seating positions: the end position, the tackle position, the guard position, and the center position.

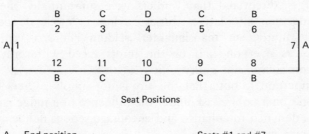

Seat Positions

A	End position	Seats #1 and #7
B	Tackle position	Seats #2, #6, #8, and #12
C	Guard position	Seats #3, #5, #9, and #11
D	Center position	Seats #4 and #10

Numbers indicate juror designations; letters indicate seat "positions."

FIGURE 5-5. Diagram of the jury table.

Hawkins analyzed the participation of jurors according to the seating position at the jury table and found that the seating position is strongly associated with the level of participation. The percentage that the average juror spoke in each position is as follows: end position (11 per cent), tackle position (8 per cent), guard position (8 per cent), and center position (7 per cent) (25).

The selection of the foreman and/or the de facto perceived leader are also positively correlated with the seating position. One major investigation showed that three times as many foremen were chosen from the end position as would have been expected by chance. The tackle position, which is next to the end position, was a distant second as the next most popular source of foremen (26).

Another assumption about juries that appears to be a myth is that the jurors wait until after the trial to make their decision. As indicated previously, the jury in reality makes its decision early in the trial; hence, the deliberation process becomes a process for formalizing commitments already made prior to the deliberation (27). Kalven and Zeisel liken the deliberation process "to what the developer does for an exposed film: it brings out the picture, but the outcome is pre-determined" (28).

Other empirical work indicated that when a jury was aligned into coalitions (e.g., proplaintiff versus prodefendant), compensating vote switching between coalitions was rare. This deliberation phenomenon revealed that the first juror to switch his vote to the opposing coalition of jurors was an almost sure indicator of the only direction in which a verdict would be made. This phenomenon occurred even when a juror from a much larger coalition shifted to a smaller coalition (29).

Vidmar, working with simulated juries in criminal cases involving murder charges, discovered that verdicts were substantially affected by the number of decision alternatives. Juries having a "moderate penalty," e.g., second-degree murder or manslaughter, seldom chose a verdict of "not guilty," whereas over one-half of the jurors faced with only a "severe" penalty option chose "not guilty" (30).

It is important to note that the jury is not simply a street corner gang. The jury works on a public task under the influence of a judge and in solemn surroundings designed to enhance and encourage serious deliberation. Kalven and Zeisel point out:

The jury . . . represents a uniquely subtle distribution of official power, an unusual arrangement of checks and balances. It represents also an impressive way of building discretion, equity, and flexibility into a legal system. Not the least of the advantages is that the jury relieved of the burdens of creating precedent can bend the law without breaking it. (31)

NOTES

1. A number of Watergate figures, including John Dean as White House Counsel, negotiated for full or partial immunity from prosecution for their own criminal activities as a condition for their testimony about the Watergate activities of others.

2. Vice President Spiro Agnew's lawyers engaged in plea bargaining with Attorney General Elliot Richardson. As a result, Agnew agreed to plead *no contest* (considered equivalent to an admission of guilt) to a single count of income tax evasion and to resign as vice-president.

3. Some attorneys hire psychiatrists and other specialists to help in the jury selection process. See Louis S. Katz, "The Twelve Man Jury," *Trial Magazine,* 4:39–40 (1968–1969).

4. C. Clyde Atkins, "Jury Voir Dire by Counsel—Let's Preserve It," *Insurance Council Journal*, 31:689 (1964).

5. Harold M. Hoffman and Joseph Brodley, "Jurors on Trial," *Missouri Law Review*, 17:242–243 (1952); and John P. Reed, "Jury Deliberations, Voting, and Verdict Trends," *Southwestern Social Science Quarterly*, 45:364–365 (1965).

6. Jerome Frank, *Courts on Trial* (Princeton, N.J.: Princeton University Press, 1949), pp. 121–122.

7. Some of these trials were realistically simulated with an actual courtroom, judge, lawyer, witnesses, and county jurors; another trial was an actual legal case with a second nonlegal jury selected for videotaping.

8. Robert F. Forston, "The Decision-Making Process in the American Civil Jury: A Comparative Methodological Investigation." Unpublished Ph.D. dissertation, University of Minnesota, 1968.

9. Ibid., p. 113.

10. Jonathan R. Laing, "Keeping Verdicts Low in Personal-Injury Suits Takes Specialized Skills," *The Wall Street Journal*, July 5, 1973, p. 10.

11. Vernon A. Stone, "A Primacy Effect in Decision-Making by Jurors," *Journal of Communication*, 19:239–247 (1969); Forston, p. 149; and H. P. Weld and E. R. Danzig, "A Study of the Way in Which a Verdict Is Reached by a Jury," *American Journal of Psychology*, 53:518–536 (1940).

12. James Marshall, *Law and Psychology in Conflict* (Indianapolis: The Bobbs-Merrill Co., Inc., 1966).

13. Charles Tucker, "Legal Practice and Communication Theory." Unpublished paper presented before the Central States Speech Association Convention, Chicago, Illinois, 1972.

14. Forston, pp. 96–102.

15. Dale W. Broeder, "The University of Chicago Jury Project," *Nebraska Law Review*, 38:751 (1959).

16. Forston, pp. 113, 150; F. Gerald Kline and Paul H. Jess, "Prejudicial Publicity: Its Effects on Law School Mock Juries," *Journalism Quarterly*, 43:116 (1966).

17. John G. Hervey, "Jurors Look at Our Judges," *Oklahoma Bar Association Journal*, 18:1508–1513 (1947); and Robert M. Hunter, "Law in the Jury Room," *Ohio State University Law Journal*, 2:1–19 (1935).

18. Robert F. Forston, "Justice, Jurors and Judge's Instructions," *The Judges' Journal*, 12:68–69 (1973).

19. Ibid., p. 68; and Robert F. Forston, "Judge's Instructions: A Quantitative Analysis of Jurors' Listening Comprehension," *Today's Speech*, 18:35–37 (1970).

20. Harry Kalven, Jr., and Hans Zeisel, *The American Jury* (Boston: Atlantic-Little, Brown, 1966).

21. Forston (1968); and Forston (1973).

22. Judge James C. Adkins, "An Art? A Science? or Luck?" *Trial Magazine*, 4:39 (1968–1969).

23. Forston (1968), pp. 75–77.

24. Joe Blade, "Professor: Juries Often Decide Early," *Minneapolis Star*, July 29, 1967, p. 9A; and Forston (1968), pp. 81–88.

25. Charles H. Hawkins, "Interaction and Coalition Realignments in Consensus-Seeking Groups: A Study of Experimental Jury Deliberation." Unpublished Ph.D. dissertation, University of Chicago, 1960, pp. 15, 21.

26. Ibid., p. 23.

27. Forston (1968), pp. 130–131.

28. Kalven and Zeisel, p. 489.

29. Forston (1968), pp. 131–133; and Hawkins, p. 155.

30. Neil Vidmar, "Effects of Decision Alternatives on the Verdicts and Social Perceptions of Simulated Jurors," *Journal of Personality and Social Psychology*, 22:211–218 (1972).

31. Kalven and Zeisel, p. 489.

STUDY GUIDE
QUESTIONS

1. What are the characteristics that distinguish mass communication from various forms of interpersonal communication?
2. What are the functions served by the mass media in our modern society?
3. What is meant by such terms as *media gatekeeper, selective perception,* and *two-step communication flow*?
4. What has mass communication research told us about short-term media effects?
5. What future implications do you see for man and his environment?

►◄ Communication and the Media

ROBERT K. AVERY

It is difficult for the college student of the 1970's to imagine living in a world without communication media. We are the product of a society that depends upon a continuous stream of messages that are transmitted via radio, television, motion pictures, newspapers, magazines, and books. In fact, the media are so much a part of our daily lives that we often take their presence for granted. Similarly, we grant them almost unlimited power in determining what current events will be brought to our attention each day. Even though we are well aware of the frequent attacks on the media by such outspoken critics as Spiro Agnew and Nicholas Johnson, we have a tendency to forget the seriousness of their accusations and return to our evening newspaper or favorite television newscast to discover what is taking place in the world "out

"Communication and the Media," by Robert K. Avery. Reprinted with permission of the author. This original essay appears here for the first time.

there." Living in a decade that has been labeled as the "age of communication" and characterized by the doubling of all human knowledge every five
years, we share a common responsibility; to develop an understanding of the
characteristics, functions, and potential impact of the mass media in our
modern society.

Human communication is the process of transmitting meaning between
individuals. It is a process that is both fundamental to man's nature and vital
to his existence. Since the birth of primitive cultures, man has been heavily
involved in expanding his capacity to express his feelings, desires, concerns,
and experiences to those around him. At first, man seemed satisfied to transmit
meaning to others in close proximity to himself, but as man developed his
intellect, he found it desirable (perhaps imperative to his very existence) to
enlarge the parameters of his communicative transmissions. Thus, man
extended the boundaries of human communication through the use of smoke
signals, jungle drums, flashes of light, and crude trumpets. Later, with the
invention of the alphabet, man transmitted his knowledge through written
communication, first using pen and ink, and later carved wooden blocks. But
it was not until the fifteenth century and the invention of movable metal type
that man developed an efficient means of providing written communication
to a mass audience in a relatively short period of time. Then, in the early
1840's, Samuel F. B. Morse, using his knowledge of electricity, developed a
device for the transmitting a code of dots and dashes over a wire that made
possible the instantaneous telegraphic transmissions of our alphabet over long
distances. Within five decades, Guglielmo Marconi had discovered the secret
of transmitting Morse's code by wireless (radio). With the turn of the century
came Lee DeForest's invention of the vacuum tube amplifier that made voice
transmission possible, thereby opening the realm of modern broadcasting.
The list of inventions and technological innovations that have contributed to
the extension of human communication from those early tribal drums and
smoke signals to today's satellite transmission seems endless. Yet it is important to note that each new development has contributed to increasing the
complexity of our modern systems of mass communication.

Students frequently respond to the question, "What is mass communication?" with such answers as "radio," "television," "newspapers," or "motion pictures." Although such responses are certainly true in part, we must
remember that the images generally evoked by these descriptors are only the
instruments or tools that make the *process* of mass communication possible.
To illustrate this important distinction, let us devise a hypothetical situation.
You are probably enrolled in a college or university that operates a closed-
circuit television system or videotaping facility of some kind. Now, let us
assume that you are given the opportunity to stand before the television
camera, record a speech, and then sit down in front of the television monitor
to watch yourself on the screen. You have just utilized many of the technical

instruments of the television medium to transmit a personal message, but has mass communication taken place? The answer is obviously, "no." However, if you carry the videotaped speech to a local television station and have it broadcast to the entire community, mass communication has taken place. In other words, it is not just the "hardware" of radio, television, and newspapers that distinguishes them as systems of modern mass communication but rather it is the special characteristics of the total mass communication process.

In other sections of this book, you were introduced to different forms of interpersonal communication. Although there may be considerable variation in how authors label or categorize these levels—dyadic, triadic, small group, and so on—they all share one important feature, the opportunity for face-to-face interaction. That is, communication that is mutually influential between the parties involved and where the receiving and transmitting of information is dynamic in nature. As one person is transmitting information, he is also receiving information in the form of head nods, restless shifting, verbal reinforcement, i.e. "I see," "you don't say," "right on," or some other form of nonverbal communication. Thus, the roles of "speaker" and "listener" are constantly changing, and each party has an opportunity to share in the human communication process.

All forms of mass communication can be distinguished from these levels of interpersonal communication by the fact that they interject an electronic or print medium into the interpersonal communication paradigm. The radio receiver, television set, newspaper, magazine, and book all serve to remove the communicator from direct contact with his audience. In other words, the instruments of the mass media eliminate the opportunity for face-to-face interaction and the changing of "speaker" and "listener" roles. With the opportunity for information sharing lost, the relationship between communicator and audience becomes much more impersonal. This is due not only to the interjection of mass media's complex technology but also to the requirements of the speaker's role as a public communicator. It is the nature of the public communicator, the nature of the audience and the communication experience itself that further distinguishes the various forms of mass communication.

Behind the warm, personal delivery of the evening television newscaster, or the fast-paced chatter of your favorite disc jockey is a formal and highly complex media organization. The establishment and regular operation of a television or radio station, for example, involves large capital investment and consequently places decision-making authority in the hands of the financial backers. The internal personnel structure of a broadcast facility is built upon certain basic policy guidelines, established by the station's owners and implemented by station management. Decision-making that determines what you see and hear does not take place in a vacuum. Pressures from federal regulatory agencies (Federal Communications Commission, Federal Trade

Commission), professional organizations (National Association of Broadcasters, Radio Television News Directors Association), trade associations (American Federation of Television and Radio Artists, Screen Actor's Guild), citizen's groups (Action for Children's Television, National Citizens' Committee for Broadcasting), and local community organizations force the media organizations to respond to normative controls and standards. In some instances, these controls impose requirements on the mass media that are far more restrictive than the usual social conventions and standards that are typical of informal, unstructured, interpersonal communication.

For anyone who has felt frustration over the cancellation of a favorite television program or dissatisfaction with the musical format of a radio station, it will come as no surprise that another distinguishing characteristic of mass communication is that the flow of information (messages) is primarily one-way. Various verbal and nonverbal feedback mechanisms do exist—letters to the editor, telephone calls to the broadcast station, correspondence with citizens' groups and regulatory agencies, circulation figures, box office receipts, and audience ratings—but the ratio of mass media output to audience input is very large. Then, too, the kinds of feedback channels that are available to members of the audience are often subject to a substantial time lag.

An excellent example is the letter to the newspaper editor or the radio and television station manager. Sometimes action in response to these letters is immediate, but more frequently it is delayed. The recent upsurge of radio's sex talk shows, "topless radio," illustrates this point very well. Many listeners who were disturbed by the open discussion of sexual issues over radio wrote letters to both the radio stations involved and the Federal Communications Commission demanding that the programs be taken off the air. The FCC responded to the outcries by conducting a closed-door inquiry to investigate the situation. At the conclusion of the inquiry, the FCC outlined definite limits for the broadcasting of sexually oriented discussions, and fined an Oak Park, Illinois, radio station $2,000 for violating a criminal statute barring the broadcast of obscene or indecent material. Between the initial letters of complaint and the commission's final action, many weeks had passed and a significant number of programs continued to be aired (in direct response to high audience ratings). Admittedly, there were some stations that discontinued their sex talk shows well in advance of the FCC decision. One such radio station in Salt Lake City, Utah, created a unique situation to elicit face-to-face audience response. This station simply encouraged listeners to drive by the downtown studios and give their reaction to the program by showing a "thumbs up" or "thumbs down" signal. When the "thumbs down" votes won by a striking margin, the program was immediately taken off the air. Thus, we have a special instance of how a newly created feedback channel greatly increased the number of audience responses and brought prompt results.

It should be obvious from this discussion that another characteristic of mass communication is that the messages of a relatively small number of communicators are widely disseminated to large audiences. Even when we combine the number of "communicators" associated with all the individual radio and television stations and the national broadcasting networks in the United States, the total is dismally small when compared with a population of approximately 205 million people. But since not everyone is a member of a given radio, television, motion picture, or newspaper audience at any one time, the natural question is, "How large must an audience be in order to qualify as a mass audience?" Certainly, an audience of 50 million television viewers watching the annual Super Bowl game would be large enough to qualify as a mass audience. But what about the thousands of fans who have packed into the football stadium to see the game in person? At this point it must become a matter of definition, and not all students of mass communication agree on what that definition should be. One well-respected scholar, Charles R. Wright, has proposed the following specification for a mass audience: "A tentative definition would consider as 'large' any audience exposed during a short period of time and of such a size that the communicator could not interact with its members on a face-to-face basis" (1). Thus, the point at which an audience is large enough to be considered "mass" is a purely arbitrary one. Perhaps more important than the matter of size are questions concerning mass audience composition.

As we consider the nature of the mass audience, we should remember that the mass media's messages are open to the public. When the technologies of printing, radio, television, or film are used for private consumption, as in the case of the private showing of our videotaped speech discussed previously, it cannot be regarded as mass communication. Obviously, unlimited open access to the message is an ideal that is seldom, if ever, achieved. Numerous technical, sociological, cultural, and economic factors influence the degree to which the mass media are available to their potential audiences. In underdeveloped countries, problems associated with multiple languages, illiteracy, and severe poverty frequently create additional barriers of media consumption.

Taking for granted that at least some of these factors will contribute to the composition of any given audience, the fact that the mass audience consists of a sampling of the general public assures that the audience for the mass media will be heterogeneous in nature. That is, it will be composed of an aggregation of individuals living under widely different conditions and occupying a variety of positions within society. There will be persons of many ages with different interests, standards of living, and levels of influence. There will be representation from both sexes, widely varying cultural and religious heritages, different races, levels of education, and so on. Yet, this gross description can be somewhat misleading. Scholars have totally rejected the notion of a single mass audience, since common sense tells us that the viewers of a television program or the readers of a newspaper are constantly changing, making it highly unlikely that the exact same mass audience will ever be assembled more than once. This fluid, dynamic characteristic prompts these scholars to talk in terms of mass *audiences* rather than audience. One suggested method of classification begins with a hypothetical *general* mass audience representing the *potential* public that is capable of being reached by the media. The general mass audience, by definition, is the largest most scattered, anonymous, and heterogeneous collectivity possible. Under this major heading is an extensive list of *specialized audiences*, each one being heterogeneous in many ways. However, these specialized audiences are composed of individuals who share some common interest or orientation, thus making a particular message appealing to all members of any one specialized audience. For example, viewers of "Hee Haw" enjoy country music, readers of *Playboy* are interested in a liberal discussion of sexual issues, listeners of Saturday's Metropolitan Opera broadcast share a taste for opera, and fans of the Monday night football telecast typically enjoy sports. Hence, with reference to the specific interest or concern that causes members of each audience to attend to the mass communicator's message (product) we can say that the audience members are homogeneous. In other words, although each specialized audience is heterogeneous in the sense that it may represent a cross section of ages, educational levels, and socioeconomic strata, there is at least one area in which there is evidence of homogeneity. Whether the existence of limited homogeneity in this respect is more or less significant than the variety of individual circumstances and backgrounds of the audience members remains a question for communication researchers.

It is important to consider that the mass media are not only capable of communicating messages to a large number of people who are located at long distances from both the communicator and other members of the audience but they are also capable of communicating these messages *simultaneously*. Naturally, the electronic media are more successful in achieving this result than are the print media, since the messages transmitted over electronic channels are transitory and therefore force all audience members to attend to the message at the same time. Newspapers, magazines, and books, on the other hand, are read at different times at the convenience of the reader. Therefore, it can be argued that the electronic media are superior in providing information instantaneously and simultaneously to a vast, widely separated audience, whereas the print media are superior in affording messages that are both permanent and capable of being received at the discretion of the consumer. Although it is true that audio- and videotape playback equipment have contributed to the permanence and convenience of receiving electronic transmissions, audience usage of such equipment for in-home recording of regularly scheduled broadcasts is still quite limited.

To summarize, we have considered six major characteristics of the mass media that distinguish them from the different forms of interpersonal communication: (1) The mass communicator does not have an opportunity for face-to-face interaction with his audience, since the communication channel is either an electronic or print medium. (2) Mass communication systems are much more complicated than interpersonal communication and require formal, complex organizations to maintain their operation. (3) The organization of the mass media permits the flow of messages in primarily one direction, with the opportunity for feedback being much more limited than in the interpersonal setting. (4) The messages of a relatively small number of mass communicators are widely disseminated to large audiences in much the same way that enormous quantities of mass-produced goods are turned out by modern manufacturers. (5) In addition to being large, the mass-media audiences are heterogeneous, anonymous, fluid, and widely scattered, although members of any particular mass audience generally share one or more interests, concerns, or orientations. (6) The mass media are capable of communicating messages to many people in different parts of the world both instantaneously and simultaneously.

With some possible exceptions, all of these characteristics should be present in varying degrees in any mass-communication situation. Taken individually, these characteristics can be viewed as either advantageous or disadvantageous when compared with the circumstances surrounding interpersonal communication. Actually, the mass media cannot be studied in isolation from interpersonal channels if one is to fully understand the total mass communication process. However, before examining the important relationship between mass and interpersonal communication, it is necessary to understand the functions served by the mass media in our modern society.

Critics and supporters of the mass media have been engaged in heated debate over the virtues and evils of the media for many years (2). Seldom has there been complete agreement on appropriate criteria for measuring their worth, let alone consensus on the major issues being debated. The most frequently agreed upon criteria evolve from the work of social scientists who have endeavored to specify the various functions normally performed by systems of mass communication. Undoubtedly, the most well-known contributor to this area of study is Harold D. Lasswell, a leading pioneer in mass communication research. Dr. Lasswell's classic paper on the structure and function of communication in modern society outlined three basic media functions: "(1) The surveillance of the environment; (2) the correlation of the parts of society in responding to the environment; (3) the transmission of the social heritage from one generation to the next" (3). Lasswell never intended to suggest that the performance of these functions were suddenly initiated with the advent of modern mass media of communication. Man has always been concerned with monitoring developments in his environment, circulating facts and opinions that would contribute to intelligent decision-making, and passing on the lore and experiences of one generation to the next. Rather, Lasswell focused our attention on the fact that the mass media had acquired these basic functions and, subsequently, caused us to ponder the possible consequences of leaving surveillance, correlation, and social transmission in the hands of the media practitioners.

Using more familiar language, the *surveillance* function refers to the collection and distribution of information about the environment or what is generally regarded as news. Other students of mass communication have labeled this the "reporting" or "watchdog" function of the electronic and printed press. Through a constant flow of information concerning events occurring around the world (and beyond), the mass media serve as a sentinel, warning us of floods, earthquakes, hurricanes, military attack, disease epidemics, and political rioting. Such everyday information as traffic reports, local weather forecasts, announcements of meetings and other institutional activities are examples of less dramatic occurrences.

Our dependence upon these daily services is not realized until we suddenly find ourselves without them. This was graphically illustrated by a research study conducted by Bernard Berelson and his associates during a New York City newspaper strike in 1945. Area residents complained of being disoriented, confused, and at a loss without their daily newspapers. Listener and viewer requests during more recent newspaper strikes in New York, Pittsburgh, and San Francisco resulted in the local broadcast media serving a much greater surveillance function until the strikes were over.

For some newsmen, the term *watchdog* has special significance with reference to monitoring our systems of government. There is probably no better example of the mass media's vital role in keeping watch over our country's political affairs than the disclosure of the Watergate cover up. As observed by prominent columnist Max Lerner, following the Senate Watergate Hearings, "The media are so crucial to everything that happens in our time that they have in effect become a fourth branch of the governing process." Two young *Washington Post* reporters, Robert Woodward and Carl Bernstein, were credited with tracking down most of the startling details from the time the Watergate burglars were apprehended. For months, Woodward and Bernstein interviewed potential news sources on the street, in people's homes, in deserted parking lots, in private offices, and over the telephone until the fragmented pieces started to fall into place. When the Senate Committee began its formal inquiry, it was again through the media, especially television, that the American people became aware of Watergate's significance.

Lasswell's second media function, *correlation*, refers to the selection, evaluation, and interpretation of the news. In effect, the mass media determine what are the most important events in our environment and, hence, what will be presented to us as "news." Kurt Lewin, another outstanding social scientist, was the first to apply the term *gatekeeper* to decision-making positions such as those held by news editors in television, radio, and the printed press. The numerous research studies growing out of this line of inquiry revealed that the editorial function of the media embodies an extremely complex process. Equally important were the findings that we are not only highly dependent upon the media for the evaluation and interpretation of the news but frequently accept, unchallenged, the media's prescription of how we should respond to it. The radio and television commentaries of Eric Sevareid, Howard K. Smith, Harry Reasoner, John Chancellor, Paul Harvey, Edward P. Morgan, and David Brinkley, and the syndicated columns of Jack Anderson, Smith Hempstone, Joseph Alsop, William F. Buckley, and James Reston are familiar examples of the media's correlation function. There can be no question that by leaving the task of evaluation and interpretation to a few qualified individuals, the majority of society frees itself from a difficult and time-consuming chore. Despite the criticism of former Vice President Agnew, it is through the "instant analysis" of television newscasters following a State of the Union message that many Americans gain their only understanding of what the President's goals and legislative objectives might mean to the country. Left to their own initiative, relatively few citizens would make the necessary effort to place important events into their proper historical and social context.

As indicated previously, the *transmission of social heritage* refers to the passing on of cultural norms, values, mores, customs, and traditions to all members of a society and from generation to generation. This is frequently described as the "socialization" or "education" function of the media. As conveyors of a society's heritage, the mass media serve as a mirror to the society itself. For example, visitors to other developed countries can often tell much about the values and priorities of the people simply by spending several days in front of a television set. Similarly, researchers have utilized the content and structure of mass-media systems in their investigation of the norms and ideologies of modern societies.

Building upon the work of Harold Lasswell, other students of mass communication have identified additional media functions. Charles Wright has suggested that *entertainment* is another primary function of the mass media. He explains that there are many "communicative acts primarily intended for amusement irrespective of any instrumental effects they might have" (4). Even a brief glance at the motion-picture listings or radio and television schedules for any given day not only offers support for Wright's contention but suggests that entertainment is probably the biggest service provided by the American mass media. The comprehensive studies of television viewing habits by Gary A. Steiner in 1960 and Robert T. Bower in 1970 clearly indicate that the primary factor influencing program selection for the vast majority of television viewers is entertainment value (5). Although it is certainly true that television ranks as the number one entertainment medium in the United States, motion pictures, radio, magazines, and newspapers are important entertainment media as well. The impact of television on the movie industry has been deeply felt since the late 1940's, but the record-breaking box office receipts from *The Godfather* are a fair indication that many people still depend upon motion-picture films as a major source of entertainment. Harold Mendelsohn's investigations of today's radio audience indicate that radio provides listeners with a constant "companion" that helps to fill the personal voids created by routine tasks and feelings of loneliness (6). Radio is entertaining in the sense that it soothes and satisfies, and affords the listener a desired psychological climate. Newspapers are generally considered the principal communicators of hard news, but readership studies have shown that some readers not only turn first to the comics section but select their newspapers on the basis of the comic strips they print. Such regular features as "Dear Abby" and "Ann Landers" must also be considered primarily as entertainment.

In his book, *Mass Entertainment*, Harold Mendelsohn links the entertainment function of the media with the socialization process. He points out that people in all social strata seek mass entertainment because some social functions are served by sharing a common entertainment experience. For instance, teen-agers identify with a particular segment of mass entertainment, which gives them the basis for rapport and group identity with other teenagers. Comedy and humor also serve significant sociological functions in that they reinforce social norms by ridiculing deviant behavior and allow us to consciously consider socially sensitive issues without involving guilt feelings. A typical example of mass entertainment that serves this function is the popular television program "Maude." Following its first year of weekly episodes that touched upon such taboo subjects as abortion, "Maude" began its second season with a socially relevant script centering on the problems of alcoholism. Using Maude's television husband, Walter Findlay, for their character study, the show's writers struggled through ten revisions of the dialogue before they were satisfied that their message would come through: "Wake up America! We're drinking too much and it is getting out of control."

Concurring that entertainment is a basic function of mass communication, Wilbur Schramm adds still a fifth function; "to sell goods for us" (7). He explains that *advertising* through the mass media contributes to a free and healthy economy in the United States. Advertising offers both opportunities and challenges to the buyers and sellers of goods and services. With the exception of public broadcasting, radio and television in America are strictly commercial operations. Without advertising as a base of support, there would be very few mass media of any kind. This is not to suggest that a nonprofit system of mass communication could not exist. Many foreign countries enjoy such systems; the most familiar being England's British Broadcasting Corporation (BBC), which is financed by license fees on radio and television receivers. But if we are to believe the opinion polls, the American public would rather endure media advertising than make a special payment for the services they presently receive free of charge (8). Figures released in May, 1973, by The Roper Organization, Inc., indicate that only 24 per cent of the 1,982 people surveyed expressed any interest in a subscription television service (Pay TV).

Adding the suggested functions of Wright and Schramm to those identified by Lasswell results in a total of five: (1) surveillance, (2) correlation, (3) social transmission, (4) entertainment, and (5) advertising. Another contributor to the study of mass communication functions, Robert K. Merton, was the first writer to warn us that any or all of these functions could have negative as well as positive effects. He called these negative consequences *dysfunctions* and proposed that there was always the possibility that they might accompany the positive effects of any single act (9). By reviewing the five media functions, it is relatively easy to recall instances when mass communication performed a disservice rather than a service to society.

Perhaps one of the most frequently cited instances of a mass medium serving a dysfunction is Orson Welles' radio broadcast of the play, "War of the Worlds" in 1938. Using a dramatic format patterned after actual news reports of the period, Welles' Halloween prank resulted in a nationwide panic. At a press conference following the broadcast, Welles claimed that he had no idea the radio audience would take the play seriously. Although the Martian invasion scare is one of the most dramatic media dysfunctions in history, it is far from being the most damaging. Just minutes after the assassination of Martin Luther King, the nation was alerted to the event by radio and television news bulletins. Within hours there were riots and demonstrations in over one hundred American cities, catching police and other law enforcement agencies completely unprepared. As a result of this and similar occurrences, the news media became the target for repeated attacks, accusing them of "fanning the flames of social unrest" (10). In response to this criticism, broadcasters and newspapers agreed to cooperate with local authorities by either delaying or avoiding news coverage of outbreaks of civil disorder.

Since the release of the Pentagon Papers and the unveiling of the Watergate conspiracy, the American public has accepted as commonplace the leaking of confidential information to the media. Yet we should be reminded that the printing and broadcast of confidential documents is a service to society only so long as it is in the public's best interest to know the information and there is a high degree of certainty that no citizen's individual rights will be jeopardized by the disclosure. Being in a position to make decisions concerning the withholding and releasing of such information, the media gatekeepers share both an enormous responsibility and far-reaching power. When Woodward and Bernstein were preparing their articles for release in the *Washington Post*, the newspaper's editors subjected each story to intensive cross-examination prior to publication. The result was a Pulitzer prize for superior investigative reporting and an eventual apology from President Nixon. However, not all gatekeepers have been quite so thorough. Columnist Jack Anderson published verbatim excerpts of testimony before the Watergate grand jury, thus possibly endangering the rights of the accused to a fair trial. In another case concerning an investigation of alleged kickbacks to Maryland officials, *Time* magazine reported that unnamed sources in the Justice Department believed the indictment of former Vice President Agnew was "inevitable" at a time when the former Vice President had not been legally accused of any crime. Unfortunate disclosures such as these are undoubtedly a product of the fierce competition existing among media organizations. We can only hope that in a large majority of situations calling for a mature, intelligent, professional judgment, the media gatekeepers will respond to the best interests of everyone.

There are numerous other instances that critics cite as examples of possible media dysfunctions. For example, instant reports of national election results and victory predictions on the East Coast may prompt West Coast citizens to stay away from the polls, feeling that their votes no longer matter. Television's persistent display of products and services within the financial reach of white middle-class America implies measures of normalcy and standards of living that can create frustration and unrest among the disadvantaged segments of our population. The frequent portrayal of racial minorities in the conflicting roles of menial laborers or heroic superstars may leave viewers with a distorted image of the normal distribution of roles that exist in our society. Finally, the perpetual complaint of popular critics is that the mass media are responsible for lowering public tastes to the lowest common denominator. In defense of the available entertainment fare, media practitioners retort, "Look at the circulation figures and audience ratings. What you read, watch, and listen to is what you'll get!"

In the limited space available here, it is impossible to adequately deal with the controversial topic of mass media effects that has been argued for many years. Claims of intemperate critics have included charges that the different media are responsible for destroying the moral fiber of the country, increasing juvenile delinquency and crime, suppressing creativity, and killing the art of conversation. Other attacks have centered around concerns that the media have fantastic persuasive powers that might make us shift our political ideologies, purchase worthless products, abandon our cultural heritage, and alter "normal" patterns of behavior in ways that would prove detrimental to a healthy family and social life. With claims of such magnitude and serious implication, it is little wonder that, long ago, critics and media practitioners alike turned to the communication researcher for help. The critic went in hopes of receiving empirical evidence that would support his charges, and the practitioner went for just the reverse. So encompassing were the questions concerning the media effects that they completely dominated the field of mass-communication research for decades.

Early research explorations coincided with the emergence of an image of society as a mass of isolated individuals who lacked any unifying purpose. It was a view that depicted the masses at the mercy of a communicator who could influence them at his will. Melvin DeFleur has described this orientation as the "mechanistic S-R theory" (11). Other writers have more commonly referred to it as the "hypodermic needle theory" because the relationship between the media and general public was seen as direct and simple: ". . . the omnipotent media, on the one hand, sending forth the message, and the atomized masses, on the other, waiting to receive it—and nothing in between" (12). That is, messages would reach every member of the audience uniformly, would be perceived in the same manner, and would result in eliciting the same response from all.

During the 1930's, scholars in various branches of the social and behavioral sciences began to turn away from mere speculation about media effects from which concepts and propositions could be inductively formulated. The developments were the result of a new stress upon objective experiments within the field of psychology as an aid in the formulation and testing of learning theories. Along with this intellectual movement came increasing recognition of individual motivation and learning differences of human perception. Hence, it became clear to students of mass communication that the audience of a given medium was not a "monolithic collectivity." DeFleur dubs this new awareness of the 1930's the "individual differences theory of mass communication" and suggests that the theory predicts that "media messages contain particular stimulus attributes that have differential interaction with personality characteristics of members of the audience . . . [and therefore] there will be variations in effect which correspond to such individual differences" (13).

Out of the behavioral research generated by the individual differences theory came new concepts that soon became familiar to every student of mass communication. The terms *selective attention, selective perception,* and *selective retention* were quickly incorporated into his working vocabulary. The principle of *selective attention* states that individuals will typically expose themselves to communications that they find pleasing and in agreement with their personal frame of reference. For example, people who enjoy listening exclusively to rock music will have little motivation to tune in radio stations that feature classical or country and western formats. Once exposed to the communication, *selective perception* will determine how the message will be interpreted by the individual. Experimental studies of human perception have revealed that an individual's predispositions, past experiences, attitudes, beliefs, values, and needs will largely determine how he selects and interprets information about the events around him. In simple terms, the principle of *selective retention* states that an individual will remember only what he wants to remember. That is, people tend to remember better messages that are compatible with their attitudes and forget messages that are not. These concepts revolutionized our thinking about the mass audience and created an awareness that such variations in the communication process as changing the communicator, the medium, the message, or the audience's environment could have a significant influence on the effectiveness achieved by mass communication. Thus, fears of unlimited persuasive powers in the hands of the media practitioners were somewhat dispelled. Researchers reported that mass communication generally served to reinforce existing attitudes, tastes, predispositions, and behavioral tendencies, but seldom, if ever, were the media responsible for changing one type of person into another.

It has been demonstrated that the media are most influential in situations where individuals have no pre-established disposition on a given subject. This was vividly illustrated by the experiences of media experts during the nonpresidential campaign year of 1970. With the amazing success of Richard M. Nixon's extensive television campaign of 1968 planted firmly in their minds, campaign strategists mapped out cleverly contrived and slickly polished promotional schemes for their political candidates. To their sad surprise, they learned that the success of Nixon's 1968 political campaign was probably the result of the mobilization of voters who were either leaning toward or already committed to the Republican ticket. The image-maker who suffered most was Harry Treleaven, a major contributor to Nixon's 1968 TV image. His record included four losses and only one win (Senator-elect William Brock of Tennessee). The conclusion reached by Treleaven and others with not so disappointing score cards was that in future campaigns, television's major image-making role would come during the primaries, when the candidate is still pretty much an unknown. Once the public meets the candidate and creates an impression of him in their own minds, television alone cannot be expected to greatly alter that image. In the words of campaign strategist, Robert Goodman, shortly after the election, "What was proved last week is that image-making can't run counter to strong national currents. TV can't overwhelm. It can only amplify."

Another major turning point in our understanding of the mass communication process, especially for students of interpersonal communication, resulted from a classic study of the 1940 presidential campaign. As you might expect from our previous discussion, researchers discovered that very few people changed their voting intentions during the campaign. However, those who did were influenced far more by family, friends, and co-workers than by direct exposure to the media. It was further realized that within every social context there were individuals who were considered "influentials" or "opinion leaders" by their peers. These opinion leaders could be identified at all socio-economic levels and in every walk of life. Not too surprisingly, they were also found to exceed noninfluentials in exposure to relevant campaign messages transmitted via the mass media. These findings led to the formulation of the "two-step communication flow" hypothesis, which proposed that influence moves from the media to opinion leaders, and from these influentials to their immediate associates. Later studies refined the original hypothesis to suggest that a complex "multi-step flow" was a more accurate depiction of the important role played by interpersonal relationships.

Since those early exploratory studies of the 1920's, the volume of research in the field of mass communication has been almost overwhelming. Unfortunately, concrete answers to many of the important questions that were posed by critics decades ago have not yet been found. The three-year, $1.5 million Surgeon General's Report that was to resolve once and for all whether the portrayal of violence and crime on television was in some way dangerous to the mental health of our nation failed to do so. One of the most conclusive statements that can be gleaned from the five-volume report issued in January, 1972 reads, "We have noted in the studies at hand a modest association between viewing of violence and agression among at least some children, and we have noted some data which are consonant with the interpretation that violence viewing produces the agression. This evidence is not conclusive, however, and some of the data are also consonant with other interpretations" (14). Several years earlier, a noted communication researcher who contributed to the Surgeon General's Report stated, "It is surely no wonder that a bewildered public should regard with cynicism a research tradition which supplies, instead of definitive answers, a plethora of relevant but inconclusive and at times seemingly contradictory findings" (15).

At this point it might be beneficial to summarize much of what has been said so far by way of a simple illustration. Figure 5-6 provides a visual representation of some of the various elements that contribute to the mass-communication process. This illustration is not intended as a communication model in the usual sense, as it does not attempt to incorporate all of the factors and characteristics that typify the mass-communication patterns of modern society. Rather, it serves to remind us of a number of important concepts: Man is being bombarded regularly by enormous quantities of messages via mass media systems. The unique characteristics of each medium influence the structure of the message and contribute to the way it will be perceived and interpreted by the listener, viewer, or reader. These communications will be received not only through direct contact with the products of the media but through second- and third-hand messages from family, friends, and other influentials as well. Our past experiences, attitudes, values, and beliefs, coupled with the interpretations and commentary of those around us, determine how each of us select, perceive, and recall the messages. Although the ratio of media output to audience input is terribly biased in favor of the media, we are constantly communicating something about ourselves to

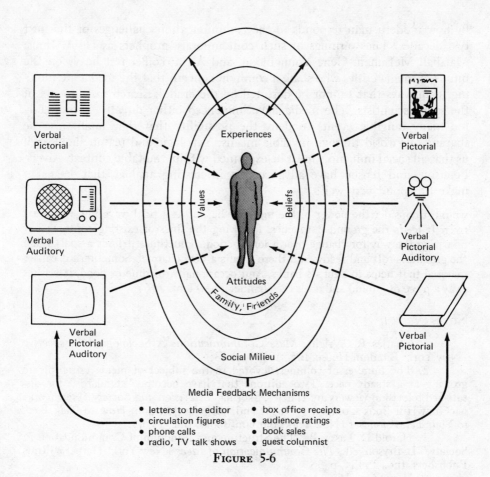

Verbal
Pictorial

Experiences

Verbal
Pictorial

Values

Beliefs

Verbal
Auditory

Verbal
Pictorial
Auditory

Attitudes

Family, Friends

Verbal
Pictorial
Auditory

Verbal
Pictorial

Social Milieu

Media Feedback Mechanisms

- letters to the editor
- circulation figures
- phone calls
- radio, TV talk shows
- box office receipts
- audience ratings
- book sales
- guest columnist

Figure 5-6

them by our choice of newspapers, television programs, or motion-picture shows. The media organizations, eager to satisfy our expression of tastes, will respond to these quantitative indicators in providing more programs, news features, or movies that appear to meet with our approval. When we wish to respond verbally to media institutions to express approval, file a complaint, or make a request, other feedback channels are available to us, although desired results are frequently slow in coming.

There can be no question that we are living in a mediated environment that is largely the product of the mass media of communication. Every indication points to the somewhat frightening prediction that in the years ahead, man will come to rely more and more on the instruments of modern technology and less and less on first-hand, personal experience. Whether the nightmares of a "1984" will eventually engulf our society will be determined by how modern man responds to the communication challenges of the next two decades. The warnings of such contemporary prophets as H. A. Innis, Marshall McLuhan, Gene Youngblood, and Alvin Toffler rest heavy on the minds of media critics who share a common concern that the media are molding us in ways that cannot be detected by the crude research instruments of the social scientists. The media have influenced either directly or indirectly too many tangible events to deny the possibility that they might also be shaping our world through invisible means. Yet, logic and reason should tell us that all social influences must be examined within a suitable context. Rivers, Peterson, and Jensen have advanced an interesting analogy that seems to make this point very well:

we must consider the power of the mass media not as a tidal wave but as a great river. It feeds the ground it touches, following the lines of existing contours but preparing the way for change over a long period. Sometimes it finds a spot where the ground is soft and ready, and there it cuts a new channel. Sometimes it carries material that helps to alter its banks. And occasionally, in time of flood, it washes away a piece of ground and gives the channel a new look. (16)

NOTES

    1. Charles R. Wright, *Mass Communication: A Sociological Perspective* (New York: Random House, Inc., 1959), p. 13.
    2. The number of volumes devoted to the subject of media criticism are growing at a steady pace. Two editions that have become "standards" for dissatisfied television viewers are Harry J. Skornia, *Television and Society* (New York: McGraw-Hill Book Company, 1965), and Nicholas Johnson, *How to Talk Back to Your Television Set* (New York: Bantam Books, Inc., 1970).
    3. Harold D. Lasswell, "The Structure and Function of Communication in Society," L. Bryson, ed., *The Communication of Ideas* (New York: Harper & Row, Publishers, Inc., 1948), p. 38.
    4. Wright, p. 16.
    5. The results of these studies appear in two published works: Gary A. Steiner, *The People Look at Television* (New York: Alfred A. Knopf, Inc., 1963), and Robert T. Bower, *Television and the Public* (New York: Holt, Rinehart and Winston, Inc., 1973).
    6. Harold Mendelsohn, "The Roles of Radio," A. Kirschner and L. Kirschner, eds., *Radio and Television: Readings in the Mass Media* (New York: The Odyssey Press, 1971).
    7. Wilbur Schramm, *Responsibility in Mass Communications* (New York: Harper & Row, Publishers, Inc., 1957), p. 34.
    8. To imply that the costs of advertising are not passed on to the public would be in error. However, few consumers stop to consider what percentage of a product's retail price goes for advertising.
    9. Robert K. Merton, *Social Theory and Social Structure*, rev. ed. (New York: The Free Press, 1957). See Chapter I, Manifest and Latent Functions.
    10. For an interesting account of the media's role in the riots and demonstrations of 1967, read the *Report of the National Advisory Commission on Civil Disorder* (New York: Bantam Books, Inc., 1968).

11. Melvin L. DeFleur, *Theories of Mass Communication*, 2nd ed. (New York: David McKay Co., Inc., 1970), p. 115.

12. Elihu Katz and Paul Lazarsfeld, *Personal Influence* (New York: The Free Press, 1954), p. 20.

13. DeFleur, p. 122.

14. *Television and Growing Up: The Impact of Televised Violence*, Chapter I. A very readable analysis of this highly publicized document can be found in a three-part article in *TV Guide* beginning November 11, 1972. A more scholarly review by Dr. James A. Anderson is printed in the Spring, 1972, issue of *Journal of Broadcasting*, pp. 224–227. *Television and Your Child: The Surgeon General's Inquiry*, an extensive evaluation, is scheduled for publication during 1974 by the Aspen Program on Communications and Society, Palo Alto, California.

15. Joseph Klapper, "The Effects of Mass Communication," B. Berelson and M. Janowitz, eds., *Reader in Public Opinion and Communication* (New York: The Free Press, 1966), p. 474.

16. William L. Rivers, Theodore Peterson, and Jay W. Jensen, *The Mass Media and Modern Society* (San Francisco: Holt, Rinehart and Winston, Inc., 1971), p. 35.

1. What major factors are involved in the political campaign process?
2. Identify the key personnel on the campaign staff. What functions does each of the personnel serve?
3. Discuss the significance of "issues" in the political campaign. How are they psychologically deployed by the campaigners?
4. Discuss the differences existing between a referendum and a contest between candidates in terms of strategies employed.
5. Identify the significant media or channels commonly utilized in political campaigns. Discuss the character, scope, and function of each medium or channel.

▶◀ Communication Perspectives in Political Campaigns

KARL W. E. ANATOL

Political campaigning in America has become a "big business enterprise." Politicians spend exorbitant sums of money to win elected positions that run the gamut from justice-of-the-peace to President of the United States. More and more, students, scholars, and researchers are being drawn to look at the rather fascinating process through which man and message are machined, packaged, and marketed to mass audiences of millions of individuals who hold divergent opinions and viewpoints. However, in spite of the vastness of the campaign industry, research conducted to date has been slow in denoting and describing the major factors that constitute the communication perspectives in the political campaign.

The analysis of communication systems or patterns in political campaigns has been predicated on rather simplistic models—for example, models descriptive of *one* man (a sort of ubiquitous rhetorical giant) swaying vast, complex audiences. Such models cause us to overlook several crucial factors that affect the outcome of the campaign. In 1969, McBath and Fisher cautioned that "no method presently exists by which campaign communication can be analyzed and evaluated to the mutual satisfaction of those who are party to the process and those who study it" (1).

"Communication Perspectives in Political Campaigns," by Karl W. E. Anatol. Reprinted with permission of the author. This original essay appears here for the first time.

In 1973, David Swanson pointed up a "new" method of analysis that may, indeed, prove to be mutually satisfying. Swanson suggested that the complexity of the modern campaign necessitates a full-blown view of campaign persuasion in which one should consider the full range of messages, influence sources, strategies, and circumstances convening upon voters (2).

POLITICAL CAMPAIGN COMMUNICATION—A MODEL

A political campaign is one form of persuasive communication designed to influence action. Dan Nimmo defines the term *campaign* as follows: "A campaign denotes the activities of an individual or group (the campaigner) in a particular context (the campaign setting) designed to manipulate the behavior of a wider number of people (the audience) to his advantage" (3).

This definition of "campaign" may be utilized to formulate a model as in Figure 5-7. This model of the political campaign process may assist us in focusing on a "full-blown" view of the persuasion process. We examine the activities, behaviors, and attitudes of campaigners and the electorate, the nature of the campaign context or setting as they are all processed together in the mills of technology and strategy. Each of the components—campaigners, message, channels, and audience—are discussed separately. The concerns of feedback, strategy, and technology permeate the entire model and *are not* discussed separately.

Campaigners

To most observers, the campaigners are the candidates for political office. This constitutes a rather shortsighted view. Very rarely does a candidate wage a one-man campaign to woo the votes of the electorate. We view the campaigners as consisting of a corps of partisan workers such as organizers, managers, agencies, consultants, specialists, and the candidates. We see the co-workers as a sort of packager and the candidate as the marketed commodity or product. We study the function of these co-workers in detail, but for the moment, let us look at the candidates.

Candidates Although any American citizen over a legally constituted age may run for political office, only a bare 1 per cent ever become candidates (4). Apparently, only those who demonstrate a cluster of traits or attributes that Nimmo terms "availability" do become candidates. According to Nimmo, availability goes beyond the mere desire to run for office and the capacity to meet specific legal qualifications (5). Several commentators suggest that the cluster of traits or attributes should include the candidates' achievements, personal qualities, contrived image, and political resources (6).

Candidates must be *attractive*. Voters must see (in them) those qual-

314

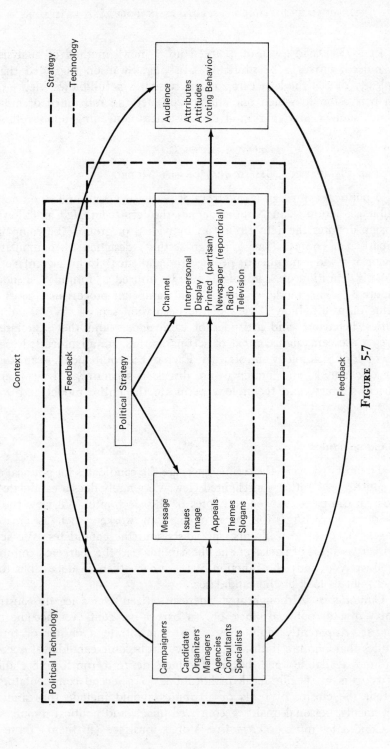

FIGURE 5-7

Legend:
- - - Strategy
- · - Technology

Context

Political Technology

Feedback

Feedback

Campaigners
Candidate
Organizers
Managers
Agencies
Consultants
Specialists

Message
Issues
Image
Appeals
Themes
Slogans

Political Strategy

Channel
Interpersonal
Display
Printed (partisan)
Newspaper (reportorial)
Radio
Television

Audience
Attributes
Attitudes
Voting Behavior

ities that are highly valued in a given culture or subculture. Unfortunately for the electorate or audience, much of this attractiveness is sometimes contrived or manufactured by the candidate's co-workers. They first find out what the voters want and then try to "make up" the candidate to fit voter expectations. If the voters desire a "conservative" type, the candidate (no matter how liberal) is sanded and polished to manifest the desired degree of conservatism. An impressive technique usually precedes the "sanding and polishing." Nimmo states that "to determine what his reputation is among the electorate, a would-be legislator, governor, or president frequently commissions an opinion-polling agency to survey voters and discover what they think of him" (7).

Candidates with widely known, respected family names—for example, the Kennedys, the Rockefellers, the Goldwaters, the Longs (Louisiana), and so on—tend to be favored by the electorate. The name seems to evoke attributions of sound qualification and political astuteness. Kamin points out, however, that the "famous name" recognition carries a greater advantage in primary elections than in general elections. Apparently, voters in a primary election are bombarded by so lengthy a string of candidates that they have little chance to learn anything about the candidates and the issues. Consequently, they select the most economical choice-stratagem—the name (8).

A candidate's *achievement* is another vital factor in his marketability. Voters are interested in knowing what qualifies a candidate for political office. Commentators argue that incumbency is the foremost asset that contributes to political success. The incumbent has the privilege of pointing out achievements in the relevant, political setting (provided that he or she has been an effective official), whereas the challenger, in most instances, can point up achievements in sometimes "nonrelevant" or "almost similar" circumstances. At best, the challenger can only offer a promise of performance. Nimmo explains the advantages and disadvantages of the "incumbent vs. challenger" contest and also suggests some other valuable spin-offs in favor of the incumbent. He writes:

Voters also are interested in a candidate's achievement; whether his experience has prepared him for public office, for example, and whether his record justifies his return to office if he is an incumbent. Few attributes contribute as much to electoral success as incumbency. Voters know that a man seeking reelection to an office possesses requisite experience; incumbency also carries with it the advantages of frequent exposure to the electorate through news coverage, sufficient previous campaign experience that an accurate assessment of successful strategies and tactics is possible, and invaluable contacts with party, group, and governmental leaders. Occasionally, however, a challenger with a celebrated name can overcome his incumbent opponent's advantages. Although politically experienced, Ronald Reagan had never held public office prior to his successful, and professionally managed, campaign against Governor Pat Brown in California in

1966. And in his first attempt at elective office, Edward M. Kennedy won the Democratic nomination for senator in Massachusetts, defeating the more experienced Attorney General Edward McCormack in the primary and the son of Henry Cabot Lodge, George Cabot Lodge, in the general election. (9)

Again, we would notice the value of "name." It serves the consumer well in the supermarket when he purchases dog food and in the political environment when he elects a representative.

Political *acumen* is yet another personal trait to be brought to the fore-front by a candidate. The dictionary describes *acumen* as: "acuteness of mind, keenness of perception, discernment, and shrewdness in practical matters." Acumen denotes a facility for undistorted perception—an ability to read political reality well. The candidate must not allow the hoopla of campaign carnival or his biases, dreams, and wishes to distort his sense of what is really happening.

Not all candidates possess the same measure of all of these attributes. However, if one is to be a serious contender, one must at least *act* as though these traits are present. (This "acting out" is perhaps the most disturbing feature in the political context.) In order to "act out" these attributes, the candidate usually selects and proclaims the most appealing of his qualities ("I single-handedly fought in the legislature in behalf of the Clean Air Act," "I carried a placard in the Mothers March on Washington," "I was in the boat following PT-109 in which Jack Kennedy sank; I helped to rescue him," and so on), but at the same time, he must cover up his weaknesses. "Acting out" of traits constitutes what is called *image projection*. The coaching for this process is usually entrusted to a professional campaign staff. Let us look at the candidate's campaign staff—the people who organize and run both the campaign and the candidate.

Organizers In addition to the need for money to wage a campaign, candidates must seek endorsements from influential citizens, newspapers, friends, well-wishers, and so on. In the process of giving the necessary assistance, these several individuals become co-campaigners or organizers. Other types of organizing personnel may include campaign management firms, campaign consultants, public-relations personnel, political pollsters, television directors and producers, fund-raisers, mass-mailing specialists, speech-writers, and others.

The *campaign managers*, for example, lay out the strategy for the overall campaign and actually oversee the delegation of contracts to specialists in fund-raising, polling, advertising, publicity, and research. The *consultants* usually work on unique "issue" problems. For instance, if tax initiative issues are important in the campaign, the campaign staff may hire the services of a tax expert to draft position papers or speeches. The *specialists* are usually those personnel who carry out such services as "working" or canvassing the precinct, preparing television documentaries, or designing and distributing mail.

Once the campaign staff has been picked, the manager and the candidate can move toward a consideration of the campaign strategy.

The Campaign Strategy

Earlier, we suggested that a campaign consists of campaigners "acting out" certain desirable images and orientations. In order to maintain consistency, a strategy is adopted. This strategy is generally guided by such questions as: What theme shall we use? What basic approach must we take? What issues must we emphasize? Broadly speaking, strategy is of utmost importance to the dissemination of messages and the utilization of the mass media. However, there is yet one other important consideration in the use of strategy. Different levels of elections (for example, a referendum versus a primary) call for different strategies.

In a referendum, for instance, personality and image play very little role; debates and contesting arguments are prominent. The strategy is to promote the idea that the passage of a certain proposition would bring benefits at "relatively little" cost to all of the parties concerned. The hard fact is that some citizens stand to lose more than others by the passage of referenda. Nevertheless, the strategy is to make the losers "blind" to the real extent of their losses.

A primary election calls for an even keener strategy. Here, the candidates are generally members of the same party. Each candidate must wage a campaign without really alienating, destroying, humiliating, or infuriating his opponents. The winner realizes that after the primary is conducted, he or she will need the support of his opponents. In a general election, the contestants may go all out in the attack but must ensure some degree of adherence to the "rules of the campaign game." Let us get back to the basic question of strategy as is hinted in the three guiding questions posed earlier. (1) What basic approach must we take in the campaign? In other words, how shall we *attack*? (2) What theme shall we use? (3) What issues shall we emphasize?

Strategies for Attack or Approach   According to Stanley Kelley, a good attack is one that helps the candidate to seize the initiative in order to avoid being on the defensive: "To attack is to press on the public issues that are to one's own advantage. To attack is not just to give one's own side of the question but to define the political situation" (10). Professional campaign staffs usually insist on having a clear-cut plan of attack devised as early as possible. Hubert Humphrey's managers, for example, were flabbergasted upon observing that as late as the time of his nomination to the Democratic party presidential ticket in 1968, the candidate had no clear-cut plan of attack for the campaign against Richard Nixon. According to eyewitness accounts, Humphrey's managers were forced to leave him on his own for the first ten days of the campaign while they feverishly sought to devise a plan of attack (11).

The Republican strategy for the presidential election of 1952 is considered to be a classic example of planning the attack. The attack consisted of two thrusts: First, it advocated retaining the votes of 20 million voters who had supported Republicans consistently in the past by appealing to the conservatives who had preferred Senator Robert Taft for the nomination. The key, in this instance, involved setting up an amicable meeting between Dwight Eisenhower and Robert Taft. Second, the plan advocated that the so-called "stay-at-home" voter be pursued. This type of voter rarely goes to the polls unless he is provoked into voting *against* something. The campaigners succeeded in getting the voter to feel "alienated" by "old politics." Consequently, he went to the polls to do something about it. According to Kelley, the campaign plan emphasized three items Americans should fight against—corruption, Communism, and the Korean War (12).

Strategies for Themes and Slogans   Political analysts contend that election campaigns are not fought on the issues but on themes and slogans. The task of the campaign advisors is to assist the candidate in emphasizing his themes and to provide him with ammunition with which to withstand the themes and slogans of the opposition.

The campaign themes and slogans must be carefully planned, since they are used to simplify complex issues into simple, memorable, recognizable statements, and since they must run through all publicity releases, ads, rallies, and so on. In some instances a theme or slogan may backfire. Barry Goldwater's "In Your Heart You Know He's Right" worked against him among certain segments of the electorate. Nimmo points out that that slogan "made possible a play on words that reinforced his extremist image rather than his sincere dedication to convictions." The slogan was one of five pretested by the MELPAR Corporation. The survey showed it to be the least preferred by evaluators; however, Goldwater chose to use it in spite of its negative reception (13).

In 1960, the managers of John Kennedy's campaign apparently chose well. Sensing that most Americans were becoming listless about the calm and complacency of the Eisenhower presidency, the campaigners elected the slogan: "Get America Moving Again." The candidate subsequently proved to be skillful in lacing most of his public utterances with that theme.

Strategies for Issues   Issues are not conjured up haphazardly. More and more, campaigners are looking to the behavioral scientists and pollsters for "hard" data on issues and voter attitudes. David Swanson observes that "the new politics seems to be undergirded by the assumption that the most effective campaign strategy is that which is grounded in 'scientific' theory and research" (14).

Political campaigners are aware that a major part of the candidate's influence may be attributable to the level of his understanding of the issues. Consequently, advisors make sure that the candidate is "well-rehearsed" and that he always presents the impression of being well-informed. The issues (researched and polished) are strung together in the so-called "campaign bible" (15).

The campaign bible contains pertinent facts, arguments, interpretations, and conclusions concerning crucial issues. It summarizes the issues on which the candidate may be interrogated by reporters or opponents. A good example of the use of strategy in dealing with the issues is pointed up by Senator John Tower's (Texas) approach. Following the trend indicated through a survey in 1965, Senator Tower was advised to appeal to women by stressing education and the cost of living, to appeal to the middle-income groups by also touching upon job security, to maintain the support of the upper-income groups by emphasizing the evils of "government interference" and taxation, and to refrain from antagonizing labor unions with any discussion of the "right to work" issue (16). Even though no Republican "was supposed" to win a senatorial seat in Texas at that time, John Tower was elected by the voters. Analysts attribute his victory to his skillful handling of the issues.

In order to get the issues out to the electorate, the campaigners try to utilize every advantage afforded by the mass media. We discuss a few of the channels or media that candidates may utilize.

Channels of Campaign Communication

The channels of campaign communication commonly employed in contemporary politics are personal or interpersonal media, billboards or display media, the printed media, radio, and television. Let us study each of these channels.

Personal and Interpersonal Media   The personal appearance is still one of the most direct and straightforward ways to get the message to the voter. Staged rallies, neighborhood coffee klatches, and press conferences constitute the format around which the candidate's personal appearance is conducted. This format allows the candidate the opportunity to demonstrate "personality" and "sincerity."

We should point out that personal appearances are sometimes risky since the disposition of the audience may not be fully known. Mindful of this uncertainty, campaign managers are rapidly adapting to a new tactic called "confrontation." The candidate, faced with a hostile, heckling crowd, invites *one* of his tormentors to share the lectern. This gesture gives him the chance to demonstrate his democratic spirit and his courage.

Display Media   The display media consist of billboards, bumper stickers, buttons, placards, and so on. A good campaign uses them effectively. In 1961, Edward Kennedy's campaign for the senate spent $47,000 on billboards and $43,500 on bumper stickers, buttons, and so on (17). The cost per billboard is relatively low, and if properly utilized to propagate the campaign theme, billboards may assist in entrenching the candidate's name in the voters memory.

The Printed Media   The printed media include such channels as "partisan" campaign literature, newspaper reports, newspaper advertising, and publicity. Let us discuss, first, the nature of campaign literature.

Campaign literature may conform to two basic types. The first type of compaign printed literature bears appeals aimed at a *mass* audience and is generally conveyed through direct-mail techniques. The second type of campaign literature is directed toward *specific* interest groups—for example, religious, economic, ethnic, and professional subgroups. The strategy of this specifically directed literature is further enhanced when selected members of the subgroups take the initiative in distributing the appeals. Eldersveld and Dodge report the availability of evidence showing that campaign literature does, indeed, promote and increase voter turnout. Their study of a local election showed that only 33 per cent of those *not contacted* went to the polls, whereas 60 per cent of those *contacted by mail* voted, and 75 per cent of those *contacted personally* voted (18).

Newspapers can also be used as an effective propaganda outlet by a skillful campaign staff—it is one of the better vehicles for "image boasting." The quality of a news item and its position or placement on the pages (first page versus last page) could make a difference. Consequently, campaign managers usually try to engage the attention of reporters and photographers in order that the candidate's visit to a children's hospital, ghetto pool hall, or mine shaft may be duly reported in a "proper" space.

Short of acquiring a committed retinue of reporters, the campaigners may also take advantage of paid newspaper advertising. A recent study indicates that 80 per cent of newspaper pages carrying advertising are read or noticed by the average reader and that men and women of all ages, income, and educational level do attend to them (19).

An important point to consider is that newspaper stories, advertising, and editorials exert great influence on the voter who is marginally interested (to begin with) in the election. Brinton and McKown suggest that the voter who feels a low involvement has very few guidelines by which to make decisions. Consequently, if he is confronted by the issues or the image in his newspaper, he may consider that information to be sufficient for his choice (20). David Swanson, on the basis of his study, reports that "results suggest that nonpartisan mass communication is an important and credible source of political information for most people, and that the assumption that campaigns should accord high priority to manipulating news coverage of the campaign is well founded" (21).

Radio Radio is fast regaining prominence as a propaganda medium. Many campaigners have minimized its value in favor of television usage. John Mitchell, campaign manager for the 1968 Nixon presidential campaign, used radio more extensively than in any previous campaign. Mitchell is reported to have said that he regrets not having spent more money to buy more radio time for his candidate.

Radio has certain advantages over other media. It is relatively less expensive for political advertising than is television. It serves as a useful tool for the candidate who may not be able to project a "good," handsome image on television. Moreover, radio absorbs a larger audience (consistently) than television does. The commuter on the way to work, the housewife, and even the "transistorized" young generation are always within earshot of political propaganda. Campaigners would do well to utilize the free publicity time afforded by interviews and talk shows, in addition to other paid political advertising.

Television Media The use of television represents the "communication blitz" in contemporary politics. The major drawback in television usage pertains to the high cost; however, the politician cannot afford to do without it. Dan Nimmo suggests that the use of television may be most beneficial to the political newcomer. He writes:

The newcomer must rely on normally inactive citizens to overcome the traditional support that regularly elects the incumbent. Because the newcomer is unknown and is appealing to persons with little active interest in politics, his managers know that voters will not come to his public appearances, peruse his literature, note his displays, or read about him in newspapers. He must therefore wage his campaign in the voters' homes when residents settle down to be entertained. As the great entertainer television provides the political neophyte a means for shattering the inattention of his desired audience. (22)

Needless to say, an incumbent also stands to gain from television exposure.

Some researchers (23) contend that the advent of color television has added yet another dimension to the politics "of images." Color, they suggest, brings a greater emotional impact to the medium of television. Also, color tends to decrease the importance of the spoken word on television. Thus, image may transcend issues. These researchers also point out that commercials on color television elicit more recall than commercials on black and white television. This factor of "recall" is quite important for, as Swanson points out, "mere exposure to partisan mass communication does not equal influence; voters must be able to retain at least a general idea of the thrust of the message" (24).

Thus far we have discussed the campaigners, the messages, and the channels used in political campaigning. The types of messages (i.e. issues, image-projection, themes, slogans, and so on) and the particular patterning of using the media both come under the scope of strategy or campaign tactics. However, we consider the *audience* or electorate to be a vital component of the model of communication in the political setting or context. The differing attitudes and voting behaviors of the audience influence the character, level, and intensity of the campaign. We discuss (1) the effects of the audience on the campaign and (2) the effects of the campaign on the audience in the next section.

The Audience in Political Campaigns

Awareness of audience attitudes generally ensures better campaign planning. Particularly, campaigners try to ascertain existing attitudes toward the political party and attitudes toward the issues.

Attitudes Toward Party   Survey data (25) indicate that three of every four American voters identify with one of the two major political parties and three of every ten are so strongly committed that they rarely ever shift to the opposition during a campaign. In a major partisan election, the candidate of the majority party must make sure that his appeals reinforce or consolidate the commitment of party loyalists and motivate them to go to the polls *en masse*. However, if the candidate campaigns through the minority party, he must strive to maintain the votes of those already committed to him, but must also work to win votes from "independents," people who tend to vote a "split ticket," or from those who are luke warm or marginal members of the other party.

Attitudes Toward Issues   The majority of voters are not well informed about the content of issues most of the time (26). Consequently, all but major public issues are eliminated for most people. By the time the campaigners get to those who care about and can discriminate among the fine points or positions on issues, it will be discovered that only about 30 per cent of the electorate is included. But, who are these people? They are the ones who are most likely to be strong party identifiers; they, of course, are not likely to shift allegiance just because of a disagreement on one or two issues. The number of issue-oriented "independents" who are left must be very small. And it is not unlikely that these people are distributed about equally on both sides of major policy questions so that the total number of votes changed by the impact of any particular issue is bound to be small (27).

What choice does the candidate have as far as the manipulation of issues is concerned? The following is Nimmo's suggestion:

One might assume that campaigners faced with a widespread indifference to issues would avoid emphasizing issues in their strategic considerations. The opposite, however, is the case; campaigners like to run "on the issues." A candidate can do relatively little about the distribution of partisanship in his constituency, but he can maneuver by articulating issues that strengthen his hand. He has at least partial control over issues. He can often relate specific issues to special interests (union workers, Irish-Americans, or soybean growers, for example) for support; he can orient his campaign to the various elites who can provide financial and organizational support as well as votes. At the same time he enunciates symbolic appeals ("Law and Order" or "Let's get America moving") to please the less informed and uncommitted citizenry. Issue positions are much easier to publicize through newspapers, television, and radio than are appeals to partisans or special groups; journalists dismiss the latter as campaign oratory, but cover the former as "policy statements" (28).

The idea that most voters are not sufficiently concerned with issues and policies to change their votes in response to policy appeals has led many commentators to suggest that campaigns have little effect on voter attitudes. We disagree with that suggestion. We believe that campaigns may bring about significant changes over the long haul—party loyalties shift, new issues are introduced, and fresh faces are introduced to the political scene. We also believe that much of the research and analysis conducted often tend to focus on the relative lack of shifting in the attitudes of voters (at the ballot boxes) and consequently overlook what may indeed be some real dynamic changes in perceptual capabilities.

The final section of this issue deals with the context or setting impinging on or surrounding the campaign. Particularly, we discuss the effects of the special characteristics of the campaign on the behavior of the electorate.

The Context of the Political Campaign

The way an individual perceives an election will influence his behavior and attitude toward the election. Some elections are more interesting than others, some broadcast issues are easier to understand than others, and, of course, some elections are more important than others. Lester Milbraith summarizes a few of the major influencing factors growing out of the context or setting. A few of the findings are as follows:

1. A perception by people that the vote will be close stimulates their interest and strengthens their belief that their votes will count.
2. People are more likely to turn out for elections that they perceive to be important.
3. The more powerful the office being contested, the more important the election is likely to be perceived. National elections are nearly

always perceived as more important than local elections, and turnout
is nearly always higher for national elections.
4. Crisis elections, which obviously are perceived as important, produce higher turnouts than noncrisis elections.
5. People are more likely to turn out for an election when clear differences are perceived between alternatives than when the alternatives
are unclear.
6. Voter participation and turnout are generally lower for referenda
and other noncandidate elections than for elections with candidates
(29).

To the extent that these aforementioned contextual factors influence
the behaviors of the electorate, it is incumbent on campaigners to fit their
strategy to the level and type of election. Certain techniques can be used to
heighten interest in elections that may be perceived as unexciting or unimportant. Every election is crucial—it is up to the campaigners to have their
constituents perceive it that way.

In this essay, we have attempted to look at political campaign communication in a manner that does justice to the scope and sophistication
of the political campaigning process. We have suggested a model of the
communication process and have developed our discussion around it.
Political campaigning has become a national industry; we can no longer use
"country store" models to describe its process. In this essay, we have described (1) the many facets of the campaign staff; (2) the importance of
image, themes, and slogans in contrast with the de-emphasis of the actual
value of issues; (3) the effects of various channels and the types of audiences
drawn to them; (4) the audience and its attitudes toward party and the issues;
and (5) the context surrounding the campaign. These factors operate at an
"observable" level; tomorrow's research may dredge up some of those factors
that lie beneath the surface of our present awareness. Moreover, commentators have only recently caught up with some of the characteristics of techniques and strategy. Since elections will always be with us (hopefully), there
is much information and enlightenment awaiting us.

NOTES

1. James McBath and Walter Fisher, "Persuasion in Presidential Campaigns," *Quarterly Journal of Speech*, 55:17–25 (1969).
2. David Swanson, "Political Information, Influence, and Judgment in the
1972 Presidential Campaign," *Quarterly Journal of Speech*, 59:130–142 (1973).
3. Dan Nimmo, *The Political Persuaders* (Englewood Cliffs, N.J.: Prentice-
Hall, Inc., 1970), p. 10.
4. Lester Milbraith, *Political Participation* (Chicago: Rand McNally &
Co., 1965), p. 19.
5. Nimmo, p. 11.

6. For a fuller discussion of the traits or attributes necessary for political candidacy, see David M. Olson, *Legislative Primary Elections in Austin, Texas, 1962* (Austin, Tex.: *Institute of Public Affairs,* The University of Texas, 1963), pp. 8–18; idem., *Nonpartisan Elections: A Case Analysis* (Austin, Tex.: *Institute of Public Affairs,* The University of Texas, 1965), pp. 20–35; Herbert Baus and William Ross, *Politics Battle Plan* (New York: Macmillan Publishing Co., Inc., 1968), pp. 7–39; David Leuthold, *Electioneering in a Democracy* (New York: John Wiley & Sons, Inc., 1968), pp. 23–31.

7. Nimmo, p. 11.

8. L. J. Kamin, "Ethnic and Party Affiliations of Candidates As Determinants of Voting," *Canadian Journal of Psychology,* 22:205–213 (1958).

9. Nimmo, p. 12.

10. Stanley Kelley, Jr., *Professional Public Relations and Political Power* (Baltimore, Md.: The Johns Hopkins Press, 1956), p. 48.

11. Theodore White, *The Making of the President 1968* (New York: Atheneum Publishers, 1969), pp. 394–395.

12. Kelley, pp. 151–156.

13. Nimmo, p. 55.

14. Swanson, p. 32. See also "Campaign Management Grows into a National Industry," *Congressional Quarterly,* 5:707, (1968).

15. Herbert Baus and William Ross, *Politics Battle Plan* (New York: Macmillan Publishing Co., Inc., 1968), pp. 184–188.

16. Nimmo, p. 92.

17. Murray B. Levin, *Kennedy Campaigning* (Boston: Beacon Press, 1966), pp. 175–176.

18. Samuel Eldersveld and Richard Dodge, "Personal Contact or Mail Propaganda?" In Daniel Katz et al., eds., *Public Opinion and Propaganda* (New York: Holt, Rinehart and Winston, Inc., 1954), pp. 532–542.

19. The Newspaper Information Committee, *A Study of the Opportunity for Exposure to National Newspaper Advertising* (New York: Bureau of Advertising, ANPA, 1966).

20. James Brinton and L. Norman McKown, "Effects of Newspaper Readings on Knowledge and Attitude," *Journalism Quarterly,* 38:187–195 (1961).

21. Swanson, p. 141.

22. Nimmo, p. 138.

23. Joseph Scanlon, "Color Television: New Language?" *Journalism Quarterly,* 44:225–230 (1967). See also Eric Schaps and Lester Guest, "Some Pros and Cons of Color Television," *Journal of Advertising Research,* 8:28–39 (1968).

24. Swanson, p. 138.

25. "Party Identification in the United States 1952–68," Survey Research Center, University of Michigan, 1968.

26. Hazel, G. Erskine, "The Polls: The Informed Public," *Public Opinion Quarterly,* 26:669–677 (1962).

27. Nelson Polsby and Aaron Wildavsky, *Presidential Elections: Strategies of American Electoral Politics* (New York: Charles Scribner's Sons, 1968), p. 14.

28. Nimmo, p. 24.

29. Milbraith, pp. 101–109.

▶◀ Man-Machine Communication: The Strategy of the Future

WILLIAM B. LASHBROOK AND MICHAEL D. SCOTT

Almost from its inception, the discipline of communication has had to fight two battles of justification in an effort to attain some resemblance of intellectual respectability. The first such encounter was largely one of approach in which the argument centered on whether the discipline should consider itself an art or a science. The second, and perhaps the most important, encounter involved reservations pertaining to substance, or the parameters restraining the disciplines legitimate knowledge claims.

Faced with a society that was increasingly characterized by individuals unable to cope with accelerated change or adapt to the complexities of the new technology, the authors of this article contend that the preceding issues have become fundamentally academic; perpetuated by practitioners of communication—e.g., the humanists and the behaviorists—abnormally preoccupied with the immediacy of the present and oblivious to the future. Indeed, it is our belief that by the year 2001, the first issue will have been relegated to an area of human concern that does not involve justification, whereas the second will diminish with time. For example, the question of approach, albeit art or science, is at best moot. The future will require all of us to become scientific, and, in being so, we will become more humanistic in outlook. This does not deny art but suggests that a commitment to the protection of man's most important values can be made only by those who are capable of recognizing that regularity and control define the human condition and that regularity and control fall within the general rubric of scientific inquiry.

The notion of substance, however, cannot be dismissed as readily. Some, in fact, might argue that it is not a question of justification but

---

"Man-Machine Communication: The Strategy of the Future," by William B. Lashbrook and Michael D. Scott. Reprinted with permission of the authors. This original essay appears here in print for the first time.

instead a temporal concern based on data stemming from what people who communicate do. We have attempted to take a more subtle position with respect to the justification of a discipline, namely, that value over time is primarily a prediction derived from statements that describe states of a system. Needless to say, this kind of determinism requires and will require a specificity of content. The fact that man communicates neither justifies the study of communication nor requires such a specificity of content. The prediction that man in the future will need to communicate in special ways with special things does provide a rationale for an epistemology of something akin to communication education. Moreover, at the very least, it *allows* for a specificity of content. Of course, when one extends this line of reasoning he finds himself vulnerable to attack from those who question the relevancy of current content to future concerns. What the discipline needs, then, is a classification of content that is capable of maintaining itself now and evolving in the future. We believe such content to be associated with information processing and see the evolution of communication into an information science.

Given this framework, we maintain that "man the communicator" can and should be conceptualized as an information processing system. As such, he is functionally related to machines that are themselves information processing systems. The term *systems* is deliberately selected as a result of an appealing point of view advanced in general systems theory. From this perspective, there is a focus on the process of communication and the relationship of its constituent elements to one another and to the environment. Furthermore, working from the vantage point of general systems theory, it is possible to reconceptualize the process of communication as a transaction rather than interaction. Inherent in this approach is a consideration of the general laws and rules of conduct that seem to govern the transfer of information between objects within a constraining environment. We hold that psychological and environmental constraints are now and will continue to be imposed by technology; that mechanistic innovations in the present and the future will intensify the demands placed on the information-processing capabilities of the individual and bring added stress to his relationship with the environment. Thus, it logically follows that a meaningful question to consider within a discipline is how does its content relate to adaptive techniques of environmental negotiation. The interface between man and machine information processing systems will involve exactly such a give and take.

In order to further explicate the preceding line of argument, we define *information* as a message unit capable of transfer between two or more processing systems. Here we have purposefully avoided semantic positions that would demand that a message unit be perceived, interpreted, or overtly responded to, in order to be classified as information. We feel such terminology to be time bound and that those concerns that influence information processing stem from a specific act and not from what is being processed. By the year 2001, we believe that it will be the quantity of information that mediates human response, rendering the meaningfulness of the specific act as inconsequential.

Let us examine for a moment the functional aspects of information processing systems such as those described previously, without regard to the nature of their components. The crucial function is transmission. Now, and in the future, issues associated with the fidelity—i.e., exactness—of information transfer between systems is a prime concern, particularly when one realizes that information processing involves commonly two levels of cross-coding. There is a negotiable kind of coding grammar that relates to the commonality between systems and a second type that is still the product of negotiation but relates to the unique aspects of each transmitting system. For example, one may now communicate with a computer in a language such as FORTRAN whose rules can be specified for both a human and machine-based system. However, to ensure that errors can be detected, this basic mode of transmission must be subsumed under a more elaborate code, which though interpretable, must, by design, maintain notions as to what cannot be processed by at least one of the systems. Errors within the first code then trigger codifiable responses in the second. But it is very important to note that the second code must include, at the primitive level, responses that tell the user that his requests are beyond the limitations of the system. Just as a man with a weak heart might be reasonably expected to renegotiate his life style as a result of his condition, so might we expect that quantity of information to be exchanged between two systems might also be so compromised. Other functional aspects of information processing—storage, retrieval, retransmission—might also be discussed in a similar fashion. That is, a processing function appears to require the transformation of codes each of which has some form of underlying calculi that via transaction simultaneously retains commonality and uniqueness. The implied ratio is analogous to a game theory type mini-max principle for judging the fidelity of information transfer.

The need to come to some type of systems resolution provides, we think, a focus for the discipline of communication, namely, that for the year 2001 its main domain will be concepts associated with machine-aided human information processing. The justification for such a position is rather straightforward. Humans, unable to cognitively process, store, and retrieve the vast amounts of information needed to successfully function, will require a scientific understanding of technologically assisted information processing for purposes of adaptation and control. Of course, the reader might find our future-oriented reasoning overly forbidding or distant from his reality. If that is, in fact, the case we suggest he consider the like reasoning of two of our contemporaries, B. F. Skinner and Alvin Toffler.

Skinner, for example, in his very human treatise, *Beyond Freedom and*

Dignity (1971), points out that the proper relationship between the controller and the controlled is reciprocal. The function of a scientist is to design his experiments in such a manner that what he manipulates can manifest affects that can be observed. His design extorts control over the kind of behavior that can be a result. On the other hand, his data base has some affect in terms of his choice of design and procedures under which information can be collected. Such a reciprocal relationship is characteristic of all social as well as physical science. In a real sense, environments to be controlled must also be obeyed. Hence, man must recognize, as he is now beginning to recognize in reference to ecology, that the sociological and psychological constraints of his environment must also be obeyed. Finally, concern for control, Skinner maintains, supersedes reservations about its effects on the freedom and dignity of the individual. For lack of control has historically meant chaos, and chaos renders a term such as *freedom* as "just another word to lose."

Toffler (1972) argues along parallel lines. In his book *Future Shock*, he talks about a state of mind that he labels *overstimulation*. Loosely, this concept refers to a psychological state resulting when a human being attempts to process information beyond his human capacities. In effect, he begins to lose control of the situation. This loss of control may be immediate or it may become patterned over time. In any event, the individual begins to manifest signs of maladaptive behavioral responses to quantities of information.

Two of Toffler's categories of maladaptive response to overstimulation appear particularly relevant to a discipline such as communication—supersimplification and specialization.

Given a complex of information systems, the maladaptive response of the supersimplifier is to collapse all of the available stimuli into a single, neat equation. From a contemporary standpoint, the supersimplifier might be best characterized by those who continue to believe that the tactics adopted by the Committee to Re-Elect President Nixon were typical of American political campaign practices or those who contend that the ecology movement is designed to subvert attention from an international communist conspiracy. By the same token, the supersimplifier is also characterized by those holding to the notion that problems concerning poverty and the distribution of wealth are the sole product of a facist elite organized for purposes of oppressing the proletariat. Finally, he is also the communication scholar advocating a linear model to justify the assumption that as communication increases the conflict between men decreases full knowing, that from an information point of view, an increase in the exchange rate could well result in an overload that might intensify a human encounter. The justification for the study of communication now and in 2001 is not based on the universal relevance of its principles to every problem that positions man in his environment. To assert that such is the case is to deny the value of a particular science. The concept of "quantity of information" as discussed previously has some degree of psychological finite-ness to it, and to suggest otherwise approaches the irrational. What is finite information is subject to negotiations—what constitutes an infinite amount of information is to quibble in the area of metaphysics.

An equally suspect form of maladaptive response to the problems associated with processing vast quantities of information is represented by specialization. On the surface it might well appear to be rational to narrow one's section of concern. Still to go after the infinite in depth offers the same problems as to go after it in breadth. But there is also an illusionary aspect to specialization that renders it a maladaptive response to *Future Shock*. The person who chooses the strategy of specialization in order to cope with information overload runs the risk of awaking one morning to find that his specialty is obsolete or else transformed beyond recognition by information outside the boundaries of his field of vision. However, we need not look to the future for examples of the specialist. In fact, you may only have to look at yourself, for the latter half of the twentieth century has been both heralded and damned as an age of specialization. It is an age that history might well record that there were no practitioners of medicine only neurosurgeons or cardiovascular specialists. It may be a period typified not by educators but Egyptologists, nuclear botanists, or attitude researchers. The point is that no speculations about the year 2001 should include guarantees that would support particular skills of inquiry beyond their capabilities to serve. The skills fostered and perpetuated by a specific system are as much a subject for negotiation as is its substance.

As easy as it is to dismiss in the abstract the categories of response labeled simplification and specialization, to do so pragmatically is difficult and even threatening. Hidden in the jargon of communication expressed in slogans such as "meanings are in people" are both classifications. First, although meanings may reside in people, it is an oversimplification to suggest that they will forever remain so embedded. Machine-based information systems can function meaningfully also. To concentrate on the meaningful narrows one's perspective to the past and the present—for it becomes the past that determines our present meanings—but is there not value in concern for what is now meaningless and yet in the future may be meaningful? The contemporaries of George Orwell, Jules Verne, and H. G. Wells, for example, in all likelihood, perceived the contents of their writings as fanciful rather than meaningful. Today, however, their speculations concerning the possibilities of a police state, interplanetary space travel, atomic warfare, and nuclear powered submarines hold profound meaning for even the youngest of schoolchildren. When we begin to consider communication as an information science, then, we can also begin to free ourselves from shortsighted demands requiring that what is currently being processed be also immediately interpretable.

Certainly, with the aid of a computerized memory bank, man can store stimuli to be used in contexts yet to be established. We admit, however, that such an ability lies beyond man alone and will require a considerable re-evaluation of principles of learning—principles we might add, the discipline of communication is just beginning to understand with respect to the human as an information processor. In the year 2001, we foresee the use of a computer to be in the repertory of all educated peoples. Three reasons suggest the rationale for such speculation. First, computers can free humans from the necessity to store all of the stimuli that they are capable of coding or transferring. Second, computers can store and retrieve informational stimuli that are not experienced by the people who might ultimately give it interpretation. That is, computers will provide future generations of mankind with the opportunity to process accurate accounts of the experiences of previous generations or interpret in the future what present capabilities deem uninterpretable.

Finally, computers can apply a multiple set of contexts for the same list of information and, as a result, optimize decisions regarding the quality of the information. In fact, present advances in the area of artificial intelligence strongly assert that by the year 2001 the act of *human* experience will no longer be a requisite for rational decision making. Rationality will require the use of a computer's core memory but not the type of normative traditions that we currently call history.

All that has been said up to this point clearly demonstrates a crucial need for some discipline to meet the challenge of producing an *effective* and *efficient* interface between a multiple complex of information processing systems. The systems of such a complex will be both human and machine based. Further, there can be little question that the effectiveness and efficiency of the interface between such systems will be a function of the fidelity of the interface defined in terms of the quantity of the information processed. The Skinnerian notion of control and the Tofflerian concern for maladaptive responses to information overload provide adequate justification for a discipline specifically concerned with the interface between information processing systems. We believe that communication now, and in the future, should be so directed. Similarly, we feel that a major adjustment should now be made in the objectives of the discipline and that it should immediately take upon itself the responsibility of educating its students and researchers to become concerned with the rules and general laws regulating information processing systems—both human and machine.

The basic rationale for an information-based communication education such as that advocated in the preceding paragraph is a simple one. It is our belief that in the future the *lack of information* on which to base decisions will be far more dangerous to the human condition than information that is simply labeled as bad. We contend, in other words, that the credibility of information is of major concern only insofar that there exists a total dependence on purposeful human participation. To *free* man from such total dependence is to allow him reciprocated control of his environments and, additionally, prevent him from committing some of the maladaptive responses forecast in Toffler's *Future Shock*.

Keeping this in mind, we can now begin to speculate about the kind of educational approach that we feel should become the focus of communication as an information science. To begin with, it is rather obvious that a future-directed education is going to encompass a wide range of data-oriented courses; that is, courses organized around vast amounts of information. Enough information, we might add, that its mere acquisition, if not impossible, is at least foreign to any behavioral notion of positive reinforcement. For far too long there has been an unnecessary if not misguided stress on the mastery of finite amounts of information and its subsequent application to an increasingly broad spectrum of human concern. Such stress has produced, on one hand, students with little chance to see beyond their own education, and on the other hand, students whose areas of specialization contain built-in obsolescence. Harsh as it may initially seem, the field of communication—particularly speech communication—while relatively new, is painfully traditional in its pedagogy.

Such courses should place strong emphasis on techniques of categorizing information for purposes of rapid storage and retrieval. It would seem paramount that this concern would involve the use of a computer. Thus, at this stage we would like to reassert our fundamental belief that electronic technology can free the individual of the necessity to consider himself a memory unit. In effect, we must replace such an analogy with one that has man asking a significant number of questions to a machine that can process large amounts of knowledge. By the year 2001, literacy will be defined in terms of asking questions and utilizing answers to those questions.

The need to utilize electronic technology in the classroom points to another avenue of content for future communication courses, namely, a stress needs to be placed on future relevant behavioral skills. All students, regardless of their majors, are going to need to master those skills that will make them efficient and effective users of machine-oriented information systems. To a large extent, even their communication with other human information systems will demand skills that are quite different from those that are limited to source/receiver functions. It seems clear that a great many of the needs of the future will involve coding skills. To this extent the delineation of the discipline of communication to so-called message variables is a step in the right direction. But also, implied by this position will be a remerger of written and oral skills within the single reference of information processing. In general, those skills that result, when mastered, in an increase in the fidelity of information transfer will be those that in the year 2001 will distinguish the educated from the uneducated. Coupled with the learning of such skills will be the need to appreciate the abandonment of outdated attributes. It has been a painful realization to most accountants that when trying to establish an efficient system for processing billing, the sooner they abandoned what they learned to do by hand the quicker they learned to count according to the constraints of the computer. The future will not protect outdated skills for information processing. The need to acquire new skills in this area will most probably require the lifelong training of all professionals. Indeed, the providing of such lifelong education will soon become the stimulus and justification for the expansion of academic disciplines such as communication and, in general, will be the saving grace for all higher education.

By the year 2001, people will not only have to continually learn new behavioral skills but they will also have to be taught to re-evaluate their time preferences. The reinforcement aspects of past and present successes will have to be transcended. There can be no resting on one's laurels. Change must be appreciated for its own sake and not for its quality ratings. This will particularly be the case for the information sciences. New informational strategies will be needed as mankind transcends an age where emphasis is placed on face-to-face contact to a less personal environment. Moreover, the behavioral abnormalities resulting from infrequent face-to-face contact and increased isolation—inevitable consequences of the future—will demand informational strategies whose powers of behavior modification far exceed those currently in existence. As new information systems and new informational strategies come into being, there will also be a need to interface them with existing ones. And this interface will be subject to negotiation and compromise between all systems regardless of their base or origin.

It should also be apparent that as new problems occur in man's environment, existing information systems will have to be adapted in order to achieve their resolve. One will not be able to focus just one system on any given problem. For example, it would be a serious and irrevocable error to continue to consider future energy crises in the environment from just the perspective of the availability of fuel. One need only turn to the dark winter mornings of 1974 to be reminded of the consequences of such shortsighted reasoning. To make judgments concerning solutions to such problems requires vast quantities of information from a multitude of storage banks. In other words, all of the available information systems must be interfaced in such a manner that no relevant information is lost in the exchange between systems. Further, these systems will need to be sensitive to the capabilities of each other system in order to determine points where additional information is needed to solve a particular dilemma. How to keep our information systems open-ended will be the most perplexing question facing communication education in the future.

Ironically, we, who are currently committed to the relevance of human communication as a social science, may find it the most difficult to consider communication as an informational science. We have fought many wars and gone through many identity crises, so many in fact that proponents of the discipline have manifested some of the characteristics of true believers. However, if we can keep in mind that it was the need to change from the intellectually sterile to the vigorous that initially fostered the discipline, then the avoidance of impotence in the year 2001 should be no problem. Communication is a discipline of and for change. Doubts that might now be held about our current place in academia need to be abandoned quickly—even those that cannot be relieved.

The symptoms of a number of our speculations are presently at hand. Problems concerning ecology, overpopulation, and energy resources, for example, are symptomatic of a failure on our part to recognize the reciprocal relationship between man and his environment—to realize that obedience to our physical and social world is the prime requisite of control. Along similar lines, maladaptive responses to *Future Shock* are not only abundant in our present culture but appear with ever increasing frequency. In a very real sense, then, we neither have the time nor the right to aimlessly ponder whether or not a present generation is ready to study the discipline we have described.

REFERENCES

Skinner, B. F. *Beyond Freedom and Dignity.* New York: Alfred A. Knopf, Inc., 1971.
Toffler, Alvin. *Future Shock.* New York: Random House, Inc., 1970.